This landmark study examines the role of gestures in relation to speech and thought. Leading scholars, including psychologists, linguists, and anthropologists, offer state-of-the-art analyses to demonstrate that gestures are not merely an embellishment of speech but are integral parts of language itself. *Language and Gesture* offers a wide range of theoretical approaches, with emphasis not simply on behavioral descriptions but also on the underlying processes. The book has strong cross-linguistic and cross-cultural components, examining gestures by speakers of Mayan, Australian, and East Asian as well as English and other European languages. The content is diverse, including chapters on gestures during aphasia and severe stuttering, the first emergence of speech–gesture combinations in children, and a section on sign language. In a rapidly growing field of study this volume opens up the agenda for research into a new approach in understanding language, thought, and society.

DAVID MCNEILL is Professor of Psychology and Linguistics at the University of Chicago. He is author of *Hand and Mind: What Gestures Reveal about Thought*.

Language, culture and cognition 2

Language and gesture

Language, culture and cognition

General editor
STEPHEN C LEVINSON
Max Planck Institute for Psycholinguistics, Nijmegen

This series looks at the role of language in human cognition – language in both its universal, psychological aspects and its variable, cultural aspects. Studies will focus on the relation between semantic and conceptual categories and processes, especially as these are illuminated by cross-linguistic and cross-cultural studies, the study of language acquisition and conceptual development, and the study of the relation of speech production and comprehension to other kinds of behaviour in cultural context. Books come principally, though not exclusively, from research associated with the Max Planck Institute for Psycholinguistics in Nijmegen, and in particular the cognitive Anthropology Research Group.

1. Jan Nuyts and Eric Pedersen (eds.) *Language and conceptualization*
2. David McNeill (ed.) *Language and gesture*
3. Melissa Bowerman and Stephen Levinson (eds.) *Language acquisition and conceptual development*
4. Gunter Senft (ed.), *Systems of nominal classification*

Language and Gesture

Edited by

David McNeill

University of Chicago

PUBLISHED BY THE PRESS SYNDICATE OF THE UNIVERSITY OF CAMBRIDGE
The Pitt Building, Trumpington Street, Cambridge, United Kingdom

CAMBRIDGE UNIVERSITY PRESS
The Edinburgh Building, Cambridge CB2 2RU, UK   www.cup.cam.ac.uk
40 West 20th Street, New York, NY 10011–4211, USA   www.cup.org
10 Stamford Road, Oakleigh, Melbourne 3166, Australia
Ruiz de Alarcón 13, 28014 Madrid, Spain

First published 2000

Printed in the United Kingdom at the University Press, Cambridge

Typeface Monotype Times NR 10/12 pt   *System* QuarkXpress™   [SE]

A catalogue record for this book is available from the British Library

Library of Congress Cataloguing in Publication data
Language and gesture / edited by David McNeill.
   p.   cm – (Language, culture, and cognition; 2)
Includes index.
ISBN 0 521 77166 8 (hardback). – ISBN 0 521 77761 5 (paperback)
1. Gesture.   2. Speech.   3. Language and languages.   4. Sign
language.   I. McNeill, David.   II. Series.
P117.L363   2000
808.5 – dc21   99–33524 CIP

ISBN 0 521 77166 8 hardback
ISBN 0 521 77761 5 paperback

Contents

Acknowledgments

The origin of this book was the conference entitled 'Gestures Compared Cross-Linguistically', held in the summer of 1995 at the Linguistic Institute, which that year was hosted by the Department of Linguistics, University of New Mexico, Albuquerque (Joan Bybee and Garland Bills, Directors). Adam Kendon was the conference co-leader. Two chapters are included from a separate conference at the 1995 Linguistic Institute organized by Sherman Wilcox. I am very grateful to the Spencer Foundation for its financial support.

Thanks to Martha Tyrone, Karl-Erik McCullough, and Nobuhiro Furuyama for their help during the conference.

Thanks to Glenda Miranda and Susan Duncan for putting the chapter references into standard form. Thanks to Karl-Erik McCullough for preparing the index.

Thanks to the authors, who have tolerated delays and answered innumerable requests, both expected and unexpected, with good humor.

Thanks to Martha Alibali and an anonymous reviewer for their advice and to Stephen Levinson for welcoming this project as part of his series on cognitive anthropology, and for crucial advice regarding publication.

And finally, above all, I wish to thank Nobuko B. McNeill for her support in every form and especially her wisdom and guidance when I unexpectedly found myself the sole editor of this volume, responsible for the publication of chapters by colleagues, a number of them young scholars just starting their careers.

Introduction

David McNeill

Departments of Psychology and Linguistics, University of Chicago

1 Introduction

The word 'gesture' needs no explanation. Yet how we use the term in this book is liable to be misunderstood. We are discussing a phenomenon that often passes without notice, though it is omnipresent. If you watch someone speaking, in almost any language and under nearly all circumstances, you will see what appears to be a compulsion to move the hands and arms in conjunction with the speech. Speech, we know, is the actuality of language. But what are the gestures? This book aims to answer this question, at least in part.

It is useful to introduce a set of distinctions to help situate our question. In the process, we will clarify the subject matter of this book and simultaneously sharpen the sense of the word 'gesture' with which we are concerned.

2 The nature of the phenomenon: four continua

I have put this title into the plural because there are several dimensions on which we need to distinguish movements that are equally well called 'gestures'. The labels for the points along the continua – "gesticulation," "pantomime," "emblem," and "sign language" – were first defined by Kendon (1982). They were lined up on a continuum termed "Kendon's continuum" by McNeill (1992). That single continuum is now subdivided into four continua, each an analytically separate dimension on which the types of gestures above can be differentiated.

2.1 Types of gesture

It will be helpful in the following to have specific examples of gestures at each of the points on Kendon's continuum.

An example of *gesticulation* is "he grabs a big oak tree and **bends it** way back" (McNeill 1992). Before making the gesture the speaker had moved his right hand forward and slightly upward while opening his hand into a kind of C-shaped grip; all of this was preparation. The gesture then took place during the boldface stretch, with the hand appearing to grasp some-thing and pull this imaginary tree back and down.

Pantomime is difficult to define, but generally means a significant gesture without speech, a dumb show (to paraphrase the *OED*). It's a movement, often complex and sequential, that does not accompany speech and is not part of a gesture 'code'. A simple example would be twirling a finger around in a circle after someone asks, "What is a vortex?"

An example of an *emblem* is the OK sign – made by forming a circle with the forefinger and thumb in contact at their tips, while the rest of the fingers extend outward – used for expressing approbation.

An example of an ASL *sign* is TREE – the dominant arm extended upward at the elbow, the fingers extended outward (a 5-hand), and the hand rotating back and forth at the wrist. The subordinate hand is extended flat and prone under the dominant-hand elbow. This sign iconically depicts a kind of schematic tree – trunk, leaves fluttering in the wind, and ground – but the iconicity is conventionalized and constrained, as will be explained below.

2.2   *The continua*

With these examples in mind, we can look at how the different kinds of ges-tures actually differ. The most concrete dimension is defined by the rela-tionship of the gesture to speech:

2.2.1   *Continuum 1: relationship to speech*

Gesticulation	→	Emblems	→	Pantomime	→	Sign Language
obligatory		optional		obligatory		ditto
presence of		presence of		absence of		
speech		speech		speech		

The bends-it-back gesture is meaningful only in conjunction with the utter-ance of "bends it back." The OK emblem can be made with speech or not. Pantomime, by definition, does not accompany speech (lack of speech is therefore trivial). With sign language, while it is possible to produce signs and speak simultaneously, doing so has a disruptive effect on both speech and gesture. Speech becomes hesitant and sign performance is disrupted at the level of the main grammatical mechanisms of the language that utilize space rather than time for encoding meanings (Nelson et al. 1993).

Associated with the speech continuum is another continuum that reflects the presence vs. absence of the characteristic semiotic properties of a lin-guistic system. This is a second continuum on which gesticulation and sign language hold down the extremes, while pantomime and emblem have exchanged places:

2.2.2   Continuum 2: relationship to linguistic properties

Gesticulation	→	Pantomime	→	Emblems	→	Sign Language
linguistic		ditto		some linguistic		linguistic
properties				properties		properties
absent				present		present

The "bends it way back" gesture lacks all linguistic properties. It is non-morphemic, not realized through a system of phonological form constraints, and has no potential for syntactic combination with other gestures. We can demonstrate the inapplicability of linguistic properties through a thought experiment. Imagine another person saying the same thing but with "it" meaning the corner of a sheet of paper. Then, rather than the hand opening into a grip, the thumb and forefinger would come together in a pinch; rather than the arm moving forward and slightly up, the pinching hand would be held slightly forward and down; and rather than pull the arm back, the pinching hand would rotate. Also, this gesture would naturally be performed with two hands, the second hand 'holding' the paper that is being bent back. That is, none of the form properties of the first gesture would be present in the second gesture, bends-it-way-back though it is. Neither gesture in fact obeys constraints within a system of forms; there are only constraints that emerge from the imagery of bending itself. The hand shape and position are creations of the moment that reflect the speaker's imagery – of a character from a story reaching up and forward to pull back a tree, of someone turning down the corner of piece of paper. The ASL sign T R E E in contrast *is* constrained by the phonological properties of the ASL language system.[1] The 5-shape is one of the standard shapes of the language; the sign could not be formed and remain intelligible with a hand shape that is not part of the language. While the 5-shape has recognizable iconicity, it is a standardized selection of iconic features that other sign languages, with signs equally iconic, do not use (Danish Sign Language traces an outline of a tree). And the sign is what Okrent calls "non-specific", in that it is used equally well for all kinds of trees and tree shapes, not just trees with long bare trunks and fluttering leaves.

Pantomime, like gesticulation, does not seem to obey any system constraints (not considering theatrical pantomime, which does have its own traditional forms and rules: Fischer-Lichte 1992). The vortex could be exhibited by twirling a finger or rotating the whole hand, and neither would be unintelligible or seem to be a violation of a system constraint.

Emblems, on the other hand, do show system constraints. There are differences between well-formed and not-well-formed ways of making the gesture. Placing the middle finger on the thumb results in a gesture with some kind of precision meaning, but it is not recognizable as the OK sign.

The OK gesture, like a word, is constrained to assume a certain 'phonological' shape. Yet these constraints are limited and don't by any means amount to a full language. There is no way to reliably reverse the OK sign, for example. Forming it and waving it back and forth laterally (another emblem that, on its own, signals negation) might convey "not OK," but it also might be seen as meaning the opposite of negation – waving the hand could call attention to the OK sign, or suggest that many different things are OK – a flexibility that is basically not linguistic in character.

Comparing Continuum 1, 'speech present' – 'speech absent', with Continuum 2, 'linguistic properties absent' – 'linguistic properties present', we see one of the basic facts of gesture life: the gesticulations with which speech is obligatorily *present* are the least language-like; the signs from which speech is obligatorily *absent* have linguistic properties of their own. This is not so paradoxical as it may seem. It reveals that 'gesture' has the potential to take on the traits of a linguistic system. This is the conclusion of thirty years of investigation of the sign languages of the deaf (see, for example, the collection of papers in Emmorey & Reilly 1995). It is also the conclusion of research on the deaf children of hearing, non-signing parents. These children are exposed to neither a sign language nor speech, and they develop their own means of gestural communication that manifests a number of important linguistic properties, such as a lexicon and basic syntax (Goldin-Meadow & Mylander 1984). In effect, their gestures move to the right of the continuum. The conclusion is that nothing about the visual–manual modality *per se* is incompatible with the presence of linguistic properties.

The comparison of the first and second continua also shows, moreover, that when the *vocal* modality has linguistic system properties, *gesture*, the manual modality, does not take on these properties. And, when it does not, speech tends to be an *obligatory* presence with the gesture. This is certainly one of the more interesting facts of gesture reality, and one that looms large in the chapters of this volume. It implies that speech and gesture combine into a system of their own in which each modality performs its own functions, the two modalities mutually supporting one another. The chapters in this volume operate on this premise and describe in detail the functions of speech and gesture across many languages and speakers.

2.2.3   *Continuum 3: relationship to conventions*

Gesticulation	→	Pantomime	→	Emblems	→	Sign Language
not conventionalized		ditto		partly conventionalized		fully conventionalized

Convention means that the forms and meanings of the gesture meet some kind of socially constituted group standard. It is because our perception is ruled by convention that only forefinger and thumb contact are recognizable as OK. At the gesticulation end of the continuum, in contrast, lack of convention is an attribute *sine qua non*. The bends-it-way-back gesture is conventional only in the broadest sense (e.g., that gesturing is acceptable in storytelling contexts). There are no conventions telling the speaker what form bending back is to take. The TREE sign, however, *is* constrained by the conventions of ASL. It must meet form standards according to which only an upright arm with an extended 5-hand is TREE.

2.2.4   Continuum 4: character of the semiosis. The fourth continuum concerns the semiotic differences between gesticulation and sign. This dimension also shows the richness that comes from combining gesticulation with speech into a unified speech–gesture system, a system that places contrasting kinds of semiotic properties in one vessel (in what sense sign–gesture systems might also exist is a topic of much current interest; for discussion, see Liddell's chapter).

The semiotic continuum is the following:

Gesticulation	→	Pantomime	→	Emblems	→	Sign Language
global and		global and		segmented		segmented
synthetic		analytic		and synthetic		and analytic

Global refers to the fact that the determination of meaning in a gesticulation proceeds in a downward direction. The meanings of the 'parts' are determined by the meaning of the whole. This contrasts to the upward determination of the meanings of sentences. In the bending-back gesture, we understand from the meaning of the gesture as a whole that the hand (one of the 'parts') equals the character's hand, the movement (another part) equals the character's movement, and the backward direction (a third part) equals the character's backward movement. These are not independent morphemes. It is not the case that the hand in general means a hand or movement backward must always mean movement in that direction (cf. Özyürek's chapter). In speech, on the other hand, the event of the character bending back the tree was constructed out of independently meaningful words or segments organized according to a standardized plan or syntax. The top-down global semiotic of gesticulation contrasts with this bottom-up mapping of the sentence. The linguistic mapping is *segmented*. The OK sign is also segmented in that it can convey approbation only when a critical 'segment' (contact of the forefinger and thumb) is present. Pantomime, on the other hand, appears to be global. The twirling finger is understood to be a swizzle stick because the gesture, as a whole, has the meaning of a vortex. ASL signs are clearly segmented in their semiotic principles.

Synthetic refers to the fact that a single gesticulation concentrates into one symbolic form distinct meanings that can be spread across the entire surface of the accompanying sentence. The single bends-it-way-back gesture displayed the actor, his or her action, and the path of the tree acted upon. In the accompanying sentence, these same semantic functions were spread across the surface – "he," "bends," "back," and "way." The mode of the sentence was analytic. Like English, ASL is also analytic. Emblems, on the other hand, are synthetic, like gesticulations. The OK meaning in spoken form could have scope over a full surface structure ("a job well done," for example). Pantomime may also be analytic, though the lack of definition of pantomime makes the attribution uncertain. The twirl of the vortex gesture is the translation of a lexical term, which suggests analyticity. Moreover, if one enacts an entire sequence of taking a pot, pouring in a liquid, and stirring it, the 'vortex' gesture refers to one step of this sequence, not the whole. The issue of whether gesticulations characteristically map onto single lexical items or are not so constrained, however, is a matter of some dispute (see the chapters by Kita, de Ruiter, and Krauss et al.).

2.3   Summary of differences along the continua

Gesticulation accompanies speech, is non-conventionalized, is global and synthetic in mode of expression, and lacks language-like properties of its own. The speech with which the gesticulation occurs, in contrast, is conventionalized, segmented, and analytic, and is fully possessed of linguistic properties. These two contrasting modes of structuring meaning coexist in speech and gesture, a fact of profound importance for understanding the nature of thought and language in general, and how they function in communication.

Signs in ASL, like words in speech, are conventionalized, segmented, and analytic, and possessed of language properties, while they are obligatorily not performed with speech. The presence or absence of speech with gesture is thus correlated with the absence or presence of conventional linguistic properties.

Emblems are at an intermediate position on the various dimensions of contrasting gestures. They are partly like gesticulations, partly like signs. For many individuals, emblems are the closest thing to a sign 'language' they possess, although it is crucial to emphasize the *non*-linguistic character of these gestures: the lack of a fully contrastive system and the lack of syntactic potential.

Pointing requires special mention. It has a form that is standardized within a given culture. Thus, in North America the standard form for pointing is the G hand shape (the index finger extended, the other fingers curled in), but in other societies one might use two fingers or an entire hand. At the same time, however, the prescribed form of pointing is not required for the pointing act to take place – the two-fingers or full-hand alternatives would definitely be understood as pointing in North America. Thus, pointing is less constrained than the OK sign, for instance. In some contexts the presence of speech with pointing may seem obligatory (de Ruiter, this volume) but pointing is fully interpretable without speech as well. The chapter by Haviland analyzes the semiotic foundations of pointing and describes in detail its use in two cultures where it is an integral part of linguistic performance – in one case because the coding of directionality is obligatory in the language, in the other because such coding is outside the normal resources of the language (neither culture is North American).

2.4   Non-redundancy of speech–gesture combinations

Considering the gesticulation end of the semiotic continuum, the bending-back gesture added a global-synthetic version of an event that was also described analytically in speech. In this co-expressed manifestation of the event, however, the gesture is not merely a global version of the analytic sentence. In bending back with a single hand, the gesture *displayed* what was, at most, only implicit in speech – that the object bent back was fastened at one end. "Bends it" could equally describe bending an object held at both ends, as it did in the paper-folding example. The addition of "way back" could conceivably be said to *implicate* an object fastened at one end. But this is not a demonstration of the fact: only the gesture does that. The preceding clause said the object was an oak tree, but this was presupposed, not encoded in the linguistic choices of "bends it way back." The gesture, on the other hand, did encode it and provided a continuation of this fact as a discourse reference. It is the one-handedness of the bends-it-back gesture, moreover, that excluded the possibility of bending back the corner of a sheet of paper. In general, speech and gesture can jointly express the same core meaning and highlight different aspects of it. Together speech and gesture present a more complete version of the meaning than either accomplishes on its own.

3   The current volume

3.1   Background

This book is a harvest of papers from a conference ('Gestures Compared Cross-Linguistically') on the role of gesture in the mechanisms of language and language use – the first conference on this topic ever held, to our knowledge. The conference took place in conjunction with the 1995 Linguistic Institute at the University of New Mexico, Albuquerque. None of the current form of the chapters, however, is as presented at the conference, and this volume is not a proceedings. All chapters have been invited because of the importance of the research they present for understanding the gesture topic. All of the chapters were written and submitted after the conference, and most were written during the 1996–97 year. Thus, the chapters have been written to appear in this book, and are current. Collectively, they cover many of the areas of contemporary gesture research. The book has a strong cross-linguistic and cross-cultural component, with chapters describing speech-synchronized gestures by speakers of Mayan, Australian, East Asian, and non-English European languages, along with many observations of English.

3.2   Topics covered

A neurological dimension is added in the chapters by Goodwin (gestures of a patient suffering aphasia) and Mayberry & Jaques (gestures during severe stuttering bouts).

An ontogenetic dimension is added in the chapter by Butcher & Goldin-Meadow (genesis of gesture–speech synchrony).

Several chapters are concerned with what can be called the 'psycholinguistics' of gesture – the implications of gestures at the gesticulation end for understanding the cognitive processes underlying speech and speech production.

Another group of chapters discusses the implications for modeling the speech process of taking into account the co-production of speech and gesture. There is in this section both agreement and disagreement – agreement that modeling is a desirable goal, disagreement over whether any steps toward this goal have been successful.

3.3   Antecedents

The modern study of gesture has seen a twofold shift away from a long tradition dating from Roman times of emphasis on rhetorical gestures (Quintilian wrote a treatise on gesture for the instruction of orators in first-century Rome) – the mannered performances of orators, with the hands and body comprising more or less deliberate gestured embellishments on spoken public performances. For sketches of the history of gesture studies, see Kendon (1982) and McNeill (1992).

With the first shift, commencing with Efron (1941) in the 1930s, gestures have come to be studied in life, as they occur spontaneously during conversation and other discourse modes. This new approach has been greatly enhanced – one might say made possible – by the advent of slow-motion film and now video, without which the careful study of gesture in relation to speech and thought would scarcely be possible. All the contributions to this book draw from modern audio-video recordings.

In the second shift, commencing with Kendon in 1972 and continuing with ever increasing vigor to the present day, gestures are regarded as parts of *language itself* – not as embellishments or elaborations, but as integral parts of the processes of language and its use. The development of this line offers new insights into the nature of speaking, thinking, remembering, and interacting with words in a social context. The chapters in this book all take the point of view that language and gesture are integral parts of a whole and present state-of-the-art descriptions and analyses of this multimodal unit that is considered as language itself.

3.4   Current state of the field

Within the modern consensus there are, naturally, differences, and in the book there are several distinct approaches with interesting theoretical tensions between them; and several of the chapters are concerned to define these differences and to suggest what can be done to overcome them. The formal structure of the book – sections on action, on thought, on models, and on signs – in part is intended to highlight the different approaches.

1. One tradition seeks to understand the function of gestures in contexts of social interaction. Gestures are instruments of human communication in this approach, and the point of view is interpsychological. The chapters in part 1 represent this approach.

2. Another tradition is that of cognitive psychology. Here the goal is to understand the origin of gestures and their interrelations with speaking in the realtime mental processes of individuals. The point of view is intrapsychological. The chapters in part 2 cover this approach.

3. A third approach is modeling. Here the goal is to outline a computational model of gesture–speech performance. The chapters in part 3 take up this question. This section, in particular, lends itself to focused controversy, and the three authors agreed to write comments on each other's chapters in which the focus is on possibilities of synthesizing their seemingly conflicting positions on this topic.

4. The final part describes ways to make the transition from gesticulation to sign. The chapters here in effect tie together the two ends of the continua above and are an appropriate way to conclude the entire work.

In summary, this book aims to provide state-of-the-art contributions across a wide range of approaches to language and thought as informed by the study of gesture, and to present these contributions side by side where they can be related to each other.

NOTE

1 I am grateful to Arika Okrent for this example and analysis.

REFERENCES

Efron, D. 1941. *Gesture and Environment*. New York: King's Crown Press.
Emmorey, K. & Reilly, J. (eds.) 1995. *Language, Gesture, and Space*. Hillsdale, NJ: Erlbaum.
Fischer-Lichte, E. 1992. *The Semiotics of Theatre*, trans. J. Gaines & D. L. Jones. Bloomington: Indiana University Press.
Goldin-Meadow, S. & Mylander, C. 1984. Gestural communication in deaf children: the effects and non-effects of parental input on early language development. *Monographs of the Society for Research in Child Development* 49 (serial no. 207).
Kendon, A. 1982. The study of gesture: some remarks on its history. *Recherches Sémiotiques/Semiotic Inquiry* 2: 45–62.
Marschark, M. & Clark, M. D. (eds.) 1993. *Psychological Perspectives on Deafness*. Hillsdale, NJ: Erlbaum.
McNeill, D. 1992. *Hand and Mind: What Gestures Reveal about Thought*. Chicago: University of Chicago Press.
Nelson, K., Loncke, F. & Camarata, S. 1993. Implications of research on deaf and hearing children's language learning. In Marschark & Clark (eds.), pp. 123–151.

Part 1

Gesture in action

Broadly speaking, the phenomenon of gesture can be viewed in two seemingly opposite ways. On one of these views, it is a 'window' into the mind, and is regarded as part of the individual speaker-gesturer's ongoing mental life. The second part of the book embodies this view. Gesture in the initial, Action, part highlights the other approach, that of gesture as part of the social interaction in which the person participates. Part of the story of gesture is the role that it performs in *inter*action: gestures as something engaged in our social lives. The chapters in this part explore the social context of gesture and the contributions to action that gestures perform in these contexts. The emphasis is on gesture as a communicative resource, how gestures affect ongoing interactions, and how interactions affect it. The opposition of 'inside' and 'outside', however, is superficial. There is no deep conflict between the inside and outside views, and both views must be taken if gestures are to be properly explained. The individual speaker is surely affected by his or her social context. This effect might extend to altering the thought processes of the individual to accord with the socially induced changes in the context. Indeed, one chapter undertakes to test this very hypothesis with positive results (Özyürek). At the same time, social interaction is not independent of the individuals participating in it. The participants are – mutually, jointly, but also individually – constituting an interaction within the constraints of cultural norms. Several of the chapters elucidate this social–individual nexus. Though conceived and prepared separately, the chapters in this part express a common theme. To state this succinctly, the theme is that in a social interaction the gestures are among the active participants – they play a part in the interaction and help to shape it, and the interaction, in turn, helps to shape them.

Haviland describes in detail the occurrences of pointing gestures in two cultures – the Mayan culture of the Tzotzil, and the Australian Aborigine culture of the Guugu Yimithirr – in which the respective language codes offer almost opposite resources for how they describe orientations in space, but both of which invoke precisely oriented pointing gestures in similar ways. Haviland argues from this convergence across cultures and languages that the use of space is a tool that makes cognition interactively available, even interactively constructed, and thus appears under contrasting linguistic conditions. That cognition is interactively constructed is the theme emphasized by Goodwin. He provides a unique exploration of the communicative solution invented by a patient suffering severe aphasia and his conversational co-participants in which gesture was used to create a new meaning in a socially distributed, group way.

Gestures are themselves shaped by the social interactive context. This is the phenomenon demonstrated by Özyürek and Furuyama in their respective chapters. As mentioned above, Özyürek tests the hypothesis that an individual's memory and thought are altered by the social context of speaking. Furuyama documents the role of gestures in instruction, discovering *listener* gestures and listener co-manipulation of *speaker* gestures, and analyzing the conditions under which these phenomena occur.

Kendon emphasizes that gestures are used to make something more precise or complete, especially the pragmatic aspects of the utterance. Kendon's chapter discusses the emblems, or, in the terminology he prefers, the quotable gestures, that figure prominently in Neapolitan interactive culture, and argues that these gestures are an integral part of the communication process, often carrying the main illocutionary load of meta-, para-, and extralinguistic effects in the conversation.

If the logical end point of gesture in action is gesture as one of the co-participants in the interaction, LeBaron and Streeck present evidence that the gesture's starting point may be an actual instrumental action. They analyze examples from recordings of adult-level instruction in the manipulation or design of material objects, to demonstrate a seamless progression of actions performed, from the manipulation of objects, to symbolic displays, to, finally, a conventionalized fixing of gestures within the local interacting group, by which time the former instrumental action has become a shared mode of symbolic reference.

1 Pointing, gesture spaces, and mental maps

John B. Haviland

Reed College and Centro de Investigaciones y Estudios Superiores en Antropología
Social (Mexico)

1 Introduction

One way people display their knowledge about space is by pointing, using a
gesture to indicate a place or a thing in a place, or perhaps a thing moving
from one place to another. Haviland (1993) argues that storytellers speaking the Australian language Guugu Yimithirr (GY) assiduously orient
pointing gestures in the 'correct' compass directions. What GY speakers
and their interlocutors know about space[1] is thus made plain in their gestures. This chapter[2] examines spatial gestures in a different speech tradition
and argues that the spaces in which gestures are performed both reflect and
constitute, as an interactive mnemonic medium, people's representations of
the spaces they inhabit, know, and talk about.

Consider two exemplary utterances[3] which appear to include 'pointing'
gestures. In the first, my compadre P, a Tzotzil-speaking corn farmer from
Chiapas, Mexico, tells about a roadside *cantina* he used to visit as a boy. He
compares its size to that of the house next to which we are sitting, extending
an index finger (Figure 1.1) in a seemingly unproblematic act of immediate
physical deixis: he appears to 'point' at the house.

(1)   yech smuk'ul chk i na chk li`e
        (It) was the same size as this house here.

Next, Maryan describes the route he used to take from the hamlet of
Nabenchauk in highland Chiapas to the distant resort town of Cancún
where he was working to pay off his debts. He has gotten his listener as far
as Palenque, a town along the way.

(2)   nopol xa li palenke
        Palenque is close by.

Maryan's index finger (Figure 1.2) points slightly downwards and roughly
north from where he sits in a house patio in Nabenchauk. In the context of
his assertion "Palenque is close" Maryan apparently means to 'point at
Palenque'.

This house
right here.

Figure 1.1.   Figure 1.2.

Pointing seems a straightforward matter: you stick your finger out in the appropriate direction, perhaps saying some accompanying words, and your interlocutors follow the trajectory of your arrow-like digit to the intended referent. Nothing could be simpler – and nothing could be farther from the truth.

2   Directional precision in language (and gesture)

One complication to the simplicity of pointing may be the demand for directional accuracy. People in many different societies, speaking such languages as Warlpiri (Laughren 1978) and GY (Haviland 1979) in Aboriginal Australia, Austronesian languages like Malagasy (Ozanne-Rivierre 1987), and American Indian languages like Wintu (Pitkin 1984), Assiniboine (Farnell 1988), and Tzeltal (Brown & Levinson 1993), are reported to keep careful track of cardinal directions, recorded in locational expressions in speech. The linguistic details vary, but frequently people use lexical roots for cardinal directions to describe things and events as points or vectors in the appropriate divisions of the horizontal plane.

There are, unfortunately, rather few descriptions of usage of the spoken reflexes of these terminological systems,[4] still fewer of the *visible* constituents of linguistic interactions in such languages. My work on narrative in GY provides one example of how gestures, too, can be precisely oriented by compass direction. Farnell (1988, 1994) gives another for the Assiniboine.

3   Gestural accuracy and linguistic precision

Haviland (1993) compares two narrative performances, separated by several years, in which a Hopevale storyteller recounts how he and a companion once had to swim three and a half miles to shore through shark-infested seas after their boat capsized. Careful spoken discrimination of cardinal directions in these GY narratives is matched by a parallel directional precision in gesture, although sometimes conceptual transpositions – mostly shifts in the narrator's perspective – are required to maintain this precision.

A particularly dramatic case of 'oriented' gestures in these GY narratives involves no explicit pointing but is an example of what Sotaro Kita has dubbed 'motion direction blends' – gestures that portray the manner[5] of a motion, but combine it with a specific orientation. The boat in question was caught in rough seas, and strong winds flipped it over in the water. On two separate tellings the narrator illustrated with different motions how the boat capsized, but in both cases he kept the orientation constant, showing that the boat rolled over from east to west.

Keeping oneself cardinally oriented is a communicative convention, a rule of proper GY with both a verbal and a gestural expression. These GY facts raise several questions, which this essay begins to address. If cardinal directions can be recovered from talk, they must figure in the 'mental representations' of the spatial configurations that are thus expressed. Moreover, the narrative transpositions to which I turn at the end of the essay suggest that these putative 'mental maps' of what 'interlocutors know' about spatial arrangements must be dynamic and shiftable (see Bühler 1982, Hanks 1990, Haviland 1991a, Engberg-Pedersen 1995). How are such transpositions managed and successfully communicated?

In languages like GY there is considerable linguistic support for directional precision, as evidenced by the obligatory and ubiquitous use of cardinal direction terms in all kinds of GY talk. Thus the orderly gestural practices of GY speakers are mutually reinforced by the insistent use of spoken compass terms. By contrast, in many other languages, among them Zinacantec Tzotzil, explicit directional terms occur rarely if at all in everyday talk. Do oriented gestures occur in such a different kind of linguistic tradition?

4   Gestural typologies and language

For ordinary interactants, gesturing is part of talking, and one learns to gesture as one learns to talk (see, for example, Bates et al. 1983). The organization of gesture is inextricably (though problematically) related to linguistic structure, as studies of the relative timing of gesture and talk suggest (e.g., Birdwhistell 1952, 1963; Kendon 1980, 1988b; Schegloff 1984). McNeill (1985, 1992) bases an entire psycholinguistic program on an argued conceptual co-dependence between gesture and speech. There may be evolutionary connections between speech and gesture, since language has evolved in the context of face-to-face interlocutors, and Armstrong, Stokoe & Wilcox (1995) find in structural elements of gesture the roots of syntax. An apparent chain of development also links spontaneous gesticulation (perhaps grounded in early motor activity, e.g., reaching and grasping [Carter 1975], to gestural 'babbling' [Petitto & Marentette 1991]) and spontaneous signs and, given appropriate communicative conditions, to systems of homesign (see, for example, Goldin-Meadow 1991), alternate sign languages (Kendon 1988a), sign-language pidgin, and ultimately full-blown (sign) language (Kegl et al. in press).

Moreover, at the level of functional interdependence, deictic gestures both substitute for and supplement spoken deictics (see Marslen-Wilson et al. 1982; Levelt et al. 1985). Several analytic consequences follow. First, as part of the interactive repertoire available to interlocutors,[6] gesture-with-speech is a vehicle of communication not only for propositional purposes but for the coordinated social action whose characteristic domain is ordinary conversation. Second, the indexical properties of gestures are potentially as central to their import and effectiveness as are those of words, since word and gesture conjointly index the spatio-temporal context of the speech event.

Typologies of gesture[7] often involve two broad cross-cutting dimensions: *representationality*, and *convention* or *autonomy*. The first dimension concerns how bodily movements that accompany speech are alleged to depict the referential content of an utterance. Some gestures seem tailored to the 'meaning' of speech, whereas others appear to be aligned to other aspects of talk.[8] The second dimension of autonomy concerns the degree to which gestural movements are *ad hoc* fleeting creations of the moment, inextricably tied to concurrent speech, as opposed to more or less conventionalized, 'language-like' signaling devices in their own right, independent of verbalization, possibly both 'glossable' and 'quotable' (Kendon 1983, 1988b, 1990a; McNeill 1987).

The notion of conventionality in gesture is too complex to treat here. There are surely elements of gestural form, even in 'pointing', that make the line between symbolic (conventional) and indexical modes of signaling problematic.[9] However, a central and striking element of 'conventionality' in GY gesture is the apparent 'fixity' of direction that accompanies pointing. When a gesture portrays location or motion, it must in a variety of ways preserve cardinal directions.

Although such a gestural convention may seem exotic, one reflex of the

Figure 1.3.

convention is probably widespread. GY speakers frequently point to the part of the sky where the sun would be visible at a certain hour to refer to the corresponding time of day. In a similar way, but using a very different pointing style, my Zinacantec compadre describes returning to a place where he had left a sick and dying horse. When he says, "it was getting late" (see (3)), he glances up at the place the sun would have been (see Figure 1.3), providing a kind of gestural metaphor for time that relies on the true cardinal direction, or local geography, to evoke the afternoon sun.

(3)   ju:ta mal xa k'ak'al u:n
         Damn, it was already getting late.

Nonetheless, it is *not* a gestural convention in my dialect of English that pointing gestures be oriented by the compass, perhaps not even to talk about sunset or sunrise. Directional precision is thus a somewhat unexpected overlay to 'conventionality' in gesture not captured by standard typologies.

5   Pointing and indexicality

Gestures are frequently classified by a familiar Peircean trichotomy. Unlike emblems, which are symbols or conventional vehicles of meaning, iconic gestures (McNeill 1987) are said to depict (by virtue of resembling in some way or other) entities in narrative. 'Deictic' or 'pointing' gestures, on the other hand, are not representational but instead act as Peircean indices, picking out their referents by virtue of a shared spatio-temporal proximity with them. Indeed, pointing gestures are the canonical and for many theorists the ontologically primeval indexical signs. (Etymology enshrines the fact that we generally point with our INDEX fingers, though people may use other body parts.)[10]

Reference is characteristically anchored in the speech event through such indexicals as pronouns, tenses, demonstratives, and so on. However, it is supposed, one can refer equally well (if not better) by showing as by saying. Accordingly deictic gestures can *replace* rather than merely accompany referring expressions. Levelt et al. (1985) consider it distinctive of certain deictic gestures that "they can be obligatory in deictic utterances" (p. 134).

Deictic terms like 'there' or 'that' . . . require the speaker to make some form of pointing gesture, for example, by nodding the head, visibly directing the gaze, turning the body, or moving arm and hand *in the appropriate direction.* (P. 134; emphasis added)

But *which* is 'the appropriate direction'? As Wittgenstein (1958) points out, ostension itself relies on what he calls a 'custom'. There is the famous example of the signpost in Wittgenstein's discussion of rules.

A rule stands there like a sign-post. – Does the sign-post leave no doubt about the way I have to go? Does it shew which direction I am to take when I have passed it; whether along the road or the footpath or across country? But where is it said which way I am to follow it; whether in the direction of its finger or (e.g.) in the opposite one?[11]

The direction of a pointing gesture can, as in ASL, start out as arbitrary but once established become both significant and enduring. Bellugi & Klima (1982: 301) describe some functions of pointing in ASL as follows:

If a referent (third person) is actually present in the discourse context between signer and addressee, specific indexical reference is made by pointing to that referent. But for non-present referents that are introduced by the speaker into the discourse context only 'verbally', there is another system of indexing. This consists of introducing a nominal and setting up a point in space associated with it; pointing to that specific locus later in the discourse clearly 'refers back' to that nominal, even after many intervening signs.

A pointing gesture, like any indexical sign, projects a surrounding context or space – let's call this its 'gesture space' – within which it can 'point'.

[E]very sign insofar as it signals indexically . . . serves as the point-from-which, or semiotic origin of a presuppositionally/entailing projection of whatever is to be understood as context. (Silverstein 1992: 36)

Note that this is a *conceptual* projection; one may point in 'real' physical space, but pointing conjures up a space oriented and populated by conceptual entities. How far an indexical sign projects, how wide or detailed the projection is, are central empirical questions.

As philosophers have been at pains to argue, what there is to point *at* is (at least ontologically) a variable thing. When an interactant 'points at something', how structured and how detailed a space that something entails (or that pointing presupposes) is neither constant nor fixed in advance. Moreover, a sequence of pointing gestures does not necessarily produce a coherent space, within which contiguous gestures may jointly be understood to point. Any coherence to the space delimited by such a sequence of indexical signs is *itself* a projection (of the indexical fact of the contiguity of the gestures), and thus the result of interpretive efforts.

6   Presupposing/entailing

Pointing gestures, like other indexical signs, may thus be placed along a continuum from relatively presupposing to relatively creative (Silverstein 1976). Where a present and 'directly' perceivable referent is the target of a pointing gesture, it is relatively presupposable: its existence, as well as its location and other salient characteristics, may be taken for granted in the speech context. You can exploit presupposable features of the actual location of a co-present referent, thus rendering the interpretability of your gesture dependent on those presupposed features. (In the absence of other information, your interlocutor must share knowledge of geographical and perhaps other relevant facts if she is to identify your gestures' referents correctly.) A gesture that 'points at' such a presupposable entity simply inserts it, and its relevant features, into the current universe of discourse.

"This Willy Woibo's father," says JB, pointing with his thumb over his shoulder, in the direction of the store where the man in question can usually be seen. JB's gesture (Fig. 1.4) draws upon the immediate environs of the speech event, within which deixis presupposes (usually observable) targets, such as local objects or geographical features, although sometimes mediated, as here, by kin relationships. Such a space is 'anchored' because the presupposable loci of such perceivable entities are immediately given in relation to the current origo, the here-and-now of the interlocutors. You locate the things you point at where they actually are. Such a situation is perhaps the primeval home that theorists imagine for deictic gestures.

This relatively presupposing strategy for pointing gestures may be adopted for *narrated spaces* as well. JB and his companion faced a long swim through rough seas from the capsized boat. JB describes the situation with a sweeping gesture to his left (Figure 1.5) – that is, southwest. He says, "You couldn't see the beach to the south; well, (it was at a distance of) three mile(s) and a half."

JB, sitting at modern Hopevale, indicates the three and a half miles to the

Figure 1.4.   Figure 1.5.

beach at Bala by pointing not in some arbitrary direction, and not north-east to where Bala actually lies from where he sits, but *southwest* – calculating from his narrated perspective near the capsized boat. He thus presupposes his interlocutors' knowledge of the geography he is describing and their ability to transpose themselves to a narrated origo from which can be projected known (presupposable) landmarks, including the named spot on the beach.

7   Relatively creative pointing gestures

Other pointing gestures – often those directed 'towards' non-present 'objects' – can by contrast be relatively creative. When your gestures themselves help create their referents – entail their existence for discursive purposes – you can often put those referents where you want them. Indeed, it may be that the 'pointing' gesture depends in no way on the location of a referent. The location may be discursively irrelevant, and the 'pointing' gesture may have only an individuating function. In such a case it may not be necessary to refer again to the same entity, so it matters little where you pointed 'at' it; and if you do have to refer to it again, the initial baptismal gesture has established a locus to which you can return.

In (4), a Zinacantec man describes how he once met a supernatural demon called *j`ik'al* 'blackman'. The man tried to grab the creature, which ran away. The narrator illustrates how the *j`ik'al* fled (Figure 1.6) and hid behind the cross in the man's patio (Figure 1.7), both times using pointing gestures. The conversation took place far from the village where the con-

Figure 1.6.   Figure 1.7.

frontation occurred. The locations indicated by the man's gestures appear
to be creative choices of the moment, not derived from the geography of the
actual events. Thus the pointing gesture in Figure 1.6 arbitrarily creates a
locus for the hiding demon, a locus that is then taken up and gesturally
elaborated when the house cross is mentioned.

(4)   1...2...........
         i -0-jatav   un
         CP-3A-run_away PT[12]
         It ran away
                             1 Turn face to right and sight to spot some dis-
                               tance away, then return gaze to front
                             2 Right arm extends out in point to R (SW), then
                               back to rest at knee

As he describes the event, the speaker surveys the local scene to gauge
how far the demon ran, pointing to his right to where the blackman fled
after he tried to grab it. In his next utterance the narrator establishes a more
definite locus.

1   3.....   4..............a....b
         te i -0 -bat   yo`   pat   krus -e
         there CP-3A-go where back cross-CL
         It went there behind the cross.
                             3 Look quickly out R again, then back
                             4 R arm lifts out R and slightly to front, (a) circles
                               anticlockwise, index finger slightly down, (b)
                               moving all slightly L and held

2   ......5................. 6........................
      k'al   yo` krus ali te vechel   krus ta
      as_far_as where cross uh there sitting_on_base cross PREP
      (It went) there to sit by the cross where . . .

                              5 R arm still extended, fingers drop to expose back
                                of hand, in anticlockwise circling motion
                              6 Circling motion of R hand repeated, then arm
                                withdrawn to rest

      ch -av-il   onox   li   j -krus   k'al   tana
      ICP-2E-see nonetheless ART 1E-cross as_far_as afterwards
      Where my cross is still today, you know.

The gesture depicted in Figure 1.7 combines both the oriented pointing that
locates the cross relative to the place where the *j`ik'al* originally fled (in
Figure 1.6), with a hand shape (and circling motion) evidently intended to
convey the spatial relationship encoded in the Tzotzil expression *ta pat krus*
'behind the cross'. The gestures here literally create their referents to populate the illustrative graphic space.

8   Gesture spaces

These two strategies for constructing indexical gestures involve different
principles for calibrating the immediate local space of the speech event with
the gesture space where the conceptual entities 'pointed to' reside. In relatively presupposing pointing, the location pointed at can be derived from
coordinating the space referred to (i.e., the space conceptually containing
the referent) with the immediate space (where the gesture is physically performed). In relatively creative pointing, a location is selected in the local
scene, as it were, arbitrarily. The gesture 'creatively' entails the referent's
existence by 'placing' it within the referent space, and it imposes a structure
on that space – including a location for the referent where such location is
relevant – with certain possibilities for subsequent reference.

There is a further consequence of the choice between these two pointing
strategies. Suppose that one explicit aim of a stretch of discourse is to establish relations, spatial and otherwise, *between* referents. An arbitrary map,
populated by means of relatively creative deictic acts of reference, may
produce arbitrary interrelationships. Or it may invoke principles other than
the geometries implied by 'actual' geographic location. Referent X may (in
the real world) stand north of referent Y, but I may put my 'pointed-at' X
and Y in some other relationship – X to the right of Y, or higher, or lower
(and there may be no need for a single consistent solution). On the other
hand, a gestural map that presupposes actual geography can directly

exploit actual presupposable geographic relations, although certain principles of transformation or rotation, zooming, and resolution may need to be invoked both to keep things straight and to achieve the required level of detail.[13]

However, choosing between relatively presupposing and creative strategies is presumably not itself an arbitrary matter. It may depend on a further convention between interlocutors, or, indeed, on a communicative tradition, part of the 'culture' of a linguistic community. My dialect of American English favors relatively creative solutions for referential gestures, 'locating' referents more or less wherever they happen conveniently to fall. For GY speakers by convention the solution is highly presupposing. It was the suspicion that Zinacantecs, despite having little overt linguistic support for precise orientation in spoken Tzotzil, also were relatively presupposing in the orientation of their gestures that prompted this closer look at Zinacantec pointing.

In addition to *local* and *narrated* gesture spaces, Haviland (1993) distinguishes a further *interactional* space, defined by the configuration and orientation of the bodies of the interactants (see Kendon 1990b). Interactional space usually comprises the intersection of the hemispheres of action and attention that project forward from the bodies of the interlocutors, especially the speaker (see Özyürek, this volume). This space has a privileged interactional character, being conjointly available to interlocutors for gesticulation. Interlocutors in a sense create this space by virtue of their interaction; they do not find it in the local surround, but carry it with them.

Although interactional space in principle can also come with cardinal directions attached, Haviland (1993) shows that even in GY discourse it is here that gestures are frequently emancipated from the compass. This is the area within which a speaker locates 'absent' referents creatively and refers to them subsequently. Interactional space may thus be free from fixed cardinal orientation.

Furthermore, when narrative recounts scenes of interaction, narrators may also quote 'free' gestures, thus invoking *narrated interactional space*: a space in which narrated interaction is located. If interactional space is unanchored by cardinal directions, then narrated interactional space may be similarly emancipated.

To repeat, in this parlance a 'space' is simply the projected spatial context for an indexical sign, the signs of interest being the loosely defined 'pointing gestures' which supposedly require at the very least spatially locatable referents. Since gestures flash by evanescently, so do their projected spaces. Thus the different kinds of gesture spaces – really complementary dimensions of projected spaces which may, in fact, be laminated one on top of another –

are swiftly instantiated and sometimes just as swiftly discarded in the inter-active flow, though rarely does an entire space disappear without leaving some usable residue. It is the multiplicity of gesture spaces, and the shifting between them, that belies the alleged simplicity of 'pointing' gestures as primitive referential devices. It is also what makes pointing gestures rich evidence about spatial knowledge – social, interactive, and individual.

9   Mental map or externalized mnemonic?

The notion of a mental map implies an internalized conceptual structure, abstracted perhaps from external, physical space, but subject to various manipulations and characterizable through linguistic categories. The inter-active practices of Mayan Indians and Australian Aborigines suggest that although physical ('real') space can be the object of linguistic and cognitive processing, it also may serve as a *tool* for such processing, a medium upon which cognition may be externalized. In particular, when conversants are actively trying to construct or agree about spatial relationships, space itself can be a mnemonic through which knowledge of land, terrain, and terri-tory can be (re)constructed and (re)calculated. The gesture spaces of con-versation constitute an interactively available – indeed, interactively constructed – analog computational device for working out spatial and other sorts of relations. Gestures, which directly exploit this spatial medium, consequently assume a special importance in such conversations.

Older GY speakers, like the narrator of the shipwreck story, show great (if quite unconscious) precision in orienting their gestures – comparable to an equal precision in the use of spoken directional terms. The same sort of gestural accuracy can occasionally be observed in the speech of much younger people, even those who liberally mix English into their GY, or who almost entirely eliminate spoken references to the cardinal directional system. One such younger man, GC, does not use spoken directionals, for example, in pseudo-experiments like retelling books or video scenarios, although older GY speakers frequently do. When it comes to his own tribal country, however, he tries to maintain careful orientation, in both word and gesture. GC is currently reclaiming rights over land expropriated by both government and other Aboriginal groups (see Haviland 1997). As a result, even otherwise innocuous interactions have been transformed into proving grounds for his traditional territorial claims.

GC is a fluent GY speaker, but one who has spent time away from the community, speaking English. He is thus out of practice with his native lan-guage, though for political reasons he cultivates its use in appropriate con-texts. He describes a site on Lizard Island, part of the traditional clan territory at Cape Flattery, which he has inherited from his patriline. The site is named after the barb of a giant stingray. According to tradition, it was also the spot where men of his lineage should be christened so as to insure their success at hunting. GC has recounted the story from the perspective of the island, which lies east of the mainland Cape Flattery camp. GC sits with his back to the east facing his interlocutor in the west. He has come to the point in his story where the ancestral figure who speared the giant stingray now turns west toward the mainland to await the birth of male children. At line 4 of fragment (6), GC points clearly to the west (see Figure 1.8), at the same time saying first "to the east," then "to the north," and finally, with a confirmatory nod at line 6, "to the west" – the word which, to judge by his oriented gesture, he was searching for.

(6) Cape Flattery
     1 well ngathi   nhaamu-:unh
        "   grandfather that -ABL
        Well, then my grandfather . . .

                 1...... a....... b
     2 nyulu   said well all right
        3SgNOM "   "   "   "
        He said, "Well, all right."

                                1 RH up in open C, rises to midchest at (a), drops
                                  at (b)

                                      2....... 3......
     3 ngathu   ganggal yii nhangu
        1sgGEN child   here 3sGEN
        My child here –

                                2 Gaze up W, staring

        ....a....b...
     4 nagaar
        east+R
        in the east –

                                3 RH starts up, two index fingers pointing: W at
                                  (a), high W at (b)

       c
     5 gunggarra
        North+R
        in the north –

                                3 (*cont.*) RH circles into body and drops to rest at
                                  (c)

Figure 1.8.   Figure 1.9.

4.....
6 guwaar . balga=-=:ya
  west+R make -REF+NPAST
  in the west, (my child) will be born.

> 4 Gaze high W, head rises slightly, staring, and
> falls

7 m; Cape Bedford?
   At Cape Bedford?
        [

        5.........
8 g;   ngayu-
        1SgNom
        "I–"

> 5 RH rises to chest height, palm in, fingers out S,
> circles clockwise and up

GC's interlocutor, knowing the geographical relationships involved, is confused by GC's words, and he hazards two incorrect guesses (at lines 7 and 10) about the place GC is talking about. Both GC's subsequent pointing gesture at line 9:6 (see Figure 1.9) and his verbal confirmation at line 11 show that GC was perfectly clear about the relative positions of Lizard Island and Cape Flattery even if he couldn't quite find the correct term. His own hand, mnemonically pointing west, may have helped him with the word search.

```
        .....  6.........7
9      gaari
       No.
```

```
                    6  Segues into RH indexes point, palm face in, up
                       high W, back to rest.
                    7  Gaze meets M, slight nod.
```

```
       ......
10 m;  McIvor
       At McIvor?
```

```
11 g;  dingaal
       At Cape Flattery.
```

10   Tzotzil narrative and oriented gestures

Tzotzil-speaking Indian peasants in the highlands of Chiapas, Mexico, also display precise bodily orientations to space despite the comparative lack of linguistic support for such precision. There are, in Tzotzil, only underdeveloped devices for talking about cardinal directions, when compared with the morphologically hypertrophied and ubiquitous cardinal direction terms in GY. Indeed, although the ancient Maya are celebrated for their calendrical and astronomical achievements, modern-day Zinacantecs have paltry lexical or grammatical resources for talking about cardinal directions. East and west are simply "place where the sun rises" and ". . . sets," or – reflecting an overall inclination of the territory dominated by the central Chiapas highlands (on the east), and the lowland Grijalva valley (on the west) – simply *ak'ol* 'up, upland' and *olon* 'low, lowland' (de León 1994a). Talk about direction is dominated by local geography rather than by celestial absolutes,[14] and directional terms are infrequent in ordinary conversation.

It may thus seem somewhat surprising that Zinacantec Tzotzil-speakers appear to maintain a division in gesture space that roughly parallels the division between *directionally anchored* local space and the *free* interactional space I have described for GY. Finding that Tzotziles, too, have their anchored spaces pushes one to search for the conceptual support that using such spaces in gesture might require.

Peasant agriculturists whose livelihood depends on intimate knowledge of the lay of the land, and especially people like my compadre P, who spent his youth leading mules on trails crisscrossing the highlands, have good reason to maintain detailed and precisely oriented mental maps of their territory.

Knowledge of routes and geography, not unlike knowledge of plants (see Laughlin & Breedlove 1993), grows naturally from tromping the trails. Older Zinacantecs are encyclopedias of place names, botanical and topographic lore, paths, routes, water holes, creeks, and settlements over a wide area that extends far beyond municipal boundaries.

Detailed knowledge of geography and terrain may have begun to fade when younger men took to trucks and buses after the arrival of the Pan American Highway in the early 1950s. However, although micro-geographic knowledge may have narrowed, the scope of Zinacantec macro-geographic knowledge has expanded. Because of economic changes in Mexico, Chiapas Indians once relatively isolated from the pressures for outmigration that have long characterized much of rural Mexico have begun to leave their communities in search of work. Zinacantecs have always traded throughout the region, but more and more individual Zinacantecs now travel far from their municipalities, sometimes never to return.[15]

Maryan described to me the route he took when, burdened by crushing debts, he fled his village and sought work in the resort city of Cancún, far from his highland Chiapas home. Although aspects of Maryan's story have great ethnographic interest, I have deliberately ignored them here to concentrate on how he carried with him to Cancún a system of directional orientation which he exhibits gesturally as he talks.

At the beginning of Maryan's performance – in which he tells me how to get to Cancún from the village of Nabenchauk where we sit – he shifts his sitting position so that the line of his shoulders runs precisely east–west. Once made conveniently available by this shift, cardinal directions in pointing seem to remain constant and significant.

Maryan describes leaving Nabenchauk and proceeding to San Cristóbal. He accompanies his words (shown at (7)) with a slow rising gesture pointing out and up to his right, due east (see Figure 1.10).

(7)   Nabenchauk to San Cristóbal
                    1   2–3 . . . *(high and retract)*
            tuk' onox ya`el cibat   ali ta
            I would go straight to . . hh . . .

            li ta . ta Jobel xkaltike une
            to . . . San Cristóbal, as we say.

The route leaves San Cristóbal and heads for another spot on the Pan American Highway called Rancho Nuevo. As Maryan describes reaching that point, his vertical flat hand, still pointing east, moves downward (see Figure 1.11), apparently indicating 'arrival'.

Figure 1.10.

Figure 1.11.

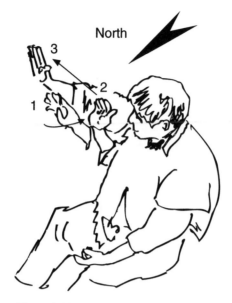

North

Figure 1.12.

(8)   Getting to Rancho Nuevo
           (1)......... 2............ *(rise and down to rest)*
           va`i un ali ja` xa li ta-
           So then, when we . . . uh . . .

                   RH up . . . rest
                       |out again to R
           yo` jtatik ali . rancho nwevo une
           when we get to where Rancho Nuevo is

From that point one "turns to the side" (9) and continues toward the next major town, Ocosingo. Maryan's expression with the verb *-k'atp'uj* means simply 'turn aside'; it makes no further specification of direction.

(9)   Turning sideways
           1   2-----3... *(high and stretch further)*
           ja` xa cik'atp'ujotik ec'el xi to cibatik .
           *that's where we turn away to the side and we go this way
           [towards Ocosingo].*

However, Maryan's gesture at this point, shown in Figure 1.12, does indicate that the direction involved is slightly east of north. He makes a pushing motion, first turning his palm to face north with the fingers slightly cupped, and then extending the hand outward in front of him (to the north-north-east), and finally extending his fingers.

One of the illustrations with which I began (Figure 1.2) is drawn from a later segment of this same route description. Maryan has located himself discursively at a crossroad just south of Palenque. His left arm is extended fully in front of his body, with the pointing finger angled slightly downward and to the right – a position that he holds as he says, "Palenque is close." The gesture is clearly transposed, in a now familiar way. *From the discursively established crossroad*, Palenque lies roughly NNW, the direction in which he now points. He has thus constructed a *narrated space*, over which he laminates the here-and-now of the conversation which supplies the required cardinal orientation.

If you look carefully at the compass directions of all Maryan's pointing gestures in this route description, you can construct a map which can be compared to, say, a road map of the same territory.

I have schematized a 'pointed' map of Maryan's Nabenchauk-to-Cancún route in Figure 1.13a. (The distances represented are only approximate interpretations of the accompanying gestural sweeps.) Comparing this virtual map with a standard road map, it is clear that Maryan's directional sense, though somewhat normalized, is close to that of cartographers (see Figure 1.13b).

Notice that Maryan's representation gives considerable local detail, naming many nearby locations, especially within the state of Chiapas, and becoming less detailed the farther he gets from home. Such differential density in representation is reminiscent of comparative findings about such externalized 'maps',[16] although it is hard to say whether this reflects Maryan's geographical knowledge or constraints of the interactive situation (where he expected his interlocutors to know more about nearby places in Chiapas than about distant points in Quintana Roo).

Maryan's gestures show directions as he proceeds from each named point to the next. However, such a point-by-point mapping of the route, if not corrected by spot sightings on unbroken roads, might be expected to produce cumulative error.[17] To judge by the ultimate tracing of paths, Maryan does not seem to have been misled by the fact that a road may leave a town in one direction, only to head ultimately in another.

These diagrams suggest that Maryan has constructed for himself an accurate representation of this macro-space, which he displays in carefully oriented gestures. Although in the whole conversation he makes hardly any *spoken* reference to cardinal directions, in his gestures he tracks his progress across the landscape with great precision.

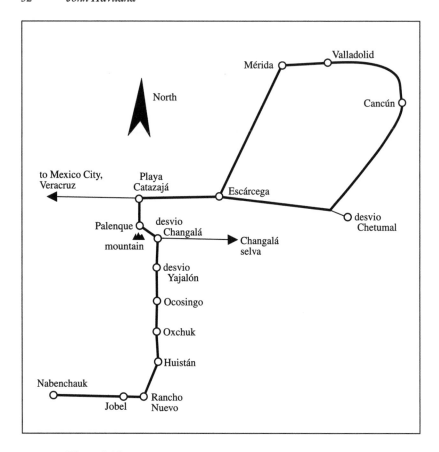

Figure 1.13a.

11   Transposition: movement among spaces

The theoretical continuum between relatively creative and relatively presupposing indexes, imported from words to pointing gestures, is complicated in practice by 'indirect' or mediated links from indexed referent to
intended referent. A narrator may, for example, point at a co-present interlocutor to refer either directly to that person as a protagonist, or indirectly
through links of kinship or historical association to some other person or
entity. More globally, pointing gestures may indicate referents which are
entirely absent, at least in the immediate physical surround.

Furthermore, skilled narrators can exploit different intertransposable
spaces, switching rapidly among them. The other gesture with which I

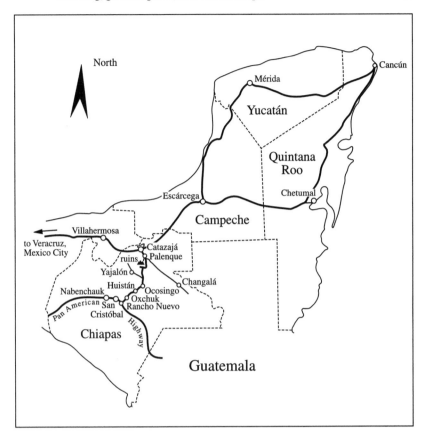

Figure 1.13b.

began (Figure 1.1) illustrates the speed with which speakers engineer (and interlocutors evidently absorb) such transpositions. P describes a roadside *cantina* where the muleteers used to drop in for a drink. Using props presented by the house patio in which we sit, he evokes this imaginary space in a remarkable sequence.

First he uses the micro-geography of his own house compound, where we sit, to establish a link between the physically co-present path and gate in *local* space – the entrance to the *sitio* (Figure 1.14) – and a *narrated gate* at the roadside bar (Figure 1.15).

(10)   1   2   4...........
1   . . oy te . ali ti` be ya`el chk li`e
         There was a gate there, just like here

Figure 1.14.   Figure 1.15.

> 1 Gaze out to right, focus on path?
> 2 Right hand up from knee, points with index
>   finger to N *(there)*
> 4 Right hand moves back W, returns E, fingers
>   curling inwards *(like this)*

	5	6

2   te jun . pwerta lek
There was a . proper door.

> 5 Right hand moves higher to above head level
>   (head turns back and down to middle) *(one)*
> 6 Fingers down, hand raised, bounces down twice
>   with palm down as gaze returns to me *(door)*

        6'.....
4   ta ti` be
at the entrance.

> 6' Right hand starts to drop, rises slightly in loose
>   hand, down to knee *(gate)*

     ...
        ....8.......................9...
7   oy tey nakal krixchano un
There were indeed people living there.

> 8 Cupped hand palm down, arm still extended,
>   taps once up and down out [N] *(living there)*
> 9 Right hand points down quickly, then (b) curls
>   back in → SW to position in front of face
>   *(people)*

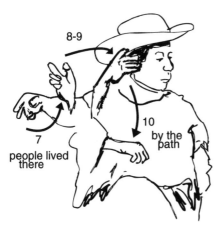

Figure 1.16.

In this transposed space his gestures (Figure 1.16) point at an imaginary fence and gate: the *tey* 'there' to which he points with the gesture shown as [8] in line 7, and the *ti` be* 'gate' which he represents with gesture [10] in line 8.

        10
8   ta ti` be
         beside the path.

                              10 Hand flat, vertical down and up motion (gaze
                                  to hand) *(gate)*

Swiftly, however, he brings his gesture back to the current here-and-now, in order to point, at [11], line 9, directly at the kitchen house beside which we are seated. "*That* house [whose gate I can point to in transposed narrative space] was the same size as *this house* [which I can point to here]." (Refer back to Figure 1.1.)

         11a   11b
9   . yech smuk'ul chk i na chk li`e
         (It) was the same size as this house here.

                              11a Right hand crosses to SW, and gaze also
                              11b and points to kitchen house before returning
                                   to rest *(size)*

Within a complex utterance he thus moves from immediate local space to a narrated hypothetical space, laminated over the former and deriving its structure therefrom, and then swiftly back again. A seemingly simple

Figure 1.17.

gesture points at once to a local building and to a narrated roadside bar long disappeared.

12   Lamination of spaces

The seemingly unproblematic notion of direction itself turns out to be unexpectedly complex. Even location by cardinal directions is not 'absolute', but relational, depending on a reference point from which a direction can be projected. Furthermore, the phenomenon of transposition makes clear that this reference point, far from being firmly anchored in the default here-and-now of the speech moment, can shift radically.

A particularly dramatic case comes from the sequence in which Maryan describes the topography of the area around the town of Palenque, which is located on a flat coastal plain running north from the central Chiapas mountain range. The famous Palenque ruins sit in the foothills of this range, in an area covered by dense jungle. He explains exactly where they are.

As we have seen, Maryan describes how one gets to the town of Palenque, and then, gesturally, he locates himself *there*. His gesture shown in Figure 1.17 establishes, in our shared mnemonic interactional space, the spot that will count as Palenque. That is where the trajectory he is about to describe starts.

(11)   *RH starts out from rest*
         | *1---2----RH moves rapidly back, and*
             | *gaze back over R shoulder*

Figure 1.18.

Suddenly he turns around rapidly to his right and makes an expansive gesture over his right shoulder (i.e., slightly to the southeast – see Figure 1.18).

(12)   1-----2--
       ali mi jtatik i Palenke
       If one gets to Palenque
       ---------3...............
           gaze back to me
           |
       xi chkom xi to vi
       (the ruins) are located this way.

He then says "(the mountains, i.e., the ruins) are located this way." After turning back to the front, he again turns to the southwest, in a further gesture.

(13)   *gaze starts back over R shoulder*
       | 1 *(points twice)*
               then rapidly back to rest
               gaze front
       k'u cha`al yochob
       like the (Nabenchauk) sinkhole.

South

Figure 1.19.

At the second line of (13) (Figure 1.19) MA turns to point straight south, at the same time focusing his gaze on a stand of rocks across the Nabenchauk lake, a place called *yochob* 'sinkhole'. Now his mental calculations are made plain. (1) Transpose yourself to the town of Palenque. (2) From *there* look that way [south]. That's where the mountains are. (3) Bring yourself back to Nabenchauk. It's the same *direction* as the sinkhole from *here*. To follow the entire performance requires the interlocutor to superimpose a map of the local terrain on the narrated spot and then calibrate positions in the latter by recalculating positions in the former (see Figure 1.20). In this spectacular feat of mental gymnastics, both location and direction are transposed, and it is the presumed constancy of compass directions that calibrates the lamination of two different spaces, one local and one narrated.

13   Morals

Space, no matter how immediate or unproblematically accessible it may seem, is always itself a construction, conceptually projected from not only where we are but who we are and what we know. Gesture makes use not of 'raw space' but of this projected conceptual entity. Gestures employ spaces for the characteristically dual ends of discourse generally: both to represent states of affairs, and to manipulate states of affairs. Let me suggest three sorts of conclusion: methodological, conceptual, and ethnographic.

Nabenchauk

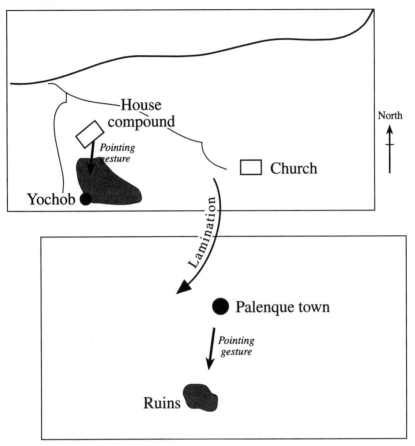

Figure 1.20.

First, the study of gestures recommends itself as ethnographic method. To unravel even apparently simple 'pointing' gestures requires cognitive and sociocultural insight: about what entities exist to be pointed at, about how to reconstruct referents from indicated locations, about why an interactant points at all (as opposed to using some other referential modality). Indeed, gestures are fleeting but accessible cognitive exhibits, playing out with the body the actions, referential and otherwise, that constitute discourse.

Second, an adequate understanding of even supposedly primeval point-ing gestures requires surprisingly complex conceptual tools. My metaphor for these conceptual tools has been the 'gesture space', distinguishing a *local* space which is relevantly *anchored* (for example, by cardinal directions, independent of the entities that may populate it) from *interactional* space, whose orientation may be irrelevant or determined solely by the relative positions of interactants. Entities in both spaces can be indexically signaled with both gestures and other deictics.

Narrated spaces are laminated over these immediate spaces, substituting for the here-and-now a narratable there-and-then. Narrated entities can in turn be denoted by indexical devices, including 'pointing' gestures, whose referents must be iconically mapped from one laminate onto another.

A narrated space can be anchored on a discursively established origo and laminated over local space so as to inherit the latter's cardinal orientation, thereby allowing referents to be located by their indicated positions, presupposably, as when relative narrated positions are (a) known to interlocutors or (b) recoverable by inference (for instance, the motion of the capsizing boat). On the other hand, what is narrated may itself be *(narrated) interactional* space, established discursively and providing an autonomous locus of reanimated narrated interactions.

All of these 'gesture spaces' can be complex constructions from knowledge that is at once geographic and social. Their lamination both enables and relies upon conceptual links that go well beyond any unproblematic spatial givenness. At the same time, the immediacy of the space that interactants share offers a vehicle for externalizing, onto the body and its surround, calculations of place and spatial relationships that might otherwise be difficult both to conceptualize and to communicate. Both Zinacantecs and GY-speaking residents of Hopevale inscribe ethnography on geography. Space itself, whether represented or simply inhabited, has an indelible social quality not captured by either topology or topography. Gesture exploits this quality of the very space it uses as its vehicle, also incorporating, indirectly, the sociohistorical evolution of spaces.

In GY country, knowledge of land traditionally involved orientational precision. As ties to land have faded in importance, such precision has also declined. Recent legal possibilities for land rights have fostered a resurgence of interest in local practices of reckoning space, which calibrate directionally anchored spaces with socially populated conceptual universes. In Zinacantán, local models of space have been exported to faraway universes, both social and spatial, perhaps contradictorily domesticating distant and dangerous places by transposing them to the here-and-now.

NOTES

1 Levinson (1992) explores some cognitive underpinnings of GY linguistic practices, and de León (1994b) discusses aspects of their acquisition.

2 A longer, multimedia version of the material presented here can be found at
http://www.cs.uchicago.edu/l-c/archives/subs/haviland-john/.

Material presented in this paper is based on work with many friends, pseudo-
kin, and colleagues, of whom I most especially would like to thank several now
deceased Guugu Yimithirr speakers from the Hopevale, viz., Jack Bambi, Bob
Flinders, and Tulo Gordon; also my friend and 'cousin' Roger Hart, my 'uncle'
Frankie Confin, and Gordon Charlie. I am also especially indebted to my com-
padres Pedro Vázquez Xuljol and Maryan Ach'eltik, from the hamlet of
Nabenchauk, Zinacantán, Chiapas, Mexico.

3 Tzotzil examples in this chapter are transcribed with an abbreviated practical
orthography, largely based on Spanish. Guugu Yimithirr is written in a standard Australianist practical orthography. Transcript lines are accompanied by a
free English gloss, and by gestural descriptions, which are synchronized with the
transcript. L, R, H, N, S, E, and W are abbreviations for left, right, hand, north,
south, east, and west, respectively. Where a transcript line is accompanied by
gestural drawings, numbers (on the drawing and set in synchrony above the
transcript line) indicate the illustrated moments of a movement.

4 An exception is Evans (1996).

5 See Talmy (1985).

6 Kendon (1994) argues that gesture has an unavoidable and naturally exploitable
communicative role. Compare Goodwin & Goodwin (1992), Goodwin (1986),
Moerman (1990), and Streeck (1993). But contrast Krauss et al. (1991).

7 Typologies on quite different principles are possible; Wilkins (1997) describes a
native Arrente classification of manual gestures, for example.

8 McNeill and his associates (McNeill & Levy 1982; McNeill 1985; McNeill, Levy
& Pedelty 1990; Cassell & McNeill 1991), drawing on the classic proposals of
Efron (1972 [1941]), propose a classificatory scheme which distinguishes iconic
and metaphoric gestures which bear a relation of resemblance to aspects of
utterance content, deictic gestures which index referents both concrete and
abstract, and beats which seem to be non-representational. See also Ekman &
Friesen (1969) and McNeill (1992).

9 The possibility of formal/functional links between gestures and the meanings
they encode complicates the dichotomy between gesticulation and emblem
or sign. See, for example, Calbris (1990), Haviland (1991b), and Kendon's
recent work (e.g., Kendon & Versante 1998) on recurrent hand shapes in Italian
gesticulation.

10 For example, see Sherzer (1972).

11 Wittgenstein (1958), sect. 85. Lest this seem like a mere philosopher's nicety,
consider Sander Adelaar's (pers. com.) anecdote about speakers of Chamic languages during World War II and the Western soldiers who pointed to a far-off
spot, asking for a place name, only to be given the name of the spot directly
below the outstretched finger.

12 Underlining connects words in phrasal glosses that correspond to single Tzotzil
words. Hyphens divide morpheme-by-morpheme breakdowns.

13 See Haviland (1991a). Habel (1990) employs the notion of resolution to model
people's knowledge of the Hamburg train system.

14 Gossen (1974) notes that Chamulans conventionally denote north as "the side of the sky on the right hand" and south as ". . . on the left hand" (p. 32). Zinacantecs often simply refer to either direction as *ta k'atal* 'sideways'. Brown & Levinson (1993) describe the cognate 'uphill' and 'downhill' system in neighboring Tenejapa Tzeltal, where the denotations are rotated 90 degrees ('uphill' denotes south).
15 See Haviland (1989) and de León (1991) for recent Zinacantec labor migration to the United States and Mexico City.
16 See Gossen (1974), who argues that as distance from Chamula increases, so do time, alienness, and danger in Chamulan ideas about the world.
17 The observation is due to Stephen Levinson.

REFERENCES

Armstrong, D. F., Stokoe, W. C. & Wilcox, S. E. 1995. *Gesture and the Nature of Language*. Cambridge: Cambridge University Press.
Atkinson, J. M. & Heritage, J. (eds.) 1984. *Structures of Social Action*. Cambridge: Cambridge University Press.
Auer, P. & di Luzio, A. (eds.) 1992. *The Contextualization of Language*. Amsterdam: Benjamins.
Basso, K. & Selby, H. (eds.) 1976. *Meaning in Anthropology*. Albuquerque: University of New Mexico Press.
Bates, E., Bretherton, I., Shore, C. & McNew, S. 1983. Names, gestures, and objects: symbolization in infancy and aphasia. In Nelson (ed.), pp. 59–123.
Bellugi, U. & Klima, E. 1982. From gesture to sign: deixis in a visual-gestural language. In Jarvella & Klein (eds.), pp. 297–314.
Birdwhistell, R. L. 1952. *Introduction to Kinesics*. Louisville, KY: Louisville University Press.
Birdwhistell, R. L. 1963. The kinesis level in the investigation of the emotions. In Knapp (ed.), pp. 123–139.
Brown, P. & Levinson, S. C. 1993. 'Uphill' and 'downhill' in Tzeltal. *Journal of Linguistic Anthropology* 3: 46–74. (Also: Working Paper no. 7, Cognitive Anthropology Research Group, Max Planck Institute for Psycholinguistics, Nijmegen, 1991.)
Bühler, K. 1982. The deictic field of language and deictic words. In Jarvella & Klein (eds.), pp. 9–30.
Calbris, G. 1990. *The Semiotics of French Gestures*. Bloomington: Indiana University Press.
Carter, A. L. 1975. The transformation of sensorimotor morphemes into words: a case study of the development of 'more' and 'mine'. *Journal of Child Language* 2: 233–250.
Cassell, J. & McNeill, D. 1991. Gesture and the poetics of prose. *Poetics Today* 12: 375–404.
DeGraff, M. (ed.) in press. *Language Creation and Change: Creolization, Diachrony, and Development*. Cambridge, MA: MIT Press.
de León, L. 1991. Achiote y fresas. *Mexico Indigena* 23: 30–31.
de León, L. 1994a. Exploration in the acquisition of geocentric location by Tzotzil

children. *Linguistics* 32: 857–884. (Paper presented at Cognitive Anthropology Research Group, Max Planck Institute for Psycholinguistics, Nijmegen, January 20, 1992.)

de León, L. 1994b. Acquisition of geocentric location by Guugu Yimithirr speaking children. Unpublished paper, Cognitive Anthropology Research Group, Max Planck Institute for Psycholinguistics, Nijmegen.

Dixon, R. M. W. & Blake, B. (eds.) 1979. *Handbook of Australian Languages*, vol. I. Canberra: Australian National University Press.

Efron, D. 1972 [1941]. *Gesture, Race and Culture*. The Hague: Mouton. (Reprinted from *Gesture and Environment*, New York: King's Crown Press.)

Ekman, P. & Friesen, W. V. 1969. The repertoire of non-verbal behavioral categories: origins, usage, and coding. *Semiotica* 1: 49–98.

Emmory, K. & Reilly, J. S. (eds.) 1995. *Language, Gesture, and Space*. Hillsdale, NJ: Erlbaum.

Engberg-Pedersen, E. 1995. Point of view expressed through shifters. In Emmory & Reilly (eds.), pp. 133–164.

Evans, N. 1996. *A Grammar of Kayardild. With Historical-Comparative Notes on Tangkic*. Berlin: Mouton de Gruyter.

Farnell, B. 1988. Where mind is a verb: sign talk of the Plains Indians revisited. Paper presented at the American Anthropological Association meetings, Phoenix, November.

Farnell, B. 1994. Ethno-graphics and the moving body. *Man* 29: 929–974.

Gibson, K. R. & Ingold, T. (eds.) 1991. *Tools, Language and Cognition in Human Evolution*. Cambridge: Cambridge University Press.

Goldin-Meadow, S. 1991. When does gesture become language? A study of gesture used as a primary communication system by deaf children of hearing parents. In Gibson & Ingold (eds), pp. 63–85.

Goldin-Meadow, S. & Mylander, C. 1998. Spontaneous sign systems created by deaf children in two cultures. *Nature* 391: 279–281.

Goldin-Meadow, S., McNeill, D. & Singleton, J. 1996. Silence is liberating: removing the handcuffs on grammatical expression in the manual modality. *Psychological Review* 103: 34–55.

Goodwin, C. 1986. Between and within: alternative sequential treatments of continuers and assessments. *Human Studies* 9: 205–217.

Goodwin, C. & Goodwin, M. H. 1992. Context, activity and participation. In Auer & di Luzio (eds.), pp. 77–99.

Gossen, G. H. 1974. *Chamulas in the World of the Sun: Time and Space in a Maya Oral Tradition*. Cambridge, MA: Harvard University Press.

Gumperz, J. J. & Levinson, S. C. (eds.) 1996. *Rethinking Linguistic Relativity*. Cambridge: Cambridge Univiversity Press.

Habel, C. 1990. Formalization of the spatial inventory. Paper presented at Workshop on Space, Time, and the Lexicon, Max Planck Institute for Psycholinguistics, Nijmegen, November.

Hammond, G. R. (ed.) 1990. *Advances in Psychology: Cerebral Control of Speech and Limb Movements*. Amsterdam: Elsevier/North Holland.

Hanks, W. F. 1990. *Referential Practice*. Chicago: University of Chicago Press.

Haviland, J. B. 1979. Guugu Yimidhirr. In Dixon & Blake (eds.), pp. 27–182.

Haviland, J. B., 1989. Tztamik ta lume, asta k'u cha`al bu chak' sat te` (Desde el suelo hasta la fruta): la migración y la información en el discurso tzotzil. Paper presented at annual meetings of the Sociedad Mexicana de Antropología, Mérida, 18 October.

Haviland, J. B. 1991a. Projections, transpositions, and relativity. Paper presented at Wenner-Gren Conference on Rethinking Linguistic Relativity, Ocho Rios, May. (Also: Working Paper, Cognitive Anthropology Research Group, Max Planck Institute for Psycholinguistics, Nijmegen.)

Haviland, J. B. 1991b. Xi chbat ta lok'eb k'ak'al: it goes towards the sunrise: sculpting space with the body. Unpublished paper, Cognitive Anthropology Research Group, Max Planck Institute for Psycholinguistics, Nijmegen.

Haviland, J. B. 1993. Anchoring, iconicity, and orientation in Guugu Yimithirr pointing gestures. *Journal of Linguistic Anthropology* 3: 3–45. (Also: Working Paper no. 8, Cognitive Anthropology Research Group, Max Planck Institute for Psycholinguistics. Nijmegen.)

Haviland, J. B. 1996. Projections, transpositions, and relativity. In Gumperz & Levinson (eds.), pp. 271–323.

Haviland, J. B. 1997. Owners vs. *bubu gujin*: land rights and getting the language right in Guugu Yimithirr country. *Journal of Linguistic Anthropology* 6: 145–160.

Jarvella, R. J. & Klein, W. (eds.) 1982. *Speech, Place, and Action: Studies in Deixis and Related Topics*. Chichester: Wiley.

Kegl, J., Senghas, A. & Coppola, M. in press. Creation through contact: sign language emergence and sign language change in Nicaragua. In DeGraff (ed.).

Kendon, A. 1980. Gesticulation and speech: two aspects of the process of utterance. In Key (ed.), pp. 207–227.

Kendon, A. 1983. Word and gesture. Paper presented at Fifth International Conference on Culture and Communication, Philadelphia, March.

Kendon, A. 1988a. *Sign Languages of Aboriginal Australia*. Cambridge: Cambridge University Press.

Kendon, A. 1988b. How gestures can become like words. In Poyatos (ed.), pp. 131–141.

Kendon, A. 1990a. Gesticulation, quotable gestures, and signs. In Moerman & Nomura (eds.), pp. 53–78.

Kendon, A. 1990b. *Conducting Interaction*. Cambridge: Cambridge University Press.

Kendon, A. 1994. Do gestures communicate? A review. *Research on Language and Social Interaction* 27: 175–200.

Kendon, A. & Versante, L. 1998. Pointing by hand in Campania and Northamptonshire. Paper presented at 6th International Pragmatics Conference, Reims, July.

Key, M. R. (ed.) 1980. *The Relationship of Verbal and Nonverbal Communication*. The Hague: Mouton.

Knapp, P. H. (ed.) 1963. *Expressions of the Emotions in Man*. New York: International University Press.

Krauss, R. M., Morrel-Samuels, P. & Colasante, C. 1991. Do conversational hand gestures communicate? *Journal of Personality and Social Psychology* 61: 743–754.

Laughlin, R. M. & Breedlove, D. 1993. *The Flowering of Man: A Tzotzil Botany of Zinacantán.* Washington, DC: Smithsonian Institution.

Laughren, M. 1978. Directional terminology in Warlpiri. In Le & McCausland (eds.), pp. 1–16.

Le, T. & McCausland, M. (eds.) 1978. Working Papers in Language & Linguistics No. 8. Tasmanian College of Advanced Education (Newnham).

Levelt, W. J. M., Richardson, G. & W. La Heij 1985. Pointing and voicing in deictic expressions. *Journal of Memory and Language* 24: 133–164.

Levinson, S. C. 1992. Language and cognition: the cognitive consequences of spatial description in Guugu Yimithirr. Working Paper no.13, Cognitive Anthropology Research Group, Max Planck Institute for Psycholinguistics, Nijmegen.

Lucy, J. A. (ed.) 1992. *Reflexive Language.* Cambridge: Cambridge University Press.

Marslen-Wilson, W., Levy, E. T. & Tyler, L. K. 1982. Producing interpretable discourse: the establishment and maintenance of discourse. In Jarvella & Klein (eds.), pp. 271–295.

McNeill, D. 1985. So you think gestures are nonverbal? *Psychological Review* 92: 350–371.

McNeill, D. 1987. So you *do* think gestures are nonverbal! Reply to Feyereisen (1987). *Psychological Review* 94: 499–504.

McNeill, D. 1992. *Hand and Mind: What Gestures Reveal about Thought.* Chicago: University of Chicago Press.

McNeill, D. & Levy, E. T. 1982. Conceptual representations in language activity and gesture. In Jarvella & Klein (eds.), pp. 271–295.

McNeill, D., Levy, E. T. & Pedelty, L. L. 1990. Gestures and speech. In Hammond (ed.), pp. 203–256.

Moerman, M. 1990. Gesticulation, quotable gestures, and signs. In Moerman & Nomura (eds.), pp. 53–78.

Moerman, M. & Nomura, M. (eds.) 1990. *Culture Embodied.* Senri Ethnological Studies no. 27. National Museum of Ethnology, Osaka.

Nelson, K. E. (ed.) 1983. *Children's Language,* vol. iv. Hillsdale, NJ: Erlbaum.

Ozanne-Rivierre, F. 1987. L'expression linguistique de l'orientation dans l'espace: quelques exemples océaniens. *Cahiers du LACITO* 2: 129–155.

Petitto, L. A. & Marentette, P. 1991. Babbling in the manual mode. *Science* (Washington, DC) 251: 1483–1496.

Pitkin, H. 1984. *Wintu Grammar.* Berkeley and Los Angeles: University of California Press.

Poyatos, F. (ed.) 1988. *Cross-Cultural Perspectives in Nonverbal Communication.* Toronto: Hogrefe.

Schegloff, E. A. 1984. On some gestures' relation to talk. In Atkinson & Heritage (eds.), pp. 266–296.

Sherzer, J. 1972. Verbal and nonverbal deixis: the pointed lip gesture among the San Blas Cuna. *Language and Society* 2: 117–131.

Shopen, T. (ed.) 1985. *Language Typology and Syntactic Description,* vol. iii: *Grammatical categories and the lexicon.* Cambridge: Cambridge University Press.

Silverstein, M. 1976. Shifters, linguistic categories, and cultural description. In Basso & Selby (eds.), pp. 11–56.

Silverstein, M. 1992. Metapragmatic discourse and metapragmatic function. In Lucy (ed.), pp. 33–58.
Streeck, J. 1993. Gesture as communication I: its coordination with gaze and speech. *Communication Monographs* 604: 275–299.
Talmy, L. 1985. Lexicalization patterns: semantic structure in lexical forms. In Shopen (ed.), pp. 57–149.
Wilkins, D. 1997. Four Arrente manual points. Unpublished paper, Cognitive Anthropology Research Group, Max Planck Institute for Psycholinguistics, Nijmegen.
Wittgenstein, L. 1958. *Philosophical Investigations*. Oxford: Blackwell.

2   Language and gesture: unity or duality?

Adam Kendon

Philadelphia, PA

1   Introduction

'Language' and 'gesture' have long been held to be different, yet at the same time a relationship between them has always been recognized. However, whether they are regarded as belonging together or not depends upon how these words are defined. Thus if, with Armstrong, Stokoe & Wilcox, we accept Studdert-Kennedy's (1987: 77) definition of 'gesture' as "an equivalence class of coordinated movements that achieve some end" (see Armstrong et al. 1995: 43), then, insofar as both speech and, let us say, gestures of the hands are comprised of "coordinated movements that achieve some end," it is possible to argue for a fundamental identity between the one and the other, as indeed they have done. On the other hand, if we insist, as some have, that a defining feature of language is that it be spoken, then this seems forever to make it impossible to see 'gesture' as part of 'language'. However, if we define language in a more abstract fashion, and allow that its medium of realization is not one of its defining features, then whether or not 'gesture' is to be seen as a part of language depends upon what other features are insisted upon. For example, if we follow Saussure's definition of language, so long as 'gestures' can be shown to be arbitrary form-meaning pairs differentiated in contrastive relationships and organized paradigmatically and syntagmatically, they can be regarded as a form of language. On these grounds, gesture systems such as primary or alternate sign languages would be included, but we might exclude such modes of expression as improvised or locally created gesturings such as may be observed in many of the gestures used concurrently with speech. On the other hand if, like William Dwight Whitney, we define language as "the means of expression of human thought" (1899: 1), which, as he goes on to say, is comprised of "certain instrumentalities whereby men consciously and with intention represent their thought, to the end, chiefly, of making it known to other men," then 'gesture' may be seen as a part of language. Indeed, Whitney is explicit on this point, since he lists among his 'instrumentalities' "gesture, grimace, pictorial or written signs, and uttered or spoken signs." Of these, the last is, according to him, "infinitely the most important"; but of gesture he says that we make use of it "on the one hand for communication where the usual conventional means is of no avail [deaf; people with different languages] and, on the other hand, for embellishing and explaining and enforcing our ordinary language: where it is of such power and value that no student of language can afford to overlook" (p. 283).

Whitney's functional definition of 'language' is not widely followed today. For one thing, it seems to many to be too inclusive, and in his own work, of course, he himself concentrated on what he referred to as "the body of uttered and audible signs by which, in human society, thought is principally expressed." From Saussure onwards, linguists have almost always defined language in structural terms, and until the advent of studies of primary sign languages, it was almost always assumed that 'language' must be spoken to be 'language'. As a consequence, very many writers use the words 'language' and 'speech' interchangeably.

This is one of the reasons why the study of gesture in any of its forms languished for so long. Whereas at the end of the last century leading writers on language such as Edward Tylor (1865), Wilhelm Wundt (1973 [1902]), and Dwight Whitney paid serious attention to it, as the structural analysis of language became more and more important, gesture, in treatises on language, at any rate, in any of its manifestations, is mentioned less and less often. If it is mentioned at all it is usually to show that it is not very interesting and can be ignored. For example, Leonard Bloomfield, in his influential textbook *Language* (1933: 39), observes that gesture accompanies speech, and remarks that it is subject to social convention, but writes that it is "obvious" in how it functions. So far as gesture languages are concerned, these for him are little more than elaborations of what he calls "ordinary gestures," and where they are more complex than this he claims they are "based on the conventions of ordinary speech."

Some linguists have shown a more interested attitude. Bolinger (1975: 18), for example, insisted that "language is embedded in gesture," and he showed, in a paper entitled 'Some Thoughts on "Yep" and "Nope"' (1946), how the boundary between what is considered 'language' and what not, is arbitrary and depends upon the extent to which the phenomena in question can be brought to order by the methodological procedures of structural analysis. Kenneth Pike, approaching the question from the perspective of his "unified theory of the structure of human behavior," insisted that language should be considered but a "phase" of human activity which should not be divorced from other "phases." In his initial and elementary demonstration of this point, in the first chapter of his major work (1967), he gives an account of a game in which the words in a sentence are progressively replaced by gestures. In this way he shows how non-spoken forms of action can be integrated structurally with spoken forms.

Despite this, little in the way of an investigation of gestures from a linguistic perspective has been undertaken, and with the reorientation of linguistics that occurred under the influence of Chomsky, which turned it into a kind of 'mental science', among those interested in language gesture appeared to disappear altogether as a topic of inquiry (Kendon 1982). Yet, curiously enough, it is really as a consequence of linguistics having come to be defined as a kind of mental science, which led directly to the development of studies of cognitive processes, that we have the situation we see today in which gesture is once again being investigated quite vigorously by those with an interest in language. If language is a cognitive activity, and if, as is clear, gestural expression is intimately involved in acts of spoken linguistic expression, then it seems reasonable to look closely at gesture for the light it may throw on this cognitive activity. This is leading to a new way in which the issue of the relationship between language and gesture can be approached.[1]

It will be clear that I am not here adopting the very radical definition of 'gesture' proposed by Armstrong, Stokoe & Wilcox that I cited at the beginning. I continue to use the term in its more usual meaning which, roughly speaking, refers to that range of visible bodily actions that are, more or less, generally regarded as part of a person's willing expression. This differentiates it from the expression of affect, on the one hand, which is typically seen as something that we cannot help, and, on the other, from those aspects of behavior such as posture and postural shifting, direction of gaze, and the like, which play a role in the processes by which participants in interaction establish and maintain their orientations to one another, but are not part of those packages of action by which greetings are exchanged, goods are bartered, stories are told, plans are laid, philosophical arguments are worked out, gossip is accomplished, and so on. There is, to be sure, no hard-and-fast line between what is 'gesture' and what is not, but there is, nonetheless, little difficulty with agreeing what it includes: handwavings or gesticulations that accompany talk and various kinds of more or less conventionalized actions which have a symbolic or semiotic function, as well as so-called gesture systems, alternate sign languages, and primary sign languages, all of which are fashioned from the same material, so to speak, and have certain features in common in consequence, but which, at the same time, may show very different kinds of organization.[2]

In this chapter I shall confine myself to a consideration of gesturing as it is found in the context of spoken interaction. I shall not consider autonomous gesture systems at all. However, I should like to point out that a comparative study of such systems, including both those of the simplest kind, as developed for use in work environments such as sawmills, where talk is impossible, to the most complex kinds of alternate and primary sign languages, provides for another way in which the question of the relationship between 'language' and 'gesture' can be investigated. Such comparative studies yield three main insights. First, that there is a close relationship between the complexity of the system developed and the degree to which the circumstances of its use are unspecialized. Second, however, for such systems to develop complexity it is also necessary that there be a COMMUNITY of users. In those few cases where we are able to look at situations where the use of a gesture system is confined to a non-reciprocated social role, the development of the system is highly limited. Third, the more unspecialized the system is in its uses, the greater the creativity to be observed within it. And it is here that we are able to find a continuum of forms ranging from forms which are locally created or improvised, through forms that are but partially lexicalized, to forms that are fully lexicalized and which participate in constructions built according to rules of syntax. The comparative study of autonomous gesture systems, thus, provides us with a way of seeing that systems that have all the structural features of a language are continually emerging through a process of evolution that depends upon appropriate circumstances of social interaction and institutionalization. This is another way in which it can be demonstrated that language is not a sharply bounded system but is, rather, something that is an emergent product of processes of semiotic and social evolution.[3]

Let me now turn to illustrations of some of the diverse ways in which gesture may be involved in acts of speaking. On the basis of these illustrations I shall argue for a functional continuity between language, as manifested in speech, and gesture. My perspective is semiotic and communicative. I shall argue that it is through the partnership between gesture and speech that we see so often in co-present conversation, that utterance meaning is achieved. I regard gesture as a mode of symbolic representation, just as spoken language is. However, in gesture, representation is achieved in ways that are different from spoken language. For example, in gesture it is possible to represent spatial relationships by means of spatially distributed displays; forms of movement can be created that can serve a variety of symbolic purposes; visible forms can be shaped that can be used as representations of concrete objects, which may serve as a means of referring to such objects either in their own right or metaphorically. Furthermore, because, as we shall see, it is possible to organize these representations concurrently with spoken forms, gesture can be used to create additional, overarching layers of meaning, overcoming, to some extent, the limitations imposed by the temporal linearity of spoken utterance. This makes it possible, for instance, for gesture to be used as a way of displaying in a continuous fashion higher-order semantic units that, of necessity, can emerge only bit by bit as they are expressed verbally. And it makes it possible for a speaker to display aspects of pragmatic meaning that govern whole stretches of discourse. This can have important consequences for how the speaker's recipients interpret what is being said.

With the exception of the first example to be presented, the examples I shall discuss come from video recordings made of naturally occurring conversations in a small town about ten kilometers inland from Salerno, in Italy.[4] Here I attempt to illustrate several ways in which gesture may operate in the context of spoken discourse in general. Whether, and in what ways, these uses of gesture are culturally specific I shall not discuss here – although some of the examples I shall show do involve the use of forms of gesture that are specific to southern Italy. But some of the others appear to have a much more widespread use.

2   Contextualizing functions of gesture: making meaning more precise

Speakers often employ gesture in such a way as to make something that is being said more precise or complete. Spoken words on their own, of course, are inherently ambiguous, and what a speaker means by the words or phrases used only becomes clear as they are set in a wider context. Such a context can indeed be created by how the expression is embedded in the spoken discourse itself. However, gesture also often plays a role in this.

The first example I shall give to illustrate this is taken from a narration in English of the fairy story 'Little Red Riding Hood'. The student doing the narration had been asked to tell the story as best she could, as if it were for an audience of children.[5]

She reaches the point in the story when the wolf, having swallowed the grandmother, is now chasing Little Red Riding Hood with the intention of eating her too. The hunter, on seeing Little Red Riding Hood rushing out of the cottage being chased by the wolf, runs up and kills the wolf. This scene is narrated in the following words:

(1)   and saw this wolf come bouncing out of the door after Little Red Riding Hood, and the hunter took his axe, and with one mighty heave, sliced the wolf's head off, and thought, 'Ha, I've saved the little girl, she should be happy now'

As she says "and the hunter took his axe" she moves both hands together as if grasping an axe by the handle; as she says "and with one mighty heave" she raises her hands above her shoulder as if enacting lifting an axe above the shoulder ready for use; and as she says "sliced" she moves both hands in a rapid downward diagonal, leftward sweep, as if to enact the action of the hunter as he struck the wolf. It is important to note the hands move downwards diagonally, as befits the sort of more-or-less downward stroke that would be appropriate for cutting off a wolf's head.

The narrator then continues by quoting Little Red Riding Hood's reaction to what had been done. Little Red Riding Hood tells the hunter that the wolf has eaten her grandmother. The story is then continued in the following words:

(2)   and the hunter said, 'Oh, that's soon remedied,' and took his hatchet, and with a mighty sweep sliced the wolf's stomach open, at which point the grandmother popped out

The gesturing that accompanies this passage is very similar to that in the previous one. Again, as she says "and took his hatchet" she acts as if she is grasping the handle of an axe or hatchet, and as she says "and with a mighty sweep" she raises and then holds her hands above her right shoulder as if in readiness to swing the weapon; and as she says "sliced" she again swings her arms rapidly leftward, as if enacting the hunter's action. But what is to be noted here is that the hands are now swung in a horizontal fashion, not on a downward diagonal. This (at least to me) conveys the idea of handling the axe so that it will produce a longitudinal cut, appropriate, perhaps, for opening a dead wolf's stomach.

Now, the thing to notice is that the speaker uses the same verb in both cases. In the first case she says "sliced the wolf's head off," and in the second case she says "sliced the wolf's stomach open." The action entailed by the task that the verb refers to in each case is different, however, and this is the difference that is made apparent in the contrast in how she performs the arm swing in each case. English offers more than one type of cutting verb. For example, she could have said *chopped* in the first case and *slit* in the second case, and in doing this she would have conveyed in a more differentiated fashion the details of the manner of action involved which the use of the verb *slice* in each case obscures. Here, however, she varies her gesture and so succeeds in conveying this additional part of the meaning.

To me, this is a useful example because we have the contrast: different gesture with what is, lexically, the same verb in each case. Yet it is clear that the verb is not, in fact, the same. The difference between the two 'local' meanings of *slice* is here made clear by the gesture.

Now I will offer two other examples which show something very similar. In these examples, an object is referred to as part of a description of something, but the way this object is arranged in space or the character of its shape or size and the way it achieves the function attributed to it, is indicated in gesture. Thus, at a dinner party, the discussion has turned to pear trees and the problem of supporting the branches when they are laden with heavy fruit. Different methods of support are described. One speaker says: "No, ci mettono le mazze sotto" ('No, they put staves underneath'). As he says "le mazze" ('staves'), with his forearm held vertically and his hand held with the fingers extended but drawn together in a bunch, he lifts his arm twice, as if to describe something vertical that is holding something up. The gesture here completes his description, for his verbal statement gives no indication of how the staves are placed under the tree or how they might serve as supports.

Another speaker, in the same discussion, says: "Io tutte le volte che andavo a Battipaglia mi colpiva questo telaio di fili che stava all'interno dell'albero" ('Every time I used to go to Battipaglia I was struck by this web of wires inside the tree'). As she says "telaio di fili" ('web of wires'), she twice lifts her hand, held with palm facing downwards and fingers spread, drawing the fingers together as she does so, providing an image of the radiating wires that suspend the branches of the pear tree from a central vertical tree or post set within the tree. In this case "telaio di fili" contains only the idea that there are many wires arranged in a 'web', but it gives no indication of the shape or orientation of this web or how, being within the tree, it could contribute to supporting the branches of the tree. With the gesture, the expression is given the context of a visual representation which immediately makes this clear.

In these examples the gesture seems to provide the context in terms of which a verbal expression is to be interpreted. Sometimes it does more than this, however, adding additional components of substantive meaning. For example, during a conversation about a robbery recorded at a bocce (indoor bowls) club, a speaker describes the condition of a door as it had been found after the break-in. He says: "Ieri mattina amma truat' rotto il pannello" ('Yesterday morning we found the panel broken'). As he says "rotto il pannello" ('the panel broken'), he turns to a door he is standing next to and uses his hands to sketch a rectangular area over the lower part of it. In this way he shows that it was the lower panel that had been broken, something he has not referred to in words at all.

Another example will show another way in which gesture can be used to add meaning. In this case, the gesture conveys an additional, more abstract, meaning that is implied by what is being said. A speaker, describing a situation which, for him, illustrates a more general idea, provides in gesture a reference to this more general idea while he provides concrete details in his speech. Thus a bus driver from the city of Salerno is lamenting the bad behavior of the youths who ride the buses he drives. He describes how boys write what he considers to be shameful phrases on the backs of the seats of the buses; that they do this in full view of the girls, who do not object. The girls are, he says, fully aware of what the boys write, and seem to be happy about it. The implication of this is that the girls are equally involved in this kind of activity; they are equally responsible for it. This implication, however, the speaker does not express directly in words but uses a gesture to suggest it. His speech is as follows

(3)   [. . .] Hanno il ragazzo a fianco/ il fidanzato o il ragazzo/ che co-continua a disegnare a pennellare e loro guardano/ non è che ci dicono: "cretino! che stai scrivendo là!"/ sono contente/ quindi sono consapevoli anche loro/ gli sta bene anche a loro questa

[. . .] they [the girls] have the boy at their side/ the boyfriend or the boy/ who co-continues to draw to paint and they look/ they don't say: "Idiot! What are you writing there!"/ they are happy/ hence they also are aware of it / It's OK also for them this

As he says "they are happy, hence they also are aware of it. It's OK also for them this" he extends his two index fingers and places them alongside one another in a gesture that is well known and is generally glossed as meaning 'equal' or 'the same'. Thus the implication of what he is saying, that the girls are equal in their responsibility for this bad behavior, equal in their participation in it, is made manifest in gesture but is not expressed in so many words in the speech. It is interesting to note that it is precisely this general implication that is picked up in his interlocutor's response, for she says "Il livello di partecipazione sociale, maschi e femmine è la stessa cosa" ('The level of social participation, males and females, it's the same thing').

3   Meta-substantive meanings in gesture

In the examples given so far I have shown some of the different ways in which gesture may contribute to the propositional meaning of an utterance. The first three examples showed how gesture often provides a context that makes a verbal expression more precise. Then I gave two examples that show how gesture can do more than this: it can contribute additional substantive content. Now I wish to illustrate how gesture is often used as a way of giving expression to pragmatic aspects of the utterance.[6] I shall introduce this use by describing an example in which a speaker repeats something he has just said. However, this repetition has nothing to do with a repair. It is done as a means of recasting what is said as a new or different speech act. We can see this not only in the way the stress pattern, intonation, and voice level alter. We also see it in the change in the gesture that is used.

The example comes from a recording of a meeting of the committee of the bocce club. The question of who will be listed as sponsors on the poster which will announce the competition is being discussed. Enzo has said that on the poster announcing the competition all the various sponsors will be listed no matter the size of their contribution. Peppe, for some reason, objects to this idea. To press his case, Enzo now takes a specific example, the poster for the competition held at San Severino. He says:

E (4)   e allor' e allor' facimm' 'na kos'
         e allora e allora facciamo una cosa
         and well, and well, let's do one thing! [Let's take an example]

(5)   'a gar' a San S'v'rin'
         la gara a San Severino
         the competition at San Severino

(6)   gara nazionale a San S'v'rin'
         gara nazionale a San Severino
         national competition at San Severino

(7)   primo trofeo provincia di Salerno
         first trophy, province of Salerno

(8)   stev' cinquant' sc'ponzorizzazion' a sott'
         c'era cinquanta sponsorizzazioni sotto
         there was [were] fifty sponsors below

(9)   cinquant' sc'ponzorizzazion' no una sol'
         cinquanta sponsorizzazioni, non una sola
         fifty sponsors, not only one

In line (8) Enzo says "there were fifty sponsors below." He says this, looking at Peppe, and as he does so, with his two hands held open and palms facing each other, he traces out on the table in front of him a sort of oval shape which seems to suggest the spatial arrangement of all the names on the poster. Peppe remains rigid at the conclusion of this utterance; he shows no change in expression whatever. Enzo now repeats what he has just said (line 9) – but this time he looks away from Peppe, actually in the direction of Giovanni, who is at the other end of the table. And now he holds up both hands, spread, palm out, moving them laterally and slightly downward as he does so. The utterance is thus redesigned, as it were, but now, instead of providing a representation of what the poster looked like with all the names printed on it, he does a gesture which expresses the notion that what is being asserted blocks whatever another might say to counter it. That is to say, in this repetition he does a gesture that now expresses the speaker's view of the role this utterance will play as a move in the rhetorical organization of the discourse.

The Palm Away Open Hands Laterally Spread gesture that Enzo uses here is an example of one of several recurrent gestural forms that have what may be called PRAGMATIC functions. They serve as markers of the speaker's attitude toward what he is saying, or they express his expectations about how what he is saying is to be dealt with by his interlocutor, or they express the nature of the illocutionary intent of the utterance of which it is a part.

Another example of a gesture of this sort is provided by the so-called 'purse hand' gesture, or *mano a borsa*. This is a well-known and widely used form that has been described a number of times in books about Italian gesture. For example, Andrea de Jorio, writing about Neapolitan gesture in 1832, described it as one of the gestures used when one asks for something. Diadori also describes it in her book, published in 1990, on gestures that should be learned by students of Italian as a foreign language. Diadori says that it is commonly associated with phrases such as *Ma che stai dicendo* 'What are you saying?' or *Ma che fai* 'What are you doing?'

Examining the contexts in which the *mano a borsa* is used in the material I have recorded, I find that it is commonly used when the speaker is asking a question that seems to have arisen because his assumptions or expectations have been undermined, when he is asking a question for which he believes no real answer is possible, or when he is asking a question that is intended to challenge or call into question actions or statements of another.

For instance, Luigi comes to tell Enzo that the telephone number he had tried in order to reach someone on bocce club business was not correct. Enzo is puzzled by this, because he thought he had given Luigi this number. Enzo asks Luigi: "Ki 'o pigljaj' 'o numm´r´ ri Kacciator´?" ('But who got this number for the Hunters?'), using the *mano a borsa* as he does so. In another instance, Sandro is puzzled because the robbers who entered the bocce club stole the telephone. Because it was a telephone rented from the state telephone company, it could not be resold, and so it seemed to be of no value to a robber. Using the *mano a borsa*, Sandro asks: "Ma a che serv´ killu telef´n´?" ('But what do you use that telephone for?') In a third example, Peppe asks Giovanni how he thinks the robber could have entered the building. Giovanni, as puzzled as Peppe, turns the question back to him as he says: "Don Pe' ma dicit´m´ vuj´, un´ ka tras´ ka dint´ ka vo 'i a 'rrubbà' ka dint´, che marjuolo è?" ('Don Peppe, but you tell me, but someone that enters in order to steal here inside, what sort of thief he is!') As he closes this utterance with "che marjuolo è?" he uses the *mano a borsa*.

The *mano a borsa*, thus, seems to be used in association with asking a question when that question arises because the speaker finds that he cannot take his expectations for granted, or when he finds that he is faced with some information, also shared by others, for which there is no apparent explanation. If the speaker asks a question simply as an attempt to gain needed information which he does not have but assumes another may possess, he does not use this gesture.

This explanation for the use of the *mano a borsa* can also be applied when, as sometimes happens, we see the gesture used when a speaker is not asking a question but making a statement in reply to a question. The instances we have observed where this happens are those in which a speaker is replying to a question that has been asked him before or which, in some other way, appears to violate the rules that govern the asking of questions in conversation. In these instances, it is as if the speaker, at the same time as he answers his interlocutor, and so provides the second part of the adjacency pair the question had created, also indicates that he is questioning his interlocutor's basis for the question he is asking. In these instances it seems that the speaker makes one kind of conversational move in his spoken reply and in his gesture, he makes another kind of move.

The first example comes from the discussion of telephone numbers. At an earlier stage of the conversation, Enzo found out from Giovanni that a certain telephone number had been passed to him by a certain person. Enzo goes to check this, and later returns in some agitation, because the number given is a number of something completely different from that which Giovanni supposed. Enzo does not explain this immediately but comes back into the room asking Giovanni, in some agitation:

E (10)   Giovà' addò 'u pigljaj' 'stu kos'?
    Giovanni dove lo prese   questa cosa?
    where did he get this thing ?

(11)   sc'kus'
    scusa
    sorry / excuse me

(12)   'stu 'stu numm'r' 'i telef'n'?
    questo questo numero di telefono?
    this this telephone number?

(13)   addò 'u pigljaj' Albert'?
    dove lo prese Alberto?
    where did Alberto get it ?

G (14)   'ngopp' a l'elenk' re società
    sull'elenco delle società
    in the list of societies
                    Gesture: *mano a borsa*

As he makes his reply (line 14) he uses *mano a borsa*. Since Enzo had already asked Giovanni this same question but a few minutes before, Giovanni is puzzled as to why Enzo should again be asking him where he got the number. His *mano a borsa* here thus appears to serve to indicate to Enzo that, even as he is giving him an answer to his question, he is at the same time asking, in effect, 'What are you asking me this for?'

The next example is similar. It again involves Enzo and Giovanni, but in this case the topic is the robbery. The question at issue is whether certain doors had been open or closed at the time when the robbery took place. Giovanni asserts that someone opened a certain door so that he could see if another door, opening on some stairs, was open or closed. Enzo, overhearing this assertion, emerges from a neighboring room to ask Giovanni who opened it, and then he asks Giovanni:

E (15)   Ma, ma l'ha aperto lui quella porta che va sul terrazzo?
             But, but he opened that door that goes onto the terrace?

– thus questioning him further as to which door exactly it was that had been opened. Giovanni replies, with a rising voice level:

G (16)   Eh! p´ gli' a v´rè –
             Yes! In order to go and see –

(17)   p´ v´rè k' 'a port´ p´ v´rè 'u purton´ ind' 'e sc'kalinat´
        In order to go to see – in order to see that the door on the stairs

(18)   si stev´ kjus´ o stev´ apiert´
        if it was closed or open

As Giovanni says (18) "si stev´ kjus´ o stev´ apiert´" ('if it was opened or closed'), he forms the *mano a borsa*. Here Giovanni is not asking a question, he is giving a reply, and yet he uses *mano a borsa*.

It is notable here that Giovanni maintains his hand in *mano a borsa* throughout three further turns in this exchange. Enzo again asks about the door opening: "Eh! aprì lui quella porta?" ('He opened that door?'); Giovanni replies "Eh!" ('Yeah!'); whereupon Enzo says "No! kill´ ric´ k' anna truat´ apert´ kella port´" ('No, he said he found that door open'). Only when Giovanni responds to this last utterance does he change from the *mano a borsa*.

Enzo had been told that Vincenzo had found the door in question open. Giovanni had been told that nothing had been found open. Enzo's close questioning of Giovanni here arises from the fact that Enzo had an understanding different from that of Giovanni. As in the previous example, at the same time as he is replying to Enzo's questions he is also saying, with the gesture, "And what are you asking me all this for?" The attitude in terms of which he is framing this entire exchange, thus, is indicated by the *mano a borsa* gesture.

In this exchange, we also see another instance of the use of gesture as an indicator of a 'para-move'. We see this in Enzo, although in his case a gesture known as the *mani giunte* is used. In this gesture the hands, with fingers fully extended and adducted, are held palm-to-palm in a gesture that looks very much like the Christian gesture of prayer (there may be a relationship between the two). The *mani giunte* is a widely used form. According to our observations, it is commonly used as a way of indicating that what is being said is a request to the other to relieve one of certain obligations or responsibilities. For instance, in a situation where a problem has been raised for discussion that a member of the group does not want to discuss, the reluctant member says: "Qua abbiamo parlato per una riunione intera l'altra volta" ('But we discussed that for an entire meeting the other time'). As he makes this assertion he uses *mani giunte*, thus indicating that what he is doing here is asking that the discussion not be held. Likewise, when Enzo has been asked to make a certain telephone call, he says: "Ma io tengo u consiglio nu momento" ('But I have a council meeting in a moment'), but as he says this he performs *mani giunte* as if to make explicit the point that the council meeting makes it impossible for him to make the telephone call, and therefore he should be relieved of the responsibility of doing it.

In the present example, Enzo uses *mani giunte* as he says: "No! kill´ ric´ k' anna truat´ apert´ kella port´" ('No, he said that they found that door open!'). As we said above, as we learn when we examine the entire dialogue, Enzo has been given to understand something different from Giovanni. He is therefore puzzled by what Giovanni has told him. The *mani giunte* here does not mark the spoken utterance as a move by which he requests any change in his obligations. Rather, at the same time as he produces his report he also indicates his puzzlement through the use of *mani giunte*. In effect, he is asking, 'Can you please explain to me why you are telling me these things and so relieve me of the difficulties I will find myself in if there is a contradiction in these accounts.'

In the examples just given, as we noted, the speaker not only formed his gesture while he was speaking, but he maintained it afterwards. He continued to hold his hand up in the form of the gesture he had used, even while the other was speaking. With gestures of the type we have been discussing, this is very common. The speaker maintains the gesture after he finishes speaking, sometimes doing so during a part or even the whole of his interlocutor's next turn. Thus, when Enzo asks Luigi: "Ki 'o pigljaj´ 'o numm´r´ ri Kacciator´?" ('Who got this number for the Hunters?'), he maintains his *mano a borsa* until, from Luigi's reply, it is clear he is not going to answer Enzo's question but is going to go on to say what happened when he called the number in question. When S asks: "Ma a che serv´ killu telef´n´?" ('But what do you use that telephone for?'), he is looking at Giovanni. He maintains his *mano a borsa* during a pause that follows, during which Giovanni continues to look at him. When Giovanni looks away without saying anything, however, Sandro drops his hand.

In all of the cases where the gesture persists after the speech, it would seem that the speaker is maintaining a display of the frame of mind or intention that informed his last utterance, and so he displays the interpretative frame in terms of which he will respond to whatever his interlocutor may say. An utterance, looked at from the point of view of its role in a conversation, always creates expectations for whoever it is who is next speaker. A current turn at talk places constraints on whoever has the next turn. These constraints may vary in their tightness, and questions of the sort illustrated here may be particularly constraining. The maintenance of the speech-act-marking gesture during the turn slot of the recipient serves to reinforce that constraint. It is a visible reminder to the recipient as to what is now expected of him. Such sustained gestures are maintained just until that point in the other's speech where the nature of his response becomes projectable – that is, to that point in the respondent's utterance where it becomes clear either that an answer is forthcoming or that the respondent is not going to take up the question. Sometimes the sustained gesture is kept up through more than one turn, and where this is so the gesturer continues, through the following turn, to pursue the issue that he raised in the first turn.

4   Conclusions

Let us now take stock of this rather complex presentation of examples. It has been my intention to illustrate some of the diverse ways in which gestures, as used in partnership with speech, participate in the construction of the utterance's meaning. I began with examples that showed how gesture can be used to provide context for spoken expression, thus reducing the ambiguity of the meaning of what is expressed. We saw, however, that gesture goes further than this. It can also add to the propositional content of the utterance. I then showed examples which illustrated how, as something spoken is recast from one kind of speech act to another, this recasting may also involve the way gesture is used. And we saw in this example how the speaker shifted the role that gesture had in the utterance. In this case it shifted from participating in the expression of substantive content (in the first utterance) to participating in expressing aspects of the pragmatic intent of the utterance (in its repetition). I then described some observations on the contexts of use of two gestural forms in widespread use which function mainly to express the speech-act status of the utterance. We saw how this is not just a matter of a kind of visual labeling of an utterance already constructed as a speech act of a certain type, however. These gestures are also found to be used as a way of accomplishing more than one speech act simultaneously. Thus we saw how Giovanni used the *mano a borsa* to show that, in the same moment as he was giving his reply, he also was questioning the legitimacy of his interlocutor's question.

There is no opportunity here for me to say anything in detail about how the gestures I have been discussing are timed in relation to the spoken phrases they are associated with. It must be sufficient here for me to say that any examination of this would make it quite clear that the gestures are organized in relation to the spoken phrases they accompany in such a way that we must say that they are part of the very construction of the utterance itself. Gesture and speech, in all the examples I have given here, are composed together as components of a single overall plan. We have to say that although each expresses somewhat different dimensions of the meaning, speech and gesture are co-expressive of a single inclusive ideational complex, and it is this that is the meaning of the utterance.

To conclude, let me return to the question posed at the outset: Do we claim a 'unity' of language and gesture, or do we claim 'diversity'? Insofar as we are concerned with what participants in conversation do as they construct utterances, it seems clear that they use gesture and speech in partnership and can shift the respective roles of gesture and speech in the utterance from one moment to the next in ways that seem rhetorically appropriate. To be sure, the way gestures are composed as semiotic forms is very different from the way spoken words and phrases are composed. This should not surprise us. The two modes of expression employ different media which have different possibilities. As we saw, gesture can be useful as a way of exhibiting overarching units of meaning, as a way of keeping visible an aspect of meaning throughout the course of a spoken utterance or even after the speech has finished. Gesture and speech, as used in conversation, serve different but complementary roles. There is, so to speak, no need for gesture to develop spoken-language-like features to any great degree, so long as spoken language is there for it to be used in conjunction with. Notwithstanding this, as readers may have noted, some of the gestures I have discussed are quite conventional in form and may, in some environments, actually function as if they are lexical items. This is true of the 'equals' gesture I illustrated in the case of the Salerno bus driver, for example. When gesture is used routinely as the only medium of utterance, however, it rapidly takes on organizational features that are very like those found in spoken language.[7]

I end, then, as I began. If, with Whitney, we think of 'language' as a complex of instrumentalities which serve in the expression of 'thought' (as he would say – one might not wish to put it quite like this today), then gesture is a part of 'language'. For those of us with an interest in language conceived of in this way, our task must include working out all the intricate ways in which gesture is used in relation to speech and of showing the circumstances in which the organization of each is differentiated from the other as well as the ways in which they overlap. This can only enrich our understanding of how these instrumentalities function. If, on the other hand, we define 'language' in structural terms, thus excluding from linguistic consideration most, if not all, of the kinds of gestural usages I have illustrated today, we may be in danger of missing important features of how language, so defined, actually succeeds as an instrument of communication. Such a structural definition is valuable as a matter of convenience, as a way of delimiting a field of concern. On the other hand, from the point of view of a comprehensive theory of how humans do all the things they do by means of utterances, it cannot be sufficient.

NOTES

1 See McNeill (1992) for an elaboration of this theme. Kendon (1997) discusses this in relation to other aspects of the gesture–speech relationship.
2 For discussions relevant to the problem of defining 'gesture', see Kendon (1981a, 1985).
3 For discussion of 'alternate' sign languages (i.e., sign languages used in speaker–hearer communities), see Kendon (1988, 1990). See also Farnell (1995).
4 I am indebted to Professor Pina Boggi Cavallo of the University of Salerno for her introductions to people and situations in which it was possible to make these recordings, and to the Wenner-Gren Foundation for Anthropological Research, Inc., for financial assistance. Maria De Simone of Salerno provided transcriptions. Further revisions of these transcriptions have been undertaken by Laura Versante of the Istituto Universitario Orientale in Naples.
5 This example was previously reported in part in Kendon (1993).
6 Some of the examples described in this section are also reported in Kendon (1995), which gives an account both of some 'illocutionary marker' gestures and 'discourse structure marker' gestures in southern Italian conversation.
7 See McNeill (1992: 69–72) for an account of an experimental demonstration of this. See also Goldin-Meadow, McNeill & Singleton (1996).

REFERENCES

Armstrong, D. F., Stokoe, W. C. & Wilcox, S. E. 1995. *Gesture and the Nature of Language*. Cambridge: Cambridge University Press.
Bloomfield, L. 1933. *Language*. New York: Holt, Rinehart & Winston.
Bolinger, D. 1946. Some thoughts on 'Yep' and 'Nope'. *American Speech* 21: 90–95.
Bolinger, D. 1975. *Aspects of Language*. 2nd ed. New York: Harcourt Brace & Jovanovich.

de Jorio, A. 1832. *La mimica degli antichi investigata nel gestire napoletano* [The gestural expression of the ancients in the light of Neapolitan gesturing]. Naples: Fibreno.

Diadori, P. 1990. *Senza parole: 100 gesti degli italiani* [Without words: 100 Italian gestures]. Rome: Bonacci Editore.

Farnell, B. 1995. *Do You See What I Mean? Plains Indian Sign Talk and the Embodiment of Action.* Austin: University of Texas Press.

Ginsburg, G. P., Brenner, M. & von Cranach, M. (eds.) 1985. *Discovery Strategies in the Psychology of Action.* London: Academic Press.

Goldin-Meadow, S., McNeill, D. & Singleton, J. 1996. Silence is liberating: removing the handcuffs on grammatical expression in the manual modality. *Psychological Review* 103: 34–55.

Kendon, A. 1981a. Introduction: current issues in the study of 'Nonverbal Communication'. In Kendon (ed.), pp. 1–53.

Kendon, A. (ed.) 1981b. *Nonverbal Communication, Interaction and Gesture.* The Hague: Mouton.

Kendon, A. 1982. The study of gesture: some observations on its history. *Recherches Sémiotiques/Semiotic Inquiry* 2(1): 45–62.

Kendon, A. 1985. Behavioural foundations for the process of frame attunement in face-to-face interaction. In Ginsburg, Brenner & von Cranach (eds.), pp. 229–253.

Kendon, A. 1988. *Sign Languages of Aboriginal Australia: Cultural, Semiotic and Communicative Perspectives.* Cambridge: Cambridge University Press.

Kendon, A. 1990. Signs in the cloister and elsewhere. *Semiotica* 79: 307–329.

Kendon, A. 1993. Human gesture. In K. R. Gibson & T. Ingold (eds.), *Tools, Language and Cognition in Human Evolution,* pp. 43–62. Cambridge: Cambridge University Press.

Kendon, A. 1995. Gestures as illocutionary and discourse structure markers in southern Italian conversation. *Journal of Pragmatics* 23(3): 247–279.

Kendon, A. 1997. Gesture. *Annual Review of Anthropology* 26: 109–128.

McNeill, D. 1992. *Hand and Mind: What Gestures Reveal about Thought.* Chicago: University of Chicago Press.

Pike, K. 1967. *Language in Relation to a Unified Theory of the Structure of Human Behavior.* 2nd ed. The Hague: Mouton.

Studdert-Kennedy, M. 1987. The phoneme as a perceptuomotor structure. In A. Allport, D. G. MacKay, W. Prinz & E. Scheerer (eds.), *Language Perception and Production: Relationships between Listening, Speaking, Reading and Writing,* pp. 67–84. London: Academic Press.

Tylor, E. B. 1865. *Researches into the Early History of Mankind and the Development of Civilization.* London: John Murray.

Whitney, W. D. 1899. *The Life and Growth of Language: An Outline of Linguistic Science.* New York: Appleton. (Originally published 1875.)

Wundt, W. 1973. *The Language of Gestures,* trans. J. S. Thayer, C. M. Greenleaf & M. D. Silberman. The Hague: Mouton.

3 The influence of addressee location on spatial language and representational gestures of direction

Asli Özyürek

Max Planck Institute for Psycholinguistics, Nijmegen

1 Introduction

How do speakers refer to their experiences of spatial relations? Verbal language is one modality through which we can express spatial relations. However, speakers' expressions of spatial relations are not limited to those of the verbal modality but are often accompanied by so-called 'iconic' or 'representational' gestures (McNeill 1992; Kendon 1980). For example, when a speaker is expressing a motion upwards, she can say "the cat climbed up the drainpipe" and move her hand upwards to represent the direction of a cat's motion upwards during her utterance.[1] If this is the case, then we have to understand speakers' use of representational gestures along with their use of spatial language in order to understand how speakers refer to spatial relations.

One way to understand spatial reference by spatial language and gestures is to assume that speakers' verbal and gestural expressions of space *represent* or *encode* the spatial relations as experienced. That is, there is a one-to-one coding relationship between the linguistic form and the representational gestures on the one hand and preexisting spatial experiences on the other. For example, some researchers argue that representational gestures derive from spatially encoded knowledge and help conceptualize the spatial relations that will be expressed in speech (Rauscher, Krauss & Chen 1996).

However, in this chapter I am going to argue and show empirically that speakers' verbal and gestural expressions of space, and specifically those of direction, cannot simply be explained by a one-to-one coding relationship between these expressions and the preexisting world of spatially encoded knowledge. Rather I will argue that reference by spatial language and gestures has to be explained *in relation to the social and spatial context* in which they are produced. I will demonstrate this by showing that speakers change their gestural and verbal expressions to refer to the same spatial content, depending on where their addressees are located during the speech event.

I will start with an example from my data to specify the nature of the problem. A speaker is talking about a cartoon event she has watched on a video screen. In this particular scene, a character (Granny) is throwing a cat (Sylvester) out of a window onto the street. As the speaker saw the cartoon on the video screen, the window was located on the left side of the screen and the street was on the right side. During her telling, the speaker had two addressees, one to her left and one to her right, and the three participants were sitting at the three points of a triangular space (see Figure 3.1).

The way this speaker expresses Granny's motion of throwing Sylvester out onto the street in her speech is as follows: "She throws him out." If we look at her gesture, we notice that she expresses additional information about this motion event. While she is uttering this sentence her arm moves from the triangular space in front of her towards the space behind her. In this way she expresses the direction of the motion in her gesture as well as in her speech.

This narrator could have expressed the same direction of motion in many different ways. For example, she could have used a different choice of preposition (e.g., "she throws the cat *across* the street") or a different gesture orientation. Instead of moving her arm from the space in front of her towards her back, she could have moved her hand forwards and towards the space in front of her. Actually, this would have corresponded to the action performed by the character, for Granny did her throwing by moving her hands forward and down.

What, then, could have motivated this speaker to choose this particular preposition of direction ("out") along with this particular gesture orientation (backwards), which did not necessarily represent the information as it is observed? If we look at her speech and gesture in relation to the extralinguistic spatial context, we notice that while she was saying "She throws him out," her gesture was not only moving backwards but also moving *out of* the triangular space shared by all the participants. That is, in order to refer to the spaces in the cartoon, she might have used the extralinguistic spatial context by moving her gesture out of the space shared by the three participants. This way, she could have created a context for the interpretation of the linguistic expression "out" and thus referred to the represented event. Therefore, this narrator may have adapted her speech and gesture orientation to the extralinguistic spatial context shared by the addressees instead of *mapping* her expression onto the information observed on the video screen.

This example illustrates the questions this chapter focuses on: Do speakers use spatial language and representational gestures of direction in relation to the social and spatial context of the utterance, specifically to the location of their addressees? If spatial context has an impact on how spatial

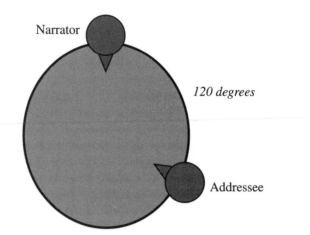

Dyadic condition

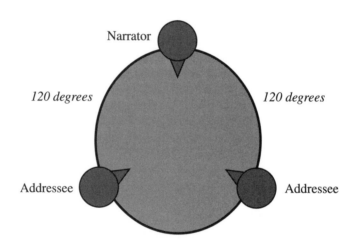

Triadic condition

Figure 3.1. Dyadic and Triadic addressee configurations used in the experimental group.

relations are expressed, then spatial reference needs to be explained with a theory of spatiality where these three aspects of the communicative event are taken into account. Speakers' construal of spatial meaning might be dependent on the integration of verbal spatial expressions, representational gestures, and the extralinguistic spatial context of the utterance.

1.1 Relationship between speech and gesture: an integrated system of two modalities

The word 'gesture' is used for a number of distinct phenomena that involve body movements in communicative situations (Kendon 1997). However, in this paper the focus will be on what McNeill (1992) has called the "spontaneous gestures" that accompany speech. These gestures are mostly hand movements performed during speaking[2] and are related in meaning to the linguistic segment they accompany. For example, when a speaker is expressing motion upwards, she can say "the cat climbed up the drainpipe" while moving her hand upwards and in this way convey the meaning of UP also in her gesture. These spontaneous gestures have characteristics different from those used in sign languages (e.g., ASL) or so-called emblems (e.g., the OK sign in American culture), where the form–meaning relationships of the gestures are socially determined and fixed. Spontaneous gestures do not have a preestablished form–meaning relationship; their meaning is determined on-line with each performance.[3]

McNeill (1992) has identified four kinds of relation between spontaneous gestures and speech used in narrative communication: iconic, metaphoric, beat, and abstract deictic. Some spontaneous gestures are 'iconic' (representational), that is, they represent objects and events by virtue of their resemblance to them. 'Metaphoric' gestures represent images of abstract referents. 'Beat' gestures are rhythmic movements of the hand that do not resemble the objects and events mentioned but index the pragmatic function of the speech they accompany, such as introduction of a new episode, and so on. 'Abstract deictics' point to locations of entities or characters within the gesture space.

1.1.1 Reference to direction by speech and gesture. This study will focus on iconic/representational gestures, especially those that accompany verbal expressions of motion events[4] and depict the direction or trajectory of the moving figure. In English, the direction of the motion event is expressed mostly by spatial prepositions or path adverbials that express the path of the moving figure (Talmy 1985). However, in many cases not only speech but also representational gestures give information about the directionality

of the motion event.[5] For example, in the utterance "the cat was running forwards," "forwards" gives information about the direction of the motion event. In uttering this sentence, the speaker might also move her gesture forwards and away from herself to refer to the direction of the cat's motion.

Representational gestures of direction can also convey meaning that is not expressed in speech. They express the viewpoints of the speakers who describe the direction (McNeill 1992). For example, describing the motion of a figure observed as going from right to left, a speaker's gesture can convey an 'observer' viewpoint if the gesture also goes along a right-to-left axis (representing the motion as it was observed). It conveys a 'character' viewpoint if it moves along a sagittal axis, that is, away from the speaker's body (representing the motion from the viewpoint of the moving figure). In most cases, the viewpoint and the direction are not expressed in speech but only in gesture. For example, the utterance "the cat was running ø" can be accompanied by a gesture in a forward orientation (character viewpoint) even though there is no mention of direction or viewpoint in speech.

Thus both speech and gesture contribute in a complementary way to the achievement of reference to direction. That is, they "express different aspects of the same meaning unit and comprise together a more complete unit of meaning than either does alone" (McNeill 1997: 2). In this chapter I will address the issue of whether the extralinguistic spatial context also has an effect on the way reference to direction is established by gesture and speech. That is, do speakers represent the direction as they have observed it, or do they change their verbal and gestural expressions of direction in relation to the spatial context of the speech event?

1.2   Relationship between language and extralinguistic spatial context

Among many others, Goffman (1974), Duranti (1992), Duranti & Goodwin (1992), Hanks (1990, 1992), and Agha (1996) have shown that the extralinguistic spatial context in which communicative activities are performed is never neutral but rather is meaningful for the encoding and interpretation of linguistic forms. For example, Duranti (1992) has shown that the performance and interpretation of the words used in Samoan ceremonial exchange are contingent upon the participants' occupation of particular positions in the house. Furthermore, with regard to spatial reference, Hanks' (1990) study of Yucatec Maya deictic particles shows that linguistic forms both encode and are dependent upon a socioculturally organized space, that is, the social space defined by the bodies of the participants in the speech event. According to Hanks, each deictic category encodes a *relation*, between some *referent* and the *indexical ground*, of the utterance. In the use of verbal deictic expressions, speakers make reference to spatial locations in relation to an indexical ground, that is, to the here-and-now of the utterance. Hanks has shown that social space among the participants is an important aspect of how the indexical ground is organized and thus determines the meaning of the deictic expressions used.

The present study attempts to go beyond the recent findings on spatial reference by gesture, speech, and spatial context in two ways. On the one hand, in contribution to McNeill's (1992) framework of speech and gesture, it tries to show that extralinguistic spatial context also serves as an important component of how speakers convey spatial meaning using speech and gesture. On the other hand, in relation to studies of language and spatial context, it attempts to show that representational gestures might also serve as a context for the use and interpretation of linguistic forms (see Agha 1996 for a similar view). Thus this study links the gap among these two lines of research by investigating whether or not speakers use their verbal and gestural expressions in relation to the extralinguistic spatial context of the utterance. Speakers' choice of representational gestures and spatial language in expressing directionality can depend upon an indexical relation to the spatial positioning of the participants in the speech event.

If speakers use their gestures and spatial language in relation to the spatial context, then they might use different spatial language and gesture orientations to express the same referential content, depending on the relative positioning of the participants in the utterance context. In order to test this hypothesis I will examine the effect of changes in addressee location on gesture orientation and spatial language using a narration task that has been extensively used in research on gesture production (the cartoon narration task used by McNeill 1992).

2   The present study

The present study tests the hypothesis that speakers use different spatial language and gesture orientation to express direction, depending on where their addressees are located. In the study, participants watched an animated cartoon and were asked to narrate it twice. The participants were assigned to two groups, one experimental and one control group. In the experimental group the addressee location was varied from having one addressee to the side of the narrator (Dyadic condition) to having an addressee on each side (Triadic condition). In the control group the addressee location was kept constant each time the narrator told the story. It was expected that the narrators would express information about the direction of motion events differently in speech (i.e., with different spatial prepositions) and gesture orientation (i.e., with different axes) in each telling of the cartoon, and that this change would be greater in the experimental than in the control group.

2.1   Method

2.1.1   Subjects. A total of sixteen speakers participated as narrators, and an additional forty served as addressees in the experimental and control groups. All the participants were native speakers of English and were chosen from among University of Chicago undergraduates.

2.1.2   Procedure. The participants were randomly assigned to the experimental and control groups. Later, participants in each group were randomly assigned to the narrator and addressee roles. Each narrator watched the seven-minute action cartoon.[6]

The task was presented as storytelling. The instruction sheet explained that a cartoon would appear on the TV screen and that the narrator would watch the cartoon and then tell it to different addressees two different times. While the narrator watched the cartoon, the addressees waited outside the experiment room. Following the cartoon, the addressees were brought in for each telling. Both tellings were videotaped.

In the Triadic experimental condition, one addressee was seated to each side of the narrator. For the Dyadic condition, a new addressee was seated on only one side of the narrator (see Figure 3.1 for the seating arrangements).

The order of conditions was counterbalanced for each narrator. Four narrators told the cartoon first when there were two addressees (Triadic condition) and retold it when there was one addressee (Dyadic condition). The remaining four narrators told the cartoon first when there was an addressee on one side (Dyadic condition) and retold it when there were two addressees (Triadic condition). Furthermore, during the tellings in the Dyadic condition, four addressees were seated to the right of the narrators, and the remaining four addressees were seated to the left of the narrators.

In the control group, one addressee was seated to one side of the narrator during each telling. The seating arrangement was exactly same as in the Dyadic condition of the experimental group. After the narrator watched the cartoon, the first addressee entered and was seated on the left or right side of the narrator. After the first telling, the other addressee was brought in and was seated at the same place as the first addressee. That is, if the first addressee was seated on the right side, the second addressee was also placed on the right side. The order of conditions was counterbalanced. Four narrators told the cartoon when their addressees were seated to their left. The remaining four narrators told the cartoon when their addressees were seated to their right.

2.1.3   Coding. Each narration was transcribed and segmented into clauses. From all clauses, those that described motion events (e.g., Granny throws Sylvester out of the window) were sorted out. (See the appendix for the list of the motion-event scenes coded in the cartoon.) For each motion-event clause, its accompanying gesture phrase was coded.[7]

Subsequently, each gesture phrase was coded for the orientation of its trajectory. Gesture orientations were classified into four categories: (a) *Lateral* (left/right), (b) *Vertical* (up/down), (c) *Frontal* (forwards/backwards), and (d) *Diagonal* (two types were identified: (i) Vertical Diagonal: from one upper side (left/right) of the body to the opposite lower side (left/right), and vice versa; (ii) Horizontal Diagonal: from one side (left/right) closer to the body to the opposite side (left/right) away from the body, and vice versa). To help obtain consistency and objectivity of classification, each gesture motion was drawn on a transparency placed on the TV screen.

For each narrator, the speech and gesture combinations that expressed the same motion-event scene (e.g., Granny throws Sylvester out the window) in both narrations were identified. If a narrator mentioned Sylvester's being thrown out of the window in both narrations, those speech and gesture combinations were selected. Next, within each gesture and speech combination, each gesture phrase was coded for whether it retained the *same* orientation or *differed* (e.g., Frontal vs. Lateral) across the two tellings for each narrator. Also, each verbal expression was coded for whether the narrator used the same or different spatial prepositions or path adverbials to refer to the same motion event in both narrations. For example, if the narrator said, "She threw him *out onto* the street" in one narration but said, "She threw him *across* the street" in the other narration, this was coded as *different*.

2.2   Results and discussion

For the first analysis, the mean percentage of total speech and gesture combinations that changed across narrations were calculated across narrators. Table 3.1 summarizes how frequently narrators changed their speech and gesture together, changed speech only, or changed gesture only, across narrations in the experimental and control groups.

The table shows that while narrators in the experimental group changed 73% of all their speech and gesture combinations across narrations, the control group changed only 53% of their speech and gesture combinations. Therefore, narrators changed their speech and gesture combinations more frequently when the addressee location varied than when it remained constant. The table also shows that the difference between the groups was mostly due to changes in gesture only. While the percentage changes in both speech and gesture (23% vs. 20%) and speech only (10% vs. 20%) were similar between groups, changes in gestures only (40% vs. 13%) were more

Table 3.1. *The mean percentage of total speech and gesture combinations that changed across narrations in the control and experimental groups*

	Both speech and gesture (%)	Speech only (%)	Gesture only (%)	Total change (%)	Total no. of speech–gesture combinations
Experimental group	23	10	40	73	103
Control group	20	20	13	53	88

frequent in the experimental group than in the control group. Thus this showed that the total difference between the experimental and control groups was mostly due to changes in the narrators' gestures only.

For a further analysis, percentage changes in gesture and percentage changes in speech were calculated separately for each narrator in the experimental and control groups. Narrators in the experimental group changed 63% of their gestures but only 33% of their speech across narrations. That is, they changed their gesture orientations more than half the time, but not their speech. However, in the control group, percentage change in gestures was similar to that of speech, and both changes happened less than half of the time; overall 33% of the gestures and 40% of the speech changed across narrations. This analysis also showed that variation in the addressee location influenced narrators' change in gesture orientation but not their speech.

Therefore, narrating a story in different addressee locations changed narrators' expressions of the same content. Yet this change was due mostly to changes in gesture rather than in speech. This was contrary to the initial expectation that spatial language would also be influenced by the changes in the addressee location. If changes in addressee location change speakers' gesture orientations, then what is the nature of these changes, and how can they be explained in relation to where the addressees are located?

2.2.1   How did narrators change their gesture orientation? Further analysis was conducted to see which gesture orientations were influenced by the changes in addressee location and how these influences were manifested. Mean proportions of total gestures perfomed along the Lateral, Frontal, Diagonal, and Vertical axes were calculated for the experimental group (see Figure 3.2).

Paired sign tests on these proportions showed that changing the addressee location between the Dyadic and Triadic conditions had an effect mainly on the Frontal (forwards/backwards) and Lateral (left/right) gesture

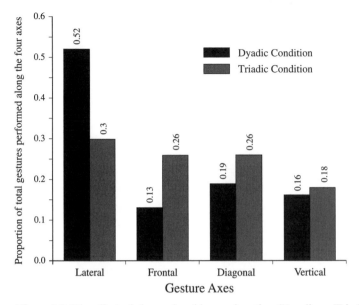

Figure 3.2. The effect of change in addressee location (Dyadic vs. Triadic) on the use of gesture orientations.

axes. Speakers used significantly more Lateral gestures in the Dyadic condition than in the Triadic condition ($p < .001$). On the other hand, they preferred Frontal gestures more in the Triadic condition than in the Dyadic condition ($p < .001$). There were no significant differences found between the Vertical and Diagonal orientations. Thus, changing the addressee location between the Dyadic and Triadic conditions influenced gesture orientation mostly along the Lateral and Frontal axes. That is, the same motion event was represented with a gesture with Lateral orientation in the Dyadic context but with a Frontal orientation in the Triadic context.

However, it is possible that the Frontal and Lateral axes are orientations that are the most likely to be altered by speakers in general, and preferences are not necessarily related to where the addressees are located. In order to rule out this factor, a similar analysis was conducted on narrators' changes of gesture orientation in the control group. Even though changes of gesture orientation occurred less than half the time in the control group (33 percent), the question still remained whether the changes that did occur were along the Frontal and Lateral axes, as in the experimental group.

For this analysis, the mean proportions of total gestures performed along the four axes were calculated for the control group (see Figure 3.3). Paired sign tests showed that repeating motion events with an addressee in

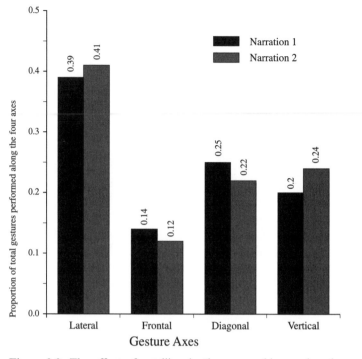

Figure 3.3. The effect of retelling in the same addressee location on gesture orientation.

the same location did not have an effect on the orientation of the gestures ($p > .05$). That is, narrators used similar proportions of Lateral (0.39 and 0.41), Diagonal (0.25, 0.22), Vertical (0.20, 0.24) and Frontal (0.14, 0.12) gestures in two narrations. Therefore, the shifts in gesture orientation along the Frontal and Lateral axes in the experimental group were not due to having told the narration twice, but were due to changes in the addressee location. Narrators in the experimental group were adjusting their gesture orientations according to where their addressee(s) were positioned.

2.2.2   Are changes in gesture orientation and speech related? How, then, can we explain the changes in gesture orientation from Lateral to Frontal axes? Why, for example, did narrators choose to express the direction of motion with a backwards (Frontal axis) gesture while saying "she throws him out" when the addressee context was Triadic but with a right-to-left gesture (Lateral axis) when there was one addressee located at the right side?

Following McNeill's theory about the integration of gesture and speech meaning, one would expect changes in gesture orientation to be related to the meaning conveyed in speech. However, we have found that speech did not change significantly with changes in addressee positioning and that only gesture did. Yet changes in gesture orientation might still be related to what is conveyed in speech and also to the spatial configuration of the space shared by the narrator and the addressees. For example, while the narrator says "she throws him out," her gesture might move backwards in the Triadic context. In this sense, her gesture would be not only moving backwards but also moving *out of* the triangular space shared by all the participants. Similarly in the Dyadic context, the space shared by the participants could be located to the side of the narrator, and her gesture could convey the meaning of "out" by moving laterally out of this shared space.

If shifts in gesture orientation are related to what is conveyed in speech and also to the space shared by the participants, then these shifts could occur when gesture accompanies certain spatial prepositions but not others. That is, gesture shifts might occur more frequently accompanying some prepositions such as *in* or *out*, where the gesture orientation could also convey meaning (e.g., OUT) by moving into or out of the shared space, but occur less frequently when they accompany such prepositions as 'across'.

However, there might be another explanation for the shifts in gesture orientation. That is, shifts in gesture might not be related to meaning conveyed in speech at all, but to their visibility by addressees. For example, one might say that the narrators used Frontal gestures in the Triadic context rather than Lateral gestures because gestures along a Frontal axis were perceived more easily by both addressees on each side. On the other hand, Lateral gestures could not have been perceived efficiently by both addressees in the Triadic context (the gesture would have been performed towards one of the addressees but away from the other at the same time). Therefore narrators could have shifted from Lateral to Frontal gestures in the Triadic context so that they could be seen better by both addressees. If this were the case, then shifts in gesture orientation would occur no matter which spatial preposition was used and thus would not be specific to what is expressed in speech.

In order to answer these questions, I selected eight motion-event descriptions in which the motion was represented along a right-to-left axis on the video screen. These motion events could be expressed along a front-to-back axis as well as on a right-to-left axis, depending on the viewpoint chosen by the narrator. (See the appendix for the description of these motion events with the orientation represented in the cartoon.) Three of these scenes represented a character's motion IN to a building or window (motion from right to left), two of them represented motion OUT of a building/window

Table 3.2. *Mean proportions of total gestures performed along Lateral and Frontal axes used for describing motion IN*

	Lateral axis	Frontal axis	Total no. of gestures
Dyadic condition	0.57	0.21	17
Triadic condition	0.21	0.61	15

(motion from left to right), and three of them represented motion ACROSS from one building to another (motion from right to left). Verbal clauses where the narrators described these scenes using spatial prepositions (*in*, *into*, *out*, and *across*) were located in all narrations. Analysis was made of Lateral and Frontal gesture orientations that accompanied verbal descriptions of these scenes.

The mean proportions of total gestures performed along Lateral and Frontal axes were found for descriptions of motion IN (see Table 3.2). Wilcoxon Signed Rank tests of these proportions showed that narrators used significantly more Lateral gestures when the addressee context was Dyadic than Triadic ($p < .05$) and more Frontal gestures when the addressee context was Triadic than Dyadic ($p < .05$). All the Frontal gestures were in the forwards orientation, that is, moving away from the narrator's body and towards the addressee.

Furthermore, an analysis was made of the location of the Lateral gestures in the gesture space in the Dyadic condition. The aim was to find out whether the location of Lateral gestures in the gesture space would change in relation to whether the addressee was seated to the right or to the left. In all the IN motion scenes, the figure in the cartoon event was moving from the right to the left on the video screen (Sylvester running into Tweety's building on the left), and all the narrators' Lateral gestures also moved from right to left. However, where the gestures were performed in relation to the narrator's body differed along with changes in the addressee location. When the addressee was seated to the left, the narrators moved the hand from the mid-sagittal line of the body towards the left (5 out of 6 Lateral gestures and three out of four narrators preferred this location). In contrast, when the addressee was seated to the right, the narrators moved the hand from the peripheral right side towards the mid-sagittal line of the body (4 out of 6 Lateral gestures and three out of four narrators). Thus, most of the gestures describing IN motion were performed *towards* wherever the single addressee was located.

A similar analysis was conducted on the mean proportions of total ges-

Table 3.3. *Mean proportions of total gestures performed along Lateral and Frontal axes used for describing motion* OUT

	Lateral axis	Frontal axis	Total no. of gestures
Dyadic condition	0.60	0.20	17
Triadic condition	0.12	0.66	15

tures performed along Lateral and Frontal axes for the descriptions of OUT motions (see Table 3.3). Wilcoxon Signed Rank tests of these proportions showed that narrators used significantly more Lateral gestures when the addressee context was Dyadic than Triadic ($p < .05$) and more Frontal (backwards) gestures when the addressee context was Triadic than Dyadic ($p < .05$). Thus, the shift between the Frontal and Lateral axes occurred for descriptions of OUT motion as well as for descriptions of IN motion. However, one difference was that all the Frontal gestures in the descriptions of OUT motion were moving backwards and away from the addressees rather than moving forwards and toward them. Even though the motion on the TV screen could not be represented by a backwards motion, narrators consistently performed backwards rather than forwards gestures.

Further analysis was made of the location in gesture space of Lateral gestures in the Dyadic condition. In all OUT motion scenes the figure in the cartoon was moving left to right across the video screen. Again, the narrators' Lateral gestures also moved from their left to their right, but the location of their gestures changed in relation to their bodies depending on where the addressee was located. When the addressee was seated to the left, the narrators moved the hand from the left side of their bodies towards the right side of their bodies (4 out of 5 gestures and three out of four narrators). In contrast, when the addressee was seated to the right, the narrators moved the hand from the right side of their bodies towards their peripheries and further right (4 out of 6 gestures and three out of four narrators preferred this location). Thus, most of the gestures describing motion OUT were performed *away* from wherever the addressee(s) was located.

Last, a similar analysis was conducted on the mean proportions of total gestures performed along Lateral and Frontal axes used for the descriptions of ACROSS motion (see Table 3.4). Wilcoxon Signed Rank tests conducted of these proportions did not show a significant difference in the use of Frontal or Lateral gestures across the conditions ($p > .05$). Furthermore, the location of the Lateral gestures in the Dyadic condition did not change consistently in relation to the addressee's location on the right or the left.

Table 3.4. *Mean proportions of total gestures performed along Lateral and Frontal axes used for describing motion* ACROSS

	Lateral axis	Frontal axis	Total no. of gestures
Dyadic condition	0.34	0.55	21
Triadic condition	0.32	0.38	16

Thus, unlike the descriptions of IN and OUT motions, the gesture orientations that accompanied verbal descriptions of ACROSS motion did not change with differences in addressee location.

These results show first of all that narrators change their gesture orientations in relation to the meaning conveyed in speech. They changed their gesture orientations accompanying their descriptions of IN and OUT motions but not ACROSS motion. Therefore, changes in gesture orientation with changes in addressee location cannot be explained by the visibility of the gestures. If the gestures had been changed to be better seen by the addressees, then we would also observe changes in the descriptions of the ACROSS motion, but we did not. Furthermore, we saw that in descriptions of OUT motion, gestures were moving *away* from the addressees and thus were *less* visible to them. Thus, narrators were monitoring the changes in their gesture orientation in relation to what they expressed in their speech rather than trying to make them more visible to their addressees.

Furthermore, these kinds of change in gesture orientation in verbal descriptions of IN and OUT motions suggest that speakers were taking the space shared by the participants into account. Gestures describing IN motion were performed *towards* wherever the addressee was located. On the other hand, gestures accompanying verbal descriptions of OUT motion were performed *away* from wherever the addressee was located (even though the backwards gestures in the Triadic condition violated what was observed on the TV screen). These findings can be interpreted to suggest that speakers' gesture orientations conveyed meaning both in relation to what was expressed in speech and also in relation to the space shared by the participants in the speech event. That is, gestures accompanying the verbal descriptions of IN motion were not only moving towards the addressees but also *into* the space shared by all the participants. For example, by saying "in" and moving the arm forwards in the Triadic condition, the narrators could also mean 'into the space we share together', in order to represent Sylvester's motion in the building. On the other hand, in the Dyadic context, the space shared by the participants could be to the side of the narrator, and a gesture could convey the meaning of "in" by moving laterally into this shared space. Similarly, gestures accompanying verbal descriptions of OUT motion were not only moving away from the addressees, but also *out of* the space shared by all the participants. For example, in the Triadic condition, backwards gestures were moving out of the space shared by the two addressees, but in the Dyadic condition they were moving laterally out of the shared space that was to the side of the narrator. In contrast, gesture orientations that accompanied verbal descriptions of ACROSS motion did not convey meaning in relation to the shared space and thus were not influenced by changes in addressee location. One explanation for this is that speakers could not convey the meaning of ACROSS by moving their gestures into or out of the space shared by the participants. That is, the meaning of ACROSS does not change with respect to shared space.[8]

3   Conclusions and general discussion

The initial aim of this chapter was to understand how speakers achieve spatial reference by using spatial language and gestures. I have shown that speakers' use of spatial language and gestures is motivated not only by spatial relations as experienced or encoded but also by the social and spatial contexts in which they are produced. That is, speakers' construal of spatial meaning is dependent upon and can be understood in terms of the way verbal spatial expressions and gestures are used in relation to the spatial context of the utterance. I demonstrated this by showing that speakers' representational gestures and the spatial language of direction can be influenced by changes in addressee location.

How did changes in addressee location influence the speakers' spatial language and representational gestures? The results of the two studies have shown that changes in addressee location changed gesture orientation but did not change what is expressed in speech directly. However, the changes in gesture orientation were not obvious. That is, they could not simply be explained by the speakers' mere global adaptation of their orientations to wherever their addressees were located. The changes could be understood, in line with McNeill's theory, only by taking into account what was expressed in speech. That is, speakers changed their gesture orientation when they were expressing in their speech the spatial relations of IN and OUT motions but not when they were expressing ACROSS motion in speech. Furthermore, the detailed analysis of the gesture shifts and the type of spatial configuration of the addressees suggested that speakers were taking the 'shared space' among the participants into account. They were changing their gesture orientations so that their gestures were moving *into* the shared space when they accompanied expressions of "in." Similarly, speakers were changing their gesture orientations so that their gestures were moving *out of* the shared space when they accompanied expressions of "out." That is, even though the narrators' speech remained the same, their gesture orientations changed in different contexts to keep the meaning conveyed by speech and gesture the same (i.e., IN, OUT). This shows that it is neither speech alone nor gesture alone but the meaning they convey *together* that is sensitive to addressee location in the speech event.

These results have further implications for, on the one hand, theories of spatial reference and, on the other, understanding cognitive processes during speech and gesture production. Theories explaining spatial reference by spatial language only (e.g., Talmy 1985; Langacker 1987; Jackendoff 1983) have to take into account not only the linguistic categories of spatial relations but also the features of gestures (such as orientation) and the features of extralinguistic spatial context (e.g., shared space). Gesture orientation was found to map onto speech semantics and not only onto the visual image of the observed event. That is, speakers' gesture orientations accompanying verbal expressions of "in" and "out" represented the direction of the motion in ways integrated to how the motion was encoded in speech instead of merely mirroring the observed event. Furthermore, the socio-spatial context is part of how this meaning is conveyed, in this case serving as a bounded region for the trajectory of the gesture to move into or out of. Last, the results of this study show that gestures and the spatial prepositions of IN and OUT motions do establish reference, at least for the scenes I have analyzed, by transposing the spatial context of the speech event, in a particular relation, to the spaces of the narrated event. That is, oriented gestures and spatial prepositions of IN and OUT motions might serve the function of 'transposition' or even 'lamination' (Goffman 1981; Haviland 1993) of the two grounds (that of the narrated event and that of the speech event). In this sense they serve the same function as that of *linguistic shifters* (Jakobson 1971 [1957]; Silverstein 1976). Thus, all these findings suggest that we can learn more about how speakers construe meaning with spatial language by taking gestures and the sociospatial context into account.

The results also have implications for theories of the cognitive processes underlying gesture and language use. Some researchers argue that representational gestures derive from spatially encoded knowledge (Rauscher, Krauss & Chen 1996; Krauss, Chen & Gottesman, this volume) or from spatio-temporal representations (de Ruiter, this volume). However, here I have shown that gestural expressions do not represent spatio-temporal representations by a one-to-one mapping onto how images are encoded. Rather they change depending on the linguistic expressions they accompany and the contexts in which they are produced. Among the models proposed so far in this volume, only the Growth Point (see McNeill & Duncan, this volume; McNeill, this volume) model seems to take into account context – that of the narrative context – as a feature that might influence the production of verbal and gestural expressions. However, this chapter has shown further that not only the narrative but also the extralinguistic spatial context influences the way spatial relations are expressed by gestures and speech. Spatial reference by gestures or language has to be explained as an integration among speech, the gestures that accompany speech, and the context of the utterance.

Appendix

Motion events in the cartoon	Direction of the motion event on the TV screen
Episode 1	
*1.1 Sylvester runs across the street from his building	Right to Left
*1.2 Sylvester runs into Tweety's building	Right to Left
*1.3 Sylvester flies out of Tweety's building (he is kicked)	Left to Right
Episode 2	
2.1 Sylvester climbs up the drainpipe	Vertical (upwards)
*2.2 Tweety flies in the window	Right to Left
*2.3 Sylvester flies in the window after Tweety	Right to Left
*2.4 Granny throws Sylvester out of the window	Left to Right
Episode 3	
3.1 Sylvester climbs up inside the drainpipe	Vertical (upwards)
3.2 Tweety drops a bowling ball down the drainpipe	Vertical (downwards)
3.3 Sylvester falls down the drainpipe with a bowling ball inside	Vertical (downwards)
3.4 Sylvester falls out of the drainpipe	Motion towards the watcher
3.5 Sylvester rolls down the street.	Left to Right
3.6 Sylvester rolls into a bowling alley	Motion away from the watcher
Episode 6	
*6.1 Sylvester swings across from his building to Tweety's building with a rope	Right to Left
6.2 He hits the wall next to Tweety's window	Motion away from the watcher
6.3 He falls down the wall	Vertical (downwards)
Episode 8	
*8.1 Sylvester runs across the wires from one building to another	Right to Left

Note:
* Motion events used in the analysis of descriptions of motion IN, OUT, and ACROSS.

NOTES

This chapter is part of a doctoral dissertation submitted to the Department of Psychology and Department of Linguistics at the University of Chicago. This research was conducted partially by means of a Spencer Foundation grant given to D. McNeill and another Spencer Foundation grant given to T. Trabasso. The writing of this article was supported by the Max Planck Institute for Psycholinguistics. I would like to give special thanks to W. Hanks and D. McNeill, and also T. Trabasso, S. Goldin-Meadow, S. Kita, J. P. de Ruiter, A. Kendon, E. Pederson, S. Levinson, J. Haviland, E. Danziger, T. Hamaguchi, and E. Özyürek for their valuable comments on and criticisms of the ideas presented here.

1 It has also been shown that speakers use representational gestures more frequently during phrases of spatial content than with other content (Rauscher, Krauss & Chen 1996).

2 Furuyama (this volume) has shown that in conversational data some gestures are produced without speech accompaniment. However, this is almost never the case in narrative communication.

3 See McNeill & Duncan (this volume) for more on the integration of linguistic and gestural meaning.

4 A motion event has been defined by Talmy (1985) as a directed motion that results in the change of a location.

5 In the narrations studied by McNeill et al., 90 percent of the motion events expressed in speech are accompanied by directional gestures (McCullough 1993).

6 For a detailed scene-by-scene description of the cartoon, see McNeill (1992).

7 Gesture coding was carried out using McNeill's (1992) conventions. According to these conventions, gestures have three phases in their production: a preparation phase, a stroke, and a retraction phase or hold. All three phases constitute a gesture *phrase* (Kendon 1980). In the preparation phase, the hand(s) move from a rest position to the position where the gesture stroke is to be executed. This is followed by the stroke, which is the main part of the gesture and is identified in both semantic and kinetic terms. Semantically, it is the main meaning-bearing part of the gesture. Kinesically, it is the part of the the gesture that is carried out with the most effort or tension. The retraction phase is when the hand returns to its rest position.

8 It is possible that speakers pointed to the locations of landmarks (e.g., buildings) in the gesture space by using abstract deictics and performed their ACROSS gestures in relation to these spaces previously pointed at. Thus space previously created by the narrator in the gesture space could have provided a context for the meaning of ACROSS, rather than the shared space among the participants.

REFERENCES

Agha, A. 1996. Schema and superposition in spatial deixis. *Anthropological Linguistics* 38, no. 4.

Basso, K. & Selby, H. (eds.) 1976. *Meaning in Anthropology*. Albuquerque: School of American Research.

Duranti, A. 1992. Language and bodies in social space: Samoan ceremonial greetings. *American Anthropologist* 94: 657–691.

Duranti, A. & Goodwin, C. (eds.) 1992. *Rethinking Context.* Cambridge: Cambridge University Press.

Goffman, E. 1974. *Frame Analysis.* New York: Harper & Row

Goffman, E. 1981. *Forms of Talk.* Philadelphia: University of Pennsylvania Press.

Hanks, W. 1990. *Referential Practice: Language and Lived Space among the Maya.* Chicago: University of Chicago Press.

Hanks, W. 1992. The indexical ground of deictic reference. In Duranti & Goodwin (eds.), pp. 43–76.

Haviland, J. 1993. Anchoring, iconicity and orientation in Guugu Yimithirr pointing gestures. *Linguistic Anthropology* 1: 3–45.

Jackendoff, R. 1983. *Semantics and Cognition.* Cambridge, MA: MIT Press.

Jakobson, R. 1971 [1957]. Shifters, verbal categories, and the Russian verb. In *Selected Writings of Roman Jakobson,* vol. ii, pp. 130–147. The Hague: Mouton.

Kendon, A. 1980. Gesticulation and speech: two aspects of the process of utterance. In M. R. Key (ed.), *The Relation between Verbal and Nonverbal Communication,* pp. 207–227. The Hague: Mouton.

Kendon, A. 1997. Gesture. *Annual Review of Anthropology* 26: 109–128.

Langacker, L. W. 1987. *Foundations of Cognitive Grammar,* vol. i: *Theoretical Prerequisites.* Stanford, CA: Stanford University Press.

McCullough, K. E. 1993. Spatial information and cohesion in the gesticulation of English speakers. Paper presented at the Annual Convention of the American Psychological Society, Antwerp, November.

McNeill, D. 1992. *Hand and Mind: What Gestures Reveal about Thought.* Chicago: University of Chicago Press.

McNeill, D. 1997. Imagery in motion event descriptions: gestures as part of thinking-for-speaking. Paper presented at Berkeley Linguistics Society meeting, February.

Rauscher, F. B., Krauss, R. M. & Chen, Y. (1996). Gesture, speech and lexical access: the role of lexical movements in speech production. *Psychological Science* 7: 226–231.

Schopen, T. (ed.) 1985. *Language Typology and Syntactic Description,* vol. ii: *Grammatical Categories and the Lexicon.* Cambridge: Cambridge University Press.

Silverstein, M. 1976. Shifters, verbal categories and cultural description. In Basso & Selby (eds.), pp. 11–55.

Talmy, L 1985. Lexicalization patterns: semantic structure in lexical forms. In Schopen (ed.), pp. 57–149.

4   Gesture, aphasia, and interaction

Charles Goodwin

Applied Linguistics, University of California at Los Angeles

1   Introduction

What is the scope of phenomena that have to be taken into account in order to describe how gesture is organized as intelligible action in human interaction? Here it will be argued that gesture as meaningful action is accomplished not by a speaker's hand alone, but instead through the relevant juxtaposition of a range of different kinds of semiotic materials which mutually elaborate each other.

The present chapter will probe the range of phenomena relevant to the organization of a gesture by looking at a rather special situation. Because of a massive stroke in the left hemisphere of his brain, Chil is able to speak only three words (Yes, No, and And).[1] However, he is able to supplement this vocabulary with limited gestures, and to understand much of what other people say.[2] His gestures have none of the syntax or other language properties of a sign language. Indeed, like his vocabulary, they seem more sparse and restricted than the gestures of people without brain damage. Despite these very severe restrictions on possibilities for expression through language, he is nonetheless able to engage in complicated conversation. How is this possible? By embedding the semiotic field constituted through his gesture in the talk and action of his interlocutors, Chil is able to both say something relevant and negotiate its meaning. His gestures do not stand alone, but instead count as meaningful action by functioning as components of a distributed process in which he creatively makes use of the language produced by others.

Crucial components of this process include (1) the embedding of gesture within a multi-party gesture space for the public constitution of meaning; (2) the placement of individual gestures within larger gesture sequences; and (3) interactive frameworks for tying talk to gesture, framing the semantic content of gestures within appropriate semiotic fields and negotiating their locally relevant meaning.[3] The present chapter's focus on socially organized frameworks for the accomplishment of meaning complements the psychological analysis of gesture found in many of the other chapters in this volume.

Chil's situation provides an opportunity to look in detail at a range of

Figure 4.1.

different kinds of meaning-making practices that are relevant to the organ-ization of gesture. It must be emphasized, however, that despite the unique-ness of the situation being examined, the practices being examined are generic ones that figure as well in the use of gesture by parties fully able to speak.

2   The sequence to be examined

Analysis in this chapter will focus on the use of gesture in a single extended sequence. Chil and his family are planning to go out for dinner. Chil is seated in a chair, and his daughter, Pat, is discussing arrangements with him. Chil's wife, Helen, and Pat's daughter Julia are seated on the couch to Chil's left (Figure 4.1).

The family agrees that all the five members present in the house will eat dinner at six o'clock (lines 1–5 in the transcript). The exchange that will be the focus of the present analysis then occurs. Chil participates in it by making a series of hand gestures with his left hand (his right hand and arm are paralyzed). In the following transcript, drawings of his handshapes are placed to the right of the talk where they were produced. A downward arrow indicates that Chil is ending his gesture and lowering his arm. To get some sense of the tasks posed for the family here, the reader is strongly encouraged to read through the transcript while using the changing hand-shapes to try and figure out what Chil wants to say.

3   Situating gestures in activity frames

With hindsight it is possible to see that Chil wants to invite two additional guests, Mack and June, to dinner. However, it takes intricate, temporally

```
 1  Pat:    So we'll see if they have  a table for five.
 2  Chil:   Ye(h)s.
 3  Helen:  When? at six a clock?
 4  Pat:    °mm hmm
 5  Chil:   Yes.
```

• • •

```
 6  Chil:   Da da:h.
 7  Pat:    When we went with Mack and June.
 8          We- we sat at a table
 9          just as we came in the: fr-ont door.
10          *hh We sat with them. (.)
11          ┌There. ┌En then we-
12  Chil:   └°mmm.└Nih nih  duh  duh. Da duh.
13  Pat:    So five of us can fit there.
14              (0.2)
15  Pat:    Six a clock.
16              (1.0)

17  Pat:    Five people,
18  Helen   Sure.
19  Pat:    ┌Its::
20  Julia:  └Seven?
21  Pat:    Seven?
22          a' clock?
23              (0.2)
24  Chil:   No(h).
```

unfolding work for his interlocutors to discover this. Through most of this sequence Pat interprets any number higher than five as a proposal about the time for dinner (lines 15, 21–22, 25, 27), not the number of people who will be going. Investigation of the sequential structures that make it possible for the numbers displayed by Chil's gesturing hand to be reframed so that his invitation is eventually recognized is beyond the scope of this chapter (but

25 Pat: *Six* a clock.

26   (0.2)

27 Pat: ⌐*Seven?*

28 Helen: └°Seven people. Who⌐ ('d they be)

29 Pat: └Five.

30   (1.0)

31 Helen: Seven people. ⌐Who *are* they.

32 Pat: └That's six.

33 Julia: Two?

34 Pat: ⌐Seven?

35 Chil: └Duh da *dah?*   *((Chil Turns and Points Toward Helen))*

36   *Ye:s.*

37   (0.2)

38 Pat: Invite somebody?

39 Chil: *Ye:s.*

40   (0.2)

41 Pat: Mack en June?

42 Chil: Yes.

43   (0.2)

44 Pat: *Oh:.*

45   (2.0)

46 Pat: *OH:.*

see C. Goodwin, in press, for such analysis). It will be simply noted that in order to give Chil's handshapes appropriate meaning, his listeners must embed them in an appropriate activity (e.g., counting people versus specifying the time for dinner). Here this activity is made visible by the semantic structure of talk that the gesture is visibly tied to. Talk and gesture mutually elaborate each other. McNeill (1992) has analyzed such a conjunction as evidence for particular kinds of psychological processes within the mind of the individual producing the gesture (e.g., the genesis of an utterance within a growth point that is subsequently given shape in different ways by at least two semiotic media: language and gesture). In the present data the gesture and the talk that it is tied to are produced by separate individuals as part of the process of accomplishing a locally relevant plan of action (going out to dinner). This provides some evidence for a social rather than a psychological motivation for the symbiotic relationship between talk and gesture. It is this ability to juxtapose into a larger whole the semiotic fields provided by gesture and language which makes possible the establishment of public, shared meaning such that courses of multi-party coordinated action can be successfully accomplished.

4   The interactive organization of Chil's gestures

For Chil, the accomplishment of meaning through gesture is a thoroughly social process, one that requires the intricate collaboration of others. Analysis will now focus on how Chil's gestures are shaped and organized as interactive processes. Phenomena to be examined will include the detailed articulation of his hand, differentiating groups of related hand movements from each other through systematic use of the arm presenting the gesturing hand, and the interactive organization of gesture space.

4.1   *Securing orientation to the gesture*

McNeill (1992: 86) defines gesture space only with reference to the body of the party producing the gesture. The present data allows us to expand his notion of gesture space and go beyond the body of the party making the gesture to focus on a multi-party interactively sustained space that provides a framework for common orientation and the production of meaning. The necessity of such a framework can be seen in a number of different ways in this sequence. For example, the place where Chil makes his gesture is organized not only in terms of his body, but also with reference to the position and changing action of his addressee. Thus, as can be seen in Figure 4.1 above, Chil places his gesturing hand squarely in Pat's line of sight. If Chil had been talking to Helen, the hand would have been placed quite differently. Gesture space is defined in terms of his interlocutor's body as well as his own.

Moreover, Chil changes the placement of his hand with reference to Pat's orientation. At the beginning of line 12 Pat is looking to her right toward Helen. Chil, who had been silent, holds up his hand in the 5-shape while producing an intonational tune (Figure 4.2). Chil's actions at the beginning of line 12 have the effect of drawing Pat's gaze to him.[4] Once she is looking at him, he raises his hand sharply into her line of sight, and this becomes the position used for gesturing throughout the remainder of the sequence. It would appear that his hand, initially in conjunction with his intonation melody, is performing two different, though interrelated, actions: first, requesting the orientation of an addressee (by announcing that he has

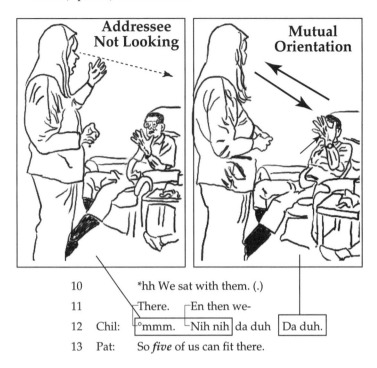

10		*hh We sat with them. (.)	
11		⌐There. ⌐En then we-	
12	Chil:	⌊°mmm. ⌊Nih nih │da duh │ Da duh.
13	Pat:	So *five* of us can fit there.	

Figure 4.2.

something to say); and second, producing a meaningful utterance, here a sequence of gestures, once his interlocutor is visibly positioned to attend to it. The process that occurs here is structurally analogous to the way in which a state of mutual orientation is negotiated prior to the production of a coherent sentence in conversation. Parties who lack the gaze of a hearer produce phrasal breaks, such as restarts, to request such gaze, and speak coherent sentences only after they have the orientation of a hearer (C. Goodwin 1981: ch. 2).[5]

In sum, the relevant framework for the analysis of Chil's gesture is not his hand in isolation, or even the entire body of the party performing the gesture, but instead a multi-party participation framework organized so as to constitute a common focus of attention.[6]

4.2 Parsing movement into coherent sequences

To count higher than five, Chil, who has the use of only one hand, has to produce a sequence of gestures: first a full hand signaling five, and then a second handshape displaying additional digits. These hand gestures have to

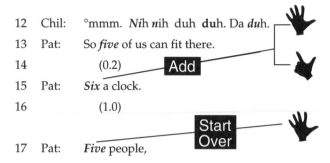

12   Chil: °mmm. *Nih nih* duh **duh**. Da *duh*.

13   Pat: So *five* of us can fit there.

14   (0.2)   **Add**

15   Pat: *Six* a clock.

16   (1.0)

                         Start Over

17   Pat: *Five* people,

Figure 4.3.

be interpreted not simply as numbers, but as numbers to be summed. This process explicitly contrasts with something else that happens here: redoing the counting sequence. In this activity another handful of numbers is also displayed. But this is not to be seen as more numbers to be added to the existing sum, but instead as the beginning of another try at getting the meaning of the number right. Thus at line 17 Pat says not eleven (an additional five added to the six she produced in line 15) but "Five" (see Figure 4.3). The separate gestures have to be grouped into relevant sequences. Correct parsing has real consequences for subsequent action: to build an appropriate next move, Chil's interlocutor performs different kinds of operations on different sequence types. How are successive hand gestures grouped into relevant sequences? It might seem that this is an interpretive problem posed for the viewer of the gestures, that is, a mental act of classification. However, making visible coherent sequences, and disjunctures between sequences, is intrinsic to the embodied work of doing gesture. The visible movements of Chil's body provide Pat with the resources she needs to parse the flow of his gestures into the separate action packages she requires in order to build an appropriate response to them. How this is done will now be investigated in detail.

The gestures that are to be summed together are consistently done in a particular way: first the five is produced with all five fingers spread apart. Then, while holding the hand in approximately the same position in space, three of the extended fingers are closed. The constant position of the hand in space provides a unifying ground, a framework, within which the successive finger displays emerge as stages in a common activity.

This contrasts quite markedly with what happens when Chil signals that Pat's interpretation is wrong, and redoes the gesture. Here Chil rapidly drops his hand, thus dismantling the stage for the hand created by the position of the arm in space, and then raises it again. In essence the stage which provides a framework for the perception of the hand is cleared, and a new stage is created. On such a stage a hand displaying numbers arrives as a fresh actor, one that is initiating a new counting sequence rather than adding to a sequence already in progress.

Why doesn't this new stage signal Pat to move to a new activity or topic? While dropping his hand and then rapidly raising it again Chil continues to stare intently at his interlocutor. The boundary between successive counting trials is thus embedded in a larger, unbroken framework of sustained focus on a continuing activity with a particular partner.

Rather than standing alone as self-contained units of meaning, Chil's handshapes are systematically informed by a nested set of hierarchical displays created by the rest of his body: first the movements of his arm which organize individual gestures into separate sequences; and second, his gaze (and the orientation of his upper body) toward an addressee, which establishes continuity across the different counting sequences made visible by his moving arm.[7]

4.3   Frameworks for constituting meaning through gesture

For normal speakers, gestures typically arrive accompanied by relevant talk. Moreover, the gesture and its lexical affiliate are not only produced by the same person, but are deeply intertwined in the development of a common structure of meaning (McNeill 1992). The accompanying talk not only provides a resource for analysts of gesture, who can investigate in fine detail the precise timing of the unfolding course of the gesture and the words it elaborates (Kendon 1983, 1994b; McNeill 1992; Schegloff 1984), but also for participants, who are easily able to find a relevant meaning in a speaker's moving hand. By way of contrast, the utterances of Chil being examined here are done entirely through gesture. Moreover, successful analysis of his gesture has real consequences for subsequent interaction. Within this process, establishing the meaning of a gesture is repetitively posed as a problematic practical task. The work done to accomplish this task throws into strong relief a range of procedures and resources used to organize gesture as a meaningful interactively sustained activity.

For descriptive purposes it can be useful to describe some of these structures in terms of a series of hierarchically embedded organizational frameworks.

- One can begin with specific handshapes. Rather than being merely expressive, Chil's handshapes are carefully organized to guide specific interpretations by their addressees.
- Second, rather than being static signs, Chil's gestures are constituted through patterns of gestural movement (Armstrong et al. 1995) which

simultaneously provide information about the operations recipients should perform on the handshapes thus framed. The hand making a display is placed and held in position by an arm. Rather than constituting a constant, amorphous ground to the meaningful figure formed by the hand, the arm is itself an important actor in the organization of Chil's gestures. Its movements delineate the boundaries of relevant sequences of gestures within a extended flow of handshapes. Such parsing of the stream of his visible activity is absolutely central to the successful accomplishment of the tasks his addressees are engaged in, since they must perform alternative types of operations (e.g., summing two numbers, as opposed to starting a count from scratch) on different arrangements of successive handshapes.

- Third, locating the lexical affiliate of a gesture does not constitute establishing its meaning. Wittgenstein (1958; see also Baker & Hacker 1980) argues that the meaning of a name is not its bearer (e.g., some version of the number five), but rather mastery of the practices required to use that sign competently in a relevant language game. Here multiple language games are at issue: first, the particular activity within which the practice of counting is embedded (i.e., time versus number of people); second, the larger projects within which an utterance such as "seven people" counts as a relevant move (e.g., a proposal that additional friends be included in the unfolding plans for dinner); and third, the frameworks and procedures that Chil and those around him deploy to make sense of his gestures in order to accomplish relevant courses of action.

- Fourth, the gesture space required for the analysis of what Chil is doing encompasses not only his own body, but also that of his addressee. Chil performs special gestural and vocal work to secure his interlocutor's visual focus on his hand, and consistently places his hand in her line of sight.

- Fifth, within this framework one party's talk can gloss and explicate another's gesture. The elements required to assemble the meaning of a gesture are distributed entities, existing in different media (the moving hand and the talk which elaborates it) and, in this case, in the activities of separate participants.

- Sixth, while an interactively sustained multi-party participation framework provides a stage for the coordinated display of gesture and talk, something more is required to constitute its meaning socially: sequential organization. Pat's glosses can be wrong. It is only through temporally unfolding processes of interaction that Pat and Chil establish a common vision of what is being said with the gesture. It is here that a range of disparate phenomena, including the talk and the visible body displays of separate people, are integrated into a common course of action.

5   Ecologies of sign systems and the communities they shape

In normal conversations, gestures frequently co-occur with talk by the party making the gesture. Since the talk carries much (though by no means all) of what is being said, it is on occasion possible for hearers to grasp the substance of an utterance while paying only passing attention to the accompanying gesture, or even ignoring it entirely.[8] By way of contrast, the utterances of Chil being examined here are done entirely through gesture, and thus must be attended to by at least one of his addressees. Chil adapts to his gestural utterances one of the basic procedures used by speakers in conversation to obtain the orientation of a hearer to an emerging strip of talk: securing the gaze of an addressee with a preliminary version of the gesture, and then redoing the gesture once mutual orientation has been established. Insofar as Chil's gestures have the status of full-fledged moves within conversation – that is, they do constitute his turns at talk – it is not at all surprising that resources used more generally to organize participation within the turn are now used to frame his gestures in ways that are not done for the gestures of participants able to speak.

The particular characteristics of the interactive community that emerge when he is a participant have other consequences as well. Despite some moves toward organizing relevant contrasts within a larger system, Chil's gesturing is not in any way comparable to the well-developed sign languages of the deaf,[9] or of speaking people prohibited from talking (Kendon 1988). Thus, his gestures are not organized into elaborate, hierarchically organized structures through syntactic processes. Moreover, unlike communication in a signing community, his interlocutors do not operate under his constraints, but instead use the full resources of talk-in-interaction. The work of Singleton, Morford & Goldin-Meadow (1995) suggests that one very strong constraint inhibiting the elaboration of syntactic relationships between hand movements, that is, the shift from isolated gestures to a signing system, is the way in which gestures remain parasitic on the structure of co-occurring spoken language. When speech is present, links between hand movements are provided by the talk and thus do not have to be built into the organization of the gestural stream. In Chil's case the issue is complicated by the question of whether damage to his brain would make syntax impossible under any circumstances. Nonetheless the work of Singleton and her colleagues leads to the very interesting possibility that the hybrid speech community that some stroke victims create with their interlocutors (e.g., one party using gestures and limited speech but tying that to the fully articulated language of others) might itself inhibit the elaboration of more syntactic organization in a stroke victim's gesturing system. Other social factors are at play here as well. Though half a million

people suffer strokes in America each year, and three million continue to
live with disability because of such trauma, most strokes (over 70 per cent)
occur in people over sixty-five years of age (Leary 1995). Unlike the situation with the deaf, which can affect the very young as well as the old, and
where concerted political action has led to the formation of viable communities and relevant educational institutions, victims of stroke typically live
out their lives disconnected from others in a similar state. Thus, instead of
there being an active, well-developed speech community using a language
like ASL together, and passing it on from generation to generation, the
communication of stroke patients develops in thousands of small, isolated
pockets, and the special adaptations each family creates die with the person
who suffered the stroke.

Chil's use of gesture is by no means the same as that of a person with
unimpaired language abilities. Nonetheless the resources that he and his
interlocutors use are generic practices for the organization of gesture
within interaction which are adapted to the specifics of his situation. Thus
his gestures make use of the same semiotic resources (gesture tied to other
meaning practices such as talk) used by normal speakers. However, in his
case the talk is produced by someone other than the person performing
the gesture (and thus has special characteristics – e.g., it is offered as a candidate understanding, with rising intonation). Chil's aphasia thus leads to
a reorganization of the ecology of sign systems implicated in the production of gesture (e.g., assigning talk and gesture to separate parties) without
however leading to a radically new type of gesture. The distributed work
of tying together signs in different modalities that is required to constitute
the meaning of a gesture is dramatically visible in Chil's case. However, it
is present as well in the talk of parties who are able to speak. Indeed, much
recent research on gesture has focused on its close ties to the structure of
the talk which accompanies it (Heath 1992; Kendon 1994b; McNeill
1992). McNeill (1992) in his work on growth points has demonstrated how
talk and gesture might emerge from a common source in the production of
an utterance. However, quite independent of the psychological origin of
such a relationship, the way in which a gesture and the talk it is tied to
mutually elaborate each other constitutes a central arena for social practice in the organization of talk-in-interaction. It provides a key resource
for participants faced with the task of making relevant sense out of the
field of action embodied in a strip of talk and the co-occurring field of
visible behavior in which it is embedded. Though gesture is typically
treated as a transparent, seamless package, conversationalists can themselves deconstruct this unity for playful and other purposes. For example,
the gestures being made by a speaker can be ridiculed by extracting them
from her talk and then reattaching them to a new, incongruent strip of

talk (C. Goodwin & Goodwin 1992). Seeing a gesture as a meaningful display characteristically involves not just orientation to someone's moving hand, but rather ongoing synthesis and mutual calibration of quite disparate kinds of information emerging through time within different modalities for expression available to the human body lodged in interaction.[10] The way in which Chil's gestures are deeply embedded in the talk of those around him provides a tragic opportunity to probe basic procedures and frameworks deployed by parties in interaction to constitute meaning together.

Throughout each day of their lives members of Chil's family face as an ongoing practical problem the task of how to constitute shared meaning so that the courses of coordinated action that make up their life world can be accomplished. Such a task, which mobilizes language, gesture and social organization for the accomplishment of action within consequential settings, sits at the very center of what it means to be human.

NOTES

I am most deeply indebted to Chil, and his family, for allowing me access to their lives. My understanding of what is happening in these data has been greatly helped by comments from Lisa Capps, David Goode, Cathryn Houghton, Sally Jacoby, Elinor Ochs, Kersten Priest, Curtis Renoe, Emanuel Schegloff, Jennifer Schlegel, Elizabeth Teas-Heaster, and most especially Candy Goodwin. An earlier version of this paper was presented as part of a plenary address at GLS 1995: Developments in Discourse Analysis, Georgetown University, February 18, 1995.

1 For analysis of Chil's use of very limited language to co-construct intricate meaning by embedding his talk in the talk of his interlocutors, see C. Goodwin (1995a).
2 His medical records at discharge in 1981 report "severe expressive and moderate receptive aphasia, moderate dysarthria and verbal apraxia."
3 The original version of this chapter included analysis of all these phenomena. However, the space limitations of the present volume make it necessary to drop the third topic, i.e., description of the sequential structures used to interactively work out the meaning of Chil's gestures. This is a crucial topic, one that is too important to gloss over in a cursory fashion. For more complete description and analysis of this process, see C. Goodwin (in press).
4 For other analysis of how parties making gestures both work to focus the gaze of their recipients on the hand(s) making the gesture and redesign the gesture after its addressee visibly misunderstands it, see Streeck (1993, 1994). For discussion of research pertaining to the question of whether gestures in conversation are in fact communicative (a position that has been challenged by some psychologists), see Kendon (1994b).
5 It is interesting to note that in both situations the item used to solicit orientation is an incomplete version of the utterance or gesture that will constitute the substance of the proposed turn.

6 See Hibbitts (1995) for an analysis of the importance of multi-party participation frameworks for the organization of gesture in the legal system.
7 The way in which Chil uses his hand to bracket sequences of gestures is quite
   consistent with Armstrong, Stokoe & Wilcox (1995), who argue that the production of gesture involves not just the hand, but many other parts of the body,
   moving through time in organized action, and in particular the arms. Kendon
   (1990) has stressed the importance of seeing the body as a locus for hierarchical
   displays of orientation.
8 This does however mean, as some psychologists have suggested, that participants in ordinary conversation entirely ignore gesture. For analysis of how
   speakers reshape emerging action to take into account displays which have been
   made through gesture, see C. Goodwin (1980) and Kendon (1994a).
9 For especially interesting analysis of the development of syntax in a sign-language system, and the way in which such a system differs radically from not only
   gesture but also more primitive signing systems, see Kegl, Senghas & Coppola
   (in press); see also Morford & Kegl (this volume).
10 The web of meaning implicated in the organization of gesture does not stop at
   the actors' skins, but encompasses as well features of their environment and historically structured representations of many different kinds (maps, images,
   graphs, computer screens providing access to worlds beyond the immediate situation, etc.) which give meaning to gesture in a variety of different ways. See for
   example C. Goodwin (1994, 1995b, n.d.), M. H. Goodwin (1995), Heath (1992),
   Heath & Luff (1992), Hutchins (1995), Hutchins & Palen (1997), LeBaron &
   Streeck (this volume), and Ochs, Jacoby & Gonzales (1994).

REFERENCES

Armstrong, D. F., Stokoe, W. C. & Wilcox, S. E. 1995. *Gesture and the Nature of
   Language*. Cambridge: Cambridge University Press.
Atkinson, J. M. & Heritage, J. (eds.) 1984. *Structures of Social Action*. Cambridge:
   Cambridge University Press.
Auer, P. & di Luzio, A. (eds.) 1992. *The Contextualization of Language*. Amsterdam:
   Benjamins.
Baker, G. P. & Hacker, P. M. S. 1980. *Wittgenstein: Understanding and Meaning*.
   Chicago: University of Chicago Press.
DeGraff, M. (ed.) in press. *Language Creation and Language Change: Creolization,
   Diachrony, and Development*. Cambridge, MA: MIT Press.
Goodwin, C. 1980. Restarts, pauses, and the achievement of mutual gaze at turn-
   beginning. *Sociological Inquiry* 50: 272–302.
Goodwin, C. 1981. *Conversational Organization: Interaction between Speakers and
   Hearers*. New York: Academic Press.
Goodwin, C. 1994. Professional vision. *American Anthropologist* 96(3): 606–633.
Goodwin, C. 1995a. Co-constructing meaning in conversations with an aphasic
   man. *Research on Language and Social Interaction* 28(3): 233–260.
Goodwin, C. 1995b. Seeing in depth. *Social Studies of Science* 25: 237–274.
Goodwin, C., in press. Conversational frameworks for the accomplishment of
   meaning in aphasia. In C. Goodwin (ed.), in press.

Goodwin, C. n.d. Pointing as situated practice. In S. Kita (ed.), Pointing: where language, culture and cognition meet. Manuscript.

Goodwin, C. (ed.) in press. *Situating Language Impairments within Conversation.* Oxford: Oxford University Press.

Goodwin, C. & Goodwin, M. H. 1992. Context, activity and participation. In Auer & di Luzio (eds.), pp. 77–99.

Goodwin, M. H. 1980. Processes of mutual monitoring implicated in the production of description sequences. *Sociological Inquiry* 50: 303–317.

Goodwin, M. H. 1995. Co-construction in girls' hopscotch. *Research on Language and Social Interaction* 28(3): 261–282.

Heath, C. C. 1992. Gesture's discrete tasks: multiple relevancies in visual conduct and in the contextualization of language. In Auer & di Luzio (eds.), pp. 101–127.

Heath, C. C. & Luff, P. K. 1992. Crisis and control: collaborative work in London Underground control rooms. *Journal of Computer Supported Cooperative Work* 1(1): 24–48.

Hibbitts, B. J. 1995. Making motions: the embodiment of law in gesture. *Journal of Contemporary Legal Issues* 6: 51–82.

Hutchins, E. 1995. *Cognition in the Wild.* Cambridge, MA: MIT Press.

Hutchins, E. & Palen, L. 1997. Constructing meaning from space, gesture, and speech. In Resnick, Säljö, Pontecorvo & Burge (eds.), pp. 23–40.

Kegl, J., Senghas, A. & Coppola, M. in press. Creation through contact: sign language emergence and sign language change in Nicaragua. In DeGraff (ed.), in press.

Kendon, A. 1983. Gesture and speech: how they interact. In Wiemann & Harrison (eds.), pp. 13–46.

Kendon, A. 1988. *Sign Languages of Aboriginal Australia: Cultural, Semiotic and Communicative Perspectives.* Cambridge: Cambridge University Press.

Kendon, A. 1990. *Conducting Interaction: Patterns of Behavior in Focused Encounters.* Cambridge: Cambridge University Press.

Kendon, A. 1994a. Do gestures communicate? A review. *Research on Language and Social Interaction* 27(3): 175–200.

Kendon, A, 1994b. Introduction to the special issue: Gesture and understanding in social interaction. *Research on Language and Social Interaction* 27(3): 171–174.

Leary, W. E. 1995. Rehabilitation focus urged in stroke cases. *New York Times*, May 28, p. 9.

McNeill, D. 1992. *Hand and Mind: What Gestures Reveal about Thought.* Chicago: University of Chicago Press.

Ochs, E., Jacoby, S. & Gonzales. P. 1994. Interpretive journeys: how physicists talk and travel through graphic space. *Configurations* 2(1): 151–171.

Resnick, L., Säljö, R., Pontecorvo, C. & Burge, B. (eds.) 1997. *Discourse, Tools and Reasoning: Essays on Situated Cognition.* Berlin: Springer-Verlag.

Schegloff, E. A. 1984. On some gestures' relation to talk. In Atkinson & Heritage (eds.), pp. 266–296.

Singleton, J., Morford, J. & Goldin-Meadow, S. 1995. The generation of standards of form within communication systems over different timespans. *Journal of Contemporary Legal Issues* 6: 481–500.

Streeck, J. 1993. Gesture as communication I: Its coordination with gaze and speech. *Communication Monographs* 60(4): 275–299.

Streeck, J. 1994. Gestures as communication II: The audience as co-author. *Research on Language and Social Interaction* 27(3): 223–238.

Wiemann, J. M. & Harrison, R. (eds.) 1983. *Nonverbal Interaction*. Sage Annual Reviews of Communication, vol. 11. Beverly Hills, CA: Sage.

Wittgenstein, L. 1958. *Philosophical Investigations*, ed. G. E. M. Anscombe & R. Rhees, trans. by G. E. M. Anscombe. 2nd ed., Oxford: Blackwell.

5 Gestural interaction between the instructor and the learner in *origami* instruction

Nobuhiro Furuyama

Department of Psychology, University of Chicago

1 Introduction

Do people gesturally interact with each other? If so, how? Is there any consistent and more or less systematic change in the way one of the participants in a dyadic communication gesturally responds to her[1] partner as the latter participant's gesture changes? These are the questions which will be pursued in the present chapter.[2]

These questions have rarely been addressed in the field of gesture–speech research. Most studies have focused on the relationship between speech and gesture in single speakers, who are merely individual participants in the narrative settings as a whole.[3] The speakers have been analyzed independently of the interaction with the communicative partner. This paradigm, which can be called a narrator-centered paradigm, has raised many important questions and brought a variety of significant insights into the field. If gestural interaction between interlocutors can also be found, and if we can determine how partners gesturally interact, the present study will shed new light on the theory of spontaneous gestures to the extent that the model of gesture and speech should take into consideration *inter*personal factors as well as *intra*personal factors (Vygotsky 1962; McNeill & Duncan, this volume).

Some researchers have already begun paying attention to and describing the phenomena of gestural interaction in a broad sense in pursuit of the question of what the listener does in a narrative setting. As one may easily imagine, even in an experimental setting the listener is actively engaged in the communication by using non-verbal behavior, such as nodding and shaking her head, making facial expressions to show whether she comprehends what she has heard, and responding to what the narrator talks about by, for example, smiling. Some of these non-verbal behaviors may be accomplished in a quite subtle way, but all of them are very important in furthering – or even impeding – the dialogue. These non-verbal behaviors by listeners are, in turn, taken into consideration by the narrator in her performance of speech and gesture in the narration/instruction that follows.[4]

For example, the narrator clarifies and/or repeats a part of the narration that is shown, by the listener's shaken head, to be unintelligible. Also, the narrator goes on to the next topic upon seeing the listener's nodding head. Furthermore, it is demonstrated that the listener, in an instructional setting such as how to follow a recipe, reproduces the partner's gestures and/or creates, out of the partner's gestures, similar gestures with additional elements (Furuyama 1993). The speaker/instructor in turn often incorporates additional elements from the listener's gestures into her own gestures in subsequent instructions (ibid.).

The present study investigates gestural interaction with regard to representational gestures, so-called iconic gestures as well as deictic gestures (McNeill 1987, 1992). In order to look at gestural interaction effectively, the experimental task should be highly demanding in terms of spatial thinking, such that the task cannot be performed by employing only verbal means. In other words, the task should be such that imagistic thinking is strongly evoked in both of the participants. *Origami*[5] instruction in the absence of using a piece of *origami* paper is one such task, and it is the task used here.

To investigate the gestural interactions that occur in dyadic communication, it is easier to focus first on the gestures of one participant and then look at those gestures in relation to the gestures of the other participant. Therefore, we will explore the learner's gestures[6] first, and then analyze those gestures in relation to the instructor's gestures.

The specific empirical questions are formulated as follows:

Question 1. What gestures are found in the learners, whose task is basically receiving information from their instructor? In a preliminary study (Furuyama 1993), the learners were found to occasionally produce gestures without speech while they received instruction on following a recipe.

Question 2. Do the learner's gestures systematically change in accord with changes in the instructor's gestures? More specifically, do the types of gestures in the learners, which are to be described in the first half of the present study, shift along with changes in the way the instructors present their gestures? Levy & Fowler (this volume) argue that speakers narrating a story mark the change from one discourse level to another, or from one topic to another, either by producing a hand gesture or by making the duration of speech longer, and that different speakers use different strategies. For these different strategies to be effective, so that the listeners appreciate the shift in discourse levels by looking at the discourse-level-marking gesture or by listening to the discourse-level-marking longer duration, the listeners must be 'attuned' to the strategy used by the narrator (Levy & Fowler, this volume). The present study will examine whether this kind of tuning can be found in how the learners gesturally respond to the instructors.

Table 5.1. *Subject information*

	Instructor subjects			Learner subjects		
Pair	Age	Sex	Experience w/ *origami*	Age	Sex	Experience w/ *origami*
1	19	F	Much	19	F	Some
2	18	F	None	18	M	None
3	20	M	Much	20	M	Some
4	18	F	Much	18	M	Some
5	20	M	Some	24	F	None
6	21	M	Much	21	F	None
7	23	M	None	42	F	None
8	19	M	None	19	F	None
9	20	M	Much	18	M	Much

2   Study of instructional gestures

In this section, the method of data collection will be described. In section 3, the learner's gestures and their relation to the instructor's gestures will be described in accordance with questions 1 and 2 above. Discussion of these questions will be followed by the description of yet other results. Section 4 provides a general discussion.

2.1   Method of data collection

2.1.1   Subjects. The subjects were eighteen students (non-psychology-major undergraduates and graduates) from the University of Chicago, who were recruited by flyers posted around the campus. All were native speakers of American English. The average age was 20.9 years (*SD* = 5.5 yr); ten were male and eight female. *Origami* experience, as reported by the subjects themselves, varied from a great deal to essentially none. Subjects were tested in pairs in which one of the subjects was the instructor and the other the learner. The assignment of roles was decided in either of the following two ways. (1) If one of the two subjects was more experienced with *origami*, that subject became the instructor. (2) If there was no substantial difference in experience between the subjects, regardless of the amount of prior experience, the assignment was decided by the flip of a coin. Table 5.1 shows the age, sex, and level of prior experience with *origami* of the instructors and learners in each pair of subjects. The subjects in pair 1 through pair 4 were

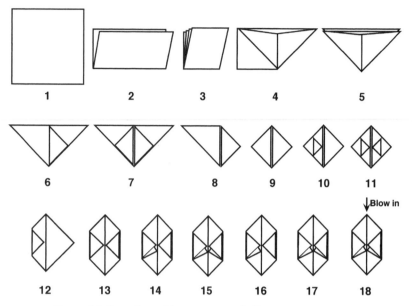

Figure 5.1. Steps in making an *origami* balloon.

acquainted with each other prior to the experiment; those in pair 5 through pair 9 were not.

2.1.2   Stimuli. The stimuli were videotaped instructions and a sheet of paper with a drawn version of the instructions (see Figure 5.1), both of which showed how to make an *origami* balloon in a detailed, step-by-step fashion. There was no verbal description of the instructions with the exception of the last step on the instruction sheet (see step 18 in Figure 5.1). Since the instructors were permitted to ask the experimenter for help when they did not understand the videotape or the instruction sheet, some instructors obtained additional demonstrations by the experimenter. These demonstrations were given only for the steps in question, and no verbal descriptions were offered in these cases.

The following is a brief description of the steps. *Step 1:* Take a square piece of *origami* paper. *Step 2:* Fold the square in half so that it is a rectangle. *Step 3:* Fold the rectangle in half so that it is a square which is a quarter the size of the original square. *Step 4:* Take the upper left-hand corner of the square and bring it to a point on the right so that the two points are symmetrical, with the right-hand edge of the square as the center line of an isosceles triangle with the base at the top. *Step 5:* Flip the whole figure over and repeat step 3 (the figure is a mirror image of the one in step 4). In other words, take the upper-right-hand corner of the square and bring it to the point on the left, which is the corner of the triangle which sticks out of the square on the back side. *Step 6:* Take the right-hand corner of the triangle and bring it to the apex on the bottom. *Step 7:* Take the left-hand corner and bring it to the apex on the bottom, which is the same apex as in step 6. *Step 8:* Turn the figure over and take the right-hand corner of the triangle and bring it to the apex on the bottom. *Step 9:* Take the left-hand corner and bring it to the apex on the bottom, which is the same apex as in step 8. After completing steps 6 through 9, there should be a square which is one-eighth the size of the original square piece of paper, but angled in a diamond shape. *Step 10:* Take the left-hand corner of the square and bring it to the center point of the square. *Step 11:* Take the right-hand corner of the square and bring it to the center point of the square. *Step 12:* Turn the figure over, take the left-hand corner of the square, and bring it to the center point of the square. *Step 13:* Take the right-hand corner of the square and bring it to the center point of the square. After completing steps 10 through 13, there should be a hexagon. *Step 14:* Take the flap on the bottom-left-hand side and tuck it into the pocket-like thing at the edge of the small triangle just created. *Step 15:* Take the flap on the bottom-right-hand side and tuck it into the pocket-like thing at the edge of the small triangle on the right-hand side of the hexagon. *Step 16:* Turn the figure over, take the flap on the bottom-left-hand side, and tuck it into the pocket-like thing at the edge of the small triangle on the left-hand side of the hexagon. *Step 17:* Take the flap on the bottom-right-hand side and tuck it into the pocket-like thing at the edge of the small triangle on the right-hand side of the hexagon. After completing steps 14 through 17, there should be the same hexagon as a whole, but with every flap on the bottom tucked into the pocket-like thing at the edges of the small triangles. *Step 18:* Now, finally, you should be able to find a tiny hole at the top of the hexagon. Blow into the hole, and the figure will puff up like a balloon.

2.1.3   Procedure. The experiment took place in three steps. (1) A learning session for the instructor. The instructor's task was to become familiar enough with the eighteen steps in making the *origami* balloon to be able to instruct her partner without using a piece of paper. The subject was permitted to practice as many times as needed and to ask for help when the instructions were unclear. The instructor was allowed to look at the instruction sheet while imparting the instructions, but could not show it to the learner. (2) The instruction session. Both subjects were told that the learner would have to make the *origami* figure after the session. The learner was permitted to ask questions and to request clarification from the instructor. Neither subject was permitted to use any utensil, such as a piece of *origami* paper, a pen, or a notepad. (3) The *origami* session. Immediately following the instruction session, the learner attempted to make the balloon using an actual piece of *origami* paper. The subject could ask the instructor for help only when hopelessly blocked. The instructor was allowed to help only for the step that the learner was having difficulty with. After the learner finished the *origami* figure, the subjects filled out a questionnaire about the difficulty of the task that both had just performed.[7]

The experimenter was present for all sessions. The subjects were videotaped during the instruction and *origami* sessions, with the camcorder set up to capture whole-body views of both.

3   Results

3.1   Observation 1: learners' gestures

3.1.1   Gestures with and without speech.[8] Observation 1 will describe the gestures performed by the learners, and will answer question 1 from the introduction. As has been well documented in the literature on gesture research (e.g., McNeill 1987, 1992), gestures by the learners tended to be synchronized with speech affiliated with the gesture in terms of meaning. In fact three-quarters of the learners' gestures were synchronized with the learner's own meaningfully affiliated speech (300 out of 400 gestures in total). In addition, the learners performed gestures without speech. This kind of gesture has rarely been found in narrative settings (see note 3). Gestures without speech are gestures that do not synchronize with speech or with any kind of vocalization by the learners themselves. Although these gestures do not synchronize with the learner's own speech, they are related to the speech and/or gesture content of the instructor or to the speech and/or gesture content of the learner at a previous or following point in the discourse. The following excerpt from the instruction session of pair 1 is an example of a learner gesture without speech and illustrates how it synchronizes with the meaningfully affiliated speech and/or the gesture of the instructor. Here, the instructor is trying to clarify her previous instruction on step 4, with which the learner is having difficulty.

(1) I: [so you **take one corner**][9] Okay.
The instructor picks up, with her right hand, the upper left corner of an imaginary piece of paper.

(2) L: {okay, take one corner}
The learner also picks up the upper left corner of the same imaginary piece of paper with her right hand, and with her left hand holds the left edge of the imagined paper.

(3) I: **[take the {<u>front corner</u>}]**
          The instructor also starts holding the left edge of the paper with her
          left hand. The learner lifts up the index finger of her right hand and
          moves it down to the front corner of the paper.

In (2), the learner's gesture synchronizes exclusively with the learner's own speech, and also is related to it in meaning. In (3), however, the learner's gesture does not synchronize with the learner's own speech. In fact, the learner does not produce any audible vocal sound while she is gesticulating in this segment. Rather, this gesture synchronizes with the instructor's speech, as the curly brackets embedded in the instructor's speech show. The learner's gesture also synchronizes with the instructor's gesture, as the curly brackets surrounded by the square brackets show. Not only that, this learner gesture is affiliated with the instructor's speech and gesture in meaning. It represents the procedure of taking "the front corner" from among four layers of paper (see step 3 in Figure 5.1). There are four layers of paper on the upper-left corner, the result of the two foldings in steps 1 and 2. This new piece of information, that one must pick up "the front corner," is crucial to complete step 3 and successfully get to step 4. Thus, it is opposed to the previously given information that one must "take one corner," which was not specific enough. It is with respect to this new information that the learner's gesture in (3) should be interpreted. It is related to a particular speech segment of the instructor's, "the front corner," and not to any other segment.

3.1.2   Collaborative gestures. Another phenomenon found in the corpus is what can be called the collaborative use of gesture. Such uses of gesture, to the author's knowledge at least, have never been observed and/or reported in narrative settings. Collaborative gestures are those which interact with the gestures of the communicative partner. They are basically not complete in themselves in terms of what they represent without the existence of the gesture of the communicative partner. The meaning of this type of gesture crucially depends on the interlocutor's gesture, since the interlocutor's gesture is a part of the collaborative gesture as a whole. One form of collaborative gesture was pointing with the index finger, for example, to the gesture of the instructor. Pointing, in general, is not complete without the object that is pointed at. Another form of collaborative gesture was the learner's touching and manipulating the parts or the whole of the gesture being produced by the instructor (including the 'object' seemingly set up in the air by the instructor with a gesture). Learners sometimes actually changed the shape, position, or direction of the instructor's gesture. They also sometimes manipulated what was drawn by the instructor in the air or on the surface of the table in front of the learner, the learner's finger tracing the instructor's gesture. In a sense, collaborative gesture is 'meta-gestural' just as language employed to talk about language is meta-linguistic (Jakobson 1960). In most cases, such collaborative gestures accompanied the learner's own speech. The following is an excerpt from the middle of the instruction at step 5, in pair 7, where the learner makes two collaborative gestures:[10]

(4) I: ['cause you have a triangle like that]
         The instructor holds his flattened left hand horizontally with the palm facing downward, and his flattened right hand slanted with the palm facing upwards, so that the two hands represent the upper-right corner of the triangle in step 5 of Figure 5.1.

(5) I: [and you#]
         The instructor, while holding the left-handed gesture in (4), picks up the upper-right corner of the triangle with his right hand. This right-handed gesture starts moving downwards, but it is interrupted by the learner.

(6) L: {and you take this corner*}
         The learner, extending her left hand between the instructor's chest and his gesture, picks up and moves the upper-right corner of the triangle downward, as rendered by the instructor.

(7) I: [bring it down#]
         The instructor, with his right hand, picks up the upper-right corner of the triangle and then brings it down to the apex of the imaginary triangle. The learner's left hand is held in front of the instructor and behind his gesture here from (6) through (8).

(8) L: {but where do you put this point?}
         The learner's left hand, with which the upper-right corner of the triangle is picked up as described in (6), beats six times at the point between the upper-right corner and the apex of the imaginary triangle. One beat co-occurred with each underlined word.

The learner's gesture in (6) is a collaborative gesture, because the learner picks up and moves the imaginary triangle rendered by the instructor. In the same way, the learner gesture in (8) is a collaborative gesture, because the learner is shaking her left hand while, with that hand, holding the same corner of the imaginary triangle made by the instructor. These collaborative gestures occurred in the space between the instructor's chest and his gesture and almost on the gesture.

3.1.3   Quantitative data analysis for the learners' gestures. It is possible in principle for collaborative gestures to occur without speech. Yet the learner subjects didn't avail themselves of this possibility. This result will be described in this section.

The analysis here focuses on the representational and deictic gestures produced by learners when the instructor's gesture was present. All of these gestures were first coded according to whether or not they synchronized with speech. (Here 'speech' refers to any utterance or any vocalization, including what are so-called filled pauses.) Then the same gestures were coded according to whether or not they were collaborative. A gesture is collaborative when it points to or manipulates the instructor's gesture. The instructor's gesture includes the gesture itself and also what is set up by the gesture, such as a figure traced by a finger in the air or on a physical surface like the surface of a table. Some learners consistently held their hands in front of them at chest level. This kind of hold gesture was counted as more than one gesture only if there were multiple strokes on the hold. When the participants talked about something other than the task itself, these parts were excluded from the object of coding.

Coding was done by the experimenter, with a randomly selected sample of gestures coded by another independent coder who was expert in gesture coding.[11] Gestures where the two codings did not match were discussed until agreement was reached. The final agreement between the two coders was 96 percent.

The bottom row of Table 5.2 shows the frequencies and percentages of learner gestures with and without speech for the whole corpus, organized according to whether they were collaborative or non-collaborative. We see that non-collaborative gestures occur most often with speech but can also occur without speech. Collaborative gestures, on the other hand, occur virtually only with speech (97%) – there are just two exceptions. Thus, although collaborativeness and lack of speech are theoretically combinable, they are in fact almost non-overlapping.

Table 5.2 also shows the patterns for individual pairs of subjects. We see the same basic tendency in all the individual pairs, with pairs 2 and 4 the exceptions. In pair 4, the learner had no gestures when the instructor's gestures were present, but this learner had no gestures at all, so it is doubtful that he should be called an exception. In pair 2, the learner produced two collaborative gestures without speech (the two exceptions to the general pattern mentioned above). Nonetheless, this subject fits the general pattern otherwise – many more non-collaborative gestures without speech than collaborative gestures without speech, for example.

Wilcoxon Matched Pairs Signed Rank sum tests show that gestures

Table 5.2. *Frequency of gesture with/without speech according to whether collaborative or non-collaborative for each learner*

	Non-collaborative		Collaborative	
	With speech	Without speech	With speech	Without speech
Pair 1	26	20	3	0
Pair 2	99	22	28	2
Pair 3	13	1	4	0
Pair 4	0	0	0	0
Pair 5	33	2	15	0
Pair 6	7	2	0	0
Pair 7	41	45	18	0
Pair 8	3	3	0	0
Pair 9	9	3	1	0
Total	231 (70.30%)	98 (29.70%)	69 (97.18%)	2 (2.82%)

without speech were more frequent when they were non-collaborative than when they were collaborative ($T = 0$ ($n = 8$), $p < .01$), and that collaborative gestures were more frequent when they accompanied speech than when they did not ($T = 0$ ($n = 6$), $p < .05$).

Though the quantity of data is limited, it seems possible to say that two dimensions of learner gestures – namely, whether or not gestures accompany speech, and whether or not they are collaborative (dimensions that are not mutually exclusive by definition) – ARE mutually exclusive in practice, for nearly all subjects. Note that this does not mean, of course, that all speech-accompanying gestures are collaborative, nor that all non-collaborative gestures are produced without speech. Nonetheless, the lack of collaborative gestures without speech is remarkable.

3.2   Observation 2: learner gestures in relation to instructor gestures

3.2.1   Question and approach. Do learner collaborative gestures and learner gestures without speech depend in any way on the instructor gestures? This should be a reasonable question, because the two distinctive modes of the learner's gestural response are actually, as we have seen above, two different ways of sharing or using the instructor's speech and/or gesture content as a resource for communication. One possible factor is whether or

Table 5.3. *The frequency of collaborative/non-collaborative gestures according to whether the focal side of the instructor's gesture faced the learner (FTL) or not (non-FTL), for each learner*

Learner's gesture	Instructor's gesture FTL		Instructor's gesture non-FTL	
	Non-collaborative	Collaborative	Non-collaborative	Collaborative
Pair 1	6	3	40	0
Pair 2	53	30	68	0
Pair 3	11	4	3	0
Pair 4	0	0	0	0
Pair 5	31	15	4	0
Pair 6	7	0	2	0
Pair 7	29	18	57	0
Pair 8	5	0	1	0
Pair 9	3	1	9	0
Total	145 (67.13%)	71 (32.87%)	184 (100.00%)	0 (0.00%)

not the focal side of the instructor's gesture faces the learner. The focal side of a gesture is the side which represents the content of what is being talked about. The focal side of the instructor's gesture was often an imaginary piece of *origami* paper at the inside of a fold, or an edge, or an imagined point on the figure. The focal side is the part of the gesture focused on and talked about by the instructor, whether or not it faces the learner. An example is the palm of the left hand representing a rectangular piece of paper, with the tip of the index finger being one corner of the rectangle and, together with the rest of the fingers, moving to the opposite corner, represented by the root of the thumb. For the palm to become the focal side of the gesture it, by definition, needs to be verbally focused on by the gesturer. An example of such focus is "This corner goes to the opposite corner of the rectangle," by which two points on the imaginary piece of paper on the palm are referred to and what is taking place there is described. The following specific question was asked: Does the frequency of the learner's gestures without speech and the learner's collaborative gestures correlate with whether or not the focal side of the instructor's gesture faces the learner?

The coding of the learners' gestures was done as in the previous section. All representational and deictic gestures produced by the instructors were coded according to whether or not the focal side of the gesture faced the learner. When the participants talked about something irrelevant to the task itself, these sections were excluded from the coding. As was done for the coding of learner gestures, the instructor gesture coding was done by the experimenter, and a randomly selected sample of gestures was later coded by another independent coder expert in gesture coding. Gestures where the two codings did not match were discussed until agreement was reached. The final agreement between the two coders was 96 percent.

3.2.2   Results. Collaborative and non-collaborative learner gestures and instructor gestures: The bottom row of Table 5.3 shows the frequencies and the ratios of the learners' collaborative and non-collaborative gestures, according to whether or not the focal side of the instructors' gestures faced the learner. We see that all of the learners' collaborative gestures occurred when the focal side of instructor gesture faced the learner.

Table 5.3 also shows the results for individual pairs of subjects. No learners' collaborative gestures were observed with pairs 4, 6, and 8 in either condition. For the rest of the learners, all collaborative gestures were observed when the focal side of the instructor's gestures faced the learner. This matches the general tendency for the whole corpus.

The Wilcoxon Matched Pairs Signed Rank sum test shows that the collaborative gestures were more frequent when the focal side of the instructor's gestures faced the learner than when they did not ($T = 0$ ($n = 6$), $p < .05$).

Learner gestures with/without speech and instructor gestures: The bottom row of Table 5.4 shows the frequencies and the ratios of learner gestures with and without speech, according to whether or not the focal side of the instructors' gestures faced the learner. We see that learner gestures without speech occurred in both conditions. Nonetheless, the ratio of learner gestures without speech was greater when the focal side of the instructors' gestures did not face the learner.

Table 5.4 also shows the patterns for the individual pairs of subjects. We see that, for pairs 1, 2, 3, 5, 6, 7, and 9, the frequency of the learners' gestures without speech was equal or greater when the focal side of the instructor's gesture did not face the learners. These individual patterns match the general pattern for the whole corpus. The opposite pattern is observed with pair 8 in terms of the ratio of learner gestures without speech in the two conditions. Again, no single gesture was produced by the learner in pair 4. Despite the deviant patterns for these two individual pairs of subjects, however, the Wilcoxon Matched Pairs Signed Rank sum test shows that gestures without speech were more frequent when the focal side of the instructors' gestures did not face the learner than when they did ($T = 1.5$ ($n = 6$), $p < .05$).

Table 5.4. *The frequency of gestures with/without speech according to whether the focal side of the instructor's gesture faced towards the learner (FTL) or not (non-FTL), for each learner*

	Instructor's gesture FTL		Instructor's gesture non-FTL	
Learner's gesture	With speech	Without speech	With speech	Without speech
Pair 1	7	2	22	18
Pair 2	78	5	49	19
Pair 3	15	0	2	1
Pair 4	0	0	0	0
Pair 5	45	1	3	1
Pair 6	6	1	1	1
Pair 7	32	15	27	30
Pair 8	3	2	0	1
Pair 9	4	0	6	3
Total	190 (87.96%)	26 (12.04%)	110 (60.00%)	74 (40.00%)

4   General discussion

In this final section, I will discuss two points after summarizing the results. The point to be discussed in section 4.1 is the tuning of the learner's gesture to the instructor's gesture. In particular, I will consider why the direction in which the focal side of the instructor's gesture faces influences the learner's gesture. In section 4.2, I will discuss the two modes of the instructor's gestures in terms of the organization of the social space (Özyürek, this volume). I will also attempt to present some possible explanations of the results, and point out problems and questions to be answered in future research.

4.1   Tuning the mode of the learner's gesture to the instructor's gesture

The instructors sometimes presented their gestures so that the focal side faced the learner, and sometimes they did not. The learners, on the other hand, sometimes produced gesture without speech and sometimes produced collaborative gestures. The present data analyses showed that (1) for a given learner's gesture, when the focal side of the instructor's gesture faced the learner, it was more likely to be collaborative than to be a gesture without speech; and (2) for a given learner's gesture, when the focal side of the instructor's gesture did not face the learner, it was more likely to be a gesture without speech than to be a collaborative gesture. These results suggest that the way the learners gesturally responded to their instructors was attuned to whether or not the focal side of the instructor's gesture faced the learner.

Given these results, the following questions arise: Why does this kind of tuning occur? Why does the direction in which the instructor's gesture faces influence the way the learner gesturally responds?

One possible explanation is that it is simply physically easier for a learner to manipulate the instructor's gesture when the focal side faces her, because the side of the instructor gesture that the learner wants to manipulate is often the focal side. However, this does not explain the collaborative gestures in (6) and (8) above, where the learner extended her hand, from almost behind the instructor, into the space between the instructor's chest and his two-handed gesture. These learners' collaborative gestures involved awkwardness, as opposed to smoothness or easiness. Moreover, these are not exceptional cases; there were many similar cases in the corpus. It thus seems that the tuning of the learner's gestures to the instructor's gestures cannot be explained on the ground that it is physically easier or harder to manipulate an instructor gesture whose focal side does or does not face the learner.

An alternative might be an explanation in terms of that which is broadly referred to as 'personal space'. Extending one's hand and manipulating the other person's gesture when the focal side does not face her might be taken as a violation of the other's personal space. But, again, this does not explain examples (6) and (8), because these collaborative gestures can also be thought of as violating the instructor's personal space. Moreover, there were many collaborative gestures by subjects who did not know each other before the experiment and/or who are different in gender. Indeed, the example in (6) and (8) is from such a pair of subjects (pair 7). In a sense, a collaborative gesture is in itself a violation of the other's personal space, especially when the learner actually touches the instructor's hands. Thus, explaining the tuning of the learner's gesture to the instructor's gesture by avoidance of violating personal space is not convincing.

Mental rotation is yet another alternative explanation. When the focal side of the instructor's gesture faces the learner, the learner does not have to mentally rotate the image represented by the instructor's gesture, and what the instructor and the learner look at is more or less the same in terms of orientation. When the focal side of the instructor's gesture does not face the learner, the learner has to rotate the mental image to assure herself that she is looking at the same image in the same orientation. However, this explanation also fails, because turning the focal side of the instructor's gesture toward the learner does not guarantee that the orientation is shared. When the instructor performs her gesture on the table between herself and the learner, often the orientation is not quite the same for both of them, yet learners produce collaborative gestures in this situation too, as long as the focal side faces them. We therefore need to consider other possibilities.

Farr (1990) argues that gesture is asymmetrical in the sense that what the speaker looks at in her own gesture and what the listener looks at in his partner's gesture are not exactly the same. Speech, on the other hand, is symmetrical in the sense that both the speaker and listener can listen to more or less the same pattern of speech. Thus Farr argues that gesture and speech are different in their status as symbols with regard to symmetry. Farr's argument explains why the learners in the present study produced gestures without speech. Because of the built-in asymmetrical nature of gesture, the learners can never fully get the information that is meant to be conveyed by the instructor's gesture. That full information needs to be regained in some other way. Learners' gestures without speech can be taken as an attempt to recover what is lost because of this asymmetry from the learner's point of view. Listeners in normal narrative settings do not produce gestures without speech, because those listeners are in most cases, if not all, not requested to do anything other than listen to a narration, a narration that is usually quite easy to understand. However, the asymmetry of gesture does not seem to be applicable to those instructor's gestures whose focal side faces the learner. Indeed, one of the major ways in which instructors turn their gestures towards the learner was to shift their own body posture or orientation so that the instructor and learner were lined up side-by-side. Another way in which instructors make their gestures face the learner is to present their gestures in lower positions: for example, on the table between the instructor and learner, where the gesture was perceivable by both from more or less the same perspective. In these ways, gestures can be made to be symmetrical in Farr's sense. This leads us to think that asymmetry is not necessarily an intrinsic attribute of gesture as a sign. Furthermore, if an instructor's gesture whose focal side faces the learner is symbolically asymmetrical, that would not motivate the learner to make a collaborative gesture. In other words, the instructor's gesture is, according to Farr, assumed to be unintelligible because of the asymmetry, and hence could not be used as a communicative resource. However, as we have seen in the present data, that was not the case.[12] From these considerations, it can be concluded that Farr's argument explains only half the present data.

In a sense, the symmetry and asymmetry of a symbol in Farr's sense is comparable to the distinction drawn by Vygotsky (1962) between outer speech and inner speech. As Vygotsky argued, outer speech is speech directed towards another person, while inner speech is speech directed towards the speaker herself. He argues that because of this basic difference between the two modes of speech, outer speech is more articulated and inner speech is less so. When one speaks to oneself, regardless of whether or not one speaks aloud, such speech (i.e., inner speech) is characterized by omissions and lack of full grammaticality, and other people may not be able to understand it.[13] To apply Vygotsky's distinction to gestural phenomena, it might be plausible to think that an instructor's gesture whose focal side faces the learner is in the 'outer-speech' mode, so to speak, and hence is 'well articulated', so that the learner can easily understand what information is being conveyed by it. On the other hand, an instructor's gesture whose focal side does not face the learner is in the 'inner-speech' mode, and hence it is not fully articulated and may not look intelligible to the learner.

Following Vygotsky, then, I would like to propose that gestures may differ in articulateness which is partly determined by their orientation towards the viewer. More specifically, a gesture in one mode may qualitatively differ from one in the other mode even if these two gestures are identical except for their orientation relative to the learner's position. If there is such a difference between the two modes of the instructor's gestures, it might explain, in part, why collaborative gestures occurred when the focal side of the instructor's gesture faced towards the learner. The explanation is that the gesture, it is supposed, was fully articulated from the learner's point of view, and the learner was able to use the partner's gesture as a resource for communication. Such a gesture is, then, 'graspable' in both metaphorical and literal senses. When the focal side of the instructor's gesture did not face the learner, however, the gesture did not afford collaboration, because, for the learner, the instructor's gesture was not articulated enough to be employed as a resource for communication. Instead, considering the complexity involved in the *origami*-making procedure, the learners had to reproduce their interlocutor's gesture by themselves, with their own hands, so that they could see in this way what the instructor was trying to convey with her speech and gesture.

4.2   *Social space and the origami instructor's gestures*

Özyürek (this volume) argues that the use of path expressions in speech and the corresponding expression of path in gesture change, depending on what kind of social space the speaker and her interlocutor have between them. That is, when the listener is located in different places relative to the speaker, the speaker tends to use path expressions and gestures in accordance with these different social spaces.

In Özyürek's study, the subjects were assigned and hence to some significant extent were fixed in one social space or the other. They were not permitted to change the social space between them. This led to gestural adjustments by the speaker to the given social space. In contrast to this prearranged setting, in the present study the subjects were basically free to work out how to arrange the social space with their interlocutors. This freedom allowed the instructors to change the orientation of their bodies and/or their gestures with respect to the orientation/position of the learner's body. In some cases they only reoriented their gestures, and in other cases they reoriented their bodies as well as gestures. This observation suggests that, in the setting in which subjects are minimally constrained with regard to social space, the communicative participants discover both a social space and orientation and/or gesture position that is the best fit for a smooth gestural exchange of information. And it was this rearrangement by the instructors that led to the shift in whether or not the focal side of a gesture faced the learner, which in turn determined how the learner gesturally interacted with the instructor.

Özyürek's study demonstrates the dependency of gestural expression on social space. And it would be quite reasonable to think that her discovery holds here for *origami* instructors (although this speculation should be examined under conditions where the subjects in her study could freely change the social space). Even if this proved to be the case, however, a further question naturally arises at this point. Namely, what underlying factors make the communicative participants change the social space? Also, considering that the orientation of the instructor's gesture is shifted along with the change in the social space in some cases, while in other cases it is shifted with the social space remaining intact, we can ask what other factors cause a change of instructor gesture orientation besides the social space. Answers to these questions, whatever they are, will be the key to understanding gestural phenomena not only for the interpersonal plane, but also for the inter- and the intrapersonal intersection. Neither Özyürek's study nor my study are designed to answer these questions. When they are answered, we will obtain a more comprehensive picture of gestural interaction than has been discussed in this chapter.

5   Conclusions

Gesture is a sign which is only realized by having, as a sign vehicle, a material form of some kind. It is further claimed that gesture can function as a 'material carrier' of thinking (McNeill & Duncan, this volume). According to this claim, gesture, together with the speech it accompanies, not only expresses thoughts but also carries out thinking-for-speaking in a material and concrete form. The present study has further argued that gesture is a 'sharable' material carrier of thinking. As we have seen, there are many questions to be answered before we fully understand the functions of collaborative gestures and gestures without speech, and the process of the learner's tuning of gestures to accord with the instructor's gestures. At the moment, the following conclusions can be drawn:

(1) Learner's gestures that do not occur with speech and learner's gestures that collaborate with the gestures of the other participant were found in *origami* instruction.
(2) Learner's gestures without speech were more likely to occur when the focal side of the instructor's gestures did not face the learner. Learner's collaborative gestures were more likely to occur when the focal side of the instructor's gestures faced the learner.
(3) These results suggest that gesture is very sensitive not only to intrapersonal factors but also to the interpersonal factors in the communication situation.

NOTES

This chapter was originally part of a paper submitted to the Department of Psychology at the University of Chicago and has been modified to be presented here. I would like to thank the department for funding which allowed me to pay subjects. My special gratitude goes to my teachers, David McNeill, Susan Goldin-Meadow, and Boaz Keyzar, and to the anonymous reviewers of this book for their invaluable suggestions and encouragement.

1 To avoid cumbersome duplications of 'his/her' pronominal references, I will adopt the convention of referring to all subjects with the feminine form unless I am referring to a real one.
2 The term 'gesture' is used here to refer to spontaneous gesture which, in most of the cases, synchronizes with speech in timing and accompanies it in meaning (McNeill 1987, 1992). As we will see later in the present study, however, spontaneous gestures do not always synchronize with speech, although they are related to speech in some way or another. Also, a single example of a spontaneous gesture by a listener in a cartoon narrative, which does not synchronize with speech, has been reported (McNeill 1992).
3 Goldin-Meadow et al.'s work (1992) is one of the exceptions; it focuses on the listener/viewer's understanding of information conveyed by gesture and speech.
4 For the relationship between these contributions by a listener and the use of gestures by a narrator, see Furuyama (1993). Özyürek (this volume) investigates the effect of different social spaces as an *inter*personal factor in the performance of gesture and speech, although the main question does not concern gestural interaction as such. Her study will be referred to once again in the discussion of the present chapter.
5 *Origami* is Japanese paper-folding art.
6 In the sense that a listener does not only listen to what a speaker is saying but is also actively involved in the communication, as mentioned above, the label 'listener' is not appropriate. Therefore, in what follows, a more general and task-specific label will be used, namely, 'learner'. In correspondence to this, the other party will be labeled 'instructor'.
7 The data obtained in the *origami* session and the questionnaires were not used in the analyses below.
8 Because we will investigate the learner's gestures in relation to the instructor's,

the description of the learner's gestures will be limited to those that occurred when the instructor's gestures were present.

9 Note on symbols used in the example: 'I' and 'L': the following speech was produced by the instructor and the learner, respectively. [ ] and { } show the starting point and ending point of the motion of the instructor's gesture and the learner's gesture, respectively. In this example, the instructor's gesture after (1) is consistently held in front of her own body at chest level throughout the excerpt, and so is the learner's gesture after (2). These holds are not covered by [ ] and { }; only the actively moving phase of the gesture is. Boldface shows the stroke phase of the instructor's gesture, and underlining shows the stroke phase of the learner's gesture. The left square bracket ([) is the onset of the preparation phase of the instructor's gesture; the left curly bracket ({) is that of the learner's. Between the stroke phase and the right bracket is the retraction phase of the gesture.

10 In this excerpt, additional symbols are used: * represents the speaker's self-interruption in speech; # indicates an audible breath pause.

11 My special thanks go to Dr. A. Özyürek, as she devoted her precious time and expertise to the coding of gesture.

12 By this, it is not meant that the learner can always fully understand the instructor's gesture whose focal side faces towards her, but that at least good portions of the information in the instructor's gesture are fairly easily graspable by the learner.

13 According to Vygotsky, inner speech is used to plan and regulate one's action (1962).

REFERENCES

Farr, R. 1990. Bodies and voices in dialogue. In Markova & Foppa (eds.), pp. 241–258.

Furuyama, N. 1993. Gesture and speech of a hearer as what makes the field of promoting action. Poster at Seventh International Conference on Event Perception and Action (ICEPA7), Vancouver, August.

Goldin-Meadow, S., Wein, D. & Chang, C. 1992. Assessing knowledge through gesture: using children's hands to read their minds. *Cognition & Instruction* 9: 201–219.

Jakobson, R. 1960. Concluding statement: linguistics and poetics. In Sebeok (ed.), pp. 350–377.

Markova, I. & Foppa, K. (eds.) 1990. *The Dynamics of Dialogue.* New York: Springer-Verlag.

McNeill, D. 1987. *Psycholinguistics: A New Approach.* New York: Harper & Row.

McNeill, D. 1992. *Hand and Mind: What Gestures Reveal about Thought.* Chicago: University of Chicago Press.

Sebeok, T. A. (ed.) 1960. *Style in Language.* Cambridge, MA: MIT Press.

Vygotsky, L. S. 1962. *Thought and Language.* Cambridge, MA: MIT Press.

6 Gestures, knowledge, and the world

Curtis LeBaron

Department of Communication, University of Colorado at Boulder

Jürgen Streeck

Department of Communication Studies, University of Texas at Austin

1   The formation of gestures and the fabrication of knowledge

Among the essential (but almost forgotten) insights of the Age of
Enlightenment was the recognition that "human understanding" (Locke
1959 [1690]) – the formation and accumulation of common knowledge – is
dependent upon the formation and accumulation of material signs:
material entities that reside, however fleetingly, in the public realm where
they may be reused and thereby shared; representations that embody a
world that may be jointly acted and reflected upon; artifacts that, while
products of minds, are nevertheless external to them, providing tools not
only for the mind, but also for labor and human self-creation; socially
shared cognitive tools that evolve over time as humanity's mind evolves
through relying on and refining them.

With this proposition, anti-Cartesian philosophers such as Condillac for
the first time directed attention to the importance of symbol systems (or
media) for human cognition, self-creation, and society. Condillac in particular recognized the inherently social character of the human mind, and he
suggested that signs and insights originate in social practice. He wrote:

> [The] history of communication will show the various circumstances under which
> signs have been formed. It will show us the true meanings of signs and . . . leave no
> doubt about the origin of our ideas. (Condillac 1746: 61)

Condillac called signs "sensations transformées," transformed sensations,
by which he meant the entire complex of affect, desire, sensory perception,
and motor action that makes up what nowadays we might call 'embodied
experience'. In his view, the incarnation of shared experiences in commu-
nally usable material signs – and the social distribution of these signs and
the knowledge embodied in them – is the core of human cultural evolution,
of the progress of the "connaissances humaines."

The formation of a symbol is a defining moment in the fabrication of shared knowledge because it allows the participants to focus upon and rein-voke previously shared experiences and to plan and conduct shared activities in their wake. An important version of this process is "langage d'action," the performance of schematic motor actions that are abstracted from actions in the material world – in a word, gestures. Gestures, in Condillac's view, constituted the original, natural language of humankind.

The method by which Condillac and his contemporaries studied the fabrication of knowledge through the formation of signs was the 'thought experiment'. Today we are equipped to investigate it through close analyses of empirical practice. In this chapter, therefore, we want to describe how gestural signs are formed and how, in this process, communal knowledge is incorporated, stored, and organized. Our aim is twofold: to ascertain several of the roles that hand gestures play in the formation and distribution of knowledge within specific "communities of practice" (Lave 1991); and to provide evidence for the foundations of symbolic gestures in practical, instrumental, non-symbolic action and experience. Our approach is guided by Condillac's vision that the fabrication of knowledge and the formation of signs are not simply dependent upon one another, but are two aspects of the same process.

Instead of solely locating gesture in the "process of utterance" (Kendon 1980) or deriving it from "mental representations" (McNeill 1985), we seek to establish its experiential foundations in activities of the hands in the material world and to explicate its indexical ties to this world. Gestures, in our view, originate neither in the speaker's mind nor in the process of speaking, even though speech and gesture are routinely coordinated. Rather gestures originate in the tactile contact that mindful human bodies have with the physical world. In other words, we propose – and claim that our data demonstrate – that conversational hand gestures ascend from ordinary, non-symbolic exploratory and instrumental manipulations in the world of matter and things, and that the knowledge that the human hands acquire (both individually and historically) in these manipulations is realized through and brought to bear upon the symbolic tasks of gestural representation. Ultimately, it is through these indexical ties of gestures to the material world that gestural signifiers can be seen and recognized: onlookers can see the motion of a configured but empty hand as (for example) a 'turning' only when they infer an object that can be turned – no matter whether the gesture refers to the object, to an act of turning it, or instead to the vehicle of a metaphor (see McNeill 1985). Without the index to the world of things, the movement of the hand could not be seen as an action, and the signifier would be lost in a sea of meaningless motions.

Our investigations have focused on gestural practices in activity-rich and cognitively complex settings such as do-it-yourself workshops and architecture classrooms, but also everyday conversational settings where practical knowledge is shared. In settings of material practice, the participants' hands are involved not only in symbolic actions (as they are in conversations) but also in practical actions with things. Hands are entangled in the world that they reach – touching objects, grasping tools, wielding instruments, managing matter. Hands are busy in many ways, shifting back and forth (sometimes rapidly) between doing things, showing things, and showing how to do things with things. Such practical and collaborative settings, we contend, are more 'foundational' and paradigmatic for studying the "communicative hand" (Bates 1974) than are the purely symbolic realms of conversation or narrative monologue. Conversation removed from hands-on interaction with things may efface the natural links between symbolic actions and the exploratory and instrumental doings that hands perform. To study gesture as only a feature of conversation is to obscure the embodied knowledge, the lived experience, that hands bring to their symbolic tasks.

Moreover, as we have examined gestures in settings of practice and instruction, we have witnessed the processes whereby gestures become conventional, shared, jointly used symbolic forms. Gestures may be regarded as mediating devices that provide a link between interpsychological and intrapsychological functioning (Vygotsky 1978); in studying gestures, one may therefore (1) look for those physical objects and experiences by which they are referentially anchored; (2) study how they organize social interaction on the one hand, and shape individual cognition on the other; and (3) explicate their social, situated, semantic histories.

By positioning our study outside a conversational framework that privileges speech, we regard gestures within the contexts of the very experiences they come to formulate and index. In settings of material practice, gestures are often contiguous to the experiences they symbolize (and comment upon, qualify, alter, and so on), and index tactile and visual experiences that the participants jointly possess from recent interaction, if only because they jointly witnessed them. Gestures also share physical space with things, most obviously those things within reach of hands.

We use the following transcript conventions:

::   colons indicate a sound stretch (vowel elongation); the more colons, the longer the stretch

–   a dash marks a 'cut-off', generally a glottal stop

(.)   a dot in parentheses indicates a 'micro-pause' (less than one 'beat')

(– –)   dashes in parentheses indicate a pause; each dash represents approximately one-tenth of a second

[square brackets indicate the simultaneity of two events, either two or more utterances or an utterance and a physical action or gesture

(( ))   double brackets mark the transcriber's description of an action

' '   single quotation marks in the description of an action signify a 'virtual' component of the action; for example, an object that is 'implied'

2   Indexing experience

The first segments we want to examine are taken from a video recording of a do-it-yourself workshop.[1] While teaching a lesson on the uses of Sheetrock, the instructor introduces a few tools for the job. He stands at the front of the room where tools and materials are spread along a countertop. He picks up a tool, labels it (a "scraper"), and moves it around in midair so class members can see the tool – and see how the teacher handles it. Such behavior is rather commonplace, a seemingly trivial scene in an ordinary classroom where teaching is done through 'showing', 'modeling', or 'mimesis'. This first stage of the teacher's lesson on scrapers is transcribed as follows (the instructor is speaking).

1.1   There's a couple of things you need for preparing Sheetrock.
       ((picks up scraper))
       [
1.2   (– – – –)

       ((puts scraper in other hand, looks at it))
       [
1.3   One of them will be the scraper of some sort.
                    ((scrapes in midair with both hands; puts it down))
                    [
1.4   This is a uh– very heavy-duty scraper.
               ((picks up other scraper; holds it up))
               [
1.5   Uh, you'd also have a scraper looks like this.

       ((begins to put it down; interrupts))
       [
1.6   (– –)

       ((scrapes, puts scraper down))
       [
1.7   Putty knife.

       ((picks up third scraper; scrapes, lowers))
       [
1.8   A little bit bigger, this is a– both a scraper and a and a tool

                    ((points scraper to wall))
                    [
1.9   you use for applying compound to Sheetrock.

Figure 6.1.   Figure 6.2.

Although this classroom moment appears commonplace, it is nevertheless a paradigmatic instance of symbol formation, for it includes the situated creation of a form–meaning pair that embodies a node of locally
produced shared knowledge. The moment exemplifies the 'transformation
of sensation' into a sign. The sign that is established here is a gesture – a
hand-configuration and movement – which signifies a class of object,
'scraper'.

The formation of this sign begins as a demonstration of a material
object, an instrument. The instrument is picked up from the table and
turned into an exhibit when it is moved from one hand to the other while
simultaneously receiving the instructor's concentrated gaze (line 2; Figure
6.1). The tool's use is then demonstrated through a schematic motion in a
virtual field of action – that is, the instructor 'scrapes', but performs in the
air (line 3; Figure 6.2).

Thus, during this first sequence (lines 2–4), one hand is configured to
hold the scraper as it would be held if actually used to work on Sheetrock.
The hand takes on the same configuration when the second scraper – i.e.,
the putty knife – is picked up and its use is demonstrated (lines 5–7). And
the same hand configuration occurs again with the third scraper (lines 8–9).
Thus, there is a natural contiguity between the members of a class of
objects (in this case, instruments) and a configuration of the hand. While
this configuration has no symbolic value during the moment above when
the different scrapers are actually being held, the hand configuration
becomes symbolic (a 'transformed sensation') subsequently, when the
instruments are implied but not literally handheld.

During a subsequent moment, transcribed below, the instructor's hands
move without holding a scraper (or any other instrument), but they remain
configured in a fashion that can now, in this context, be recognized as an

Figure 6.3.   Figure 6.4.

index of scrapers, at least by those who have witnessed the prior scene: the handshape makes sense only vis-à-vis the instruments that this hand has previously held, and it simultaneously conjures up the image of these instruments. While the tools are physically absent from the instructor's demonstration, their 'virtual' or symbolic-cognitive presence can be jointly inferred by all recipients of this communicative act. The handshape turns into a socially shared symbol.

Having put the scrapers down, the teacher now raises an empty hand that is shaped 'as if' holding a scraper (line 1 below). The hand moves in midair and thereby initiates a more complex demonstration: an absent scraper is used to distribute invisible mortar on a non-existing surface so as to make virtual piles of the compound, as described simultaneously (albeit vaguely) through speech (lines 1–4 below). While the hand moves with precision, the verbal instructions are quite inexplicit. Without touching the tools that remain visible on the countertop, the instructor's hands move to make the scrapers 'present' through an indexical implication.

((raises right hand))
[

2.1   So that's the idea behind those (– – –) (notches).
        ((scrapes 'compound' up))

        [
2.2   No matter how much you put in
        ((continues))

        [
2.3   if you scrape it
        ((scrapes 'compound' off 'instrument'))

        [
2.4   and scrape it off

Here the instructor demonstrates a complex skilled activity. In a sequence aimed at demonstrating the importance of applying the right amount of compound to Sheetrock, he shows how excess compound can be scooped up with and removed from the scraper. The instructor's movements are swift and precise, and for those who have some visual familiarity with this line of construction work, it is easy to 'see' not only the scraper but also the compound and the surface (i.e., the Sheetrock), as well as another unnamed tool which is used to remove the compound from the scraper. We 'see' how compound is scraped up to make a pile which is then lifted off the Sheetrock and scraped to the other tool.

Thus, from the teacher's initial handling of the scraper, a pattern of movement is abstracted – that is, a gesture. Performed publicly, it constitutes a communal sign, a convention, in which a shared experiential nexus or bit of knowledge about the world is embodied. The gesture evolves as a situationally transparent, symbolic construction through which practical knowledge may be handed about. It emerges in two stages of what might be called an 'indexicalization schema': originating in the hands-on manipulation of the material world within reach, the abstracted gesture retains an indexical link to it, which can be used in both directions – the gesture presupposes the material world for its intelligibility, but can also and by the same token evoke it. The sign is now available to invoke a nexus of practices, things, and relations between them, and is potentially applicable to infinite communicative purposes, syntactic contexts, and semantic roles. By simply raising a hand with a recognizable shape, a complex of actions, objects, instruments, and so on may be denoted by the teacher or other participants.

The sign is also available to be folded back upon itself, for the layering on of further information: for example, to denote manners, possible mistakes, or more elaborate lines of action. In this fashion, the shared knowledge of the community can grow via the invention, reuse, and transformation of an ephemeral, but nevertheless material, sign. A pattern of muscular movement has been abstracted from the hands' entanglements with concrete worlds and can be used in other contexts, including strictly symbolic or representational ones such as conversation. But to function in these contexts, audiences must be able to 'fill in' indexical background: in these episodes, recipients of the instructions initially had to 'see' a countertop as a symbolic representation of Sheetrock and subsequently – on the basis of locally produced knowledge – recognize that a hand was configured in a certain way because it represented the holding of a scraper. (Compound also had to be filled in.)

3   Emerging conventions

Our focus now shifts from the do-it-yourself workshop where hands engage in (symbolic) instrumental actions from which gestures are then derived, to a university classroom where a professor's hands manipulate a material, spatial object in an exploratory fashion. The professor's movements made in this process are subsequently abstracted as gestures that do not represent actions or instruments, but rather features of the object explored. While the signifier is a motion, the signified is a fixed, immutable structure in space.

As part of his undergraduate course on architectural design, the professor critiques miniature buildings made by students using cardboard and glue. The students sit arranged in a large circle, all oriented toward the middle of the classroom where the professor sits on an elevated stool, next to a large table. One by one, the students step forward and place their cardboard models on the table, making them available for others to see, and available for the professor's critique. Here we focus on one cardboard model: introduced by the student as a "tunnel shape," it is subsequently described as a "sewer-like" culvert by the professor, who first explores it, then interprets it, and thereby critiques it.

Before talking about the model, the professor silently explores its three-dimensional features. He leans forward and over the model to look inside; he moves his body to see the sides; then he touches it, lifts it, and slowly turns it in midair, observing it from various angles (Figure 6.5) and at the same time feeling with his fingers the architectural shapes created by the student's hands. The professor's exploration might be called a 'primary' stage of knowledge formation – and hence a 'necessary' stage of symbolic action. As he encounters the cardboard model for the first time, his hands become entangled with it. He has a series of visual and tactile experiences, made possible by his practical actions upon the object that he begins to grasp. He becomes knowledgeable regarding the cardboard model through the very experiences that his subsequent gestures will formulate and index. At the same time, the professor's lived experience is a shared experience: as he explores, he also shows. By turning the model in midair to observe its various angles, he enables his students to do likewise; and he directs their attention toward the model through his orientation, gaze, and extended fingers, which all function like pointing gestures (Scheflen 1976). Moreover, the professor's exploration may be regarded as a demonstration. By sitting in the middle of the room, at the center of the group, he makes his own experience an object of attention, a public performance, a potentially vicarious experience. His behaviors are both private and self-conscious, appearing as practical precursors of the group's symbolic tasks. His solo actions are a form of social practice as he interacts with a material world – something the instructor with his scraper only implied. In short, his hands mediate between thing and thought.

Eventually the professor begins talking about the cardboard model as his hands continue to move in relation to it. His exploring hands are also pointing fingers that direct the students' attention toward specific spatial features, thereby highlighting shapes of the model being discussed. For instance, the professor slowly slides an extended index finger along one edge, finding and highlighting its curved shape (Figure 6.6), creating a figure–ground separation that informs students how to see the model. At the same time, the professor may be teaching students how to see his hand – his behavior may serve to highlight the movement of his hand, not just the shape of the model.

With increasing frequency over a ten-minute period, the professor's hands move without actually touching the cardboard model. That is, his hands perform shapes in the air that are physically separated from the material object that they index. The following transcription represents such a moment.

((curved touching))
[
3.1   . . . you have (.) uh– uh long bent
((curved gesture))
[
3.2   sort of uh– uh linear experience

While touching the cardboard model, the professor describes it. He refers to its "long bent" form (line 1) and highlights the same by touching the model with his extended index finger (Figure 6.6). His speech is organized (i.e., he says "long" before he says "bent") according to the shapes that his finger encounters as it slides upon a long, straight edge before moving around a bend. Immediately after highlighting the model's "long bent" shape, the professor reproduces this shape in the air – mere inches above the cardboard, but nevertheless separated from it (Figure 6.7). This is a defin-ing moment. The midair motion is recognizable as a gesture, because its shape is performed apart from the tangible influence of its referential anchor. The gesture emerges as a natural extension and an incipient feature of practical actions upon an object. The new convention is shared, under-stood by those participating (perhaps vicariously) in the hands-on activity. Moreover, the new symbol heralds knowledge formation that the speech also marks: as touch moves to gesture, concrete talk turns abstract; the words "long bent" (line 1) describe tactile and visible features that are quickly recast as a "linear experience" (line 2), and the professor begins to discuss the full-body consequences of the hand-sized shape. In sum, the emerging gesture shows a close connection with a material object, which serves as a springboard into interaction about imagined experience – alto-gether a sort of transformed sensation.

Continuing for several minutes, the professor's hand gestures evolve as his critique unfolds. Sometimes his movements are relatively small: with a flick of his wrist, he outlines a "long bent" shape in the air, approximately

Figure 6.5.

Figure 6.6.

Figure 6.7.

Figure 6.8.

the size of the architectural model (hand-sized) and located only inches above it (see Figure 6.7). Other times, his movements are big: "long bent" shapes performed at eye level, where his whole arm extends, separated from the model by feet rather than inches (Figure 6.8). The following transcription represents such a moment.

```
                   ((large gesture begins))
                        [
4.1      . . . you can see the wall at the back

4.2      it's lit it goes (– –) way far back
                   ((large gesture ends))
                        [
4.3      (.) it disappears around the corner
```

The professor's descriptions become vivid as he expounds upon the full-body consequences of the hand-sized model. When he talks about seeing "the wall at the back" (line 1), he extends his right arm fully so that his flat palm may be regarded as a distant surface (similar to Figure 6.8). As he describes what "you can see" (line 1), he draws his gesturing hand toward his eye and lightly touches the side of his face. Then his hand moves outward from his eye and straight along his line of vision, which "goes" (line 2) parallel with the imaginary passage. As he says "back" (line 2), his arm becomes fully extended again, and then his hand hooks to the left (Figure 6.8) when he says "disappears around the corner" (line 3). Altogether, the professor outlines a "long bent" shape, created in midair but referentially anchored in the model on the table below his arm. At the same time, he performs a 'lived' experience: gazing off 'into space', he talks

Figure 6.9.

himself along the hallway that he imagines and motions, using present-tense language to describe architectural details as they spatially and temporally unfold. Because his performance is public, the professor provides – at least potentially – a vicarious experience to seated students, as suggested by the pronoun "you" (line 1).

Group knowledge forms as "long bent" gestures occur and evolve to embody the unfolding shape of the professor's critique. Shared understanding is especially evident when students participate in the class discussion and also perform "long bent" gestures to articulate their views, which build upon the group's understanding. For instance, consider the following excerpt. Immediately after the professor ends his comments and invites other opinions, a student performs a large gesture while giving a favorable critique of the architectural model:

5.1   ... you kno::w (– –) where to go:
5.2   you're not– you're not (.) wandering
5.3   around (– – –) and (.) you ha:ve
          ((large gesture))
          [
5.4   (.) u:h dire:ction to it

To articulate his view, the student uses behaviors that may be recognized by other classroom participants. With the utterance "u:h" (line 4), he lifts his right hand to his right eye; while describing the "dire:ction" (line 4) of the architectural structure, his hand moves outward from his eye and straight along his line of vision; and once his arm is fully extended, his hand hooks to the left (Figure 6.9). Altogether, the student outlines a "long bent" shape in midair that is referentially anchored in the model on the table – largely through the professor's prior public performance. Moreover, the student's gesture occurs as he expounds upon the full-body consequences of the hand-sized model. Like the professor, the student uses present-tense language to describe an imaginary 'lived' experience. The student's behavior is a potentially vicarious experience for others in the classroom, as suggested by the pronoun "you" (lines 1, 2, and 3).

The architectural model is different from the do-it-yourself scraper, for reasons that have consequences for the formation and recognition of gestures. On the one hand, the scraper is lifted and used. It is treated as a tool, an instrument to be employed, an extension of the human hand that subjects implied objects to performed actions. On the other hand, the model is lifted and explored. It is regarded as an object, an entity with properties to be discovered, a thing understood through the human actions that its shape implies and guides. Although material things may embody instructions for how they are to be used or regarded (Norman 1988), differences between the scraper and model are instantiated through behaviors during the 'primary' stage of knowledge formation. Wielded again and again, the scraper is never mistaken for a miniature building. Although cardboard is capable of scraping mortar, the professor initially and immediately moves his body relative to the architectural model, projecting fixedness upon it. As a consequence of primary behaviors, gestures eventually emerge imbued with verb-like and noun-like attributes. In the workshop, the teacher's gestures are verb-like, with the implied scraper in the role of instrument: his hand movements are recognizable as hand actions – a rather low-level abstraction. In the classroom, by contrast, the professor's gestures become large and semantically complex: his hand movements are noun-like as they outline (in the air) three-dimensional features discovered in the model; these same hand movements are at the same time verb-like as they represent a person's movement through the imaginary building being outlined – a rather high-level abstraction. Moreover, the professor's gestures serve as a heuristic device, enabling him to translate the hand-sized model into a full-size architectural experience that becomes grounds for his critique. Furthermore, his gestures serve as a teaching device, helping students to read the cardboard shape as a representation of an embodied experience, vicariously lived and critiqued.

Our analysis of these episodes has demonstrated at least three things. First, the interactions in the classrooms exemplify the step-by-step processes by which embodied – manual – action in the world of matter and things may be transformed into symbolic action. That is, activities within and upon the material world may be abstracted, schematized, and converted into components of the shared communicative repertoire of a local 'community of practice'. In short, our analysis has traced the experiential, practical roots of individual gestures. Second, our analysis shows how the shared knowledge of these communities grows through the formation of these gestures. Like all signs, the gestures comprise cognitive and communicative features and functions: they do not only represent or express, they *constitute* socially shared knowledge. The further growth of knowledge in these communities is dependent upon and made possible by the shared possession of newly formed signs, which can then be modified and elaborated so as to represent proper modes of action, possible mistakes, compound activities, and so on. Finally, the episodes demonstrate that the proper seeing and understanding of these signs requires the material world as an indexical background: the configurations and motions of the hands make sense only by virtue of their contiguity to things, and it is by reference to these things that the motions of the hands can be recognized as schematic actions (or manipulations). In short, seeing a gesture requires knowledge of the world.

4   Background knowledge and the perception of gestures

In the instructional situations we have examined, such knowledge is available from the course of recent interaction; the publicly visible material experiences and activities of the hands from which the gestures have been derived are part of the local, shared memory of all participants. Some might object, therefore, that these incidents are uncharacteristic of gestures as they are used in the exclusively symbolic realm of everyday conversation, 'conversation pure', which is more often than not predicated upon the absence of the material events and states of affairs that constitute its topics. Moreover, it might be objected, symbolic communication in the absence of things constitutes the more astonishing and more important human achievement.

However, it is our contention that gesture – certainly descriptive or 'iconic' gesture – necessarily involves indexical links to the material world, even though these links are rarely established or explicated in the communicative situation itself. Rather, in conversational contexts that are detached from the talked-about world, participants must fill in encyclopedic knowledge (ranging from universal bodily experiences to highly specific cultural practices) to see and recognize gestures. Phenomenally, there are only motions of the hands. What is perceived, however, is typically not motions but actions and, simultaneously, implied objects acted upon. Thus, we do not see two flat hands moving apart, but we see them dividing a substance (or a substance being divided) – which, in the given conversational context, may signify a group of friends, dough, or the mélange of issues that will have to be discussed. To see the hands engaged in a schematic act of dividing, and to 'see' a something that is being divided, our eyes must be intelligent, experienced in the ways of the world of the hands. Without chipping in our "beholder's share" (Gombrich 1961), we could not see the gesture, that is, the signifier – let alone identify the signified.

We briefly illustrate these indexical underpinnings of iconic gestures by examining two excerpts from a series of conversational stories about car accidents. In the videotaped recording (which was made in Germany), two Japanese friends, having discussed the difficulties of obtaining a German driver's license, proceed to tell one another about their involvement in various accidents that resulted from the drivers' inattention to the road. As is common in such narratives, the narrators' bodies variously reenact the protagonist's actions while driving the car, shift to render the behavior of the cars on the road, or move to represent the setting. More specifically, their hands are used in semiotically different ways to represent different 'players' in the event, enabling the two interlocutors to speak from constantly shifting perspectives: at times, in 'the first person', they reenact the acts of the protagonist's hands; at other times, in 'the third person', their hands serve as symbolic tokens for the moving and crashing cars; at yet other times, their hands are extraneous producers of symbolic constructs – sequentially rendered ephemeral three-dimensional shapes – which represent components of the setting. In the following, these components, in particular, deserve our attention.

The first of the two fragments is a narrative segment told 'in the first person'. The speaker, Satomi, describes how she was absentmindedly driving along a straight road, when she realized that she had to turn to the right. At this point in the story, she puts down the teacup that she has been holding in her hands, readies her hands by moving them to her stomach, and says:

6.1   Nde ne douiu wakeka sugoi:
       And I don't know why but

       ((two hands hold and turn 'steering wheel'))
       [
6.2   ko kirrisugitan da yo ne.
       I turned the steering wheel too much, like this.

Along with the lexical description of her turning of the steering wheel, Satomi makes a large two-handed gesture which international audiences unfailingly recognize as an enactment of car-driving: holding her two hands in a 'grip shape' parallel to her chest, she moves one diagonally up and the other one diagonally down and thereby shows the turning of a steering wheel (Figures 6.10–11). The gestural portrayal is consistent with

Figure 6.10.   Figure 6.11.

the lexical description, and the gesture appears to add little to the narrative, except perhaps visual precision (i.e., how far she turned the wheel).

And yet we may ask how it is that we can so easily identify the gesture – and the action that the gesture denotes as well as the object that is involved in the action – all of this despite the fact that we do not understand the language. In fact, it is this gesture (which is performed several times during this narrative) that enables people who do not understand Japanese to 'see' a story about driving cars and accidents. Here is the simple yet significant explanation: we recognize the gesture to the extent that we share the material culture that the speaker is drawing upon. Throughout the world, as in Japan, there are few objects (if any) that are routinely handled – held and turned – in the fashion of a steering wheel, other than the steering wheel itself: the gesture can therefore only be about driving a car. We recognize the action that is abstractly performed by the configured motions of the configured hands because we are culturally familiar with the material world where such an action could 'really' be performed. Our perception of the gesture as a schematic action requires our beholder's share, that we 'fill in' generic objects to which the motions of the hands may relate.

In the 'steering wheel' instance above, our encyclopedic knowledge of the material world – what kinds of things are handled in the fashion seeable in the gesture? – enables us to recognize the signified. In other cases, world knowledge enables us to see the gestural signifier – the seeing of a motion as an action – even when this action has no correspondence in the event that is signified. For example, through a version of the method of "documentary interpretation" (Mannheim 1959) we manage to see that, for example, the motion pattern of the hands could relate to a specifically shaped object – that they are virtually holding a bowl (see Scheflen 1974). Thus, we 'see' a bowl – and disregard the 'holding' (which has no correspondence in the event). The schematic act of holding – the gestural signifier – would be an

Figure 6.12.

exclusively descriptive or pictorial, not a referential, device. Nevertheless, to perceive it, we must know about basic embodied acts and their generic objects.

This applies to the following segment, in which Satomi's friend and conversational partner, Tomoio, also shows a round object that can be turned; she shows it by performing a one-handed gesture. But this is an object that could not be manipulated using the action pattern from which the gesture is formed; the motion here serves descriptive purposes, and no action corresponds to it in the event that is reported. The object shown by the gesture is a worn-out tire skidding on a slippery road.

7.1   TOMOIO: h de kou hashitteta no (.) 'hh (shitara) sa ame ga furi
hajimete

7.2   sono kuruma ga sa: 'hh akseru funde sa
The driver stepped on the gas and

7.3   SATOMI: nng

                  ((one hand 'turning a round object'))
                  [

7.4   TOMOIO: subetta yo taiya ga bo:zu datta no
skidded. The tires were worn out.

During her utterance at line 7.4, Tomoio opens her right hand wide and rotates it a few times back and forth so that her wrist provides an axis (Figure 6.12). She performs a schematic manual action to evoke a particular kind of object – an object that is round and can be rotated around an axis. To see the gesture this way, onlookers must possess and fill in basic experiential knowledge about relationships between acts of turning, round shapes, and rotating things. Using this knowledge, they can 'see' in the speaker's hand a round object and recognize the hand's rotation as a description of the object's behavior, skidding, rather than as a schematic action. The signified (the car's tire), of course, could not in reality be turned in this fashion by a single human hand, because it is so much bigger. But this is a matter of contextual specification: what matters here is that the object was round and that it rotated, not what size it had. To use grammatical terminology: while Satomi's gesture would be understood as having the grammatical shape of a transitive verb plus nominal undergoer (steering a steering wheel), Tomoio's has that of a nominal subject modified by an intransitive verb (a tire skidding). This distinction is not inherent in the gestures' shapes, but rather is a seeing that is achieved in a context and informed by knowledge about the material world. We must know that there are things that can be turned back and forth, and that they may be round and rotating around an axis. Tires are objects that have these features. Thus, by moving from the schematic act of the hand to the object and back to the hand, onlookers know to abstract from the hand's action: here, it is only a component of the signifier, not of the signified; there is no hand or human agent in the moment described, just a worn-out tire skidding on a slippery road.

In both of these segments, the gestures achieve their pictorial effects through a presupposed indexical link between the hand and the world of things. In the first case, we 'see' the object that the protagonist's hands actually manipulated in the event; the gesture is a virtual action which represents an instrumental action in the depicted scene. In the second example, the gestural motion enables us to 'see' a kind of object: one that is round and rotating. This narrative hand has no correspondence in the event; there is no hand that holds and turns a tire (nor could there be).

Iconic gestures of this kind have been described throughout the literature on gesture (cf. Calbris 1990; McNeill 1992; Wundt 1975 [1911], among others), but little attention has been devoted to what they tell us about the roots of gesture in non-symbolic action or to the role that these experiential roots – and, thus, our experiential, embodied knowledge about the material world and its manipulations – play in our ability to see and understand gestures. Our suggestion here is that an essential component of the pictorial language of gesture – of the logic by which 'iconic' (or descriptive) gestures achieve their communicative effects – are the tactile, indexical ties that the hands and their motions have and retain to the material world that they can reach, explore, know about, and act upon. Before we learn how to gesture, we learn how to handle things. This knowledge is incorporated in our hands; we use it and we appeal to our interlocutor's possession of it when we represent the world gesturally and invite our interlocutors to understand our gestures accordingly. Gestural communication is mediated by shared experiential knowledge about the material world.

5   Conclusion

Our aim in this chapter has been to examine processes of symbol formation (Werner & Kaplan 1963) and use within communities of practice and
to regard these processes as native to the performance and recognition of
gestural representations in conversations abstracted from hands-on interaction with things. Initially, we investigated the orchestration of linguistic
and embodied communication in 'material-rich' learning settings such as
do-it-yourself and architecture classrooms and suggested that the evolution of bodies of knowledge is a communal process of forming symbols
that embody experiences that have emerged in situated action. The contiguity of gesture and experience in these contexts enables us to examine
the indexicalization practices (a term suggested to us by John Gumperz)
through which gestures are made meaningful and gradually become 'independent' meaningful symbols within a (however limited) community of
practice. At the same time, we displaced gesture, specifically iconic gesture,
from the bipolar logical space in which it is almost exclusively situated and
studied when it is examined in the context of abstract narrative or conversation. Our studies therefore also reveal something about the ways in
which generally representational gestures emerge and are understood. In
'pure' conversations, gesture is typically assumed to correspond either to a
mental image or to objects, actions, or events 'out there' (beyond the immediate setting) with which it is alleged to share similarities of form. Neither
mental image nor referent is available in the documented situation.
However, in practical settings where gestures share the situation with the
experiences that they formulate, we can begin to see the important indexical underpinnings of the pairings of form and meaning, of signifier and
signified: here these underpinnings are the situated histories of practical
and symbolic action in which tactile, practical acts – manipulations – are
gradually abstracted into 'free-standing' symbols which can then signify
not only acts but also manners and mistakes as well as objects acted upon
and their features. We believe that these gestures' socially-situated emergence may reflect, generally, the way humans interactively constitute and
use gestural forms.

The experiential grounding of conversational gestures is typically not
available to interlocutors in the situation at hand, but it is presupposed.
These gestures have lost the immediate connection to the material experiences from which they may have derived, and circulate in social life as
purely symbolic, gestural forms. They appear self-contained because their
situated emergence and existence extends beyond the situated humans who
use them. But many of the gestural shapes that people recognize in talk-in-
interaction may have originally been devised in some prior situation of the

kind that we have described above and from which they were abstracted and passed on. And competent members of human societies are capable of recognizing these links between gestures and objects because they are familiar with the basic actions of which gestures are abstract versions, as well as with the world that affords them. Moreover, the speaker's hands know how to do things other than gesticulation, and it seems unlikely that the skills that the hands bring to bear on their symbolic tasks are entirely separate from those that they have acquired while handling things. Rather the patterns that are at hand when there is a need to gesture appear to be made from the same fabric as those that are required in instrumental action. And this 'producer's knowledge', too, is socially and culturally shared.

In the picture that emerges from these studies, then, gesture is not a symptom of mental events, and it does not derive its communicative potential from a hypothetical relationship to images in the speaker's mind. Rather it is an embodied and therefore public symbolic practice, kinesthetically known by its makers, visually known by its beholders, and derived from and embedded in an objective world within which mindful hands operate. Gestures do not represent by virtue of any similarity to their denotata. Rather they are abstracted from – and are interpreted vis-à-vis the backdrop of – the realm of material action. Hands learn how to handle things before they learn how to gesticulate. They are knowing signifiers and bring embodied schematic knowledge, acquired through physical action, to the diverse symbolic tasks of gesticulation. Gestures, designed as they always are for particular recipients, appeal to those recipients' knowledge, knowledge that may have been acquired over the course of the current situation or in a cultural and physical world that is in some part the shared property of the members of a single society or cultural group, and in other parts common to all human beings.

NOTE

1 We wish to thank Cam Tew for allowing us to make use of this material.

REFERENCES

Bates, J. A. V. 1974. The communicative hand. In Benthall & Polhemus (eds.), pp. 175–194.
Benthall, J. & Polhemus, T. (eds.) 1974. *The Body as a Medium of Expression*. London: Allan Lane.
Calbris, G. 1990. *The Semiotics of French Gestures*. Bloomington: Indiana University Press.
Condillac, E. 1746. *An Essay on the Origin of Human Knowledge, Being a Supplement to Mr. Locke's Essay on the Human Understanding*. London: J. Noursse.

Gombrich, E. H. 1961. *Art and Illusion: A Study in the Psychology of Pictorial Representation*. 2nd ed. Princeton, NJ: Princeton University Press.

Kendon, A. 1980. Gesticulation and speech: two aspects of the process of utterance. In Key (ed.), pp. 207–228.

Key, M. R. (ed.) 1980. *The Relationship of Verbal and Nonverbal Communication*. The Hague: Mouton.

Lave, J. 1991. Situating learning in communities of practice. In Resnick, Levine & Teasley (eds.), pp. 63–83.

Locke, J. 1959 [1690]. *An Essay concerning Human Understanding*. New York: Dover.

Mannheim, K. 1959. *Essays on the Sociology of Knowledge*. London: Routledge & Kegan Paul.

McNeill, D. 1985. So you think gestures are nonverbal? *Psychological Review* 92: 350–371.

McNeill, D. 1992. *Hand and Mind: What Gestures Reveal about Thought*. Chicago: University of Chicago Press.

Norman, D. 1988. *The Design of Everyday Things*. New York: Doubleday.

Resnick, L. B., Levine, J. M. & Teasley, S. D. (eds.) 1991. *Perspectives on Socially Shared Cognition*. Washington, DC: American Psychological Association.

Scheflen, A. 1974. *How Behavior Means*. Garden City, NY: Anchor.

Scheflen, A. 1976. *Human Territories*. Englewood Cliffs, NJ: Prentice-Hall.

Vygotsky, L. S. 1978. *Mind in Society: The Development of Higher Psychological Processes*, ed. M. Cole, V. John-Steiner, S. Scribner & E. Souberman. Cambridge, MA: Harvard University Press.

Werner, H. & Kaplan, B. 1963. *Symbol Formation*. New York: Wiley.

Wundt, W. 1975 [1911]. *Völkerpsychologie: Eine Untersuchung der Entwicklungsgesetze von Sprache, Mythus und Sitte*. Aalen: Scientia Verlag.

Gesture in thought

The shared theme of the chapters in this part is the topic of language and mind. The part develops and justifies a rationale for viewing speech-synchronized gestures as windows into the on-line processes of thinking and speaking.

The view through this window, we believe, is striking. Unlike the picture assumed through decades of psycholinguistics research – research focused on the inscribable aspects of speech – the speech–gesture window reveals a wider panorama. In addition to the analytic processes that are embodied in words and syntax, there is imagery. The principal concept that underlies part 2 is that the linguistic code and gesture imagery work together as a single system (a concept assumed in several of the part 1 chapters as well). Utterances possess two sides, only one of which is speech; the other is imagery, actional and visuo-spatial. To exclude the gesture side, as has been traditional, is tantamount to ignoring half of the message out of the brain. The chapters in this part describe ways to examine the full complexity of utterances in this wider framework.

The main difference of part 2 from the first is the approach, which here is that of cognitive psychology. The emphasis is on the mental processes *in* individual speakers and listeners. This 'inside' or process view does not conflict with the 'outside' or interaction view of part 1. Every researcher must pick some aspect of speech and gesture on which to focus attention. The terms 'inside' and 'outside' describe research approaches, not the phenomenon itself. We face a complex phenomenon with both its inside and outside aspects, and there are various routes to fathoming the relationships between them.

The chapters in this part cover theories of speech–gesture integration (McNeill & Duncan; Kita), speech–gesture timing (Nobe; Mayberry & Jaques), the relationship of speech–gesture synchrony to speech parameters in discourse (Levy & Fowler), and the ontogenesis of speech–gesture integration during the single-word period of language development (Butcher & Goldin-Meadow). Several of the chapters advance theoretical ideas for explaining the dynamics of utterance formation. An important issue concerns the sense in which gestures and speech are related; and two views are represented. In the McNeill & Duncan chapter, gesture and speech are united into single idea units, gesture and speech, as if two sides of a single coin. In the Kita chapter, gesture and speech are conceptualized as parallel but basically separate streams of cognition (a conception similar to that of Paivio 1971). The two chapters agree that speech and gesture co-occur and work together through a dialectic: they differ in whether synchronous speech–gesture combinations comprise single idea units. This issue has hardly been discussed, and much remains to be uncovered. As far as the contributions to this book are concerned, the joint emergence of speech and gesture as a developmental milestone (Butcher & Goldin-Meadow) and the unbreakability of speech–gesture unity during stuttering (Mayberry & Jaques) seem to be evidence in favor of the unity theory.

REFERENCE

Paivio, A. 1971. *Imagery and Verbal Processes*. New York: Holt, Rinehart & Winston.

7 Growth points in thinking-for-speaking

David McNeill

Departments of Psychology and Linguistics, University of Chicago

Susan D. Duncan

Department of Psychology, University of Chicago; Laboratory for Cognitive Neuropsychology, National Yang Ming University, Taipei

1   Introduction

Many bilingual speakers believe they engage in different forms of thinking when they shift languages. This experience of entering different thought worlds can be explained with the hypothesis that languages induce different forms of 'thinking-for-speaking' – thinking generated, as Slobin (1987) says, because of the requirements of a linguistic code. "'Thinking for speaking' involves picking those characteristics that (a) fit some conceptualization of the event, and (b) are readily encodable in the language" (p. 435).[1] That languages differ in their thinking-for-speaking demands is a version of the linguistic relativity hypothesis, the proposition that language influences thought and that different languages influence thought in different ways.

Thinking-for-speaking differs from the so-called strong Whorfian version of the linguistic relativity hypothesis, as we understand it. The latter (Whorf 1956; Lucy & Wertsch 1987; Lucy 1992a, b) refers to general, *langue*-wide patterns of 'habitual thought', patterns that, according to the hypothesis, are embodied in the forms of the language and analogies among them. The thinking-for-speaking hypothesis, in contrast, refers to how speakers organize their thinking to meet the demands of linguistic encoding on-line, during acts of speaking – what Saussure (1959) termed *parole* rather than *langue*. The thinking-for-speaking version and the Whorfian version of the linguistic relativity hypothesis are not mutually exclusive, but neither are they identical. The distinction between them parallels the characterization of Whorf as 'synchronic' compared with Vygotsky (1987) as 'diachronic' that was offered by Lucy & Wertsch (1987). Following them, we will regard the thinking-for-speaking hypothesis as having a diachronic focus on *thinking* rather than a synchronic focus on *habitual thought*.

Slobin outlined three approaches to demonstrate linguistic relativity in this thinking-for-speaking sense. One is to find the stages at which children talk about experience in ways that appear specifically shaped by the linguistic system they are acquiring; another is to identify the difficulties that second-language learners have in adapting their thinking to the new language; the third is to look at languages historically – the elements most resistant to change being possibly those most deeply ingrained in thought. In each of these approaches, spoken language is the only source of information, and none of them breaks into the logical circle of language representing itself. Child speakers of different languages acquire expressive habits that mirror the semantic-structural differences among their languages (Choi & Bowerman 1991). A skeptical view, however, could hold that these differences operate only at the level of linguistic expression. To counter such a view, some way is needed to externalize cognition in addition to language. In this chapter, we consider speech and gesture jointly as an enhanced 'window' onto thinking and show how the co-occurrences of speech and gesture in different languages enable us to infer thinking-for-speaking in Slobin's sense.

2   The gestures we analyze

2.1   Co-expressive and synchronized with speech

Detailed observations of the gestures that accompany speech show that gesture and speech are systematically organized in relation to one another. The gestures are meaningful. They form meaningful, often non-redundant combinations with the speech segments with which they synchronize. A speaker raises her hand upward to mean that a character in a story is climbing up. The rising hand expresses upwardness, and so does the speech, "[and he climbs **up the pipe**]." The specific phase of the gesture depicting upwardness coincides with the semantically most congruent parts of the utterance (the stroke phase shown in boldface). The confluence of speech and gesture suggests that the speaker was thinking in terms of a *combination* of imagery and linguistic categorial content; 'thought' was in the form of a holistic image of the character rising upward coordinated with the analytic, linguistically categorized meanings of "up" and "the pipe." The contents of the gesture and the synchronized speech need not be identical, and indeed they usually are not. An upward gesture combined with "up" might be regarded as redundant, but the same gesture continued through "the pipe" – a related but distinct concept. The term we use to denote such related but not identical meanings is 'co-expressive'. This means that the gesture and its synchronized co-expressive speech express the same underlying idea unit but do not necessarily express identical aspects of it. By looking at the speech *and* the gesture jointly, we are able to infer characteristics of this underlying idea unit that may not be obvious from the speech alone.

2.2   Unique semiotic properties

2.2.1   Idiosyncratic. The gestures we analyze are 'idiosyncratic' in the sense that they are not held to standards of good form; instead they are created locally by speakers while they are speaking.[2] The forms of such gestures are driven almost entirely by meaning. The hand rising upward expresses upwardness; upward at an angle expresses upwardness at an angle. The system is graded, not categorial. Idiosyncratic gestures differ from arbitrary sound-meaning pairings in which meaning plays no role in determining signifier shape. By virtue of idiosyncrasy, co-expressive, speech-synchronized gestures open a 'window' onto thinking that is otherwise curtained. Such a gesture displays mental content, and does so instantaneously, in real time (as prosody also functions to display content; cf. Bolinger 1986). Idiosyncratic gestures should be distinguished from gestures of the kind that Kendon has called "quotable" and others have called "emblems" (Kendon, this volume, 1992; Morris et al. 1979; Ekman & Friesen 1969) – gestures that must be configured according to preestablished standards of form in order for them to function as signs, such as the OK sign among North Americans or the *mano a borsa* or purse-hand among Neapolitans (Kendon, this volume). The OK sign made not with the forefinger but with the middle finger touching the thumb is not recognizable as the same sign or as a graded approximation to it, even though it differs but minimally from the official sign.

2.2.2   Global and synthetic. The way in which idiosyncratic gestures display their mental content is unlike the sign mechanisms of speech. The terms 'global' and 'synthetic' characterize how gestures differ as semiotic entities.

Global: The meanings of the 'parts' or the features of gestures are determined by the meaning of the whole. The meaning determination is whole-to-part. The global property contrasts with the 'compositional' property of speech. In speech, whole meanings are built up out of independently meaningful parts (morphemes) and the semiotic direction is part-to-whole. It is not the case that the hand in the 'up' gesture, or its movement or direction separately from this gesture, meant the character, his movement, or direction. These 'parts' received their meanings because they were the parts of a gesture that meant, as a whole, the character rising up. 'Global' in this sense does not refer to the contextualization of meaning, but to how the meanings of the parts are determined by the meanings of wholes.

Synthetic: Distinguishable meanings in speech converge into one symbolic form, the gesture. The synthetic property contrasts with the analytic distribution of meanings across the surface structures of sentences. Putting the semantic components of actor, action, and path direction in a sentence, "he climbs up the pipe" spreads them out analytically. The upward-rising gesture compresses them into one symbol, synthetically.

Thus, when gesture and speech combine, they bring into one meaning system two distinct semiotic architectures. Each modality, because of its unique semiotic properties, can go beyond the meaning possibilities of the other, and this is the foundation of our use of gesture as an enhanced window into mental processes (cf. Kita, this volume, for a related approach).

3   The growth point

The growth point (GP) is the name we give to an analytic unit combining imagery and linguistic categorial content. We center our analysis on this hypothesized unit (a preliminary version of the GP concept was presented in McNeill 1992).

3.1   *Composition and integrity of growth points*

GPs are inferred from the totality of communicative events with special focus on speech–gesture synchrony and co-expressivity. Following Vygotsky (1987), a GP is assumed to be a *minimal* psychological unit; that is, the smallest unit (in his analysis) that retains the essential properties of a whole, in our case the whole of an image and a linguistically codified meaning category, such as we see in the speech–gesture window. We use the gesture's semantic content and its synchrony (that is, the synchrony of the gesture stroke phase) with speech to infer the GP. For example, to locate the GP of the following[3]

(1)   and Tweety Bird runs and gets a bowling b[all and Ø <u>drops</u> **it**
         do<u>wn the drainpipe]</u>

(where the two hands appear to form a large round object and move it down)[4] we refer to both gesture and speech. The GP was embodied in both the image and the synchronized linguistic categorial content. The image was of a cartoon character dropping something down (a bowling ball). The categorial content was the linguistic segments "it" and "down." The gesture suggests visuo-spatial/actional thinking in which the downward movement of the ball due to the action of an agent was central. Such imagery is important. It grounds the linguistic categories in a specific visuo-spatial context (the gesture itself is not the 'context'; see section 3.2). The downward content of the gesture is a specific case of the general linguistic category 'down' – a specific visualization of it. The linguistic categorization is also crucial, since it brings the image into the system of categories of the language.

The psycholinguistic reality of the GP is seen in the fact that it strongly resists forces trying to divide it. For example, delayed auditory feedback grossly disrupts speech timing, but speech–gesture synchrony remains intact (McNeill 1992: ch. 10, first DAF experiment). Synchrony is disrupted only if speech and gesture are drained of meaning through repetition; i.e., such that GPs may be circumvented in their production (second DAF experiment). Neither does clinical stuttering interrupt speech–gesture synchrony, despite massive disruptions of speech. Gestures during stuttering bouts freeze into holds (Mayberry & Jaques, this volume; also Nobe, this volume). On the reception side, listeners, after a brief delay, cannot tell whether information was conveyed in gesture or in speech; the two are unified (McNeill et al. 1994). In each case, the meaningful linkage of gesture and language resists division.

3.2 Growth points as psychological predicates and the context of speaking

A thread that runs through all examples of GPs is the following: GPs inferred from speech–gesture synchronizations are the elements in the immediate context that are presented as newsworthy; they are points of departure from preceding discourse, what Vygotsky called *psychological predicates* (as opposed to grammatical predicates).

The concept of a psychological predicate illuminates the theoretical link between the GP and the context of speaking. Defining a psychological predicate (and hence a GP) requires reference to the context; this is because the psychological predicate and its context are mutually defining. The GP:
1. marks a significant departure in the immediate context; and
2. implies this context as a background.
We have in this relationship the seeds for a model of realtime utterance generation and coherent text formation.

Regarding the GP as a psychological predicate suggests a mechanism of GP formation in which differentiation of a focus from a background plays an essential part. Such differentiation is validated by a very close temporal connection of gesture strokes with the peak of acoustic output in speech. Nobe has documented this connection instrumentally: "The robust synchrony between gesture strokes and the peaks of acoustic aspects suggests that the information the gesture stroke carries has an intrinsic relationship with the accompanying speech information prominently pronounced with these peaks. The manifestation of the salient information seems to be realized through the synchronization of these two modalities" (1996: 35).

Regarding the GP as a psychological predicate also clarifies the sense in which we use the term 'context'. This term has a host of meanings (cf. Duranti & Goodwin 1992), but for our purposes 'context' is the background from which a psychological predicate is differentiated. This background indexes and is constrained by external conditions, both social and material, but the background is also under the control of the speaker; it is a *mental construction*, part of the speaker's effort to construct a meaning. The speaker shapes the background in a certain way in order to make possible the intended significant contrast within it. Background and contrast are both necessary and are constructed together.

3.3   Growth points in thinking-for-speaking

Though seemingly antithetical, image and language category are equally indispensable to thinking-for-speaking. The opposition between them is the key that unlocks speech. As image and language interact, they are able to influence one another – the "continual movement back and forth" of which Vygotsky spoke in his evocation of the dialectic of language and thought. This mutual influence enables language to influence imagery, and imagery to influence language as the utterance unfolds in real time. Speech is not a translation of one medium, image, into another, language. To grasp it, we should not replace the minimal unit possessing antithetical poles with a succession of single poles. In keeping with Vygotsky's conception of inner speech, the GP with its dual imagistic–categorial nature, is the mediating link between individual cognition and the language system.

3.4   Unpacking growth points

The dialectic continues during what Werner & Kaplan (1963) termed "microgenesis" and we will call "unpacking." The surface utterance works out the implications of the GP and finds a grammatical framework in which to fit it. Thought undergoes continuous change during this process, thus shaping thinking while speaking.

Linguistic categorization may select for classification only some aspects of the image. The gesture, being global and, especially, being synthetic, is likely to contain information pertaining to more than one component of meaning. The segment(s) of speech with which the gesture stroke synchronizes, however, need not categorize all this information. Since the gesture in (1) displayed two hands releasing or thrusting down, it could logically have been categorized with "drops." However, the stroke of the gesture was withheld during this verb, even though the hands were in position to perform it. In GP terms, the core concept excluded the act of dropping, which was an action by the character, Tweety. This fits with the narrative goal, which was to explain how the bowling ball got inside Sylvester and flushed him out of the pipe. In this logic, the emphasis was on the bowling ball, and the key transformation was attributed to it. "Drops," therefore, the action not of the ball but of Tweety, was not part of the GP, and the gesture stroke, accordingly, excluded it. To identify the gesture as "drops" would have been meaningful had What Tweety Was Doing been the significant opposition, rather than What the Bowling Ball Did.[5]

What processes of unpacking resulted in the verb "drops," then? This latter component characterized Tweety's action, not the bowling ball's. Thinking subsequently shifted to categorize the action of this agent and supplied a verb referentially motivated by it. According to this explication, a verb is not the only way to anchor a sentence. In this example the verb was essentially *derived* from the GP's complex of meanings. In the course of unpacking the GP, thinking shifted and acquired an agentive cast. In such a case the verb, though uttered first, would arise in the sentence-generation process after the GP itself. The dynamics of thinking-for-speaking during unpacking thus highlight the distinction between action by the agent and the other object's path, a distinction appropriate in the discourse context of this GP.[6]

3.5   Linguistic relativity

This distinction may come easily to thinking that is being formulated in English and similarly organized languages, in which path and agent are separably encoded meaning components, but it is not easily achieved in other languages – Georgian, for example. In one narration in this language, a downward gesture stroke corresponding to (1) was categorized by a verb that includes both path and agentivity content (*chagdebs* 'throws-down').[7] In other words, Georgian does not make available a path word outside the verb to categorize just this feature. The image inevitably is categorized for agentivity as well. The Georgian-speaker's thinking-for-speaking would thus differ in this respect from the English-speaker's, though the imagery was effectively the same.

3.6   Summary of the growth point

To sum up, a G P is neither word nor image. It is thinking in global imagery and linguistic categories simultaneously. Its essential feature is a dialectic of these forms of thinking, and it gives rise to speech and gesture through their collaboration ("convergence" – Kita, this volume). Speech–gesture synchrony is therefore explained genetically, as an inevitable consequence of how the idea unit itself took form and its resistance to interruption during unpacking. Speech–gesture synchrony could not be otherwise with an initial organizing impulse of this sort. Thinking, according to this hypothesis, is both global *and* segmented, idiosyncratic *and* linguistically patterned. The implied model of language production is therefore not G (imagery)→L; that is, language is not a translation of imagery. Nor is it L→G, meaning that the gesture depends "sequentially and organizationally" on language.[8]

4   Motion in three languages

With the G P framework now described, we will illustrate its application in three languages. We shall search for differences in thinking-for-speaking as embodied in G Ps in English, Spanish, and Chinese (we have already mentioned Georgian). This approaches, via observable speech and gesture, the experience of having different forms of thinking in different languages.

4.1   Motion events

We focus on a particular semantic domain, the motion event. This domain offers the advantage of allowing us to borrow much current linguistic and psycholinguistic analysis. In particular, Talmy's (1985, 1991) motion-event componential analysis provides a cross-linguistic schema in which motion is analyzed into a set of semantic components and languages are compared and grouped according to how they package these into linguistic forms (see also Aske 1989; Slobin 1987; Choi & Bowerman 1991). According to Talmy, a prototypical motion-event expression has these components, among others:

- A moving object, called the 'figure', as in "drops *it* down," where the "it" indexes the bowling ball, the object in motion;
- A reference object, called the 'ground', as in "drops it down *the drainpipe*," where the downward trajectory occurs in relation to a non-moving object, the drainpipe;
- A trajectory, or 'path', as in "drops it *down*," where the bowling ball moves on a downward trajectory;

- A 'manner', as in "it *rolls* down," where the motion is performed in a certain way.

According to Talmy, each given language has a characteristic way of packaging such motion-event components. The languages we discuss here fall into two classes that Talmy has classified as "satellite-framed" and "verb-framed." The category depends on how the path component of the motion is packaged. English is satellite-framed, meaning that path is coded in a so-called satellite – i.e., an adjunct to the verb, like *down*. Path is coded outside the main verb. Spanish is verb-framed in that path information is bundled into the verb itself. Talmy (1985) classifies Chinese as also satellite-framed, like English, although other writers have placed it on a continuum somewhere between English and Spanish (Slobin & Hoiting 1994).

Manner and how it is presented is a second important difference between the verb- and satellite-framed types. In contrast to path, manner in a satellite-framed language is encoded in the main verb, and indeed both English and Chinese have rich lexicons of manner verbs (e.g., distinctions of bipedal locomotion – *walk*, *run*, *stroll*, etc.). Manner is prepackaged in many English and Chinese verbs.

Because of this relentless presence of manner, English-speakers appear sometimes to go out of their way to avoid it. We find that deictic verbs like *go* and *come* have a use in English discourse as a way of avoiding manner, when including it may be an undesirable overspecification in the motion-event description; for example, saying "he comes out the pipe" when "he rolls out the pipe" would have been referentially appropriate but might seem an overspecification in the context (where only the fact of motion was significant). We will show that gesture provides another means by which English-speakers exclude manner.

With Spanish, in contrast, path is bundled into the verb, while manner is often introduced constructionally outside the verb, in a gerund, a separate phrase, or clause. The gerund is a frequent pattern, illustrated by *sale volando* 'exits flying', in which path is in the main verb and manner is in a gerund. Slobin (1996) has discovered an effect of this typological difference – novels written originally in English lose as much as half their manner coloration in Spanish-language translations, presumably because including manner is rhetorically cumbersome. As we will show, a somewhat more complex picture emerges when gestures are considered.

4.2   Motion-event gestures in English and Spanish

4.2.1   Gestural manner. As mentioned above, there is sometimes an embarrassment of riches in English with respect to manner, and the problem is how to downplay it. We present here a snapshot of how gesture can downplay manner even when the speaker employs a manner verb in speech. Spanish-speakers are an interesting contrast case, for they do not face this same problem.

In English we see two alternating patterns. In one, there is a focus on manner through gesture; in the other there is use of gesture to downplay manner. The following examples illustrate these patterns with the verb *rolls*:

(2)   [but it **rolls**] him out
        Hand wiggles: manner information.

(3)   [and he rolls . . . **down** the drain spout]
        Hand plunges straight down: path information only.

In (2), which is from one speaker, a wiggling-hand gesture synchronized with "rolls" in the utterance. We infer that the GP of this utterance consisted of manner imagery (here shown with gestural 'agitation') categorized as rolling. In (3), from another speaker, the gesture lacked manner and did not synchronize with "rolls" at all. Instead the gesture skipped the verb and synchronized with path, "down," and ground, "the drainspout" (via the post-stroke hold).

In other words, even when the same verb occurs, gestures can differ. From this we infer different GPs and thinking-for-speaking. In one pattern, the core idea includes manner, whereas in the other it does not, and the manner in the verb is made to recede in the face of a gesture without manner that may be synchronized with other content, as in (3). We might suspect that these differences of focus occur in contrasting immediate contexts – in (2) a context in which the rolling manner of the ball is a significant opposition, versus a context in (3) in which manner is not treated as significant. There is some support for this prediction. The speaker of (2) was focusing on the motion of the bowling ball, while the speaker of (3) focused on Sylvester. The framework of significant oppositions was therefore different, and the gesture placements (and inferred GPs) shifted accordingly.[9]

In Spanish, we find the opposite situation, cases where gestural manner appears without a linguistically encoded anchor and has the potential to appear at several places in a motion-event description, something like a manner 'fog'. A manner fog is defined as manner in gesture that is not also coded in speech. Although Spanish speakers often omit manner from their speech, manner is abundant in their gestures and combines with other linguistic categories, typically path (verb) and/or ground (nominal phrase).

(4.1)   e entonces busca la ma[ner**a (silent pause)**][10]
          and so he looks for the way
          Gesture depicts the shape of the pipe: the ground.

(4.2)   [de **entra**][r / **/ se met**][e **por el**]
         to enter REFL goes-into through the
         Both hands rock and rise simultaneously: manner and path (left
         hand only through "mete").
(4.3)   [de**sague** *//*] [/ / si?]
         drainpipe ... yes?
         Right hand continues to rise with rocking motion: path + manner.
(4.4)   [de**sague entra** /]¹¹
         drainpipe, enters
         Both hands briefly in palm-down position (clambering paws) and
         then rise with chop-like motion: path + manner.

Gestural manner (either a climbing or a winding, 'corkscrewing' motion) was articulated throughout this description.¹² Each GP in this bit of discourse could embody manner, but this manner, unlike that in the English example in (2), was not categorized as manner by any linguistic unit. Rather, manner imagery was categorized in non-manner ways – path: "*mete*" 'goes-into' in (4.2), ground: "*desague*" 'drainpipe' in (4.3), and path again: "*entra*" 'enters' in (4.4). GPs thus brought manner in gesture into the Spanish categorial system through routes other than manner as a category itself. The question is how manner is categorized in Spanish when there is no clear focus for manner given in the verb system. These gestural-manner combinations with Spanish path or ground are GPs, no less than GPs are with manner verbs in English. In Spanish, we say, GPs with manner are categorized and enter the linguistic system as path and/or ground. That manner in gesture goes with path and/or ground is an empirical observation that may say something about the interrelations of motion-event concepts themselves, especially manner and path/ground.

Thinking in relation to manner thus can move in opposite directions in English and Spanish. In English, gestural manner focuses at a specific point (the verb) if it is part of a core idea; otherwise it is omitted and the gesture stroke can skip the verb, thus downplaying the manner component. Alternatively, speech finds its way to a non-manner-encoding expression, such as *comes out of*. In Spanish, gestural manner, far from appearing only when it is categorized as manner, can appear in the absence of spoken manner and be categorized instead as a kind of path (4.2 and 4.4) or a kind of ground (4.3).

We interpret this difference between Spanish and English as arising from thinking-for-speaking adaptations. In English, gesture and verb jointly highlight manner when it is part of the speaker's focus. When manner is not in focus, gesture does not encode it and need not synchronize with a manner verb, even if one is present. Thus gesture modulates the lexical system of

English, and while it may include manner it also may exclude it. Spanish, with its non-obligatory manner, does not require modulation. Manner appears in Spanish speech presumably only when it is a focused component, and it is often omitted even when it is potentially significant. Finding a way to include manner is the challenge in Spanish. Gesture, again, adds to thinking-for-speaking, but in the opposite direction from English. This analysis suggests that differences in the dynamics of thinking-for-speaking can be traced to typological differences between languages.

4.3   Motion-event gestures in English and Chinese

Talmy (1985) includes Chinese in the class of satellite-framed languages. Like English, it has a large lexicon of manner verbs and high-frequency constructions that parcel out the components of motion events in ways similar to English. Path, for example, is typically not encoded in the verb but expressed instead in particles associated with the verb. In the gestures of Chinese-speakers we find no cases of manner fogs, as in Spanish. Thus gestural evidence, too, aligns Chinese and English in this framework.

4.3.1   Speech–gesture framing. In Chinese, however, we find a language-specific pattern of gesture and possibly of thinking-for-speaking. The hallmark of this Chinese pattern is a gesture that occurs earlier in the temporal sequence of speech than the timing facts of English and Spanish would lead us to expect. This suggests a difference in GP possibilities. An example is the following:

(5)   lao tai-tai[na -ge da   **bang hao**]-xiang gei   ta   da-xia
       old lady hold CLASSIFIER big stick seem   CAUSE him hit-down
                                                               verb-satellite

   'The old lady apparently knocked him down with a big stick'

The gesture (a downward blow) that accompanied the spoken reference to the stick was expressively redundant with the verb and satellite, "*da-xia*" 'hit-down.' As the speaker said "*da bang*" 'big stick', she performed a downward-blow gesture. Her hand then promptly relaxed and went to the rest position well before the verb phrase emerged in speech. This timing pattern is often found in our Chinese data. It presents a quite different picture from the sentential-predicate-(verb-) focused gestures we see with English- and Spanish-speakers. It is as if the gesture shifts forward in the surface speech stream, in the direction of the utterance-initial position characteristic of topic statements in Chinese speech. We do not consider such speech–gesture pairings to be 'errors' of synchrony; there is nothing random about them.

We find, in every such case, an idea unit with clear semantic coherence. In terms of thinking-for-speaking, we interpret this pattern of synchrony as evidence of imagery that forms with speech-idea units based on framing constraints: units that specify upcoming domains of reference before they are articulated in speech. In English and Spanish, in contrast, the tendency is to think in terms of the kinds of event transformations embodied in the grammatical predicates of subject–predicate constructions. Chinese shows the latter pattern in many instances as well, but adds this further pattern that may resemble topicalization in its framing effects.[13]

Chinese is what Li & Thompson (1976, 1981) have termed a "topic prominent" language. English and Spanish, in contrast, are "subject prominent." Utterances in the latter are founded on subject–predicate relations. In line with this typological distinction, we find cases like (5), in which gesture provides one element and speech another element to jointly create something analogous to a topic frame.[14] Again, therefore, we see the possible impact of language type on thinking in that language.

4.3.2   English in contrast. The Chinese-specific character of this use of imagery for thinking on the topic-like frame level becomes clear when Chinese is compared with English. In English too a gesture depicting an event yet to be expressed in speech occasionally gets ahead of speech in production. But the precocious imagery appears to be regarded by the speaker as an error, something to be repaired. In (6.1), a gesture that shows the result of an action synchronizes with speech describing the cause, a semantically appropriate pairing:

(6.1)   [so it **hits** him on **the hea**][d

(6.2)   and he winds up **rolling down the stre**]et

The two gestures in (6.1) depicted Sylvester moving down the street, an event not described until (6.2). In (6.1) they synchronized with a description of the initiating condition for the gestured event; the pairing therefore is similar to that in the Chinese example. The difference between the languages is apparent at the next step. Unlike the Chinese-speaker, this English-speaker held and then repeated the gesture in a larger, more definite way when the target linguistic segments emerged in speech (6.2). Thus, an important difference between Chinese and English thinking-for-\speaking dynamics is exposed by this contrast between seemingly similar speech–gesture combinations. No hold or repetition occurred in the Chinese example. The subsequent enhanced repeat in the English example indicates the relevance of the gesture to the predicate. This is what makes it look like a gestural 'repair'. In other words, the speaker retained the imagery at (6.1) for the GP of (6.2). She did not use it, as did the Chinese-speakers, as a self-contained framing unit.

4.3.3   'Enslaved' to predication. Gestural evidence that links the typological distinction of topic- versus subject-prominence with different patterns of thinking-for-speaking indicates that Chinese-speakers are able to create a topicalizing frame with conjoined gestures and speech, something that appears to be beyond the ken of English- (and presumably Spanish-) speakers. The packaging of motion information in English (and presumably Spanish) is encased in the grammatical structure of the sentential predicate to a degree not found in Chinese. In English, given one component of a motion event, others are bound to be included in a structure more or less preordained, particularly by the predication structure and its linkage to other parts of the sentence. We can think of English and Spanish as in this sense 'enslaved' to predication, because they need to find machinery (grammatical, morphological, gestural) to link predicates to their subjects. In the English example above, there is a linking gesture hold, which functions as a kind of anaphoric reference. In terms of the GP hypothesis, the expatiation of GPs in English and Spanish is satisfied by structures typically organized as sentential predicates. This constituent is thus at the heart of thinking-for-speaking in these languages. In Chinese, in contrast, the *"da-xia"* 'hit-down' verb-satellite assembly in (5) was dissociated from gesture and intonationally destressed, as if its role in speech were largely formal. Thinking-for-speaking in Chinese therefore seems less tied to specific predicate-based constructions.

4.4   Summary of motion-event expression

We have seen evidence of the following:
1. The GP is a unit of analysis applicable in all languages.
2. The minimal GP unit of thinking is irreducibly imagery and a linguistic category.
3. Describing the same motion events, languages encourage different forms of thinking. English and Spanish (as well as Georgian) are predicative in their focus, but thinking differs in how motion-event semantics are focused. Chinese induces thinking in which the focus is a frame for other information. Observations thus show an effect of linguistic organization on thinking on two levels – predicative and discourse – and different patterns on both.
4. As a model of thinking-for-speaking, the GP embodies thinking that exists because of the linguistic code. Thinking emerges via the GP with language categories built in.

5   Embodied cognition and being

Why do we perform gestures at all? In what sense are gesture and speech embodied cognition? What functions do gestures serve for thinking-for-speaking? In the cases we have described, we can see that the relationship of gestures to speech is shaped by language. Researchers have asked if gesture is motivated mainly or entirely by a desire to convey narrative- or discourse-pragmatic-level information that is less than adequately conveyed by the linguistic code. If this is the role of gesture, certain phenomena must be carefully explained. Gestures occur, famously, in the absence of a face-to-face audience – on the phone, for example.[15] Further, they often do not reflect the deliberateness of speech. They do not occur invariably, so there is some selection principle. As well, when they occur they may be more or less elaborated as kinesic performances.

Several proposals can be mentioned to explain the occurrence of gestures, among them that they are the remnants of an earlier stage of language evolution (Armstrong et al. 1995; Donald 1991), and that they have their own communicative effects. Speech–gesture patterning is undoubtedly heterogeneous in origin; it is shaped by culture and possibly by evolution, and it includes social-interactional as well as individual factors. In developing a theory of language production centered on the GP as a unit of analysis, we wish to address the implications of the idea that gesture, the actual kinesic event itself, is a dimension of thinking.

Gestures are *material carriers* of thinking – a phrase used somewhere by Vygotsky. Note that in the GP model, speech is equally a dimension of thinking. The same sense of a material carrier is thus invoked. Speech and gesture are best thought of, we argue, not as the packaged communicative outputs of a separate internal production process but rather as the joint embodiment of that process itself. One approach to the material-carrier concept is found in Werner & Kaplan (1963), who wrote of the "organismic" foundations of symbolization; of our capacity to represent the world symbolically by capturing it in a kind of imitation carried out in bodily movements made possible by ". . . this *transcendence of expressive qualities, that is, their amenability to materialization in disparate things and happenings*" (p. 21). The development of an individual child in this view is, in part, a process of adding semiotic distance between movement and the expressive qualities it can have: "The act of denotative reference does not merely, or mainly, operate with *already formed* expressive similarities between entities. Through its productive nature, it brings to the fore latent expressive qualities in both vehicular material and referent that will allow the *establishment of semantic correspondence* between the two entities. It is precisely this productive nature of the denotative act that renders possible a symbolic relation between any entity and another" (pp. 21–22; emphasis in the original in both passages). We see this creation of meaning in gesture.

A more radical extension of the material-carrier concept carries it past the realm of representations. This is to give the concept an interpretation on the level of cognitive being. To the speaker, gesture and speech are not only 'messages' or communications, but are a way of cognitively existing, of cognitively being, at the moment of speaking. By performing the gesture, the core idea is brought into concrete existence and becomes part of the speaker's own existence at that moment. The Heideggerian echo in this statement is intended. Gestures (and words etc. as well) are themselves thinking in one of its many forms – not only expressions *but thought, i.e., cognitive being, itself.* The speaker who creates a gesture of Sylvester rising up fused with the pipe's hollowness is, according to this interpretation, embodying thought in gesture, and this action – thought in action – was part of the person's being cognitively at that moment. To make a gesture, from this perspective, is to bring thought into existence on a concrete plane, just as writing out a word can have a similar effect. The greater the felt departure of the thought from the immediate context, the more likely its materialization in a gesture, because of this contribution to being. Thus gestures are more or less elaborated depending on the importance of material realization to the existence of the thought. Such a correlation of gesture elaboration with less continuous/predictable references in speech has been observed (McNeill 1992: 211).

There are, however, deep and hitherto unexplored issues here, and possibly some contradictions. If to the speaker the gesture and linguistic form are themselves forms of being cognitively, there would seem to be no room in this process for the presentation of symbols; the signifier–signified distinction that constitutes semiosis is lacking. A semiotic relation appears when an observer is taken into account – a listener who participates or a coder who looks at the communicating individual. Dreyfus (1994), in his invaluable exposition of Heidegger, explains Heidegger's treatment of symbols in a way that suggests a rapprochement. To cope with signs is not to cope just with them but with the whole interconnected pattern of activity in which they are embedded (this still has the viewpoint of a listener/observer; from the speaker's viewpoint, we should say that producing a sign *carries the speaker* into a "whole interconnected activity"). Heidegger, according to Dreyfus, says that signs point out the context of a shared practical activity – and this is the key to the rapprochement. To have your thoughts come to exist in the form of signs is to cause them to exist in a context of shared practical activities. A sign signifies only for those who 'dwell' in that context. This we can recognize is a recipe for the GP: sign and context are inseparable, and this context must be dwelled in. This brings the

GP and the social-interactive context together as joint inhabitants of the context (and it is the speaker who always must be the one dwelling there the best). The communication process is then getting the other to dwell there on her own. In this way the GP model can be seen to map 'external' interactive contexts into internal units of functioning, a convergence of this mode of theorizing with Vygotsky's model of two planes, the interpsychic and intra-psychic.[16]

In a GP, the gesture, as one dimension of a material carrier, is as much a part of the linguistic process as are the familiar linguistic objects of words, phrases, and clauses. The gesture adds substance to the speaker's cognitive being. When, by gesture, language is extended, narrowed, or adapted to exploit a linguistic feature, cognitive being itself is changed.

6   Conclusion

We have argued in this chapter that speakers of different languages create language-specific modes of thinking-for-speaking. Gesture contributes material carriers to thinking-for-speaking, and these take different forms in different languages. Speech and gesture together can be conceptualized as bringing thinking into existence as modes of cognitive being. This concept explains the occurrence of gestures, and explains why they are more frequent and more elaborate where the departure of the meaning from the context is felt to be greater.

NOTES

Parts of this chapter were presented at the University of Buffalo and the Max Planck Institute for Psycholinguistics. Our research has been supported by grants from the National Science Foundation, the National Institutes of Health, and the Spencer Foundation. We are grateful for help and advice from Susan Goldin-Meadow, Stephen Levinson, Elena Levy, Karl-Erik McCullough, Tatiana Naumova, Asli Özyürek, Jan Peter de Ruiter, Jürgen Streeck, Sandra A. Thompson, and the members of the gesture class at the 1995 Linguistic Institute. We especially wish to acknowledge the eye-opening lecture expounding Heidegger given by Barbara Fox at the Linguistic Institute (Fox 1995) and Shaun Gallagher for commenting on our Heidegger section.

1 The expression 'thinking-*for*-speaking' suggests a temporal sequence: thinking first, speaking second. We posit instead an extended process of thinking-*while*-speaking, but keep the thinking-*for*-speaking formulation to maintain continuity with Slobin and his writings, and to capture the sense of an adaptive function also conveyed by use of *for*, with the caveat that we do not mean by this a thinking–speaking sequence.

2 'Idiosyncratic' in this use does not mean unique or bizarre. Two speakers can non-uniquely perform similar non-bizarre (even mundane) gestures and both be 'idiosyncratic', that is, not meet external standards of well-formedness.

3   All examples in this paper are from narrations by adult speakers retelling a seven-minute animated color cartoon to a naive listener. Neither speaker nor listener was aware that the speaker's gestures were of interest. For details of the method and transcription, see McNeill (1992) and Duncan et al. (1995).

4   Square brackets show when the hands were in motion; boldface marks the gesture stroke phase, the phase of 'effort' that bears the semantic content of the gesture; and double underlining marks a hold – the hands held in place in midair – which in this case included both a 'pre-stroke' and a 'post-stroke' hold (Kita 1990).

5   To describe a gesture as displaying components of motion at all is, in a sense, an oxymoron, in that it takes linguistically segmentable meanings and attributes them to a quite different kind of semiotic entity. The holistic stroke in "drops it down" was seamlessly all these motion components at once: 'pathgroundfiguremanner'. The synchronized speech brought into segmented existence the first three components of this amalgam.

6   See McNeill, this volume, for analysis of contexts in GP formation.

7   We are grateful to Kevin Tuite for this example.

8   To use a phrase of Schegloff's (1984). The GP can also be compared to his concept of a "projection space." While evidently related, projection space and GP are not identical. They apply to different empirical domains – conversational interaction and the microgenesis of individual speech and thought, respectively. Although addressing different domains, we can answer Schegloff's question, What is 'in play'? It is *the very GP itself* that is 'in play' (not a word or lexical affiliate, therefore, but a linguistically categorized image).

9   Example (2) was at the end of a series of references to the bowling ball where it and what it was doing would have been highlighted.

and he drops a [bowl]ing ball [in**to** <u>the rain spout</u>]
[and it **goes down**]
and it* [/] ah*
you [**can't tell if the bowl**<u>ing ball</u> /] [is un* <u>/</u>] [is **und**<u>er Sylvester</u>
<u>or</u> **ins**ide of him]
[but it **rolls him out**]*   (= 2)

Example (3) appeared in a series that began similarly but then shifted to Sylvester and his path. The shift took place before (3) and continued beyond it, and would have created a context in which the bowling ball and its manner of motion would be downplayed.

[the canary] # [th**rows***] # [puts a # [bowling] [ball] #
into] # [the **drain** <u>spout as the</u>]
[**cat** <u>is climbing up /and</u>] [it goes <u>into his</u>] [mouth] /   (switch to Sylvester)
[and **of course**] # [**into** <u>his</u> stomach] #
[and he rolls # **down** <u>the drain</u> spout]   (= 3)
[and [**across**] [the **street**] into [the bowling] alley #]

10 Kendon (pers. com.) believes that when speech halts like this, listeners have a tendency to shift their gaze to the speaker, and this could be such an occasion.

11 We are grateful to Lisa Miotto, Karl-Erik McCullough, and Gale Grubman-Stam for transcribing and translating this example. The example is from Grubman-Stam's data.

12 In the grammar of Spanish, the combination of manner and path is confined to paths that do not end with the moving object entering a specifically configured state (Aske 1989; Slobin & Hoiting 1994). In example (4), however, path *does* end in a 'specifically configured' ground state – the drainpipe; yet it appears with gestural manner. The G P, as a dual imagery–language unit, can expand the resources of the language at such points (cf. Kita, this volume).

13 Chafe (1976) stated our intended sense of topicalization: "What the topics appear to do is limit the applicability of the main predication to a certain restricted domain . . . the topic sets a spatial, temporal, or individual framework within which the main predication holds" (p. 50; also quoted by Li & Thompson 1976).

14 Gestures may be recruited for topicalization precisely where they can expand the resources of the linguistic system. Duncan (1996) found that accompanying gesture reflects the particular semantic link between the case-marking grammatical particle *ba* and the nominal it marks. Duncan is now exploring the possibility that gestures are recruited at points of incipient grammaticalization. Example (5) represents such a point involving the verb *na* 'to pick up', which often appears, as in the example given, where speech and gesture jointly specify the framework within which the main predication holds. The verb *na* may have an incipient grammaticized role of marking instrumentality (the big stick mentioned).

15 Although the number of gestures is reduced when a social presence is lacking, as in speaking to a tape recorder (Cohen 1977).

16 The Vygotskian model of two planes, the 'interpsychic' and the 'intrapsychic', helps clarify the relationship of individual cognition to the social context of speaking. In Duranti & Goodwin's (1992) discussion of Vygotsky, however, the focus is exclusively on the interpsychic plane (Harré 1986 performs a similar 'intraectomy'). This transmogrification of Vygotsky removes any basis for considering the relationship of individual cognition to social context.

REFERENCES

Armstrong, D. F., Stokoe, W. C. & Wilcox, S. E. 1995. *Gesture and the Nature of Language*. Cambridge: Cambridge University Press.

Aske, J. 1989. Path predicates in English and Spanish: a closer look. In Hall et al. (eds.), pp. 1–14.

Aske, Jon, Beery, Natasha, Michaelis, Laura & Filip, Hana (eds.) 1987. *Proceedings of the 13th Annual Meeting of the Berkeley Linguistics Society*. Berkeley, CA: Berkeley Linguistics Society.

Bolinger, D. 1986. *Intonation and Its Parts*. Stanford, CA: Stanford University Press.

Chafe, W. L. 1976. Givenness, contrastiveness, definiteness, subjects, topics, and point of view. In Li (ed.), pp. 25–55.

Choi, S. & Bowerman, M. 1991. Learning to express motion events in English and Korean: the influence of language-specific lexicalization patterns. *Cognition* 41: 83–121.

Cohen, A. A. 1977. The communicative functions of hand illustrators. *Journal of Communication* 27: 54–63.

Donald, M. 1991. *Origins of the Modern Mind: Three Stages in the Evolution of Culture and Cognition*. Cambridge, MA: Harvard University Press.

Dreyfus, H. L. 1994. *Being-in-the-World: A Commentary on Heidegger's Being and Time, Division I*. Cambridge, MA: MIT Press.

Duncan, S. D. 1996. Grammatical form and 'thinking-for-speaking' in Chinese and English: an analysis based on speech-accompanying gestures. Unpublished Ph.D. dissertation, University of Chicago.

Duncan, S. D., McNeill, D. & McCullough, K.-E. 1995. How to transcribe the invisible – and what we see. In O'Connell et al. (eds.), pp. 75–94.

Duranti, A. & Goodwin, C. 1992. *Rethinking Context: Language as an Interactive Phenomenon*. Cambridge: Cambridge University Press.

Ekman, P. & Friesen, W. V. 1969. The repertoire of nonverbal behavioral categories: origins, usage, and coding. *Semiotica* 1: 49–98.

Fox, B. 1995. On the embodied nature of grammar: embodied being-in-the-world. Paper presented at the International Conference on Functional Approaches to Grammar, University of New Mexico, Albuquerque, July.

Gahl, S., Dolbey, A. & Johnson, C. (eds.) 1994. *Proceedings of the 20th Annual Meeting of the Berkeley Linguistics Society*. Berkeley, CA: Berkeley Linguistics Society.

Hall, K., Meacham, M. & Shapiro, R. (eds.) 1989. *Proceedings of the 15th Annual Meeting of the Berkeley Linguistics Society*. Berkeley, CA: Berkeley Linguistics Society.

Harré, R. 1986. Mind as social formation. In Margolis et al. (eds.), pp. 91–106.

Hickmann, M. (ed.) 1987. *Social and Functional Approaches to Language and Thought*. Orlando, FL: Academic Press.

Kendon, A. 1992. Some recent work from Italy on quotable gestures (emblems). *Journal of Linguistic Anthropology* 2: 92–108.

Kita, S. 1990. The temporal relationship between gesture and speech: a study of Japanese–English bilinguals. Unpublished master's thesis, Department of Psychology, University of Chicago.

Li, C. N. (ed.) 1976. *Subject and Topic*. New York: Academic Press.

Li, C. N. & Thompson, S. A. 1976. Subject and topic: a new typology of language. In Li (ed.), pp. 447–489.

Li, C. N. & Thompson, S. A. 1981. *Mandarin Chinese: A Functional Reference Grammar*. Berkeley and Los Angeles: University of California Press.

Lucy, J. A. 1992a. *Grammatical Categories and Cognition: An Historical, Theoretical, and Empirical Re-evaluation of the Linguistic Relativity Hypothesis*. Cambridge: Cambridge University Press.

Lucy, J. A. 1992b. *Grammatical Categories and Cognition: A Case Study of the Linguistic Relativity Hypothesis*. Cambridge: Cambridge University Press.

Lucy, J. A. & Wertsch, J. V. 1987. Vygotsky and Whorf: a comparative analysis. In Hickmann (ed.), pp. 67–86.

Margolis, J., Krausz, M. & Burian, R. M. (eds.) 1986. *Rationality, Relativism and the Human Sciences*. Dordrecht: Martinus Nijhoff.

Maxwell, J. & Heritage, J. (eds.) 1984. *Studies in Conversation Analysis*. Cambridge: Cambridge University Press.

McNeill, D. 1992. *Hand and Mind: What Gestures Reveal about Thought*. Chicago: University of Chicago Press.

McNeill, D., Cassell, J. & McCullough, K.-E. 1994. Communicative effects of speech-mismatched gestures. *Research on Language and Social Action* 27: 223–237.

Morris, D., Collett, P., Marsh, P. & O'Shaughnessy, M. 1979. *Gestures: Their Origins and Distribution*. New York: Stein & Day.

Nobe, S. 1996. Representational gestures, cognitive rhythms, and acoustic aspects of speech: a network/threshold model of gesture production. Unpublished Ph.D. dissertation, University of Chicago.

O'Connell, D. C., Kowal, S. & Posner, R. (eds.) 1995. *KODIKAS/CODE* (Special issue on signs for time: *Zur Notation und Transkription von Bewegungsabläufen*) 18.

Saussure, F. de, 1959 [1916]. *Course in General Linguistics*. New York: Philosophical Library.

Schegloff, E. A. 1984. On some gestures' relation to talk. In Maxwell & Heritage (eds.), pp. 266–296.

Shibatani, M. & Thompson, S. A. (eds.) 1996. *Grammatical Constructions: Their Form and Meaning*. Oxford: Oxford University Press.

Shopen, T. (ed.) 1985. *Language Typology and Syntactic Description*, vol. III: *Grammatical Categories and the Lexicon*. Cambridge: Cambridge University Press.

Slobin, D. 1987. Thinking for speaking. In Aske et al. (eds.), pp. 435–445.

Slobin, D. 1996. Two ways to travel: verbs of motion in English and Spanish. In Shibatani & Thompson (eds.), pp. 195–219.

Slobin, D. & Hoiting, N. 1994. Reference to movement in spoken and signed languages: typological considerations. In Gahl et al. (eds.), pp. 487–505.

Sutton, L. A., Johnson, C. & Shields, R. (eds.) 1991. *Proceedings of the 17th Annual Meeting of the Berkeley Linguistics Society*. Berkeley, CA: Berkeley Linguistics Society.

Talmy, L. 1985. Lexicalization patterns: semantic structure in lexical forms. In Shopen (ed.), pp. 57–149.

Talmy, L. 1991. Path to realization: a typology of event conflation. In Sutton et al. (eds.), pp. 480–520.

Vygotsky, L. S. 1987. Thinking and speech, trans. N. Minick; ed. R. W. Rieber & A. S. Carton. In *The Collected Works of L. S. Vygotsky*, vol. I: *Problems of General Psychology*, pp. 39–285. New York: Plenum.

Werner, H. & Kaplan, B. 1963. *Symbol Formation: An Organismic-Developmental Approach to Language and the Expression of Thought*. New York: Wiley.

Whorf, B. L. 1956. *Language, Thought, and Reality: Selected Writings of Benjamin Lee Whorf*, ed. J. B. Carroll. Cambridge, MA: MIT Press; New York: Wiley.

8   How representational gestures help speaking

Sotaro Kita

Max Planck Institute for Psycholinguistics, Nijmegen

1   Introduction

The purpose of this chapter is to discuss the speaker-internal motivation to produce representational gestures. Consequently, the communicative aspects of gesture will be backgrounded in the following discussion, and the main focus will be on the cognitive functions of representational gestures. Representational gestures are defined here as iconic gestures and abstract deictic gestures (McNeill 1992). In an iconic gesture there is a certain degree of isomorphism between the shape of the gesture and the entity that is expressed by the gesture. An abstract deictic gesture points to a seemingly empty space in front of the body, as if establishing a virtual object in the gesture space or pointing at such a virtual object. Because these gestures have a relatively transparent form–function relationship, they play an important role in communication.

However, it is known that people also produce representational gestures without visual contact with the interlocutor, although under such a condition the frequency decreases (Rimé 1983). This cannot be fully explained as a habit formed during more frequent face-to-face interactions. This is because certain types of gestures that are meant to be seen are not produced if there is no visual contact with the interlocutor. For example, waving a hand to mean "Bye-bye" at the end of a phone conversation feels extremely unnatural. Bavelas et al. (1992) experimentally demonstrated that 'interactive gestures', whose signification function involves other participants in the speech event, are produced less frequently when there is no visual contact between the interactants.[1] In contrast, the frequency of 'topic gestures', which signify story-line-level information, does not change. Speakers therefore selectively suppress gestures that are meant to be seen by the interlocutors. These studies suggest that representational gestures have cognitive functions in addition to communicative functions.

There have been two related proposals as to how representational gestures help speaking: the Image Activation Hypothesis and the Lexical Retrieval Hypothesis. According to the Image Activation Hypothesis, gesturing helps to maintain an image (Freedman 1977; de Ruiter 1995, 1998). Freedman argues that a representational gesture 'buttresses' an image and cements the image's connection to the word. De Ruiter (1995, 1998) maintains that some spatial features are activated and reactivated by gesturing, while the language formulation processes encode the spatial features. Both Freedman and de Ruiter claim that an image is kept activated while a linguistic connection is made with the image.

According to the Lexical Retrieval Hypothesis, gesturing helps lexical retrieval (Rauscher et al. 1996; Krauss et al. 1996). Krauss and his colleagues have argued that the production of representational gestures helps the speaker retrieve, on the basis of conceptual specification, a lexical entry with morphosyntactic information (i.e., a lemma in Levelt 1989) by cross-modal priming. They remain open as to the details of the priming, but they accept as a possibility Hadar & Butterworth's (1993) proposal that "gestural representation serves to 'hold' the conceptual properties of the sought-for lexical entry in memory during lexical search" (Krauss et al. 1996: 421). According to Krauss et al., the execution of a gesture keeps certain spatio-dynamic features activated; in other words, it keeps a spatio-dynamic image activated. These features, in turn, keep a set of conceptual properties activated while a proper lexical item is being retrieved. Thus, the theory of Krauss et al., with its 'holding' idea, could be seen as a combination of the Image Activation Hypothesis and the Lexical Retrieval Hypothesis, where the aspect of speech production that benefits from the boosting of an image is localized in lexical retrieval.

The purpose of this chapter is to argue for an alternative view which expands on the idea that "[g]estures, together with language, *help constitute thought*" (McNeill 1992: 245; emphasis in the original).

Information Packaging Hypothesis

1. The production of a representational gesture helps speakers organize rich spatio-motoric information into packages suitable for speaking.
2. Spatio-motoric thinking, which underlies representational gestures, helps speaking by providing an alternative informational organization that is not readily accessible to analytic thinking, the default way of organizing information in speaking.
3. Spatio-motoric thinking and analytic thinking have ready access to different sets of informational organizations. However, in the course of speech production, the representations in the two modes of thinking are coordinated and tend to converge.

The plan of the chapter is the following. The two modes of thinking are defined in section 2, and the interplay between them is elaborated in section

5. Sections 3, 4, 5, and 6 will present the evidence that supports the Information Packaging Hypothesis.

2   Analytic thinking and spatio-motoric thinking

Analytic thinking organizes information by hierarchically structuring decontextualized conceptual templates (henceforth, analytic templates).[2] An analytic template can be either non-linguistic in nature, such as a 'script' (Schank & Abelson 1977), or linguistic in nature, namely, semantic and pragmatic specifications of a lexical item, their clause-level combination, and a more abstract combinatoric template (e.g., English transitive template, NP-Nominative Verb NP-Accusative).[3] Analytic templates are decontextualized in that they are not modality-specific. In other words, the activation of analytic templates does not necessarily involve activation of 'peripheral' modules such as visual, tactile, and motoric modules, or 'non-combinatoric' modules such as affect. However, translation between analytic templates and modality-specific information is possible. Since some of the analytic templates are associated with a linguistic expression, the package of information prepared by analytic thinking for verbalization is partially, if not fully, linguistically specified.[4] This is the default mode of thinking that underlies speaking.

Spatio-motoric thinking organizes information with action schemas and their modulation according to the features of the environment. This is the type of thinking normally employed when people interact with the physical environment, using the body (e.g., the interaction with an object, locomotion, and imitating somebody else's action). It involves automatic uptake of the information that determines possible modulation of action schemas and in some cases induces a new action schema. It is similar to what Gibson (1986) called the picking up of "affordances." For example, when you grasp an object with a novel shape, your body can figure out a stable grip. When you explore an object by looking at it and handling it, spatio-motoric thinking takes up different possibilities for touching and manipulating the object. When an object moves against a stable background, our eyes detect the change, their foci jump to the object, and the object's movement is followed by turning the head and eyes.

To carry out a particular body movement toward a target entails an analysis of environmental information. A particular part of the environment is picked up as relevant for the body movement, such as the shape and orientation of the contact area for grasping and touching, or a displacement vector for tracking a moving object. A set of possible body movements in a particular environment constitutes an organization of the environmental information in terms of spatio-motoric structuring.

I hypothesize that spatio-motoric thinking can also be applied to the virtual environment that is internally created as imagery. Representational gestures are actions in the virtual environment (Streeck 1996 and Müller 1996 maintain a related view that representational gestures have their origin in practical action). Note that the word 'action' refers to a body movement oriented towards an object (e.g., grasping an object, orienting the gaze to an object) and to a body movement that is autonomous (e.g., limb movements in walking). The virtual environment is not an accurate reproduction of the physical environment that has been experienced. Rather it is an array of modality-specific analog information, including aroused affect, which is isomorphic to (but may not be accurate copies of) reactions to a certain external event or state. It is flexible in the sense that various construals of the same event or state can be represented (e.g., the same event could be observed from different perspectives).

When spatio-motoric information has to be conveyed, especially when the richness of the information requires further processing (e.g., selecting certain aspects, breaking them down into smaller chunks and regrouping the chunks, and construing the event at a different level of abstraction), both default analytic thinking and spatio-motoric thinking are evoked. The two modes of thinking collaboratively organize information for the purpose of speaking (this follows the idea that two different structures of information interact to constitute the speaker's thought, in the Growth Point theory developed in McNeill 1992, 1997; McNeill & Duncan, this volume). There are two mechanisms involved in the collaboration, which leads to the convergence of the contents of the two modes of thinking (Kita 1993: p. 54; see also section 3 in McNeill & Duncan, this volume). One mechanism assesses the degree of match between the representations in the two modes of thinking. The other is a related mechanism that 'translates' representations in one mode of thinking into those in the other insofar as representational resources in each mode of thinking (such as lexicon) allow.[5] Through these mechanisms, the two modes of thinking feed information to each other, and their contents are modified toward the convergence in the course of utterance planning. Note that the Lexical Access Hypothesis and the Image Activation Hypothesis presume that the direction of influence is one way: from gesture to language. In other words, they presume that imagery is translated into a language, but the representational constraints of the language do not change the kind of imagery evoked.

The key idea in the Information Packaging Hypothesis is that the speaker has access to a wider range of possible organizations because two modes of thinking have ready access to different organizations of information. The two modes of thinking are always in mutual check and influence each other's representation. In the next two sections, I will survey the evidence in the literature for this mutual influence on representation.

3   Influence of gesture on speaking

There have been reports that the production of speech is not as smooth when gesturing is inhibited. Rauscher et al. (1996) report that the inhibition of gesturing affects the fluency of speech. Graham & Heywood (1975) also report that inhibition of gesture increases the proportion of time spent pausing, excluding the pauses associated with demonstrative words. These reports suggest that gesturing helps speaking in some way. Rimé et al. (1984) report that the inhibition of gesture has a more profound effect on speaking than changing fluency: inhibition of gesture also changes the content of speech. They compared subjects' speech performance when the arm, the head, the leg, and the feet were immobilized and when the subjects could move their bodies freely. Speech was essentially free conversation. They report that during immobilization the imagery index of speech was lower than when the body could be moved freely. Content analysis of the speech indicated that utterances in the activity/movement category decreased during immobilization, but those of other categories (sensations, emotions, social behavior, concrete concepts, and abstract concepts) did not change.

4   Influence of language on gesturing

The Information Packaging Hypothesis predicts an influence of language on the content of gesture and the convergence of the contents of language and gesture. In contrast, this type of phenomenon provides evidence against the assumption, implicit in the Image Activation Hypothesis and the Lexical Retrieval Hypothesis, that the underlying image of a representational gesture is generated independently of properties of the language being spoken (Freedman 1977; de Ruiter 1995, 1998; Krauss et al. 1996). Some authors stressed the opposition between the private nature of the underlying imagery and the public nature of language (Freedman 1977).

According to this assumption, iconic gestures would not vary among speakers of different languages, given that they would be talking about the same spatio-motoric experience. There are some reports that seem to support this prediction. For example, McNeill (1992) summarizes what he observed in representational gestures by Georgian-, Swahili-, Mandarin Chinese-, and English-speakers, depicting the same scene in a stimulus animation: "A remarkable thing about iconics is their high degree of cross-linguistic similarity. Given the same content, very similar gestures appear and accompany linguistic segments of an equivalent type, in spite of major lexical and grammatical differences between the languages" (p. 212). However, this observation seems to hold only as a first approximation. Evidence for language specificity of representational gestures is emerging (e.g., Kita 1993; McNeill & Duncan, this volume).

Kita (1993) compared English and Japanese descriptions of a scene from an animated cartoon,[6] in which English and Japanese speakers are forced to linguistically package information differently. The scene involves spatial information that is difficult to verbalize in Japanese because of the lack of an appropriate lexical item. The descriptions of the scene by eleven Japanese- and eleven American English-speakers were compared (for more information about the methodology, see chapter 4 of Kita 1993).

The animated-cartoon scene in question is the following. A cat and a bird are across the street from one another in the windows of different high-rises. Attempting to catch the bird, the cat swings across the street on a rope that we must imagine is attached somewhere in the air above the street.

In the Japanese language, there is no straightforward way to encode agentive change of location with an arc trajectory. There is no verb that corresponds to the English intransitive verb *to swing (to)*, as in *the cat swings across the street*. There is no easy paraphrase for it either. So this is not only a lexical gap but is also a more general expression gap in the language. Note that this gap is quite idiosyncratic. It is not the case that Japanese in general cannot express the trajectory shape. For example, Japanese has a non-agentive intransitive swing *hureru* (e.g., a pendulum swings), and also the transitive swing *huru* (e.g., I swing a pendulum).

The eleven English-speakers all used the word *swing*. In contrast, none of the Japanese-speakers lexically encoded the arc trajectory. Examples of speech simultaneous with the stroke phase and the post-stroke hold phase[7] of the gesture depicting the swing scene include *tondeku mitai na koto* 'do something like go-flying', *kara biru e* 'from (a building) to another building', *tobi uturoo to sita*, 'tried to jump over to', and *kotori no hoo o megake te ikun desu* 'go to the direction of the bird'.

The gestures that express the change of location of the cat in the swing scene exhibit both cross-linguistic similarities and differences. Japanese-speakers on average made twice as many gestures as English-speakers (Table 8.1). Since all the gestures were produced simultaneously with a segment of speech, more gesture tokens indicate more verbal material uttered. This suggests difficulty in verbally expressing the scene in Japanese. A more striking difference is that the Japanese-speakers produced a large number of 'straight gestures' that do not encode a down-then-up arc. More than half of the Japanese-speakers produced at least one straight gesture (Table 8.2). Japanese-speakers are more likely to produce at least one

Table 8.1. *Gesture tokens with an arc-shaped stroke and a straight stroke in English and Japanese*

	Japanese	English
Arc gesture	20	14
Straight gesture	12	1

straight gesture than English-speakers (one-tailed Fisher exact test, $p = .0045$). On the other hand, most speakers of both languages produced at least one arc gesture for this one scene (Table 8.2).

Most of the Japanese-speakers produced at least one straight gesture, which is in a sense a less accurate rendition of the swing scene than anatomy would have allowed. However, most of the Japanese-speakers also produced an arc gesture. This suggests that representational gestures are shaped by two competing forces. One force shapes the representational gesture so as to make it as isomorphic as possible with a spatio-motoric model of the stimulus scene.[8] The other shapes the representational gesture so as to make its informational content as compatible as possible with linguistic encoding possibilities. These two forces shape the gestures in the same direction in English utterances, but in Japanese utterances they are in competition. The Japanese arc and straight gestures exhibit the two forces at work. Thus, representational gestures are produced at the level of the language-cognition interface mechanism, where a compromise is sought between the to-be-talked-about 'raw material' in cognition and the encoding possibilities of the language. Representational gestures emerge from the process, in which spatio-motoric thinking comes up with alternative organizations of information that can be utilized in the generation of an analytic message underlying speech.

5   **The interplay of analytic thinking and spatio-motoric thinking**

In order to speak, the information to be conveyed has to be regimented in the way required by the obligatory morphological marking of the language (Slobin 1987). It is also necessary that the information to be conveyed is organized so as to make it more compatible with the linear nature of speech and the limited capacity of the speech-production system. Rich and complicated information has to be organized into smaller packages so that each package has the appropriate informational complexity for verbalization within one processing cycle of speech production, which yields an utterance.

Table 8.2. *English- and Japanese-speakers categorized by types of gestures produced*

	Japanese-speakers	English-speakers
Only arc gestures	4	10
Both arc and straight gestures	5	21
Only straight gestures	2	0

The Information Packaging Hypothesis maintains that this process of informational organization is helped by representational gestures. It is helped because the production of representational gestures involves a different kind of thinking (namely, spatio-motoric thinking) from the default thinking for speaking (namely, analytic thinking).[9] Spatio-motoric thinking provides alternative organizings of information that are not readily accessible via analytic thinking.

In the context of speaking, spatio-motoric thinking and analytic thinking continuously interact, with a common goal of organizing rich and complicated information into a series of packages that can be verbalized within one planning unit of speaking (considered to be roughly the size of a clause; see Levelt 1989 for a summary of the evidence). The collaboration between the two modes of thinking might proceed in the following way, in the context of stimulus-elicited narrative as used in the study reported in section 3.

1. First, the speaker selects a 'scene', or a stretch of story that is coherent in terms of causal and spatio-temporal contiguity of events and the plan–goal structure of the protagonists. The scene is informationally small and coherent enough so that the speaker can without difficulty retrieve it as a whole or as a sequence of events. A scene contains multiple informational formats, including spatio-motoric and analytic representations.

2. Spatio-motoric thinking and analytic thinking search for a construal of the scene that can be verbalized within one speech production cycle.[10] If the scene is too rich and complicated, alternative organizations are sought: focusing on certain parts of it, segmenting it into smaller chunks, regrouping chunks, and construing it at a different level of abstraction. In the course of such organization, the two modes of thinking exchange information about their respective contents at each given moment, and both analytic and spatio-motoric contents are modified so as to minimize discrepancies (Kita 1993: 54; see also section 3 of McNeill & Duncan, this volume).

3. When a certain level of match is achieved, the package of information

begins to be externalized (Kita 1993: 54). Such a package, or message, is a complex, consisting of coordinated multiple informational formats such as analytic and spatio-motoric representations (equivalent to a "growth point" in McNeill 1992, 1997; McNeill & Duncan, this volume).[11] The level of match required before launching an utterance can be lowered for certain reasons such as interactional pressure to keep talking (Kita 1993: 54). In such cases, it is more likely that an utterance will be produced with relatively discordant gesture and speech.

4. An utterance (i.e., a speech–gesture complex) is produced. At a first approximation, the content of analytic thinking manifests itself as speech, and the content of spatio-motoric thinking as gesture. Note, however, that the content of spatio-motoric thinking can also be expressed in speech with expressive prosody and imagistically loaded linguistic forms such as mimetics (Kita 1997).

When the two modes of thinking interactively work in parallel in this way, more organizational possibilities are available to the speaker. Consequently, the generation of a message, and thus an utterance, is more efficient.

The dialectic between two types of representation is the key component of the Growth Point theory of speech and gesture production (McNeill 1992, 1997; McNeill & Duncan, this volume). The two types are a "global-synthetic image" underlying gesture and "linear-segmented hierarchical linguistic structure" (McNeill 1992: 245). The Information Packaging Hypothesis follows the idea that the constant interaction between two distinct representational systems helps constitute thought. However, it differs from the Growth Point theory in the assumption of what underlies a gesture. In the Growth Point theory, what underlies a gesture is visual, spatial, and actional imagery (McNeill 1997). In the Information Packaging Hypothesis, what underlies a gesture is an action in virtual environment. In other words, in the Growth Point theory, what underlies a gesture is *representational*, and in the Information Packaging Hypothesis it is *actional* (see, however, the discussion of "material carriers" in McNeill & Duncan, this volume, for a more actional view on gesture in the Growth Point theory).

The actional view of gestures does not deny that gestures are signs. The actional view makes a further commitment as to the formation of a gestural sign. A gestural sign is formed by the cognitive system that is also used in the movement of the body in the physical environment. Note also that even the gestures that do not have an obvious enactment component, such as abstract deictic gestures, are also formed by spatio-motoric thinking. The production of abstract deictic gestures, which point to a seemingly empty location in front of the speaker or move as if to track a moving object, could be related to the ability to orient our body parts (e.g., gaze and the hand) toward a target in the physical environment, and to the ability to track the target when it moves.

The Information Packaging Hypothesis stipulates that what generates a gesture is spatio-motoric thinking, which has a *raison d'être* independent of speaking. Consequently, it is expected that gestures and speech have a certain degree of independence from each other. That gestures and their synchronized speech are held to be independent systems is another important difference between the Information Packaging Hypothesis and the Growth Point theory. Gesturing during silence or meaningless vocalization and a semantic mismatch between gesture and speech during transition phases of conceptual development, both of which will be discussed below, are important supporting cases for the hypothesis. The independence allows spatio-motoric thinking to explore different organizations of information, in some cases without fully coordinating with analytic thinking. Gestures and speech are produced by two independent (but often tightly coupled) processes, which collaborate toward the common goal of organizing information to be conveyed into a more readily verbalizable shape.[12]

6   Cases of externalized interplay between the two modes of thinking

The collaborative convergence of the two modes of thinking is usually done internally, and there is no overt vocalization or body movement. However, it is occasionally externalized. Let us consider the following examples from the cartoon narratives analyzed in section 3. The two examples were produced by two English-speakers. In these examples, the following chronology of events holds.

1. A complicated spatial event is gesturally depicted, and there is no meaningful concurrent vocalization.
2. Part of the gesture in (1) is recycled, and this time the speech is more substantive.
3. If the speech and gesture contents do not match sufficiently, the shape of the gesture is slightly modified and more co-expressive speech is produced (Example 2 only).

The gesture is modified until co-expressive concurrent speech is produced. I take this to be an externalization of the feedback loop between analytic thinking and spatio-motoric thinking to achieve convergence.[13] The change in gestural representations is a gradual one (readily derivable in spatio-motoric thinking), but the concomitant change in speech is a cataclysmic one. This illustrates an advantage of two parallelly running modes of thinking.

In Example 1, gesture (1.4) was produced during a filled pause, and the last part of it is recycled in gesture (1.5). Repeated gestural features are in small capitals. Boldface indicates that the stroke phase of the gesture synchronized with these words. Underlining indicates synchronization with a gesture hold phase. Square brackets delimit the gesture phrase, beginning with the onset of preparation and ending with the end of retraction or with the onset of another gesture. RH, LH, and G stand for right hand, left hand, and gesture, respectively. "/" stands for a silent pause.

Example 1

Scene in the cartoon:
Sylvester (a cat) sets up a seesaw-like device underneath the window several floors up where Tweety (a canary) is. Sylvester stands on one end of the seesaw with a heavy weight and throws it to the other end. The weight catapults him up to the window. He snatches Tweety and comes back down to the same spot on the seesaw, which in turn catapults the weight up. Sylvester runs away with Tweety in his hand, but the weight lands on top of him and Tweety gets away.

Preceding context:
Speech: *and he grabs the bird and then when he comes down again um*
RH: clenched above head to enact grabbing, then brought down to waist level, and then held there with the same hand shape.

(1.1)   [the **weight**]
          RH: continues to be held.
          LH: open hand, palm facing slightly up & right, knuckles pointing slightly left & away from body; located above the left thigh; moves slightly up and back down.

(1.2)   [**follo-**]
          RH: continues to be held.
          LH: open hand, palm facing slightly up & right, knuckles pointing slightly left & away from body; located above her left thigh; moves up in the same manner as (1.1) but reaches a higher point than (1.1).

(1.3)   [**ws him**]
          RH: continues to be held.
          LH: open hand, palm facing right and knuckles pointing away from body; moves from above the left thigh to the center of the torso, at the chest level; moves in an arc, first up and then gradually to the right, reaching the summit in a quarter of a circle.

(1.4)   [*I* eh ehm]
          RH: continues to be held.
          LH: G continues from end position of the previous G. At chest height, open hand, palm facing right and knuckles pointing away

from the body; moves in an arc and traces the second quarter-circle by moving right and increasingly downwards. (A PART OF THE FOLLOWING REAPPEARS IN (1.5).) LH LANDS ON TOP OF RH. LH IS STILL AN OPEN HAND, AND WITH PALM FACING DOWN AND KNUCKLES POINTING RIGHT.

(1.5)   [um and he **gets** <u>clobbered by the weight</u>]
           LH: lifted slightly during the preparation phase and then continues to be held as before.
           RH: REPEAT OF THE LAST PART OF (1.4). AN OPEN HAND WITH THE PALM FACING DOWN AND THE KNUCKLES POINTING RIGHT. LH MOVES DOWN 5 CM AND LANDS ON RH.

In this example, the crucial transition is from (1.4) to (1.5). The gesture in (1.4) is an elaborate expression of the spatial model of the scene. The right hand represents the location of the cat with the canary in his hand, and the movement of the left hand represents the falling of the weight (which got shot up by the cat's landing on the seesaw) from up in the air onto the cat. No substantive speech is concurrent with this gesture, presumably because of the complexity of the spatial information that the speaker has activated. In constrast, in (1.5), the speaker focuses only on the final portion of the movement that is represented in (1.4), namely, the impact of the weight on the cat. This is a readily derivable change for spatio-motoric thinking; however, the change allows the speaker to package the spatial information into a compact linguistic form. More substantive speech, referring only to the impact, accompanies gesture (1.5) than gesture (1.4).

In the following example, the stroke of gesture (2.4) is synchronized with a meaningless vocalization. The initial part of gesture (2.4) is recycled in gesture (2.5). Then the same movement feature is blended into gesture (2.6), which is not a simple repetition of a sub-segment of any preceding gesture. The final part of gesture (2.6) is recycled in (2.8). As the spatial information gets reorganized, more substantive speech is uttered concurrent with the gestures.

Example 2
Scene in the cartoon:
Sylvester is on the ground, underneath the window several floors up where Tweety is. He gets inside the opening of a drainpipe which leads to the window. He climbs up through the pipe. Tweety notices this, takes a bowling ball, and puts it into his end of the drainpipe. The bowling ball hits Sylvester, and he is pushed down through the pipe out onto the street. He has swallowed the ball. His round body rolls down the street down and into a bowling alley. There is the sound of bowling pins being knocked down.

174   *Sotaro Kita*

Preceding context:
Speech: *Tweety Bird un sees him coming and drops a bowling ball down the rain barrel*

(2.1)   [so **it hits** <u>him on</u>]
RH: palm faces left & toward body; hand moves straight down.

(2.2)   [**the head**]
RH: palm faces left & toward body; hand moves straight to right (slightly up)

(2.3)   [and he winds up **rolling down the str-**]
RH: palm faces left and then turns down; hand moves in a down-then-up arc to the right.

(2.4)   [eet because it / **aaaa** /]
RH: TO REAPPEAR IN (2.5): THE PALM FACES TOWARD BODY AND THE KNUCKLES POINT UP. THE HAND MOVES TOWARD THE THROAT; PALM FACES RIGHT AND KNUCKLES POINT TOWARD BODY; HAND MOVES DOWN TO BELLY LEVEL. TO REAPPEAR IN (2.8): THE WRIST ROTATES IN THE DIRECTION OF THE LITTLE FINGER, SO THAT THE PALM FACES RIGHT AND THE KNUCKLES POINT AWAY FROM BODY. THEN THE HAND MOVES RIGHT. (The above-mentioned movements are performed in a smooth sequence.)

(2.5)   well [actually what happ<u>ens is he I / you</u> **assume**]
RH: A SEGMENT OF (2.4), ALSO TO BE INCORPORATED IN (2.6): PALM FACES TOWARD BODY AND THE KNUCKLES POINT UP; HAND MOVES TOWARD THROAT.
LH: held with palm facing the body and knuckles pointing up.

(2.6)   [that **he swallows** / <u>this bowling</u>]
RH & LH: AN INCORPORATED FEATURE OF (2.5): PALM FACES TOWARD BODY AND KNUCKLES POINT UP; HAND MOVES TOWARD THROAT as the wrists rotate so that the palms face down and the knuckles point contralaterally.

(2.7)   [ball **and he comes**]
RH & LH: palms face each other and knuckles point up (and away from the body); hands move down slightly and to the right.

(2.8)   [**rolling out** <u>of the bottom of the rain barrel</u>]
RH & LH: palms face each other and knuckles point away from body; hands move slightly down and right. A PART OF (2.4): RH WRIST ROTATES IN DIRECTION OF LITTLE FINGER SO THAT PALM FACES RIGHT AND KNUCKLES POINT AWAY FROM BODY; HANDS MOVE SLIGHTLY UP AND RIGHT.

(2.9)   [**and rolls down the street**]
RH: palm faces down and the knuckles point right.

LH: palm faces up & right and knuckles point to the right.
LH & RH bounce up and down repetitively and at the same time move to the right.

The complexity of the gestural movement in (2.4) indicates that the speaker attends to a complex sequence of events at one time, too complex a sequence to be verbalized within a planning unit of speech. The gestural movement is broken into smaller pieces, and they are incorporated in the following sequence of gestures. This is a readily derivable modification of representation for the spatio-motor thinking; however, this is a drastic change from the viewpoint of linguistic packaging of spatial information. The spatial information is chunked into small enough pieces for each to be verbalizable within one planning unit of speaking. The size of the chunk is not the only factor that is relevant for linguistic packaging. The discursive appropriateness of the chunk is also important. The transition from (2.5) to (2.6) illustrates this point. The gestural movement of the right hand in (2.6) is the initial portion of the gesture in (2.5), which is a readily accessible modification of representation for spatio-kinesic thinking. However, this informational chunk – namely, the bowling ball approaching the cat's mouth – is not taken to be discursively appropriate by the speaker. Judging from how the speech changes from (2.5) to (2.6), the speaker takes the swallowing of the bowling ball, which causes a series of events that lead up to the climax of the episode, to be the discursively appropriate information at this point in the story. The speech synchronized with gesture (2.5) is a meta-narrative statement that is not co-expressive with the gesture, which encodes the story-line-level information. In gesture (2.6), a movement to the throat similar to gesture (2.5) is blended with a downward component, realized by the wrist rotation. The resulting movement is a better match to the linguistic concept of 'swallow something'. This is a minor modification in spatio-motoric thinking, but it made a crucial difference in the degree of match with the discursively appropriate linguistic expression.

The examples above illustrate the advantage of running two modes of thinking in parallel. A small modification in the spatio-motoric representation can be a significant change from the viewpoint of linguistic packaging. A similar coordination presumably took place (externally, as in the example above, or internally) in the shaping of the gesture and speech contents in the descriptions of the swing scene discussed in section 3.

7   Further evidence: gesture–speech discordance produced by children

A phenomenon that further supports the Information Packaging Hypothesis is systematic gesture–speech discordance which is found in children when they explain their solutions to problems (Church & Goldin-Meadow 1986; Goldin-Meadow et al. 1993). This gesture–speech discordance appears specifically during the transition phase toward the acquisition of a new concept. I propose that this discordance appears because spatio-motoric thinking explores organizings of information that analytic thinking cannot readily reach.

The phenomenon in question is the following. Church and Goldin-Meadow tested children between the ages of five and eight years with Piagetian conservation tasks, and asked them to give explanations for their judgments. In the liquid-quantity-conservation task, water in a tall glass was poured into a wide, flat dish and children were asked whether the amount of water in the glass and the amount of water in the dish were the same or different. A number of children in this age range said "different"; that is, they were non-conservers. The non-conservers could be divided into two groups on the basis of the contents of their speech and gestures in their explanations of their answers. One was the Concordant Group, in which the contents of speech and gesture match. For example, the height of the containers can be discussed "in both speech ('there is less water in the dish because the dish is short and the glass is tall') and in gesture (the child demarcated the heights of the two containers of water with his palm)" (Goldin-Meadow et al. 1993: 284). The other was the Discordant Group, in which the contents of speech and gesture did not match. For example, "one child focused on the height of the container in speech ('the dish is lower than the glass') but focused on the width of the container in gesture (the child produced a wide C hand near the dish and a narrower C near the glass)" (ibid.).[14] Church and Goldin-Meadow demonstrated, by testing the two groups again after giving them training, that the Discordant Group learned the concept of liquid-quantity conservation more readily than the Concordant Group. They concluded that gesture–speech discordance is an indication that the child's concept of conservation is in a transition phase.

In a similar study involving mathematical equivalence problems, such as $3 + 4 + 5 = 3 + \_\_$, Goldin-Meadow et al. (1993) found that children in the transition phase have a larger repertoire of 'procedures' (strategies that focus on certain aspects of a problem, such as referring to all three numbers on the left-hand side) in gesture than in speech.[15] Before solving such problems correctly, children often expressed a correct procedure only in their gestures. This suggests that gestures had privileged access to alternative construals of spatially arranged clues that led to the correct solution to the problem. In other words, an organization of clues that is not accessible to analytic thinking was discovered in spatio-motoric thinking.

I propose that how discordant utterances are produced is similar to the examples discussed in section 5, in that spatio-motoric thinking serves as an exploratory mechanism for alternative organizings of spatial information. The two cases differ in how spatial information relates to the goal of the discourse. In the explanation of a solution, potential building blocks of the explanation are spatially arranged in front of the speaker. The discourse to be produced is not mere description of the spatial arrangement. Rather it is a higher-order logical organization of the building blocks, which is a realm of analytic thinking. This difference leads to discordant gestures of a type that seems unusual from the viewpoint of adult gestures during narrative.

In the early stage of the development of certain concepts, children often produce concordant gestures in the explanation of their incorrect answers. In this type of explanation, the spatial descriptions used in the explanation are correct (e.g., "the dish is short and the glass is tall"), but how these pieces of spatial information are logically deployed is incorrect. The children at this stage presumably are content with their logic, just like adults solving the same problem; and thus there is no reason to trigger relative independence of spatio-motoric thinking from analytic thinking. In the transition phase of concept acquisition, however, meta-monitoring detects an inadequacy of the logic in analytic thinking. This triggers spatio-motoric thinking to relatively independently explore alternative organizations of the spatially arranged potential building blocks. Discovery of various alternatives does not immediately lead to concordant utterances, since higher-order analytic thinking does not necessarily succeed in finding the right logical organization of the building blocks.

Note that the Image Activation Hypothesis and the Lexical Retrieval Hypothesis do not explain why gesture–speech discordance arises during the transition phase in conceptual development.

8   The evidence that has been claimed to support the Lexical Retrieval and Image Activation hypotheses

In sections 4, 5, and 6, phenomena for which only the Information Packaging Hypothesis provides an explanation were discussed. In this section, the evidence that is said to support the Lexical Retrieval and the Image Activation Hypotheses will be examined to see whether it is compatible with the Information Packaging Hypothesis.

8.1   Evidence for the Lexical Retrieval Hypothesis

The Lexical Retrieval Hypothesis is based on a model of speaking in which a message is constructed pre-verbally, and then lemmas (morphosyntactic specifications of lexical items) are retrieved on the basis of conceptual specifications of the message, as proposed by Levelt (1989). The hypothesis states that gesturing helps the retrieval of lemmas but has nothing to do with the packaging of rich information into chunks appropriate for speaking (Krauss et al. 1996).

There are four lines of empirical support for the Lexical Retrieval Hypothesis. I maintain that they are all compatible with the Information Packaging Hypothesis. First, Rauscher et al. (1996) found that gesture frequency increases as certain restrictions are imposed on speech. The effect was localized in phrases with spatial content (i.e., phrases containing spatial propositions). Speech was restricted by requiring subjects (1) to use obscure words and (2) to avoid using words containing the letter 'c'. These manipulations not only make lexical access more difficult, but also call for an exploration of alternative construals of a rich array of information to be described. The Information Packaging Hypothesis predicts that this is precisely the situation in which more representational gestures will be evoked.

The second line of evidence for the Lexical Retrieval Hypothesis is that inhibition of gestures leads to a lower speech rate and a higher dysfluency rate only in phrases with spatial content (Rauscher et al. 1996). However, a lower speech rate and higher dysfluency may arise not only because of difficulty in accessing lemmas with spatial content. They could also arise from difficulty in organizing spatial information into chunks appropriate for speech-formulation processes.

Rauscher et al. also demonstrate that the proportion of non-juncture-filled pauses (hesitations with vocalization such as *er* that fall within a clause rather than at the boundaries of clauses) to the total number of filled pauses increases when gesture is inhibited. They maintain that non-juncture-filled pauses are related more to lexical access problems than to the problem of organizing conceptual information for speaking. Their argument leading to this assumption, however, is far from watertight. First, they argue that problems in lexical access lead to filled pauses, citing results from Schachter et al. (1991) that the filled-pause rate is correlated with a high type–token ratio for words. However, a high type–token ratio suggests that more alternatives are being considered not only in lexical selection but also in the organization of the information to be described. They also cite Boomer & Dittmann (1964), who demonstrated that the filled-pause rate increases when subjects are asked to speak without using words with a certain letter. As I noted above, this restriction causes not only lexical difficulties but also conceptual difficulties in finding alternative construals. Second, Rauscher et al. argue that non-juncture pauses are primarily due to problems in lexical access. This argument is based on the fact that when speech is rehearsed, the proportion of pauses falling at grammatical junctures increases (Butterworth 1980; Chawla & Krauss 1994). They assume that rehearsal makes only lexical access easier. This assumption is not tenable, since in rehearsal one repeats not only the process of lexical access but also the organization of conceptual information. In sum, there are no grounds for assuming that filled non-juncture pauses reflect lemma-access problems more than problems in conceptual organization.

The third line of proposed evidence involves familiarity ratings of the lexical affiliates of a representational gesture.[16] The lower the familiarity rating, the longer the asynchrony between the onset of the gesture and its lexical affiliate (Morrel-Samuels & Krauss 1992). According to Krauss et al. (1996), the Lexical Retrieval Hypothesis predicts that the onset of representational gestures "precedes inaccessible lexical affiliates by a longer interval than lexical affiliates that are highly accessible" (p. 424). The problem here is that the familiarity rating of a word could also correlate with the accessibility of a certain organization of information at the level of message generation.

A fourth line of evidence is claimed to support a theory that combines the Lexical Retrieval Hypothesis and the Image Activation Hypothesis. Morrel-Samuels & Krauss also found that the duration of a representational gesture tends to be longer when the asynchrony between the onset of the gesture and its lexical affiliate is greater. Krauss et al. (1996) suggest that this is evidence that a representational gesture "serves to maintain conceptual features in memory during lexical search." However, there is no reason to assume that the delay in speech onset is caused exclusively by lexical access. The data are also compatible with the idea that a representational gesture is lengthened until the problem in organizing information at the conceptual level is resolved.

8.2   Evidence for the Image Activation Hypothesis

Empirical support for the Image Activation Hypothesis is provided by de Ruiter (1995, 1998). De Ruiter had subjects describe a configuration of geometric figures to another person, from whom the subjects were separated by a curtain. The person behind the curtain drew the configuration on the basis of the description. De Ruiter had two independent variables. One was the stimulus presentation. In one condition, the subject described the configuration while looking at the stimuli, and in the other condition the subject described it from memory. De Ruiter hypothesized that if representational gestures help in holding an image while its content is being verbally expressed, then the frequency of representational gestures should increase for the memory condition. This is because the image that underlies a gesture is constantly reinforced by visual input in the viewing condition but not in the memory condition. He found that the frequency of representational gestures does indeed increase in the memory condition, and concluded that they help keep an image active while its content is verbally expressed.

This observation is compatible with the Information Packaging Hypothesis. De Ruiter's data show that representational gestures and viewing the stimulus at the moment of speaking share the same function at some level. I suggest that the shared function is the organization of rich information via spatio-motoric thinking. In the viewing condition, the configuration of geometric figures affords certain gaze movements (i.e., gaze gestures). The gaze shifts according to the attention-drawing features of the configuration. Neurological evidence also suggests that movement of the eyes and other body parts toward a sensory target is driven by a similar mechanism (Stein 1992). The neural substrates for both types of behaviors are in the posterior parietal cortex, where "sensory stimuli may accordingly be interpreted in the light of one's intentions and current movements to locate objects with respect to the observer" (p. 700).[17] Thus, de Ruiter's results are compatible with both the Image Activation Hypothesis and the Information Packaging Hypothesis.

9   Conclusion

The Information Packaging Hypothesis states that gesturing helps the speaker organize information in a way suitable for linguistic expression. When a person speaks and gestures, analytic thinking and spatio-motoric thinking are collaboratively organizing information. The two modes of thinking have easy access to different sets of possible informational organization; consequently, the collaboration between the two modes provides speakers with wider possibilities to organize thought in ways suitable for linguistic expression.

This hypothesis can provide an explanation for the phenomena that have been presented as evidence for the Lexical Retrieval Hypothesis and the Image Activation Hypothesis. Furthermore, the Information Packaging Hypothesis can explain phenomena for which neither the Lexical Retrieval Hypothesis nor the Image Activation Hypothesis has any explanation. Thus I maintain that the Information Packaging Hypothesis alone suffices to explain the cognitive functions of representational gestures.

It is not the case that the Information Packaging Hypothesis is more vague in its formulation and thus automatically covers all the cases supporting the Lexical Retrieval Hypothesis and the Image Activation Hypothesis.[18] The Information Packaging Hypothesis is empirically dissociable from the other two hypotheses. For example, the Information Packaging Hypothesis predicts that:

(1) the speaker is cognitively compelled to produce more representational

gestures if the spatio-motoric event to be verbally conveyed does not readily lend itself to linguistic structuring, regardless of the difficulty in retrieving relevant lexical items or in activating an image of the described event;[19]

(2) the frequency of representational gestures does not change if the difficulty in the linguistic packaging of the information to be conveyed is kept constant, and the difficulty in retrieving relevant lexical items or in activating an image of the described event is varied.

NOTES

The data presented in section 2 are from my dissertation (Kita 1993), completed at the University of Chicago. English data were made available to me by David McNeill, and a large portion of it was transcribed by Karl-Erik McCullough and Desha Baker. I would like to acknowledge David McNeill, who provided me with the research facility and intellectual support throughout my Chicago days. Many of the ideas for this chapter were developed at the Max Planck Institute. Discussions with the members of the Gesture Project at the Max Planck Institute have also been very helpful. Jan Peter de Ruiter, Adam Kendon, Asli Özyürek, Martha Alibali, David Wilkins, and David McNeill read the manuscript and gave valuable comments. Of course, all remaining errors and shortcomings are mine.

1 Interactive gestures include beats and batons.

2 Analytic thinking is similar to "the contribution of language" to thought in the process of speaking (McNeill 1992: 253–56), but differs in that it includes non-linguistic elements.

3 These linguistic units are equivalent to the structural side of a "construction" in Goldberg's (1995) sense.

4 In other words, I do not posit the concept of a "pre-verbal message" (Levelt 1989). This is tantamount to the elimination of the distinction between a lexical concept and a lemma, contrary to what Roelofs (1993) proposes.

5 Just like translation between two languages, translation between the two modes of thought is never perfect: some information drops out and new information gets added.

6 See the appendix in McNeill (1992) for the details of the stimulus.

7 A gestural movement can be decomposed into phases. The stroke phase is the part where the most force is exerted, and a post-stroke hold the hand held at the final position of the stroke (see Kendon 1972 and Kita et al. 1998 for more discussions of phases). These two phases are considered to be semantically active (Kita 1990).

8 Japanese arc gestures are counterevidence for the hypothesis that "a lexical item generates an iconic gesture through one or more of its semantic features that can be interpreted spatially" (Butterworth & Hadar 1989: 172). This position entails that a gesture always contains less information than the affiliated lexical item. However, there is no semantic feature of the words in the concurrent speech that could be the source of the arc trajectory in Japanese.

9 The representational system for analytic thinking was called the "analytic

dimension" of representation in Kita (1993, 1997). That for spatio-motoric thinking was called the "synthetic dimension" in Kita (1993) and the "affecto-imagistic dimension" in Kita (1997).

10 In addition to the two modes of thinking, discursive thinking has influence on how an utterance is constructed. Each utterance should contribute to the goal of discourse in a structured way. Discourse thinking is also active in step 1, where a scene is selected from an episode.

11 The spatio-motoric part of a message is a version of the affecto-imagistic dimension, the concept of which is developed more fully in Kita (1993, 1997), simplified for the sake of concise presentation. In the affecto-imagistic dimension, sensory, spatial, motoric, and affective information is bundled as a unit called "proto-event," which subjectively bears vivid experiential quality. A proto-event underlies expressive prosody and some lexical items such as mimetics and onomatopoeias.

12 Joint expression of an idea for the purpose of communication is also a common goal of speech and gesture.

13 The convergence between the two modes of thinking is presumably done internally in most cases because the threshold for the content match between speech and gesture is normally high enough not to allow a grossly mismatching speech–gesture complex such as a gesture without meaningful speech.

14 "C hand" refers to the handshape where all the fingers are curled and the thumb is opposed to the other four fingers, creating a C-like shape with the thumb and index finger.

15 In the case of liquid conservation, comparing the height of the two containers would be a 'procedure'.

16 The "lexical affiliate" of a gesture was determined by asking subjects who watched a video recording of gestures and speech to "underline places in their transcript where the meaning of a word or phrase was related to the meaning of the gesture" (Morrel-Samuels & Krauss 1992: 618).

17 This could be the crucial neural substrate for the production of representational gestures. According to Stein (1992), the neurons in this area get (1) sensory inputs (e.g., somaesthetic, proprioceptive, vestibular, auditory, and visual), (2) movement information of the oculomotor system, head, limb, and the locomotor system, and (3) the limbic system, which is often implicated in intention and affect. Elsewhere I argue for a similar convergence of information on the basis of a semantic analysis of a class of Japanese words called mimetics, which are almost always accompanied by a representational gesture in narrative (Kita 1997). It was argued that representational gestures are generated from a "proto-event," where sensory, motoric, and affective information are all co-present and bundled as a unit.

18 An example of a vagueness relationship between hypotheses would be the following. Hypothesis X, 'representational gestures help speaking', is more vague than hypothesis Y, 'representational gestures help lexical retrieval in the course of speaking'. Any supporting evidence for hypothesis Y would automatically support hypothesis X.

19 Note that this prediction is independent of the issues of being communicatively compelled to gesture when the speech is failing, namely, the issues of the speaker deciding (consciously or subconsciously), "I cannot express what I want to

convey to the interlocutor in the speech, so I will use gesture to convey it.".A way to retain the cognitive compulsion while at least partially suppressing the communicative compulsion may be to have a visual barrier between the speaker and the interlocutor (see, for example, de Ruiter 1998).

The prediction is also independent of the issues of the extent to which gesturing in fact leads to better performance in speaking. The quality of spatiomotoric thinking comes into play as an additional factor here. It is possible that there are some gestures that help organize your thought better than others. The tendency of "less elaborate and poorly-formed gestures [to go] with muddled and dysfluent speech and more elaborate gestures with better-formed speech" (David McNeill, pers. com.; see also Duncan 1997) is not contradictory to the Information Packaging Hypothesis.

I would like to thank David McNeill for pointing out these two related issues.

REFERENCES

Aske, J., Beery, N., Michaelis, L. & Filip, H. (eds.) 1987. *Proceedings of the 13th Annual Meeting of the Berkeley Linguistics Society*. Berkeley, CA: Berkeley Linguistics Society.

Bavelas, J. B., Chovil, N., Lawrie, D. A. & Wade, A. 1992. Interactive gestures. *Discourse Processes* 15: 469–489.

Biemans, M. & Woutersen, M. (eds.) 1995. *Proceedings of the Center for Language Studies Opening Academic Year '95–96*. Nijmegen: Center for Language Studies.

Boomer, D. S. & Dittmann, A. T. 1964. Speech rate, filled pauses and body movement in interviews. *Journal of Nervous and Mental Diseases* 139: 324–327.

Butterworth, B. 1980. Evidence from pauses in speech. In Butterworth (ed.), pp. 155–176.

Butterworth, B. (ed.) 1980. *Language Production*, vol. I. New York: Academic Press.

Butterworth, Brian & Hadar, Uri, 1989. Gesture, speech, and computational stages: a reply to McNeill. *Psychological Review* 96: 168–174.

Chawla, P. & Krauss, R. M. 1994. Gesture and speech in spontaneous and rehearsed narratives. *Journal of Experimental Social Psychology* 30: 580–601.

Church, R. B. & Goldin-Meadow, S. 1986. The mismatch between gesture and speech as an index of transitional knowledge. *Cognition* 23: 43–71.

de Ruiter, J. P. 1995. Why do people gesture at the telephone? In Biemans & Woutersen (eds.), pp. 49–56.

de Ruiter, J. P. 1998. Gesture and speech production. Unpublished dissertation, University of Nijmegen.

Duncan, S. 1997. An alternative view to gestures as a communicative resource. Paper presented at the 'Embodied Cognition' symposium at the Annual Meeting of the National Communication Association, Chicago, November.

Freedman, N. 1977. Hands, words, and mind: on the structuralization of body movements during discourse and the capacity for verbal representation. In Freedman & Grand (eds.), pp. 109–132.

Freedman, N. & Grand, S. (eds.) 1977. *Communicative Structures and Psychic Structures: A Psychoanalytic Interpretation of Communication*. New York: Plenum.

Gibson, J. J. 1986. *The Ecological Approach to Visual Perception*. Hillsdale, NJ: Erlbaum.

Goldberg, A. E. 1995. *Construction Grammar*. Chicago: University of Chicago Press.

Goldin-Meadow, S., Alibali, M. W. & Church, R. B. 1993. Transitions in concept acquisition: using the hand to read the mind. *Psychological Review* 100: 279–297.

Graham, J. A. & Heywood, S. 1975. The effects of elimination of hand gestures and of verbal codability on speech performance. *European Journal of Social Psychology* 5: 189–195.

Hadar, U. & Butterworth, B. 1993. Iconic gesture, imagery and word retrieval in speech. Unpublished manuscript, Tel Aviv University.

Kendon, A. 1972. Some relationships between body motion and speech: an analysis of an example. In Siegman & Pope (eds.), pp. 177–210.

Kita, S. 1990. The temporal relationship between gesture and speech: a study of Japanese–English bilinguals. Unpublished master's thesis, Department of Psychology, University of Chicago.

Kita, S. 1993. Language and thought interface: a study of spontaneous gestures and Japanese mimetics. Unpublished Ph.D. dissertation, University of Chicago.

Kita, S. 1997. Two dimensional semantic analysis of Japanese mimetics. *Linguistics* 35: 379–415.

Kita, S., van Gijn, I. & van der Hulst, H. 1998. Movement phases in signs and co-speech gestures, and their transcription by human coders. In Wachsmuth & Fröhlich (eds.), pp. 23–35.

Krauss, R. M., Chen, Y. & Chawla, P. 1996. Nonverbal behavior and nonverbal communication: what do conversational hand gestures tell us? In Zanna (ed.), pp. 389–450.

Levelt, W. J. M. 1989. *Speaking*. Cambridge, MA: MIT Press.

Levelt, W. J. M. (ed.) 1993. *Lexical Access in Speech Production*. Oxford: Blackwell.

McNeill, D. 1992. *Hand and Mind: What Gestures Reveal about Thought*. Chicago: University of Chicago Press.

McNeill, D. 1997. Growth points cross-linguistically. In Nuyts & Pederson (eds.), pp. 190–212.

Morrel-Samuels, P. & Krauss, R. M. 1992. Word familiarity predicts temporal asynchrony of hand gestures and speech. *Journal of Experimental Psychology: Learning, Memory, and Cognition* 18: 615–622.

Müller, C. 1996. Gestik in Kommunikation und Interaktion: eine Studie zu Formen und Funktionen des Gestikulierens in interkulturellen Gesprächen. Unpublished Ph.D. dissertation, Free University, Berlin.

Nuyts, J. & Pederson, E. (eds.) 1997. *Language and Conceptualization*. Cambridge: Cambridge University Press.

Rauscher, F. H., Krauss, R. M. & Chen, Y. 1996. Gesture, speech, and lexical access: the role of lexical movements in speech production. *Psychological Science* 7: 226–230.

Rimé, B. 1983. The elimination of visible behaviour from social interactions: effects on verbal, nonverbal and interpersonal variables. *European Journal of Social Psychology* 12: 113–129.

Rimé, B., Schiaratura, L., Hupet, M. & Ghysselinckx, A. 1984. An effect of relative immobilization on the speaker's nonverbal behavior and on the dialogue imagery level. *Motivation and Emotion* 8: 311–325.

Roelofs, A. 1993. A spreading-activation theory of lemma retrieval in speaking. In Levelt (ed.), pp. 107–143.

Schachter, S., Christenfeld, N., Ravina, B. & Bilous, F. 1991. Speech disfluency and the structure of knowledge. *Journal of Personality and Social Psychology* 60: 362–367.

Schank, R. C. & Abelson, R. P. 1977. *Scripts, Plans, Goals, and Understanding*. Hillsdale, NJ: Erlbaum.

Siegman, A. & Pope, B. (eds.) 1972. *Studies in Dyadic Communication*. Elmsford, NY: Pergamon.

Slobin, D. 1987. Thinking for speaking. In Aske, Beery, Michaelis & Filip (eds.), pp. 435–445.

Stein, J. F. 1992. The representation of egocentric space in the posterior parietal cortex. *Behavioral and Brain Sciences* 15: 691–700.

Streeck, Jürgen, 1996. How to do things with things: objets trouvés and symbolization. *Human Studies* 19: 365–384.

Wachsmuth, I. & Fröhlich, M. (eds.) 1998. *Gesture and Sign Language in Human–Computer Interaction: International Gesture Workshop, Bielefeld, Germany, September 17–19, 1997, Proceedings*. Lecture Notes in Artificial Intelligence, vol. 1371. Berlin: Springer-Verlag.

Zanna, M. (ed.) 1996. *Advances in Experimental Social Psychology*, vol. XXVIII. Tampa, FL: Academic Press.

9 Where do *most* spontaneous representational gestures actually occur with respect to speech?

Shuichi Nobe

Department of English, Aoyama Gakuin University, Tokyo

1 Introduction

Speech-accompanying spontaneous gestures have attracted the attention of psycholinguists and cognitive psychologists in recent years. Theorists assert that spontaneous gestures, along with the speech they accompany, are a window into the nature of speakers' mental representations and processes (Goldin-Meadow et al. 1993; Kendon 1986; McNeill 1985, 1987, 1992). Researchers have shown that speech-accompanying gestures are inextricably intertwined temporally and semantically with speech (Kendon 1980; McNeill 1992). Various models of production of speech and representational gestures (i.e., iconics, metaphorics, and abstract deictics) have been presented (Beattie & Aboudan 1994; Butterworth & Hadar 1989; Kita 1993; Krauss et al. 1996; McNeill 1989, 1992; Nobe 1993, 1996).[1]

There have recently been debates on the credibility of each model (see Hadar & Butterworth 1997; Hadar & Yadlin-Gedassy 1994; Hadar et al. 1998; and other chapters in this book). Unfortunately, the current chapter does not have any space (and thus it is not the writer's intention) to evaluate all models mentioned above. It is, however, a fact that many agree that the temporal relationship of representational gestures and speech is very significant in constructing gesture- and speech-production models. Moreover, the 'tendency' of gestures to occur with respect to their accompanied speech does matter. This chapter reports on how the timing between gestures and speech is measured, and how this gesture tendency is calculated and presented as evidence for the construction of speech and gesture models.

Comprehensive models of speech and gesture should account for as many gestures as possible. If the number of gestures which are accounted for by a model is rather small, we should not regard it as a general theory (Nobe 1996). In particular, this chapter reports that the timing and the tendency to produce gestures may not be well represented in some contributions to the literature, owing to their adopting a measurement involving 'ratios'. I do not intend to claim that this unit is useless; I agree that it is useful in some cases. However, the ratio measure may sometimes ignore a substantial number of gestures.

Ratios were used to support an inference by Beattie & Aboudan (1994) that the potentially different social contexts of experiments might cause us to observe different databases. Although differing social contexts may influence the production of gestures, using this type of measurement alone may have the effect of not explaining many observed gestures. I would like to point out that if researchers try to construct comprehensive theories which explain as many gestures as possible, they should be aware of the fact that such measurements and presentations involving ratios may fail to achieve this important goal. The following sections will discuss these issues in detail.

2   Baseline problems

Our concern is to examine the precise temporal relationship between gestures and speech. For this relationship is "fundamental to the theoretical claims made about the relationship between speech and gesture" (Beattie & Aboudan 1994: 243). Beattie & Aboudan stated:

what is especially interesting is that the people who use gestures to argue for these different types of models disagree on almost everything about the relationship between gestures and speech. McNeill (1985), for example, argued that the majority of gestures occurred during the speaker's actual speech articulation, whereas Butterworth and Hadar (1989), employing a very different model of language production, asserted that certain kinds of gestures (namely iconics) tend to have their onset in pauses in fluent phases of speech, and hence preceded the onset of related speech material. Both sets of researchers seem to imply that gestures are verbal, but they disagree on something as fundamental as where gestures actually occur with respect to speech. (P. 242)

There are at least two reasons to be cautious in accepting Beattie & Aboudan's interpretation of the temporal relationship between speech and gesture reported above. First, Butterworth and his colleagues (Butterworth & Beattie 1978; Butterworth & Hadar 1989) and McNeill (1985, 1992) have discussed different phases of gestures.[2] The former discussed the onset of gestures, but the latter emphasized the stroke and the pre/post-stroke hold. McNeill wrote:

The decisive component of the gesture . . . is the stroke phase. If the stroke coincided with speech, the gesture was counted as coinciding with speech even if there was silence during the preparation or retraction phases; conversely, if the stroke coincided with silence, the gesture was counted as coinciding with silence even if there was speech during the preparation or retraction phases. With beats (which have only two phases), the entire gesture had to coincide with speech to be counted as occurring during speech . . . 90% of all strokes occurred during the actual articulation of speech. (1992: 92)

In spite of this evident difference of criterion, the interpretation by Beattie & Aboudan (1994) was that those two parties reported contradictory phenomena.

Second, the frequency of representational gestures was measured in Butterworth & Beattie (1978) and Beattie & Aboudan (1994) in a particular way that could influence the apparent speech–gesture timing relationship. Butterworth & Beattie (1978) analyzed randomly selected speech data from monologues and from academic interactions. Alternating patterns of relatively hesitant phases (with high pause/speech ratios) and relatively fluent phases (with low pause/speech ratios) were identified in their corpus. They found that representational gestures tended to have their onsets during the silent pauses in fluent phases, and hence preceded the onset of the related speech material. The rates of representational gesture production (per unit time: 1,000 sec.) during silent pauses and phonations in hesitant and fluent phases were measured, with the result that the gesture rate during silent pauses in hesitant phases was 59.2; during phonations in hesitant phases, 44.3; during silent pauses in fluent phases, 280.1; during phonations in fluent phases, 106.9.

However, this type of data presentation might be misleading. McNeill has pointed out that

their way of presenting data is not directly comparable to [this result, that is, 90% of all strokes during the actual articulation of speech and only 1% to 2% during filled and unfilled pauses] . . . which shows the percentage of gestures made during speech and hesitation, not rates per unit of time. To normalize during hesitations and speech to get equal baselines of time might be useful for some purposes but it gives a grossly distorted picture of the actual distribution of gestures during narrations since speech is, by far, more copious than hesitation. (1992: 92)

Beattie & Aboudan (1994) addressed this concern by making use of "per unit unfilled (silent) pause" and "per unit word" baselines instead of that of "per unit time." They asserted:

it was necessary to compute the ratio of the number of gestures per unit unfilled pause and number of gestures per unit word in order to determine if gestures were more common during unfilled pauses than during actual articulation . . . When this was done it became immediately apparent that gestures originated more frequently in pauses than during actual articulation. (P. 261)

Note that the very logic held by McNeill above applies to this switching of baselines into 'per unit silent pause' and 'per unit word'. Beattie & Aboudan reasoned that these baselines were needed "because speakers spend a greater portion of time articulating than they do in silence" (1994: 261). However, the assumption that one word is equivalent to one silent pause – rather than one phrase, one clause, etc. – has not been justified

(McNeill, pers. com.). Moreover, it is no wonder that they observed the gesture rate per silent pause to be higher than the gesture rate per word. It will be pointed out later that this difference is ensured by the very switching of these baselines. Because these gesture rates have two different denominators (i.e., the number of silent pauses and number of words), which have inherently skewed distributions, as suggested by Beattie & Aboudan (1994: 254–55), the word-to-pause comparison may give a distorted picture of the frequency of gestures.

I have made the following points thus far: first, it might be misleading to conclude, at least right now, that Butterworth & Hadar (1989) and McNeill (1992) contradict each other, as Beattie & Aboudan (1994) suggest, about where representational gestures actually occur with respect to speech, because they are discussing different phases of representational gestures. Second, the rates of representational gestures 'per unit time', 'per unit unfilled pause', and 'per unit word' might be misleading, especially when the actual frequency of representational gestures is being discussed. I believe, as emphasized in Nobe (1996), that one of the most important criteria for a model of gesture production is the number of gestures it can account for. Beattie & Aboudan's form of data presentation, involving the switching of baselines, may fail to explain many gestures.

In spite of these problems, the presentation of Butterworth & Beattie's (1978) database has prevailed for years without scrutiny by the gesture-research community. For example, Morrel-Samuels & Krauss (1992) wrote that "Butterworth and Beattie (1978) claimed that speech-related gestures are initiated during such production pauses [as speakers seek unusual and unfamiliar words in memory]" (p. 617), and Feyereisen & de Lannoy (1991) that "Butterworth and Beattie (1978) proposed . . . [that] . . . Representational gestures were more often observed during hesitations, especially in the execution phase" (pp. 82–83).[3] These researchers try to construct their models based upon this report of the temporal relationship between gestures and speech. The measurement and presentation of ratios thus directly influence the report and do matter. I will point out that such measurement fails to capture many observed gestures.

Recently, Beattie & Aboudan (1994) have suggested that the difference between McNeill's and their results come from the influence of the social contexts in which the two kinds of samples were collected. They compared all types of gestures, including representational gestures and beats, which subjects produced in narrating a cartoon under three different conditions. The first was a 'non-social condition' in which "speakers were left alone in a room and asked to tell the story in a situation without any audience being present." Second was a 'social/monologue condition' in which "an interviewer was present in the room listening to the subject without any

interruptions or any verbal exchange." In other words, this was a monologue in the presence of an audience. Last was a 'social/dialogue condition' in which "an interviewer was present in the room and interacted
verbally with the subject, asking questions, seeking clarification, and generally using interruption to achieve these ends."

It was reported first that the onsets of gestures were significantly more
frequent in silent pauses in the social/dialogue condition than in either the
non-social condition or the social/monologue condition, when the overall
number of silent pauses was taken into account. Second, gestures were significantly more common in the social/dialogue condition than in either the
social/monologue or the non-social conditions. Last, only in the social/dia-
logue condition were there significantly more gestures originating in silent
pauses than during actual phonation, when the overall amounts of pausing
and phonation were taken into account. Note that in all these conditions
the ratios of gestures were measured per unit silent pause and per unit
word. Beattie & Aboudan concluded that there was a dramatic effect of
social context both for the onset of gestures and the frequency of gestures,
and claimed that the speaker produced gestures as "attempt-suppressing
signals" (Duncan 1972; Duncan & Fiske 1977) to maintain the turn.[4] It was
implied that the data collected by McNeill were not from a social/dialogue
condition, in which case, they concluded, it is no wonder that the data
reported by McNeill and by Butterworth and his colleagues represented
different tendencies.[5] Beattie & Aboudan remarked:

> It would be nice to learn something about the interaction dynamics of Anansi folk-
> tales, or mathematicians discussing their work, or college students describing
> Tweety Bird and Sylvester the Cat cartoons, because these dynamics are extremely
> likely to exert a very profound impact on the nature of any data on gesture collected.
> (1994: 260–61)

Note that the attempt-suppression-signal theory was advocated to explain
gestures whose onsets originate during silent pauses. As Beattie & Aboudan
stated:

> gestures originated more frequently in pauses than during actual articulation . . . but
> . . . this difference only reached significance in the case of the social/dialogue condi-
> tion . . . This, of course, makes perfect sense because only in that condition would
> certain critical interpersonal functions accrue to gesture – namely, the maintenance
> of the turn for the current speaker, the gesture acting as an attempt-suppression
> signal. (1994: 261)

I have no intention of claiming here that there are no attempt-suppression
functions with representational gestures. However, I will raise the question
of whether most representational gestures can be explained by the attempt-
suppressing theory alone.

3   The current study

In the current study, part of the cartoon narration database collected by McNeill is reanalyzed to verify the following two points. One is the timing relationships between the onset of representational gestures and the accompanying speech, not only focusing on the frequencies of these gestures, but also using the 'per unit silent pause' and 'per unit word' baselines, although these baselines are problematic, as pointed out above. Then it is pointed out that the attempt-suppressing function alone does not account for many representational gestures. This discussion will lead, in particular, to a reinterpretation of one of the Beattie & Aboudan results, that only in the social/dialogue condition were there significantly more gestures originating in silent pauses than during actual phonations, when the overall amounts of pausing and phonations were taken into account.

3.1   Method

3.1.1   Participants. This experiment involved six subjects (five females, one male). They were native speakers of English and University of Chicago graduate students.

3.1.2   Materials and procedures. Each speaker was shown a stimulus, an animated color cartoon of the Sylvester and Tweety Bird series, consisting of twelve episodes.[6] All episodes have basically the same theme, i.e., Sylvester tries to capture Tweety but is thwarted by Tweety or Granny, but with considerable surface variation of details. After watching the cartoon, the speaker immediately recounted the story from memory to a listener who did not have prior knowledge of the stimulus and did not see it. The speaker was told to present the story in as clear and complete a fashion as possible, for the listener would have to retell it later to a third person. The narrations were videotaped, but neither the speaker nor the listener knew that gestures were of interest, and the instructions did not mention them (see McNeill 1992).

In the social/dialogue condition, as described by Beattie & Aboudan (1994), an interviewer was present in the room and interacted with the subject verbally, asking questions, seeking clarification, and generally using interruption to achieve these goals. Following this definition, it is logical to call the current situation of narrating a cartoon also the social/dialogue condition. In the current study, as evidenced in the recorded sessions, the listeners nodded and produced many back-channel signals and asked questions when needed. It was certainly not the social/monologue condition, in which the interviewer was present in the room listening to the subject without any interruption or any verbal exchange.

Table 9.1. *Where gestures start*

	Pauses	Articulation	Total
The social/dialogue condition in Beattie & Aboudan (1994): all gestures included	50	124	174
The current study: representational gestures alone	38	121	159

The difference from the Beattie & Aboudan social/dialogue condition, however, was that they had the interviewer intentionally interrupt the speaker's narration. This could lead to either more or more severe than usual interruptions in their social/dialogue condition, and this factor might impact the results significantly. One possibility is that speakers might feel that their turns were severely threatened, and they might then produce more gestures, according to the attempt-suppression-signal theory. In our current study the listeners were not given any instructions about how to interact with their speakers in any specific ways.

Analyses of speech, speech/silent-pause timing, and gestures were conducted following Beattie & Aboudan (1994).[7] However, only representational gestures were counted in the current study. The gestures and the verbal narrations which the subjects produced, beginning with the first scene of the stimulus and ending with the scene "Sylvester's rolling down into the bowling alley" (the first three episodes depicted in the stimulus), were analyzed.

3.2   Results and discussion

Table 9.1 gives an overview of the results and compares them with those of Beattie & Aboudan (1994). It presents the temporal relationship between representational gesture onsets and their accompanying speech and pauses. Out of 159 representational gestures in the corpus, 38 had their onset during silent pauses (23.9%). The proportion in Beattie & Aboudan (1994) was similar: out of 174 gestures (including beats and others) in the social/dialogue condition, 50 had onsets during silent pauses (28.7%). Although the number of non-representational gestures was not reported in Beattie & Aboudan, the number of representational gesture onsets which started during silent pauses alone must have been fewer than 50. However, because their onsets do not start during silent pauses, the 124 gestures whose onsets started during articulation in the Beattie & Aboudan social/dialogue condition in Table 9.1, and the 121 representational gestures in the current corpus in Table 9.1, cannot be explained by the attempt-

Table 9.2. *Frequency of silent pauses and number of words in the social/dialogue condition in Beattie & Aboudan (1994)*

Subject	Silent pauses	Words
1	128	689
2	96	515
3	105	791
4	103	637
5	118	625
6	72	396
mean	103.7	608.8

Table 9.3. *Frequency of silent pauses and number of words in the current study*

Subject	Silent pauses	Words
SV	22	262
SL	26	164
SJ	17	253
SC	17	209
SD	16	122
SS	34	177
mean	22.0	197.8

suppression-signal theory alone. Most representational gestures (more than 70%) were initiated during speech.

Tables 9.2 and 9.3 show the frequency of silent pauses and the frequency of words in Beattie & Aboudan (1994) and in the current study. The 'per unit silent pause' and 'per unit word' baselines were applied to these tables, and Tables 9.4 and 9.5 show the frequency of gestures originating in silent pauses and during articulation per unit pause and per unit word, respectively.

Similar tendencies were revealed in the current study and in Beattie & Aboudan (1994). In both studies, the rate of representational gestures whose onset occurred during silent pauses was higher than those whose

Table 9.4. *Number of gestures originating in silent pauses and during articulation per unit pause and per unit word, respectively, in the social/dialogue condition in Beattie & Aboudan (1994)*

Subject	Gestures per pause	Gestures per word
1	0.14844	0.06096
2	0.00000	0.00971
3	0.02857	0.00379
4	0.15534	0.06750
5	0.03390	0.02080
6	0.11111	0.04545
mean	0.08038	0.03394

Table 9.5. *Number of gestures originating in silent pauses and during articulation per unit pause and per unit word, respectively, in the current study*

Subject	Representational gestures per pause	Representational gestures per word
SV	0.045	0.069
SL	0.420	0.128
SJ	0.352	0.106
SC	0.294	0.110
SD	0.438	0.172
SS	0.234	0.062
mean	0.297	0.108

onset was during articulation (Tables 9.4 and 9.5). This difference was significant (Wilcoxon Test, $p < .05$, 1-tailed).

Some readers may notice that this similarity of results supports the inference that McNeill's database of cartoon narrations was in fact recorded in a social/dialogue condition. If Beattie & Aboudan's implication that this database had been monologic was correct, the rate of gestures originating in silent pauses should not have been significantly higher than those originating during actual articulation. However, that the rate was significantly higher suggests that their implication might be problematic.

Although similar tendencies were revealed in the current and Beattie &

Table 9.6. *The mean rate of silent pauses/number of words in Beattie &*
Aboudan (1994) and in the current study

Condition	Social/dialogue in Beattie & Aboudan (1994)	The current study
mean	0.1728	0.1188

Aboudan (1994) studies, this does not support the widespread claim that gestures originate more frequently in pauses than during actual articulation. Their form of data presentation, involving the switching of baselines, failed to explain many representational gestures (see Table 9.1). The seeming statistical preponderance of onsets in pauses is probably an artifact arising from switching baselines, as argued earlier.

The ratio of gestures originating in silent pauses to those originating during actual articulation was about one to three in Table 9.1. Table 9.6 shows the mean rates of silent pauses/number of words in two conditions: the social/dialogue condition (in Beattie & Aboudan 1994) and the current study. Skewed distributions appeared: these rates correspond to a frequency of silent pauses to number of words of about one to six in the social/dialogue condition, and of about one to eight (i.e., 8.4 words were produced per silent pause) in the current study. When the gesture rate is calculated in these circumstances, it is no wonder that the gesture rate per word looks smaller than the gesture rate per silent pause in Tables 9.4 and 9.5. This form of data presentation (i.e., a comparison of the rate of the number of gestures per unit silent pause and number of gestures per unit word) produces a distorted image of the production of representational gestures that leaves many gestures unexplained.

4   Concluding remarks

The current data analyses reveal that the onsets of most spontaneous representational gestures did not start during silent pauses in the current database. Rather, their onsets occurred during speech articulation. I have shown that this conclusion is consistent with the seemingly contradictory claim made by Beattie & Aboudan (1994). Switching baselines (per unit silent pause and per unit word) gives a distorted picture of the actual distribution of representational gestures. The prevailing misconception that most representational gestures start during silent pauses in fluent phases is therefore disproved. The conclusion is drawn that models based on this misconception (including the attempt-suppression-signal model) explain only a small number of gestures in our and, apparently, in Beattie & Aboudan's database.

I am not claiming that attempt-suppression signals do not occur with representational gestures. Some such uses of gestures may occur, and all representational gestures may have such a function inevitably.[8] An alternative model (i.e., a network/threshold model) of the production of representational gestures was presented in Nobe (1996). It accommodates the attempt-suppression functions, too. Although the details of the model needs further discussion, it accounts for much more representational gesture than other models based on the misconception I discussed above.

NOTES

I would like to thank David McNeill and Karl-Erik McCullough at the University of Chicago for allowing me to use their database for this chapter. I am grateful to David McNeill for very helpful comments on drafts of the chapter.

1 According to McNeill (1992), iconics, which display, in their form and manner of execution, concrete aspects of the same information that speech is also presenting; metaphorics, which display, in the form and manner of execution, abstract concepts and relationships; deictics, which (abstractly) point to a location in gesture space that stands for an abstract concept or relationship.

2 A gesture (or a gesture phrase) is divided into one or more movement phases, i.e., preparation, holds, stroke, and retraction (Kendon 1980; Kita 1990, 1993; McNeill 1985, 1992). The following definitions come from McNeill (1992: 83). The preparation phase is a period where the limb moves away from its rest position to a position in gesture space where the gesture stroke starts. A hold is any temporal cessation of movement, and the pre-stroke hold is a limb hold at the position and hand posture reached at the end of the preparation itself. The stroke is the peak of effort in a gesture. The meaning of the gesture is expressed in this phase. The post-stroke hold is the final position and posture of the hand reached at the end of the stroke. The retraction is the return of the hand to a rest position. By definition, a gesture does not exist without a stroke; the other phases are optional.

3 On the contrary, Nobe (1996) found that the onsets of most representational gestures started during speech phonations in fluent (execution) phases in the database he analyzed.

4 An attempt-suppressing signal displayed by the speaker maintains the turn for him, regardless of the number of yielding cues concurrently being displayed. Auditors almost never attempted to take their turn when this signal was being displayed. The attempt-suppressing signal consists of one or both of the speaker's hands being engaged in gesticulation (Duncan 1972: 287).

5 Note, however, that the database collected by Butterworth & Beattie (1978) includes gestures observed in monologues, which cannot be explained by the attempt-suppressing-signal theory.

6 The data for this experiment were collected by David McNeill and his graduate students. Much of the data transcription was conducted by Karl-Erik McCullough with the assistance of Desha Baker.

7 One exception is the definition of silent pauses. Silent pauses were defined as perceptible gaps in the speech (with an 85.4% interobserver reliability) in Beattie & Aboudan (1994), but they are defined as any non-phonation periods longer than 0.2 seconds (Henderson et al. 1966) in the current study. I do not believe that this difference caused a significant problem in comparing the result reported by Beattie & Aboudan (1994) with my own. An investigation revealed that 90% of the silent pauses measured by machine in the current database were the perceptible gaps identified by two native speakers of English.

8 DeVito (1995: 28) wrote that "in general, communication in an interactional situation is inevitable, because you are always behaving; but the behavior must be perceived in some way by some other person for this behavior to be considered communication."

REFERENCES

Beattie, G. & Aboudan, R. 1994. Gestures, pauses and speech: an experimental investigation of the effects of changing social context on their precise temporal relationships. *Semiotica* 99: 239–272.
Butterworth, B. & Beattie, G. 1978. Gesture and silence as indicators of planning in speech. In Campbell & Smith (eds.), pp. 347–360.
Butterworth, B. & Hadar, U. 1989. Gesture, speech, and computational stages: a reply to McNeill. *Psychological Review* 96: 168–174.
Campbell, R. N. & Smith, P. T. (eds.) 1978. *Recent Advances in the Psychology of Language: Formal and Experimental Approaches*. New York: Plenum.
DeVito, J. 1995. *The Interpersonal Communication Book*. 7th ed. New York: HarperCollins.
Duncan, S. 1972. Some signals and rules for taking speaking turns in conversation. *Journal of Personality and Social Psychology* 23: 283–292.
Duncan, S. & Fiske, D. W. 1977. *Face-to-Face Interaction: Research, Methods and Theory*. Hillsdale, NJ: Erlbaum.
Feyereisen, P. & de Lannoy, J.-D. 1991. *Gestures and Speech: Psychological Investigations*. Cambridge: Cambridge University Press.
Goldin-Meadow, S., Alibali, M. W. & Church, R. B. 1993. Transitions in concept acquisition: using the hand to reach the mind. *Psychological Review* 100: 279–297.
Hadar, U. 1989. Two types of gesture and their role in speech production. *Journal of Language and Social Psychology* 8: 221–228.
Hadar, U., Burstein, A., Krauss, R. & Soroker, N. 1998. Ideational gestures and speech in brain-damaged subjects. *Language and Cognitive Processes* 13: 59–76.
Hadar, U. & Butterworth, B. 1997. Iconic gestures, imagery, and word search retrieval in speech. *Semiotica* 115: 147–172.
Hadar, U. & Yadlin-Gedassy, S. 1994. Conceptual and lexical aspects of gesture: evidence from aphasia. *Journal of Neurolinguistics* 8: 57–65.
Henderson, A., Goldman-Eisler, F. & Skarbek, A. 1966. Sequential temporal patterns in spontaneous speech. *Language and Speech* 9: 207–216.
Kendon, A. 1980. Gesticulation and speech: two aspects of the process of utterance. In Key (ed.), pp. 207–227.

198   *Shuichi Nobe*

Kendon, A. 1986. Some reasons for studying gesture. *Semiotica* 62: 3–28.
Key, M. R. (ed.) 1980. *The Relationship of Verbal and Nonverbal Communication*. The Hague: Mouton.
Kita, S. 1990. The temporal relationship between gesture and speech: a study of Japanese–English bilinguals. Unpublished master's thesis, Department of Psychology, University of Chicago.
Kita, S. 1993. Language and thought interface: a study of spontaneous gestures and Japanese mimetics. Unpublished Ph.D. dissertation, University of Chicago.
Krauss, R. M., Chen, Y. & Chawla, P. 1996. Nonverbal behavior and nonverbal communication: what do conversational hand gestures tell us? In Zanna (ed.), pp. 389–450.
McNeill, D. 1985. So you think gestures are nonverbal? *Psychological Review* 92: 350–371.
McNeill, D. 1987. *Psycholinguistics: A New Approach*. New York: Harper & Row.
McNeill, D. 1989. A straight path – to where? Reply to Butterworth and Hadar. *Psychological Review* 96: 175–179.
McNeill, D. 1992. *Hand and Mind: What Gestures Reveal about Thought*. Chicago: University of Chicago Press.
Morrel-Samuels, P. & Krauss, R. M. 1992. Word familiarity predicts temporal asynchrony of hand gestures and speech. *Journal of Experimental Psychology: Learning, Memory, and Cognition* 18: 615–622.
Nobe, S. 1993. Cognitive processes of speaking and gesturing: a comparison between first language speakers and foreign language speakers. Unpublished master's thesis, Department of Psychology, University of Chicago.
Nobe, S. 1996. Representational gestures, cognitive rhythms, and acoustic aspects of speech: a network/threshold model of gesture production. Unpublished Ph.D. dissertation, University of Chicago.
Zanna, M. (ed.) 1996. *Advances in Experimental Social Psychology*, vol. XXVIII. Tampa, FL: Academic Press.

10 Gesture production during stuttered speech: insights into the nature of gesture–speech integration

Rachel I. Mayberry
School of Communication Sciences & Disorders, McGill University

Joselynne Jaques
School of Communication Sciences & Disorders, McGill University

1   Introduction

Some of our clearest insights into how the mind constructs language come from the investigation of challenges to the sensory, motor, and/or neural mechanisms of the human brain. The study of stroke and diseases of the central nervous system has led to enormous, but still incomplete, knowledge about the neural architecture of human language. Investigation of the sign languages that spontaneously arise among individuals who are deaf has revolutionized psycholinguistic theory by demonstrating that human language capacity transcends sensory and motor modality. The studies we describe here follow in this long research tradition.

We have been investigating the gesture–speech relationship in individuals with chronic stuttering in order to gain insights into the nature of the relationship between the two in spontaneous expression. Stuttering, the involuntary and excessive repetition of syllables, sounds, and sound prolongations while speaking, is highly disruptive to the production of speech. This provides us with an opportunity to observe what happens to the temporal patterning of gesture against the backdrop of a fractionated speech stream. Our studies have garnered striking evidence that gesture production is, and moreover must be, integrated with speech production at a deep, neuromotor planning level prior to message execution. The expressive harmony of gesture patterning relative to speech patterning is so tightly maintained throughout the frequent and often lengthy speech disruptions caused by stuttering that it suggests a *principle of co-expression* governing gesture–speech execution (Mayberry, Jaques & Shenker 1999). Before describing the research that led us to these conclusions, we briefly discuss

199

some current hypotheses as to how gesture and speech are related to one another in extemporaneous expression.

2   The gesture–speech relationship

Exactly how gesture and speech are related to one another during the act of spontaneous expression is not fully understood, and there are competing hypotheses as to what the nature of this relationship is, or indeed, if there is a relationship beyond coincident production. One hypothesis holds that gesture and speech are autonomous and separate communication systems (Butterworth & Beattie 1978; Butterworth & Hadar 1989; Feyereisen & deLannoy 1991). In this hypothesis, which we call the 'independent systems' framework, gesture functions as a backup or auxiliary system for the temporary absence or failure of speech, such as in coughing, having a mouth full of food, or being unable to put words to thoughts. The hypothesis requires speech to fail in order for gesture to appear in the speech stream. Note that this hypothesis implies that there are links of a feedback nature between speech production and gesture such that when speech fails or is about to fail, gesture begins. With respect to stuttering, the independent-systems hypothesis predicts that stuttered speech will be accompanied by *more* gestures than will fluent speech. This would be due to the frequent failure of speech production during stuttered speech and relative lack of failure during normally fluent speech. This is because gesture is hypothesized as compensating for speech breakdown.

A related hypothesis (Goldin-Meadow, McNeill & Singleton 1996) proposes that gesture serves a compensatory role for speech, as exemplified by the home sign gestures of deaf children and the related phenomenon of sign languages. This proposal, unlike the independent-systems hypothesis, focuses on the compensating role gesture plays in the complete absence of speech, as in profound deafness. This is clearly not the case in stuttering, however, where speech remains the primary mode of expression. Nonetheless, stuttered speech can severely restrict spoken expression and sometimes halt speech for very long intervals. The question we address in our studies is whether gesture compensates for speech when speech is present but its expression is difficult.

An alternative hypothesis is that gesture and speech together form an integrated communication system for the single purpose of linguistic expression (Kendon 1980; McNeill 1985, 1992). In what we call the 'integrated system' framework, gesture is linked to the structure, meaning, and timing of spoken language. Thus, speech and gesture would always be co-expressed. With respect to stuttering, the integrated-system hypothesis predicts that stuttered speech will be accompanied by fewer gestures than fluent speech, so long as the stuttered speech results in appreciably less spoken language content.

Investigating the nature of the gesture–speech relationship in terms of the production timing of gesture and speech in fluent speakers has led to findings that have been interpreted as supporting both the independent-systems hypothesis and the integrated-system hypothesis. For example, Levelt, Richardson & La Heij (1985) examined the relationship between voice onset time and the gesture apex (the movement extension of a point gesture) in subjects who were asked to point at a series of lights while simultaneously saying, "That one" or "This one" in Dutch. Gesture apex and voice onset time were found to co-vary with one another by a matter of milliseconds across a variety of conditions. When gesture production was hampered by putting weights on the hand, speech did not stop so long as the gesture interruption occurred within milliseconds. The time limit corresponded closely to the reaction time of saying a word. When the weight was placed after this time limit, speech halted. These findings were interpreted as showing that once word production was initiated, it could not be stopped even though the gesture was halted and thus as providing evidence for an autonomous view of speech and gesture.

In another study, Morrel-Samuels & Krauss (1992) found gesture movement to precede the co-expressed speech in English by milliseconds as a linear function of the lexical familiarity of the word or phrase being spoken simultaneously. Duration of gesture movement was likewise highly correlated with gesture–speech execution asynchrony. These findings were interpreted as supporting the integrated-system hypothesis.

Despite different interpretations, the basic findings of these studies were similar. Except when hand movements were impeded, the timing of gesture and speech execution were highly correlated with one another. Gesture and speech execution occurred within milliseconds of one another in a principled fashion, even though the execution of gesture and speech was not precisely simultaneous, which would be an unrealistic expectation given the gross differences in the articulators and motor systems involved: the vocal tract versus the upper torso, hands, and arms. Nonetheless, ambiguity remains as to the degree to which gesture and speech are linked in extemporaneous expression or, conversely, whether the appearance of being linked is an illusion caused by the fact that both modes are expressing similar meanings within the same time frame and communicative act.

We turned to the speech disorder of stuttering to shed light on this question (Mayberry, Jaques & DeDe 1998; Scoble 1993). In stuttering we can observe gesture production in the context of a highly disrupted speech stream. If gesture and speech are fundamentally linked in a deep way at the level of message planning as well as at the level of production, then gesture should keep full pace with stuttered speech, just as has been observed for fluent speech. However, if gesture and speech are truly autonomous and only appear to be synchronous because both modes are expressing similar meanings at the same time, then gesture production would be expected to break away from speech production during the highly extended stuttering blocks associated with chronic stuttering. Our experiments were designed to test these competing hypotheses and predictions. Before describing these studies, we give a thumbnail sketch of stuttering.

3   Stuttering

Stuttering is a speech disorder of unknown etiology that affects approximately 1 percent of the population. It usually begins in childhood with a gradual onset between the ages of two and five; 80 percent of childhood stutterers spontaneously recover (Bloodstein 1993). Stuttering appears to be sex-linked, affecting more males than females, at a ratio of 3:1 and tends to run in families. Both these facts suggest a strong heritable component to stuttering (Smith 1990). Stuttering does not dart randomly in and out of the speech stream, however. To the contrary, research has found that the appearance of stuttering in speech shows a systematic relationship to language structure: first sounds and syllables of words are more likely to be stuttered, as well as the first words of sentences and clauses, and content words as contrasted to closed-class words (Wingate 1988). The patterning of stuttering with the structure of language and speech appear to reflect neuromotor planning junctures where the information and coordination load is the highest for the central nervous system and hence the most vulnerable to breakdown in the speaker with a fluency disorder.

No previous studies have investigated the speech-related gestures of individuals who stutter, perhaps because gesture has traditionally been thought to fall outside the domain of speech and hence outside the domain of the disorder. A few studies have investigated the effects of stuttering on what has been called non-speech behavior, or more specifically, head, eye, and lip movement (Schwartz, Zebrowski & Conture 1990). Conture & Kelly (1991) note in passing that the hand may freeze in association with stuttering but give no other details. This observation is one of the effects of stuttering on speech-related gesture that we discovered and describe below.

4   Gesture in fluent and disfluent speech

In our first study, we adapted the experimental paradigm used by McNeill (1992) and his colleagues to elicit extemporaneous speech and gesture, the cartoon-narration task. We used an animated cartoon and, to avoid any memory problems that might potentially be associated with having to narrate an entire cartoon, divided its presentation into three equal segments with respect to duration and the number of action episodes contained in each segment.

Subjects were tested individually. They viewed the first segment of the cartoon and then narrated the story line to an unfamiliar, neutral listener. By neutral, we mean that the listener made no comments other than "Anything else?" and produced *no* gesture. This procedure was repeated two additional times. The subjects' narration was videotaped and then transcribed. After the cartoon-narration task, the subjects who stuttered were asked to complete a brief protocol of reading, speaking on the phone, and speaking spontaneously. These tasks are standard clinical procedures for measuring stuttering severity (Johnson, Darley & Spriesterbach 1963).

Twelve English-speaking adults participated in the first study. Six subjects identified themselves as stutterers and had a childhood onset of the speech disorder. Five subjects were males and one was female; they ranged in age from 21 to 51 years, with a mean of 36 years. The stuttering severity of the subjects, as determined from a speech sample of one hundred words taken after completion of the first study, was mild for two subjects (0 to 5% of words stuttered), moderate for two subjects (5% to 10% of words stuttered), and severe for two subjects (greater than 10% of words stuttered). Six additional subjects with no history of stuttering were matched by age, sex, and highest level of education to the subjects who stuttered. The highest level of education for four of the subjects who stuttered was an undergraduate degree, and for two others it was a high school diploma. Likewise, four of the control subjects had an undergraduate degree, and two controls had a high school diploma.

We transcribed the narrations of the second and third segments of the cartoon for each subject. These were transcribed and coded for gesture, speech, and the temporal concordance between the two, always in the same order for all subjects. To ensure the validity of our transcriptions, the gesture transcription was completed first without reference to speech, i.e., with the audio portion of the videotape turned off. Each instance in which the subject moved his or her hand/s from rest to action was noted and categorized into one of three categories: (1) a self-touching movement or manipulation of an object, (2) a non-representational beat – moving the hand up and down – or (3) a representational gesture – gestures where the movement and/or hand shape is iconic, as in using a grabbing hand with a downward stroke to depict a woman 'swatting' a cat with an umbrella, or metaphoric, as in sweeping the hands across space to signify that the cartoon ended. The first category, self-touching and object manipulation, was analyzed no further because it was not considered to be gesture. The gesture coding was based on a coding system previously developed for sign language research (Mayberry & Eichen 1991). During the production of gesture, the hand/s sometimes made more than one gesture before returning to rest, as in making a 'swatting' gesture immediately after a 'grabbing' gesture. Thus, the number of gestures produced within each gesture unit was noted also, following conventions we had developed to measure and count morphology in American Sign Language (Mayberry & Eichen 1991).

In a similar fashion, we made the speech transcription without reference to gesture, i.e., with the video portion of the videotape turned off. The transcript included all words spoken in addition to all speech disfluencies. Each disfluency was categorized as being one of two types: (a) stuttered disfluencies, which included sound and syllable repetitions and audible and inaudible sound prolongations, or (b) normal disfluencies, which included word and phrase repetitions, word and phrase revisions, pauses, and interjections, such as "um" or "uh." The number of words, clauses, and cartoon story-line details the subject gave in his or her spontaneous speech sample was also noted.

Finally, we ascertained the temporal concordance between gesture and speech by combining the previous two transcripts with reference to both the audio and video portions of the videotape. The boundaries of each gesture were demarcated with respect to the words and disfluencies that were simultaneously produced with it. Gesture onset was defined as initiation of the hand/s' movement from rest; gesture offset was defined as movement cessation when the hand/s returned to rest. The precise temporal locus of each speech disfluency was determined as co-occurring with one of six sequential phases in gesture production taken from Kendon (1980) and Kita (1993): (1) the preparatory stage (raising the hand in order to execute a gesture), (2) the pre-stroke hold (an optional pause before initiation of the gesture movement), (3) the gesture onset (the initiation of gesture movement), (4) the gesture stroke (the movement of the gesture itself), (5) the post-stroke hold (an optional pause before returning the hand to rest), and (6) retraction (return of the hand to rest). Owing to the brief nature of beat gestures in contrast to representational ones, our analyses here are primarily concerned with the latter gesture type.

When we analyzed the fluency of the speech uttered by the two groups, we found, as expected, that the main difference between the two groups was the amount of stuttered disfluency that appeared in their speech and not the amount of normal disfluency. Stuttered versus normal disfluency turns out to be an important distinction when investigating the gesture–speech relationship, as we shall later explain.

Although the narration task was open-ended in the sense that the subjects could speak for as long as they wished, there was a strong effect of stuttering on the length and content of the subjects' narrations. The control subjects said on average about 35 percent more words in 50 percent less time than did the subjects who stuttered. These findings underscore the fact that chronic stuttering renders the production of spoken expression difficult.

The difficulty stuttering imposes on spontaneous expression was also shown by a significant negative correlation between the degree of stuttering in the subjects' speech stream and the richness of narrative detail and complexity of sentence structure. Hence, the subjects who stuttered tended to give fewer narrative details with fewer clauses in simpler sentence structures (less embedding and complementation).

In keeping with the predictions generated by the integrated systems hypothesis, the reduced speech output of the subjects who stuttered was accompanied by only half the number of gestures produced by the control subjects in their narrations, with an average of 152 total gestures for the control subjects and an average of 82 gestures for the subjects who stuttered.

The reduced frequency of gesture expression that we observed in association with stuttered speech was not a simple function of less speech being uttered on the part of the subjects who stuttered. This was apparent when we examined the percentage of words the subjects spoke that were accompanied by gesture. The controls accompanied 78 percent of their words with gesture, but the subjects who stuttered accompanied only 30 percent of their words with gesture. This difference between the groups was also reflected in the amount of time that the subjects gestured, or, put another way, the amount of time that their hands were in the air while they spoke. The control group gestured for 70 percent of the total time they spoke, whereas the group that stuttered gestured for only 20 percent of the time they spoke.

The interruptions of stuttering on speech production have a clear attenuating effect on spontaneous expression with respect to linguistic content and structure: less is said in simpler sentences in more time than is typical of fluent speech. The gesture that accompanies stuttered speech, rather than compensating for reduced content and structure, shows an even more marked reduction than does the speech. Stuttered speech is accompanied by even fewer, and not more, gestures than fluent speech, with simpler forms and meanings (Mayberry et al. 1999). Thus we see that stuttering attenuates gesture production above and beyond what would be expected given the reduced speech content and structure. This suggests that some factor above and beyond 'amount of talk' affects the degree to which individuals who stutter gesture. Indeed, we have observed pre-adolescent children with severe stuttering not to move their hands at all on this narration task, something we have never observed in normally fluent children. Clearly much more research is required to investigate this complex finding. Next we examined the timing relationship between gesture production and fluent and stuttered speech.

5   Gesture is co-produced with fluent but not disfluent speech

We located all instances of normal and stuttered disfluencies in the speech stream of the subjects' narratives and then determined whether or not gesture was co-produced with each disfluency. This analysis showed that the normal disfluencies of the control subjects and those who stuttered were co-produced both with and without gesture with equal frequency.

In contrast to the maintenance of the gesture–speech relationship we observed for normal disfluencies, gesture was rarely co-produced with stuttered disfluencies. In the very few instances when a gesture was co-produced with a stuttered disfluency, the gesturing hand could be observed to fall to rest during the moment of stuttering and then to rise again and resume gesturing within milliseconds of resumption of speech fluency. In a few instances, the gesturing hand could be observed to stop moving during the moment of stuttering and to resume movement within milliseconds of the recovery of speech fluency. In fewer instances still, the hand began to gesture but abandoned the gesture by falling to rest and remaining at rest throughout the remainder of the spoken clause. These observations provide strong support for the integrated-system hypothesis and are not predicted by the independent-systems hypothesis.

In order to more closely examine the precise timing relationship between gesture execution and type of speech disfluency, we located every instance in which either a normal or a stuttered disfluency co-occurred with a representational gesture. We chose representational gestures for this analysis because the duration of representational gestures was of sufficient length to observe precisely the relationship between the motor-execution phase of the gesture and the speech disfluency with a high degree of accuracy without instrumentation.

The results of this analysis showed that stuttered disfluencies, that is, syllable and sound repetitions and prolongations, almost never co-occurred with the onset of the gesture stroke. By stroke onset, we refer to the movement-initiation point of a representational gesture that occurs after the handshape of the gesture is positioned in the air. This is in direct contrast to the normal disfluencies of both the control subjects and those who stuttered. The distribution of normal disfluencies for both groups occurred with comparable frequency across the pre-stroke, stroke-onset, and stroke phases of gesture execution.

In direct contrast, stuttered disfluencies occurred after the stroke onset of the gesture, toward the end of the gesture (that is, during the gesture movement and retraction phase). There was a marked absence of stuttered disfluencies at the stroke onset; no stuttering disfluencies accompanied the stroke onset. Four stuttered disfluencies occurred at the preparation phase of the gesture. In three instances the gesturing hand froze in midair during the stuttering bout and resumed moving only when fluent word production resumed after the stuttering bout ended. In one instance when a stuttering bout began during the preparatory phase of a gesture (raising the hand from rest), the hand immediately fell to rest and remained there throughout the stuttering bout. When the stuttering bout finally ended and fluent speech resumed, the hand immediately flew from rest and executed the stroke of the representational gesture in temporal co-expression with the now fluently produced word.

The same general tendency characterized the relationship between beat gestures and disfluency. However, six out of forty-seven beat gestures were executed simultaneously with the onset of stuttering disfluency, whereas no representational gestures were, so far as we could ascertain with the naked eye. Thus, there is a preliminary suggestion that the onset of the movement (or stroke) of a representational gesture requires fluent word production and beat gestures less so. A more detailed examination of this question is required with instrumentation, because beat gestures can be executed very quickly with much briefer duration than representational gestures.

One striking example illustrates the phenomenon well. One man who stuttered was narrating a cartoon sequence where the character Tweety Bird runs across a road. His spoken clause was "ran across the road," and his representational gesture accompanying the clause indicated a 'movement across a flat surface' (the palm, with straight and closed fingers, was face down and moved back and forth from in front of the torso outward). The man began to stutter on the word "ran" with multiple repetitions of the initial phoneme /r/. Just prior to the stuttering bout, his hand had moved from rest and assumed a flat, closed handshape but had not yet initiated the gesture stroke – the back and forth movement indicating 'across the surface'. At the moment when he began to stutter on the word "ran," his hand froze in space before initiating its (to and fro) movement; his hand remained motionless in space throughout the prolonged stuttering bout. When finally the stuttering ceased and he fluently uttered the clause "ran across the road," his hand simultaneously unfroze and initiated the gesture movement (to and fro) completely and co-temporaneously with the fluently spoken clause.

These findings and observations suggest that there are at least two important features that underlie the initiation of gesture movement, or the stroke onset, in representational gestures. One feature is that initiation of the gesture movement, or the stroke onset, appears to be functionally equivalent to the onset of word production. This is suggested by the finding that gesture production can be interrupted by speech stuttering throughout the preparatory phases of gesture production up to the *initiation* of gesture movement, i.e., the stroke onset. Once the movement of the gesture has been initiated, stuttering no longer interrupts gesture production. The second feature indicated by these data and observations is that the onset of the gesture stroke appears to be directly linked to the onset of fluent word production. This is suggested by the finding that gesture production co-occurs only with fluent word production. Gesture production is halted during bouts of stuttering.

Normal speech disfluencies do not show this link to the stroke onset of representational gestures. One appealing explanation is that word and syllable production and stress and prosody patterns are all maintained throughout normal speech disfluencies – the 'ums' and 'uhs' and word repetitions that are common in fluent speech. During this type of speech disfluency, gesture flow proceeds mostly unaffected. Stuttered disfluencies, by contrast, disrupt the flow of speech. Words and syllables are fragmented, and stress and prosody patterns collapse. Gesture production ceases until the speech stream fluently resumes. Clearly, gesture production is linked to fluent word production. If our interpretation is correct, then we would predict that speaking conditions other than stuttering that disrupt the flow of the speech stream, particularly with respect to word production, would also disrupt gesture production.

The robust correspondence between fluent speech production and maintenance of gesture production suggests that gesture and speech are planned and integrated by the central nervous system at some point prior to their actual physical execution. Moreover, there must be multiple feedback links between gesture and speech throughout extemporaneous expression. In other words, gesture and speech are an integrated system in language production. When speech stumbles and stops as a result of stuttering, the hand always waits for speech so that the meanings being expressed by the hand in gesture always coincide with the meanings being expressed by the mouth in speech, even when the gesture must wait for a very long time. Gesture and speech production are clearly not autonomous. We believe that the implications of these findings are significant and discuss them in greater detail below after describing our second experiment.

6   Only speech-related gesture is disrupted by stuttering

As provocative as our results were, we needed to exclude a purely manual-motor shutdown explanation for the phenomenon. While it has been long observed casually that individuals who stutter do not move their hands and arms while stuttering (A. Smith, pers. com.), it was nevertheless essential for us to demonstrate that the absence of gesture during the stuttering moment was due to a co-expression principle that governs gesture and speech execution rather than to some underlying inability to move the hands and arms during stuttering. The stuttering blocks of some of the subjects were so prolonged and disruptive to speech that a naive observer could readily envisage that a massive motor shutdown was taking place at the moment of stuttering.

In order to rule out a purely motor-shutdown explanation for the phenomenon, we asked three subjects who participated in the first study to participate in a second one where they narrated a second cartoon under three dual-task conditions (Mayberry et al. 1999; Scoble 1993). In the first dual task, the subject narrated a cartoon and simultaneously pressed a button continually. In the second dual task, the subject pressed a button to signal that he or she was stuttering. In the third task, the subject took a pencil and wrote the word being stuttered. All three subjects were able to carry out the simultaneous tapping and signaling dual tasks with no apparent disruptions during moments of stuttering. Moreover, all three subjects gestured with the free hand while simultaneously speaking extemporaneously and tapping with the other hand! Only one subject was able to write the word being stuttered during the stuttering moment. This was because the stuttering blocks of this subject, but not the other two, were of sufficient duration to permit word writing.

These findings completely rule out the possibility that at the moment of stuttering hand and arm movement is not possible. Rather, individuals who stutter are fully able to execute manual, non-gesture motor actions during the moment of stuttering, but they do not execute speech-related gesture during the moment of stuttering. During the moment of stuttering, speech is not being executed, and gesture is not being executed either, but the hand can scratch the head and grasp a pen.

These findings indicate that gesture and speech are tightly linked in extemporaneous expression. Gesture and speech were always co-expressed in all our data sets despite the frequent and often lengthy interruptions caused by stuttering – interruptions as frequent as one out of every ten words ranging in duration from milliseconds to minutes. The fact that the temporal concordance between gesture and speech execution is always maintained throughout stuttered and fluent speech suggests that the complex neuromotor patterns of gesture and speech are coordinated and integrated prior to their production in extemporaneous expression. What might the mechanism of gesture–speech integration be? We now address this question.

7   **The neuromotor coordination of gesture and speech**

One hypothesis as to how movements originating from disparate motor systems are coordinated is the "Dynamic Pattern" perspective. In this theoretical framework, the coordination of movement of different limbs is thought to arise from interactions between oscillatory processes themselves rather than from central representations (Kelso, Tuller & Harris 1981).

Smith and her colleagues (Smith, McFarland & Weber 1986; Franz, Zelaznik & Smith 1992) have discovered that simultaneously produced cyclic movements of the mouth, arm, and fingers harmonize with one another during meaningless, non-linguistic motor repetition tasks. Movements of separately controlled motor systems (the mouth and the finger, for example) eventually come to be harmonized with one another and then are co-produced in cyclic coordination. Such a mechanism could be the means by which the gesture–speech co-expression principle is achieved by the central nervous system. If so, this would mean that, in addition, the cyclic coordination that harmonizes the complex motor patterns of the gesture system with those of the speech system is ultimately coordinated by and integrated with the output of the conceptual and linguistic systems.

Although we can observe cycles of oscillation for the mouth and finger while each is engaged in simply repeating a single action, it is more difficult to imagine what the underlying cycles are in speech and gesture production that become harmonized to such a degree that they become a single expression of gesture–speech. The concept is especially difficult to imagine if speech is, a priori, conceptualized as having a linear, sequentially organized form with one word following another, and gesture is conceived of as having a spatial, simultaneous form, with gestures being three-dimensional masses placed in various spatial arrangements. But of course this may not be the case at all.

Thus we ask, Where are the cycles of speech and gesture that become harmonized in gesture–speech co-expression? One candidate possibility raised by our observations of subjects who stutter and the research of McClave (1994) and Nobe (1996) is that the oscillatory cycles of speech are contained in the prosodic patterns of the speech stream and that the oscillatory cycles of gesture are contained in the stress patterns of gesture movement. Speech prosody clearly rises and falls and reflects, to some degree, both the clausal structure of spoken language and the foregrounding and backgrounding of discourse and conceptual structure. Gesture movement likewise clearly rises and falls in relation to elements in conceptual, discourse, and linguistic structure and harmonizes with speech prosody. One germane observation from stuttering and gesture production that supports this hypothesis is that the onset of the gesture stroke was always produced concurrently with the onset of fluent word production. Stuttered disfluencies almost never coincide with the onset of the gesture stroke.

In the examples where the gesturing hand waits for fluent speech production, we observe that the onset of the gesture stroke requires a fully formed and intoned word in order for both the gesture stroke and the uttered word to be executed together within milliseconds of one another. These findings are in keeping with those of Morrel-Samuels & Krauss (1992), who observed gesture and speech execution to be coordinated within milliseconds of one another in normally fluent speakers of English.

The exciting possibility added by the "Dynamic Pattern" perspective of motor-control theory to an explanation of how gesture and speech come to be so highly coordinated is that the harmonizing of cycles of speech and gesture during motor execution requires no central representation to achieve this remarkable feat of elegant cross-modal coordination. Instead, the neuromotor coordination of gesture–speech can occur on-line as spontaneous expression is being constructed and produced. It is important to note here that yet a third (or more) process is being harmonized with the cycles of gesture and speech, namely, the meanings being expressed by narrative and sentence structure.

How is this type of information wed with speech prosody and gesture tempo? It is possible that speech prosody and gesture tempo are part and parcel of propositional meaning and not separate systems that have to be coordinated and integrated with language meaning. From the earliest of ages and stages of language acquisition, children produce gesture and speech in a synchronized fashion. For example, Masataka (2000) and colleagues have discovered that the babble of Japanese babies is more canonical, or syllable-like, when they simultaneously flap their arms/hands as compared with when they do not. Nicholadis, Mayberry & Genesee (1999) have found that very young children co-produce iconic gestures with speech propositions shortly after putting words together for the very first time, and not before. Thus, there is certainly developmental evidence suggesting that arm/hand movements and representational gestures are co-produced and synchronized with speech from the very beginning of language development.

The key elements required for gesture–speech harmonization in production by the "Dynamic Pattern" perspective are that both the speech stream and the gesture stream have oscillatory movement, or cycles. Tuite (1993) has proposed that a rhythmic pulse underlies gesture and speech production. This rhythmic pulse may be the harmonizing cycles of gesture and speech coordination within the framework of the dynamic-pattern perspective. Our observations of individuals who stutter has led us to hypothesize that stuttering disrupts and/or destroys the temporal cycles that organize the speech stream, as suggested by the sometimes flat prosodic patterns common in the speech of individuals who stutter. For example, one subject who stuttered was mostly fluent but spoke in a monotone. This subject produced scant gestures. Hence, oscillatory cycles in the speech stream (in the form of prosodic patterns) may be necessary to glue gesture production to speech. While only speculative at this point, our working hypothesis as to how gesture and speech are integrated and coordinated at a deep neuromotor level prior to execution explains the striking effects of stuttering on gesture production that we have observed and documented here and elsewhere (Mayberry, Jaques & Shenker 1999; Mayberry, Jaques & DeDe 1998; Scoble 1993). In current work, we find the same phenomenon to characterize the gesture–speech production of pre-adolescent children who stutter in comparison with children who are normally fluent (Scott 1999).

In summary, the results of our studies strongly suggest that gesture and speech production are governed by a deep principle of co-expression in extemporaneous expression. As previous research has discovered, the structure and content of gesture parallels the structural and semantic properties co-expressed in speech. Our work extends these findings by suggesting that a principle of co-expression produces the tight temporal relationship observed in gesture–speech expression. Gesture execution starts and stops in temporal lockstep with speech execution throughout and despite the highly frequent and sometimes massive interruptions caused by stuttering. The resistance of gesture–speech co-expression to temporal uncoupling during severe bouts of stuttering broadens our view of the expressive act. The speaker's mind coordinates the complex patterns of the gesture system (finger, hand, arm, shoulder, and joint neuromuscular patterns) and integrates them with the complex patterns of the speech system (orofacial, laryngeal, and respiratory patterns) while weaving all this together with the complex mental structures of thought and language. The integration and timing the mind produces are so highly coordinated that all these vocal and gestural actions appear as one seamless image in the same moment of expressive time.

NOTE

The research reported here was supported by a grant from the Natural Sciences and Engineering Research Council of Canada (Grant #171239) to R. Mayberry. We thank Ann Smith for helpful discussions about speech–motor control; any errors in interpretation, however, remain our own. We also thank the individuals who volunteered as subjects for this research.

REFERENCES

Bloodstein, O. 1993. *Stuttering: The Search for a Cause and Cure*. Norwalk, CT: Allyn & Bacon.

Butterworth, B. & Beattie, G. 1978. Gesture and silence as indicators of planning in speech. In Campbell & Smith (eds.), pp. 347–360.

Butterworth, B. & Hadar, U. 1989. Gesture, speech, and computational stages: a reply to McNeill. *Psychological Review* 96: 168–174.

Campbell, R. N. & Smith, P. T. (eds.) 1978. *Recent Advances in the Psychology of Language: Formal and Experimental Approaches*. New York: Plenum.

Chamberlain, C., Morford, J. & Mayberry, R. I. (eds.) 2000. *Language Acquisition by Eye*. Mahwah, NJ: Erlbaum.

Conture, E. & Kelly, E. M. 1991. Young stutterers' nonspeech behaviors during stuttering. *Journal of Speech and Hearing Research* 34: 144–156.

Cooper, J. A. (ed.) 1990. Research needs in stuttering: roadblocks and future directions, *ASHA Reports* 18. Rockville, MD: American Speech–Language-Hearing Association.

Feyereisen, P. & deLannoy, J. D. 1991. *Gestures and Speech: Psychological Investigations*. New York: Cambridge University Press.

Franz, E., Zelaznik, H. & Smith, A. 1992. Evidence of common timing processes in the control of manual, orofacial, and speech movements. *Journal of Motor Behavior* 24: 281–287.

Goldin-Meadow, S., McNeill, D. & Singleton, J. 1996. Silence is liberating: removing the handcuffs on grammatical expression in the manual modality. *Psychological Review* 103: 34–55.

Iverson, J. & Goldin-Meadow, S. (eds.) 1998. *Nature and Functions of Gesture in Children's Communication*. San Francisco: Jossey-Bass.

Johnson, W., Darley, F. & Spriesterbach, D. 1963. *Diagnostic Methods in Speech Pathology*. New York: Harper & Row.

Kelso, J. A. S., Tuller, G. & Harris, K. S. 1981. A 'Dynamic Pattern' perspective on the control and coordination of movement. In MacNeilage (ed.), pp. 137–173.

Kendon, A. 1980. Gesticulation and speech: two aspects of the processes of utterance. In Key (ed.), pp. 207–227.

Key, M. R. (ed.) 1980. *The Relation between Verbal and Nonverbal Communication*. The Hague: Mouton.

Kita, S. 1993. Language and thought interface: a study of spontaneous gestures and Japanese mimetics. Unpublished Ph.D. dissertation, University of Chicago.

Levelt, W. J. M., Richardson, G. & La Heij, W. 1985. Pointing and voicing in deictic expressions. *Journal of Memory and Language* 24: 133–164.

MacNeilage, P. F. (ed.) 1981. *The Production of Speech*. New York: Springer-Verlag.

Masataka, N. 2000. The role of modality and input in the earliest stages of language acquisition: studies of Japanese Sign Language. In Chamberlain, Morford & Mayberry (eds.), pp. 3–24.

Mayberry, R. I. & Eichen, E. B. 1991. The long-lasting advantage of learning sign language in childhood: another look at the critical period for language acquisition. *Journal of Memory and Language* 30: 486–512.

Mayberry, R. I., Jaques, J. & DeDe, G. 1998. What stuttering reveals about the development of the gesture–speech relationship. In Iverson & Goldin-Meadow (eds.), pp. 89–100.

Mayberry, R. I., Jaques, J. & Shenker, R. 1999. Stuttering on the hands: the relation of speech fluency to spontaneous gesture. Unpublished manuscript.

McClave, E. 1994. Gestural beats: the rhythm hypothesis. *Journal of Psycholinguistic Research* 23: 45–66.

McNeill, D. 1985. So you think gestures are nonverbal? *Psychological Review* 92: 350–371.

McNeill, D. 1992. *Hand and Mind: What Gestures Reveal about Thought*. Chicago: University of Chicago Press.

Morrel-Samuels, P. & Krauss, R. M. 1992. Word familiarity predicts temporal asynchrony of hand gestures.' *Journal of Experimental Psychology: Learning, Memory, and Cognition* 18: 615–622.

Nicholadis, E., Mayberry, R. I. & Genesee, F., 1999. Gesture and early bilingual development. *Developmental Psychology* 35: 514–526.

Nobe, S. 1996. Cognitive rhythms, gestures, and acoustic aspects of speech. Unpublished Ph.D. dissertation, University of Chicago.

Schwartz, H. B., Zebrowski, P. M. & Conture, E. G. 1990. Behaviors at the onset of stuttering. *Journal of Fluency Disorders* 15: 77–86.

Scoble, J. 1993. Stuttering blocks the flow of speech and gesture: the speech and gesture relationship in chronic stutterers. Unpublished master's thesis, McGill University.

Scott, L. 1999. The gesture–speech relationship in children who stutter. Unpublished master's thesis, McGill University.

Smith, A. 1990. Factors in the etiology of stuttering. In Cooper (ed.), pp. 39–47.

Smith, A., McFarland, D. & Weber, C. M. 1986. Interactions between speech and finger movements: an exploration of the dynamic pattern perspective. *Journal of Speech and Hearing Research* 29: 471–480.

Tuite, K. 1993. The production of gesture. *Semiotica* 93: 83–105.

Wingate, M. E. 1988. *The Structure of Stuttering: A Psycholinguistic Analysis*. New York: Springer-Verlag.

11   The role of gestures and other graded language forms in the grounding of reference in perception

Elena T. Levy

Department of Psychology, University of Connecticut; Haskins Laboratories

Carol A. Fowler

Department of Psychology, University of Connecticut and Yale University; Haskins Laboratories

1   Introduction

Humans acquire knowledge in two major ways – by perceiving their environment and by perceiving and comprehending communications involving language. In principle, some knowledge acquired by perceiving the environment can be certain knowledge, because perception of the environment can be 'direct' (e.g., Gibson 1979). Knowledge acquired by language is likely to be less certain, because it cannot convincingly pass the tests for directness of perception.

We will suggest, however, that speakers do provide some directly perceivable information to listeners. The information takes the form of increases and decreases in what we will call the energy expended to communicate. This is manifested as the occurrences of longer or shorter, more carefully or more casually articulated lexical expressions accompanied or not by manual gestures. Energy peaks (long carefully articulated expressions accompanied by a gesture) mark topic shifts. Peaks and troughs can help to specify reference.

Before presenting the data, we clarify our distinction between direct perception and less reliable means of acquiring knowledge. Next we discuss sources of information about reference and topic shifts.

2   Direct perception and less reliable ways of acquiring knowledge

Perception of the environment is direct if it is unmediated by construction of covert representations of the environment being perceived and if it is unmediated by guessing that is required when stimulus information is insufficient to specify its source. Here is how perception of the environment can be direct.

Components of the environment lawfully structure media such as light and air; the light and air in turn impart their structure to the perceptual systems of perceiver/actors. Because the structure is lawfully caused by components of the environment, and because distinct components of the environment structure media distinctively, the structure in media can specify – that is serve as wholly reliable information for – its causes in the environment. Perceivers use structure in light and air as information for its environmental causes and thereby acquire certain knowledge of specified parts of the environment. As we will elaborate in section 7, direct perception achieves a relation of 'parity' (identity) between components of the environment and what is perceived.

Not everything that perceiver/actors need to know about the environment is specified in this way, and in these cases, achievement of parity is less reliable than when perception can be direct. For example, although some human actions may render the intentions that fostered them transparent, some may not. Accordingly, some knowledge acquired by perceiving behavior can be less certain than knowledge acquired by perceiving the inanimate parts of the environment.

This may be especially true if the behaviors include human language. When listeners attend to speech, generally they hope to learn what the speaker means or intends by what he or she says; they hope to achieve communicative parity. But the meaning does not immediately structure a medium, such as light or air, so that it may be specified to perceivers. Rather it is encoded, in part, into a sequence of linguistic forms that have the meanings and conjoint meanings they do by cultural convention.

By analogy with the lawful structuring of light and air by properties of the environment, we suppose that meanings are encoded into linguistic forms systematically according to culturally determined conventions. Further, distinct meanings tend to be encoded into distinct sequences of forms so that the forms can, perhaps, specify the meanings, enabling achievement of communicative parity. However, for a variety of reasons, they may not do so. For example, because the structuring of forms to convey meanings is not by physical law, but rather by culture, and because conventions vary from place to place and from social group to social group, the listener's and talker's conventions may not be wholly shared. Even when they are shared, talkers are likely to begin speaking without knowing exactly what meaning they are trying to convey. Finally, even when talkers know what to say, they are not guaranteed to package their meanings interpretably, because the structuring of forms by intended meanings is not causal.

To the extent that knowledge acquired by perceiving linguistic utterances is uncertain, we might expect speakers to augment their linguistic utterances with behaviors that can provide certain knowledge. As the chapters in this volume show, communications that include linguistic utterances are richer in information than a typescript of the utterances reveals. For example, speakers gesture, and they vary systematically both the transparency and the intelligibility of words they produce. We will show one way in which deployment of these activities is systematic and potentially informative, and we will suggest that the patterns that their systematic deployments create can be directly perceived. Accordingly, their occurrence with and in speech increases the opportunities for listeners to acquire certain knowledge of speakers' intended meanings, that is, to achieve communicative parity.

Our focus in this chapter is on the communicative activity of making reference. Most accounts of reference have focused on one type of relationship between word and referent, that is, on the referential function of semantic information encoded in conventional and arbitrary lexico-grammatical categories. Pragmatic information, encoded by non-arbitrary links between word and referent, has for the most part been overlooked or has been treated as secondary to the central role played by semantics.[1] This asymmetry in the supposed relative importance of semantic and pragmatic information follows from the 'objectivist' assumption that language understanding is mediated by abstract symbols that are internal representations of external reality (Lakoff 1987). From this point of view, processing systems are symbol manipulators (Fodor 1983) that assign meaning to utterances by relying on decontextualized symbols to access stored representations. In the absence of contextual information, however, processing models encounter significant problems such as unresolvable ambiguity and the escalating of semantic entailments. As Dreyfus (1992) and others have pointed out, for a computational system to process language, the semantic domain to which the interpreting device has access must be narrowly defined (a 'micro-world'). However, human language-users live in a macro-world; by implication, human language understanding involves something more than symbol manipulation; the something more on which we will focus is context in the form of indexical information.

When interpretation of linguistic utterances takes place in the context of ongoing activities, the problems of ambiguity posed by objectivist accounts are minimized or eliminated. In context, speakers and listeners are likely to know their reasons for speaking, and their shared intersubjective understanding constrains how they interpret individual references (see Tomasello 1992 for a related argument with respect to early word-learning). As we will show, identification of referents can be further constrained by pragmatic indexical signals provided by patterns of gesturing, of articulatory reduction, and of choices of longer and shorter (and correspondingly more and less transparent) referring expressions. Generally, identification of a referent is conjointly determined by lexico-grammatical and indexical information. If indexical and lexico-grammatical information is interdependent (cf. McQuown 1971) and listeners use both sources of information, then a realistic processing model must reflect that.

3   Reference, the origo, and topic structure

From a social-pragmatic perspective (Tomasello 1992), every naturally occurring act of referring is grounded in indexicality. Reference is possible only with respect to a system of coordinates the origin of which Bühler (1990 [1934]) calls the "origo." In the simplest case, when a speaker is making reference to entities that are perceptibly present so that they can, in one way or another, point to them ("ocular deixis" in a translation of Bühler's terminology), the origo is at the speaker and is the personal and spatio-temporal locus denoted by the expressions *I, here,* and *now.*

Hanks (1992) suggests that deictic referring expressions such as these can encode up to four kinds of information. Two of the four information types in Hanks' taxonomy are RELATIONAL and INDEXICAL. Relational information specifies the relation of the referent to the origo, and indexical information locates the origo itself. For example, the deictic term *this* is used to pick out an entity proximal to the speaker. 'Proximal to' is the relational information provided by use of *this*; that the locus of the origo is at the speaker is the indexical information.

Hanks offers an interesting example of the sort on which we are focusing in which relational and indexical information is provided interdependently by the choice of referring expression and by directly perceivable information. In the example, two Maya men out of each other's sight are searching for a lost tool. One asks the other whether the tool is *tol o?* (approximately "there"). The other answers *hàah, way yan e?.* ("Yeah, it is here (where I am)"). The expression *way e?* means "at this place including me." By understanding this expression, the first speaker can know where the tool is, but only if he localizes the speaker's voice. That is, the choice of referring expression specifies the location of the tool only if the listener can determine where "this place including me" is. In the example, this information is provided by the (direct) acoustic specification of the speaker's location.

The origo is not always at a speaker's 'here and now'. In story or film narrations that we have studied, the origo is likely to be in the here-and-now of the characters in the story (and reference involves anaphora and "imagination-oriented deixis" in Bühler's terminology). This might appear to eliminate any role for directly perceivable information in identification of referents or in situating them in the events of a story. However, we will suggest that it does not.

Much of a narration consists of narrative statements (McNeill 1992) that tell the events of a story. In these statements, the origo is typically in the here-and-now of characters in the story. However, as McNeill (1992) has observed, narrators also use METANARRATIVE STATEMENTS in which the origo shifts back to an experiencer of the story's initial viewing or telling. The italicized phrases in (1) (from Levy & McNeill 1992) are metanarrative; the phrases in plain text are narrative.

(1)(a) *and then a little later you see a scene where* they're all in the dining hall
(1)(b) *OK so now we go back to* the picnic

Metanarrative statements tend to occur where there is a topic shift in the story and so, typically, a shift in the origo at the narrative level of description as well. Following these multiple shifts in the origo (from the narrative level to the metanarrative and back; and a shift at the narrative level as well), referents tend to be treated as new even though they may be highly familiar to the listener.

We and other investigators have found differential indexical marking of new and old information generally. Several studies have shown that gestures are more likely to occur in conjunction with presentation of unexpected than of expected lexical information (Kendon 1980; McNeill 1992; Levy & McNeill 1992; Marslen-Wilson, Levy & Tyler 1982). At the articulatory level, utterances are more carefully produced (and so are durationally longer and more intelligible) when words provide unexpected or unpredictable information (Bolinger 1963, 1981; Fowler & Housum 1987; McAllister, Potts, Mason & Marchant 1994). Lexically, there is a graded continuum of referring expressions, with attenuated forms occurring (all other things being equal) when the signal is in a relatively redundant context, and longer forms occurring when the discourse context is non-redundant (see Givón 1991; Levy & McNeill 1992).

Our research findings summarized below suggest that these devices are used after metanarrative statements even in conjunction with referents that are already well known to the listener. We will suggest that, along with the metanarrative statements, they serve to mark a topic shift. In addition, along with the lexical choices of referring expressions, they help to identify referents.

The indexical devices on which we focus are not the only topic-shifting indexical devices that have been observed. Kendon's (1972, 1980) analysis of a spontaneous conversation suggests that waves of body motion and intonation contours mirror the hierarchical structure of discourse topics. The patterning of these indexical forms indicates that "gesticulation may, in various ways, make visible the organization of the discourse; at times one may observe gesticulatory patterns that appear to have this function particularly." Likewise, increases in pitch range (Hirschberg & Pierrehumbert 1986) and self-repairs (Schegloff 1979) tend to occur at points of topic change. (See Duncan & Fiske 1979 for other examples of indexical topic-shifting devices.) The devices on which we focus are associated specifically with referring expressions.

Because referents introduced after metanarrative statements are treated as new even when they are familiar, words introducing new topics are marked by patterns of greater energy (in our research, occurrences of gestures, of careful productions of words, of lexically long and transparent referring expressions). In contrast, words referring to topics that have already been established are marked by patterns of lesser energy. We propose specifically that energy peaks associated with referring expressions provide directly perceivable evidence for a topic shift that is redundant with evidence for shifts provided by metanarrative statements. In addition, because these energy peaks are associated with referring expressions, they can delimit the possible referents of these expressions. In particular, energy peaks mark a referent as new; this eliminates as possible referents (all other things being equal) entities previously introduced following a topic shift. In contrast, a decrease in energy expenditure associated with referring expressions (that is, an absence of gesturing, a reduced articulation of a transparent referring expression, or choice of a short expression such as a pronoun) likewise provides a directly perceivable restriction on the identity of the referent; it must be one of the entities already introduced after the topic shift.

We present evidence in the next section that speakers mark topic shifts and that they differentially mark new and familiar discourse entities using variations in energy at different levels of description of a speech event. We propose that energy peaks and troughs provide directly perceptible information for topic introduction (including introduction of discourse entities) and topic maintenance (in part by references to previously introduced discourse entities), respectively, to listeners.

4   Empirical support for the proposal that patterns of greater and lesser energy mark topic structure in connected discourse

To show that a systematic relationship holds among gestural, articulatory, and lexical pragmatic devices, on the one hand, and the discourse function of shifting and maintaining topics, on the other, we take explicit metanarrative statements (italicized in (1a) and (b) above) as an operationalization of topic structure. The data on which we draw are monologues in which a listener is physically present but the referents in question are not.

4.1   Correlation of gestures with metanarrative statements

Levy & McNeill (1992) report three analyses that reveal a relation between gesturing and metanarrative statements. The first analysis is based on a narration that is part of a larger study in which a series of narrators retold a story that they had seen on film.

The narration was orthographically transcribed and then segmented into episode units, using explicit metanarrative statements, as in (1) above. In all, there were thirty-five episode units in this narration. All animate referring expressions were coded as explicit or inexplicit forms, such as proper names or pronouns, respectively. All gestures made by the narrator that precisely co-occurred with her articulation of explicit referring terms were then transcribed.

A description of the coding procedure will help to clarify what Levy & McNeill meant by a gesture. Their six-point coding scale was based on a principle of contrast: a lower number represented a higher degree of contrast with the environment. Category (1) represented instances of strict temporal co-occurrence between gesture and referring expression, and (6) represented instances with a complete absence of gesturing.

More specifically, categories (1) and (2) represented instances in which the hand both began and ended in rest position (cf. Kendon's 1980 "gesture units"). In category (1), the gesture co-occurred with (either 'precisely', beginning and ending with; or 'closely', extending over at least the syllable with primary stress) the articulation of the referring expression. Category (2) was a weaker form of (1), in which the gesture co-occurred with at least the syllable of greatest stress in the referring term, but extended slightly longer in time than the articulation of the referring expression (either beginning somewhat before or extending slightly beyond it). For categories (3) through (5), the hand did not both begin and end in rest position (cf. Kendon's 1980 "gesture phrases," but not "gesture units"). Category (3) represented those instances in which there was a discrete gesture that precisely accompanied the articulation of the referring expression, but also a discrete gesture that accompanied an adjacent word or phrase. The two gestures differed in form, spatial location, or temporal duration. Category (4) applied to gestures that constituted a series of beats. That is, the gesture that accompanied the target referring term was one of a series of formally similar or identical gestures. Gestures in category (5) extended substantially longer in time than the articulation of the referring term itself. Category (6) represented an absence of gesturing, and so included self-adaptors. Note

Table 11.1. *Metanarrative constraints on gestures*

	Gestures[a]	
Position in episode unit	+ G	− G
English narration of film		
Position 1	22 (63%)	13 (37%)
Position 2–last	17 (27%)	47 (73%)
English narration of comic book		
Position 1	8 (86%)	1 (14%)
Position 2–last	4 (22%)	14 (78%)
Georgian narration of film		
Position 1	12 (80%)	3 (20%)
Position 2–last	18 (19%)	78 (81%)

Note:
[a] Gestures that co-occur with references to characters made
with full Noun Phrases.

that only those gestures were coded that consisted minimally of movement
of the whole hand; finger movement was not coded as gesture.

For purposes of analysis, the 6-point scale was collapsed to a binary
scale: categories (1)–(3) were classified as +GESTURE, and categories
(4)–(6) as −GESTURE.

Loglinear analyses were run using the variables Position in an episode
unit (either position 1 or positions 2 through last), and Gesture (presence
vs. absence). The results, reproduced from Levy & McNeill in the first part
of Table 11.1 ("English narration of film"), show that gestures occur more
often in the first position of an episode unit than in subsequent positions ($p < .003$). This is illustrated in (2).

(2.1)   and then a little bit later you see a scene where they're all in the
dining hall
(2.2)   and [this pompous officer] comes in
(2.3)   and the friend of the officer whose name I don't remember the guy
that I told you he was sort of joking with but that is obviously his
superior, well he's also in the same dining area
(2.4)   and this pompous officer comes in
(2.5)   and sees the guy

In this example, the first reference to a character (*this pompous officer* in
2.2) that follows a metanarrative statement (*you see a scene* in 2.1) is accom-

panied by a gesture, marked by square brackets; the second reference (in 2.4) is not. The results of the analysis suggest that the greater energy employed in producing a gesture helps, along with metanarrative statements, to signal a topic shift and corresponding transformation of the origo.

Two other analyses, also appearing in Table 11.1, support this finding. Both narrations were segmented into episode units using explicit metanarrative statements. The data from the English narration of a comic-book story (reanalyzed from Marslen-Wilson, Levy & Tyler 1982) show that the distribution of gestures relative to metanarrative statements is similar to that in the Levy & McNeill study. The table also shows similar results from a narration of a Hitchcock movie told in the Georgian language (transcribed and translated by Kevin Tuite).

These studies indicate that gestures co-occurring with referring expressions tend to follow metanarrative statements that shift the origo. Expressions referring to characters already introduced following a metanarrative statement are not accompanied by gestures. Accordingly, the occurrence of gestures in conjunction with referring expressions can contribute to a shift in the origo; the occurrence or nonoccurrence of gestures can restrict the possible identities of a referent.

4.2   Word duration and metanarrative statement

To look for an association of metanarrative statements with careful articulations of words, we (Fowler, Levy & Brown 1997) used the four film narrations studied by Levy & McNeill (1992) and two others of the eight originally collected that also provided a sufficient quantity of word pairs to measure. We segmented the narrations into episode units using metanarrative statements. This gave us between ten and fifty episode units per narration.

We picked out references to main characters in the film that met either of two criteria. Either both members of a repetition pair occurred within an episode unit and were first and second utterances of the expression within that episode, or the members of a pair occurred on opposite sides of a metanarrative statement and were serially adjacent in the narration (that is, no other utterance of the expression intervened). For the four narrators who remembered the names of both main characters, we included all utterances of both names that met either of the two criteria. One narrator remembered just one of the names, and we included here criterial mentions of just that one name. One narrator remembered neither name, but used consistent descriptions (*the narrator* and *the blonde*); we included her criterial mentions of those descriptions in place of character names. The number of pairs included in the analyses ranged between eleven and fifty-three per narrator. We measured in milliseconds the durations of the acoustic signals corresponding to each reference.

In an analysis of the durations of these expressions, we found that narrators shortened expressions referring to the main characters when they were second mentions within an episode. However, they lengthened expressions that were first in an episode but followed a mention in an earlier episode. Five of the six narrators showed shortening within an episode; five also showed lengthening between episodes. Overall, names that were first in an episode averaged 536 ms in duration. This compares with an average duration of 496 ms for words that occurred second in the same episode and 491 ms for words that occurred last in a previous episode.

This analysis provides support for our proposal that expenditures of energy mark shifts in a topic with corresponding shifts in the origo, as we also find for use of manual gestures. Expressions that serve to introduce characters after a topic shift are marked by expenditures of energy; those that maintain a topic are marked by reductions of energy expenditure. As for gestures, we have shown that increases in the energy expended to produce a referring expression can provide information for a topic change and a corresponding shift in the origo. Expenditures of energy to produce a referring expression signal that a character has not yet been introduced into an episode; decreases in energy signal that the referent is among those already introduced after the topic shift.

4.3   *Lexical length and explicit metanarrative statements*

There is evidence that, in addition to articulatory length, the lexical length and hence the transparency of referring expressions is greater immediately following metanarrative statements than when the expressions serve to maintain an already introduced topic.[2] Levy & McNeill (1992) report an analysis of four of the film narrations described above, in which the lexical length of referring expressions was correlated with the position of the reference in an episode unit. Included in the analysis was a coding of each reference's relationship to its immediate linguistic context: if a referent was relatively predictable relative to its immediate context, it received a coding of COREFERENTIAL; if relatively unpredictable, it was coded NON-COREFERENTIAL. (See Levy & McNeill 1992 for a description of the algorithm used in this coding procedure.) In three narrations, length of referring expressions was statistically associated with position in an episode unit. In the fourth narration this association was marginally significant ($p < .0567$). In all narrations, longer forms (such as proper names) were more likely numerically than shorter forms (such as pronouns) to occur in initial than in subsequent position in an episode unit. Shorter forms tended to occur in positions after the first. The finding that longer forms occur episode-initially held even in those cases in which, based on the immediate context, a shorter form such as a pronoun would have been referentially unambiguous.

As for gestures and word durations, then, we find higher-energy referring expressions occurring following metanarrative statements and lower-energy forms occurring for repeated mentions.

4.4   *Summary*

These findings show that increased expenditure of energy marks topic change at all three levels of description: gestural, articulatory, and lexical. At each level, more coding material tends to appear in contexts that follow a topic shift and, therefore, are high in COMMUNICATIVE DYNAMISM (see McNeill 1992). This suggests that indexical devices at these three levels can contribute to transforming the origo. In addition, at each level, high energy expenditures and decreases in energy relative to those increases can restrict the identity of a referent respectively to an entity not yet mentioned after a topic shift or to one of those already introduced.

Perceiving the occurrences of gestures or their absence, perceiving articulatory carefulness or reduction, and possibly perceiving that referring expressions are long or short can be direct (see note 2). However, knowing exactly which referent is being marked in one of these ways typically requires interpretation of the lexical form used to refer. Accordingly, as in the case described by Hanks of localizing a tool that was present, direct perception in "imagination-oriented" reference contributes interdependently with information obtained by interpretation of linguistic forms to a listener's ability to situate a referent in a past, present, or fictional event.

5   Multi-channel participation in delineating the indexical ground

As our findings suggest, our proposal that communicatively dynamic information is marked by an increase in energy does not imply that, at any given point of high communicative dynamism such as at a point of topic shift, all linguistic forms show a marked increase in energy. Rather differences across narrations suggest that different narrators, at least in particular situations of speaking, use only a subset of possible linguistic devices to mark information that is communicatively dynamic. For example, in one film narration that we (see also Levy & McNeill 1992) examined (narration A in Table 11.2), topic shifts (as measured by the occurrence of metanarrative statements) tend to co-occur both with gestures and with increases in lexical

Table 11.2. *Discourse devices used by two narrators (data on types of metanarrative statements, gesture, and lexical length from Levy & McNeill 1992)*

	Narration A	Narration B
Type of metanarrative statement	'Cinematic'	'Fluid'
Assoc. of metanarrative statements with		
Gesture	Signif.	None
Articulatory duration	None	Signif.
Lexical length	Signif.	Marginal

length, but not with increases in articulatory duration. In contrast, a second film narration (B in Table 11.2) shows no association of topic shifts with gestures and only a marginal association with lexical length, but it does show an association of topic shifts with articulatory duration.

Perhaps these patterns of form–function relationships constitute, as Levy & McNeill (1992) suggest, strategies that reflect a speaker's perspective on the sequences of narrated events. In fact, Levy & McNeill report that the metanarrative statements themselves of speakers such as A and B differ in kind. The former consist of propositions composed of mental-state verbs with references to a generalized 'film viewer' in subject position and references to structural components of the film in the predicate, as in *then you see the scene* and *you get a flashback*. This creates an impression of the film as object, whose components move in relation to a stationary viewer (a CINEMATIC perspective). Narrator B, in contrast, tends to use primarily deictic discourse markers, such as the summarizing deictic in *this I didn't understand*, or clauses with verbs of motion, as in *he went back into the narrative* (a FLUID perspective). Through these and other devices, this speaker creates an impression that the narrator is 'traveling through' the story, moving from one temporal/spatial location to another.

It is likely that, as more levels of information are taken into account in an analysis, the function of sets of formal devices as indicators of topic structure will become increasingly clear.

6   Why do patterns of energy expenditure vary, and does the variation communicate?

We have reviewed our evidence that narrators exhibit a systematic relation between the occurrence of metanarrative statements and indexical devices that signal information about referents. Energy varies in respect to the occurrence or non-occurrence of gestures accompanying vocal referring expressions, the carefulness and hence duration of articulatory activities that produce words, and lexical choices themselves. When we have proposed that information at least of the first two kinds can be directly perceived and that, therefore, direct perception may contribute to a listener's understanding of a communication involving language, we have assumed that listeners are sensitive to these sources of information and detect what they signify. In fact, however, relevant research findings are slim. We review what evidence there is.

We can imagine two origins for directly perceivable marking of topic shifts and maintenance. On the one hand, the greater energy expended by speakers to refer to discourse entities immediately after a topic shift may reflect the newness of the entities to the speaker himself or herself. In a sense, the energy expenditure may be an 'unreflective reflection' of the ease or difficulty of a speaker's access to a discourse entity. In this case, the information is not intentionally made available to listeners, and listeners may or may not use it. Perhaps compatibly with this proposed origin, Krauss and colleagues, among others, find that gestures occur even when listeners cannot see speakers (e.g., Krauss, Dushay, Chen & Rauscher 1995). Likewise, with respect to word intelligibility, Bard, Sotillo, Anderson, Doherty-Sneddon & Newlands (1995) report that speakers produce less-intelligible word forms when they have produced the forms recently, whether or not the listener has heard the forms recently. Consequently the reduction of articulatory effort that must underlie the reduction in intelligibility appears to have an egocentric origin.

Despite this evidence, however, there is evidence as well that speakers attempt to shape their communications to the audience. Accordingly, on the other hand, a second reason for the observed energy peaks and troughs in spoken communications might be that they are provided on behalf of the listener. Gestures occur more frequently when listeners and speakers are in visual contact than when they are not (e.g., Krauss et al. 1995). Compatibly, durational shortening of repeated words does not occur in a non-communicative setting in which speakers read a list of words into a microphone (Fowler 1988), and more shortening occurs in a referential communication task when speech is directed to a listener who is present (and can provide evidence of understanding) than in speech that is recorded ostensibly to be played to a listener at some later time (McAllister et al. 1994). Finally, in a referential communication task in which speakers provided information to listeners about the identity of more and less familiar public figures, Fussell & Krauss (1992) found significant, though weak, evidence that directors provided more lexical information about public figures who they judged were less identifiable to their addressees than about more identifiable figures.

Whether or not speakers intend their systematic increases and decreases of energy expenditure to communicate to a listener, do the patterns communicate? They might provide two kinds of information. We have proposed that they might help the listener pick out a referent. The occurrence of a reduced articulation of a referring expression or the occurrence of a pronoun, neither accompanied by a gesture, should tell the listener that the referent must already have been introduced following a topic shift. The occurrence of a clear utterance of a referring expression or of an explicit expression, either one accompanied by a gesture, implies a new referent – not one already introduced.

Second, an increase in energy expenditure can serve to shift the origo. The occurrence of an overly explicit (or overly clearly articulated) referring expression accompanied by a gesture can, particularly in the context of a metanarrative statement, announce a change in the reference frame such that previously presupposed referents no longer are such.[3]

The literature provides some evidence that patterns of energy expenditure may communicate in these ways. As for gestures, Krauss, Morrel-Samuels & Colasante (1991) showed viewers videotapes (without sound) of speakers describing pictures of objects, people, or scenes. Viewers were better than chance at choosing which of two lexical affiliates had accompanied the gesture on the sound track. (Distracter lexical affiliates had originally occurred with some other gesture.) Likewise in a following experiment, judges rated written interpretations of gestures as more similar to the gestures' own lexical affiliates than to other lexical affiliates. Accordingly, we have some indirect evidence that gestures can help pick out their referents. However, our questions more specifically ask whether or not the occurrence or non-occurrence of a gesture, whatever the gesture's specific form may be, signals to a listener reference respectively to a currently backgrounded or foregrounded referent and whether or not the occurrence of a gesture in reference to a currently foregrounded referent may serve to shift the origo. We know of no research addressing these questions.

As for durational shortening, we know that listeners can tell by the way a word is produced whether it is a speaker's first utterance or a repetition (Fowler & Housum 1987). Accordingly, high- and low-energy renditions of a word have the potential to communicate. However, the literature does not tell us whether or not the appropriate occurrence of a high- or low-energy rendition of a word fosters identification respectively of a backgrounded or foregrounded referent, or whether or not an otherwise unnecessarily clear production of a word can foster a shift in the frame of reference.

Finally, as for lexical choice, we know that a pronoun referring to a focal referent fosters faster retrieval of information about the referent than does an explicit referring expression (Cloitre & Bever 1988). Accordingly, we can conclude that an appropriately opaque referring expression can help to pick out its referent better than an inappropriately explicit one. Further, we know that use of a prompt for story continuation that is either a full noun phrase or a pronoun that refers to a currently foregrounded referent stimulates respectively continuations in which scene shifts occur or do not (Vonk, Hustinx & Simons 1992). Here we have some evidence suggesting a positive answer to our second question: whether or not increases in energy expenditure can provide information for a shift in the origo.

7   How patterns of energy expenditure might communicate: a bridge between language comprehension and perception

Despite the paucity of evidence currently available as to whether patterns of energy expenditure do communicate to listeners, here we take the view that they will be shown to, and go on to address the question of how they might serve their communicative function. We see this as an important question, because the answer may reveal a new sense in which language comprehension may be grounded in perception.

Perceivers of the non-linguistic environment have to be realists; that is, they have to perceive those aspects of their environment that are critical for their survival. Realist perceiving involves achieving parity – a relation of identity – between those critical aspects of the environment and what is perceived. Perceptual systems function to foster achievement of parity. As we outlined in the introduction, in visual perceiving, for example, perceptual systems exploit the facts that objects and events in the environment causally structure light and that different objects and events structure light distinctively. In consequence, there is a specificational relation between structure in light and the objects and events that caused it. The visual perceptual system uses specifying information in light as such, and, therefore, perceivers see properties of the environment, not properties of the light that stimulates the visual system. By the same token, the auditory perceptual system uses specifying structure in air as information for its causal source in the environment.

Achievement of parity is also a goal of communication systems, including language. When a speaker produces an utterance, he or she generally intends to accomplish something by talking, and accomplishment of that something requires achievement of communicative parity. If A produces the utterance "Please sit down" to B, he intends that B shall at least know what he wants her to do; more than that, he intends that she do as instructed and sit down. Parity is achieved if B knows from A's utterance what he intends. In a different example, if A describes an event to B, he intends at least that she acquire knowledge of the aspects of the event he chooses to describe. Parity is achieved if the properties of the event that *B* comes to know about are the same as those that *A* attempts to convey.

In direct perception, structure in stimulation at the sense organs is immediately about a causal environmental source. Some direct perception can occur in listening to spoken utterances, because structure in the acoustic signal is immediately about the vocal-tract gestures that caused them. However, acoustic structure is not immediately about the speaker's intended message, and so perception of the message cannot be direct based on the speaker's words. How can parity achievement be fostered in language understanding?

We briefly proposed one important part of the answer in the introduction. We suggested that speakers' choices of words and their sequencing of words into syntactically structured sentences to convey a particular message or to implement a particular speech act are determined by cultural necessity. That is, if members of a language community want to communicate, they must use the words that members of the community use to convey messages, and they must use the community's syntactic conventions to sequence or properly inflect the words. To an extent, cultural necessity can serve the role in language use that lawful causation serves in direct perception of the environment. Further, the language forms can, in principle, specify the message that they encode because, in languages, distinct sequences of forms are used to convey distinct messages.

The need for something more to buttress language understanding derives at least in part from the differences between lawful causation and conformity to cultural conventions. Physical laws cannot be broken, whereas conventions can be breached. Physical law holds everywhere, but conventions vary from geographic location to location and from social group to social group. We have proposed that the something more is provided by directly perceivable indexical signals.

In language-learning, direct perception may play a much larger role than it does in skilled communication by language. Much of speech to very young children occurs during routinized activities such as bedtime, mealtime, or bathtime (Nelson 1985; Bruner 1990). In these cases, caregivers may not only foster language acquisition but, more locally, may foster comprehension of their linguistic utterances by talking about events in the here-and-now. The pajamas or the toothbrush being discussed are visible, that is, directly perceivable. In a sense, we might say that caregivers take some of the burden off the child's undeveloped linguistic system by talking about events in the here-and-now. Direct perception can stand in for language understanding in part, and achievement of communicative parity may thereby be fostered. In ocular deixis, we may see something similar happening in the speech and associated activities of linguistically highly competent communicators. For example, speakers may point to a referent. Similarly, Hanks' example above, in which a speaker says of a tool *it is here*, may be considered an example of 'aural deixis' in which a listener can localize the speaker directly and thereby localize a referent.

Of course, however, the power of linguistic communications is in their not being tied to provision of information about what is present in the here-and-now. Can direct perception lighten the burden of parity achievement on a linguistic utterance even when the utterance is not about events occurring in the here-and-now – that is, in imagination-oriented deixis? Perhaps it can. It can be no accident that energy peaks accompany reference to less accessible (new) information and troughs to more accessible information. We doubt, for example, that narrators in other cultures would show the opposite association of energy and accessibility (cf. the Georgian study to which we alluded earlier). Perhaps, then, energy peaks may provide directly perceivable evidence of a narrator referring to something relatively inaccessible; troughs may provide evidence of reference to something relatively accessible.

8   Summary

Our major purpose has been to show that there is a non-arbitrary relation between some properties of communicative activities and the messages that the activities convey. Specifically, we have surveyed a range of findings that reveal an association between the occurrence of metanarrative statements and the use of longer, more transparent referring expressions, of durationally longer words, and of gestures. In our terms, 'energy peaks' follow metanarrative statements relative to troughs that occur elsewhere. Metanarrative statements appear to serve the function of transforming the indexical ground, and they should, therefore, render some previously familiar or accessible referents less accessible. The occurrence of energy peaks at these points of high communicative dynamism, and of troughs elsewhere, provides redundant information for the transformation, and it provides information for the identity of referents themselves against which referents are identified. The energy peaks and troughs are particularly interesting in this respect because they can provide directly perceptible information for these components of discourse. If listeners make use of that information (an essentially unresearched issue), then direct perception of information for referents can serve to reduce listeners' dependence on information conveyed by means of lexico-grammatical forms.

NOTES

We thank Nobuhiro Furuyama for comments on an earlier version of this manuscript. Preparation of the manuscript was supported in part by NICHD grant HD01994 to Haskins Laboratories.

1 As Lakoff (1987) puts it, semantics has been supposed to be central, because it specifies "connections between language and the objective world" (p. 117), whereas pragmatics is peripheral information that is not concerned with objective reality but "merely" with human communication.

2 We include the variable lexical length in our presentation even though it may be questionable whether lexical length can be directly perceived. We include it because long expressions, such as full noun phrases, require greater energy expenditure than short ones, such as pronouns, and because lexical length patterns in ways similar to the patterning of gestures and word duration with respect to metanarrative statements. Clearly, however, lexical length can only contribute to a listener's assessment of energy expenditure if the listener has identified the expression as a referring expression that could have been shorter (or longer).

3 We have weak evidence that different narrative strategies influence the listener's perception of what she has heard. In Levy's original study (1984) of the film narrations we have described, each listener rated the narration she had heard on a 5-point scale according to how entertaining the story was. The only narrations rated as '5' ("very entertaining") were those of B and of a second narrator who, like B, showed an association between metanarrative statements and word duration. Narration A, differing on all dimensions from B, was rated '3'.

REFERENCES

Bard, E., Sotillo, C., Anderson, A., Doherty-Sneddon, G. & Newlands, A. 1995. The control of intelligibility in running speech. In Elenius & Branderud (eds.), pp. 188–191.

Bolinger, D. 1963. Length, vowel, juncture. *Linguistics* 1: 5–29.

Bolinger, D. 1981. *Two Kinds of Vowels, Two Kinds of Rhythm*. Bloomington: Indiana University Linguistics Club.

Bruner, J. 1990. *Acts of Meaning*. Cambridge, MA: Harvard University Press.

Bühler, K. 1990. *Theory of Language: The Representational Function of Language*, trans. D. F. Goodwin. Amsterdam: Benjamins. (Originally published 1934.)

Cloitre, M. & Bever, T. 1988. Linguistic anaphors, levels of representation and discourse. *Language and Cognitive Processes* 3: 293–322.

Dreyfus, H. 1992. *What Computers Still Can't Do: A Critique of Artificial Reason*. Cambridge, MA: MIT Press.

Duncan, S., Jr. & Fiske, D. W. 1979. *Face-to-Face Interaction: Research, Methods, and Theory*. Hillsdale, NJ: Erlbaum.

Duranti, A. & Goodwin, C. (eds.) 1992. *Rethinking Context*. Cambridge: Cambridge University Press.

Elenius, K. & Branderud, P. (eds.) 1995. *Proceedings of the XIIIth International Congress of Phonetic Sciences*. Stockholm: Arnes Stromberg Grafiska.

Fodor, J. A. 1983. *The Modularity of Mind: A Monograph on Faculty Psychology*. Cambridge, MA: MIT Press.

Fowler, C. A. 1988. Differential shortening of repeated content words produced in various communicative contexts. *Language and Speech* 31: 307–319.

Fowler, C. A. & Housum, J. 1987. Talkers' signalling of 'new' and 'old' words in speech and listeners' perception and use of the distinction. *Journal of Memory and Language* 26: 489–504.

Fowler, C. A., Levy, E. T. & Brown, J. M. 1997. Reductions of spoken words in certain discourse contexts. *Journal of Memory and Language* 37: 24–40.

Fussell, S. & Krauss, R. M. 1992. Coordination of knowledge in communication: effects of speakers' assumptions about what others know. *Journal of Personality and Social Psychology* 62: 378–391.

Gibson, J. J. 1979. *The Ecological Approach to Visual Perception*. Boston: Houghton Mifflin.

Givón, T. (ed.) 1979. *Syntax and Semantics 12: Discourse and Syntax*. New York: Academic Press.

Givón, T. 1991. Isomorphism in the grammatical code: cognitive and biological considerations. *Studies in Language* 15: 85–114.

Hanks, W. F. 1992. The indexical ground of deictic reference. In Duranti & Goodwin (eds.), pp. 43–76.

Hirschberg, J. & Pierrehumbert, J. 1986. The intonational structuring of discourse. In *Proceedings of the Twenty-fourth Annual Meeting of the Association for Computational Linguistics*. New York.

Jarvella, R. J. & Klein, W. (eds.) 1982. *Speech, Place and Action*. Chichester, Sussex: Wiley.

Kendon, A. 1972. Some relationships between body motion and speech: an analysis of an example. In Seigman & Pope (eds.), pp. 177–210.

Kendon, A. 1980. Gesticulation and speech: two aspects of the process of utterance. In Key (ed.), pp. 207–227.

Key, M. R. (ed.) 1980. *The Relationship of Verbal and Nonverbal Communication*. The Hague: Mouton.

Krauss, R., Dushay, R., Chen, Y. & Rauscher, F. 1995. The communicative value of conversational hand gestures. *Journal of Experimental Social Psychology* 31: 533–552.

Krauss, R., Morrel-Samuels, P. & Colasante, C. 1991. Do conversational hand gestures communicate? *Journal of Personality and Social Psychology* 61: 743–754.

Lakoff, G. 1987. *Women, Fire, and Dangerous Things: What Categories Reveal about the Mind*. Chicago: University of Chicago Press.

Levy, E. T. 1984. Communicating thematic structure in narrative discourse: the use of referring terms and gestures. Unpublished Ph.D. dissertation, University of Chicago.

Levy, E. T. & McNeill, D. 1992. Speech, gesture and discourse. *Discourse Processes* 15: 277–301.

Marslen-Wilson, W., Levy, E. T. & Tyler, L. K. 1982. Producing interpretable discourse: the establishment and maintenance of reference. In Jarvella & Klein (eds.), pp. 339–378.

McAllister, J., Potts, A., Mason, K. & Marchant, G. 1994. Word duration in monologue and dialogue speech. *Language and Speech* 37: 393–405.

McNeill, D. 1992. *Hand and Mind: What Gestures Reveal about Thought*. Chicago: University of Chicago Press.

McQuown, N. A. 1971. *The Natural History of an Interview*. Microfilm Collection of Manuscripts on Cultural Anthropology, 15th ser. Chicago: University of Chicago, Joseph Regenstein Library, Department of Photoduplication.

Nelson, K. 1985. *Making Sense: The Acquisition of Shared Meaning*. New York: Academic Press.

Schegloff, E. A. 1979. The relevance of repair to syntax-for-conversation. In Givón (ed.), pp. 261–286.

Seigman, A. & Pope, B. (eds.) 1972. *Studies in Dyadic Communication*. Elmsford, NY: Pergamon.

Tomasello, M. 1992. The social bases of language acquisition. *Social Development* 1: 67–87.

Vonk, W., Hustinx, L. G. M. M. & Simons, W. H. G. 1992. The use of referential expressions in structuring linguistic discourse. *Language and Cognitive Processes* 7: 301–333.

12 Gesture and the transition from one- to two-word speech: when hand and mouth come together

Cynthia Butcher
Department of Psychology, University of Chicago

Susan Goldin-Meadow
Department of Psychology, University of Chicago

1 Introduction

Despite the fact that they are produced in different modalities, gesture and speech form a unified communication system in adults. To explore whether symbolic communicative gesture and speech form a single system in young children, three girls and three boys were observed longitudinally during the transition from one- to two-word speech. Initially, gesture tended to be produced without speech, and, on the rare occasions when it was combined with speech, that speech was meaningless and not synchronized with the accompanying gesture. The two characteristics that define integration in adult speakers – semantic coherence (combining gesture with meaningful and related speech) and temporal synchrony (producing gesture in synchrony with speech) – were found to emerge in the children's communications at the same moment and prior to the onset of two-word speech. The onset of gesture–speech integration thus occurs during the one-word period and before words are combined with other words.

Adults and children typically express their thoughts in speech, and, along with that speech, they spontaneously produce gestures. Despite the fact that they are produced in different modalities, gesture and speech deliver a coherent message to the listener (Alibali, Flevares & Goldin-Meadow 1997; Goldin-Meadow & Sandhofer 1999; Goldin-Meadow, Wein & Chang 1992; McNeill, Cassell & McCullough 1994) and thus can be said to form a single unified communication system (Goldin-Meadow 1997; Goldin-Meadow, Alibali & Church 1993; McNeill 1985, 1992). According to McNeill (1992), this coherence is possible because gesture and speech share a common cognitive representation; that is, before the communication

unfolds, gesture and speech are part of a single idea. As expression proceeds, the message is parsed, with most information channeled into speech
but some information channeled into gesture. The coordination of gesture
and speech to convey a single message, and particularly the origins of such
coordination, form the cornerstone of this study.

1.1   *Gesture and speech form an integrated system in adult speakers*

Evidence that gesture and speech form a single, unified system in adult
speakers comes from two sources. First, gestures and speech are semantically and pragmatically co-expressive. When people speak, they produce a
variety of gesture types (iconics, metaphorics, beats, cohesives, deictics; cf.
McNeill 1992), and each type of gesture has a characteristic type of speech
with which it occurs. For example, iconic gestures have a transparent relationship to the ideas they convey; iconics accompany utterances that depict
objects and events and fulfill a narrative function (i.e., they accompany the
speech that 'tells the story'). As an instance, a speaker produced the following iconic gesture when describing a scene from a comic book in which a
character bends a tree back to the ground: the speaker grasped his hand as
though gripping something and pulled his hand back. He produced this
gesture as he uttered the words "and he bends it way back," a concrete
description of an event in the story.

In contrast, metaphoric gestures are also pictorial but represent an
abstract idea rather than a concrete object or event; metaphorics accompany utterances that refer to the pragmatic structure of the discourse as a
whole. As an instance, a speaker produced the following metaphoric gesture
when announcing that what he had just seen and was about to recount was
a cartoon: the speaker raised his hands as though he were offering an object
to the listener – a pictorial representation of the cartoon as a whole, but not
a concrete one. He produced this gesture as he said, "It was a Sylvester and
Tweety cartoon," an utterance which set up and introduced the topic of discussion rather than forming part of the storyline. Other gesture types similarly have their own parallels with speech (see McNeill 1992: ch. 7),
suggesting a linked relationship between the two modalities.

It is important to note that, although the information conveyed by
gesture is, for the most part, related in some way to the information conveyed by speech, the particular information conveyed by the two modalities
need not be identical. For example, when describing Granny's chase after
Sylvester in a cartoon narrative, a speaker moved her hand as though
swinging an object while saying, "She chases him out again" (McNeill
1992). Speech conveyed the ideas of pursuit and recurrence, but gesture
conveyed the weapon used (an umbrella) during the chase. Thus, the two

modalities may present different aspects of the same event, suggesting that gesture and speech share a common cognitive representation at some point during the speech act.

The second source of evidence that gesture and speech form a unified system comes from the fact that the two are almost always synchronous. Gesture is rarely produced on its own in adults (except in the form of an emblem, e.g., the OK sign; see Kendon 1981 for discussion). Indeed, McNeill (1992) found that 90 percent of gestures in adults were produced when the gesturer was speaking. Thus, acts of speaking and gesturing are bound to each other in time at a general level. Moreover, gesture and speech are synchronized temporally at another, more refined level as well; even within a single utterance, the gesture and the linguistic segment representing the same information as that gesture are co-temporal. Specifically, the gesture movement – the 'stroke' – lines up in time with the equivalent linguistic segment. As an example, in the description of an iconic gesture above, the speaker produced the stroke of the gesture just as he said, "bends it way back" (see Kita 1993 for more subtle examples of how speech and gesture adjust to each other in timing; Morrel-Samuels & Krauss 1992 for evidence that the timing of gesture and speech is related to the rated familiarity of the spoken word; and Mayberry, Jaques & DeDe 1998 for evidence that gesture and speech are synchronized even when, as in stuttering, the speech-production process goes awry). Such synchrony implies that the speaker is presenting the same meaning in both channels at the same moment and that gesture and speech form a single integrated system.

These findings strongly suggest that gesture and speech work together to convey a single message integrated in both time (synchrony across the two modalities) and meaning (semantic coherence across the information conveyed in the two modalities) in adults. However, there is little work exploring the origins of such a system in children at the earliest stages of language development. Is gesture–speech integration characteristic of the earliest communications of young children, or does integration across the two modalities emerge at a consistent point in the young child's linguistic development? We explored this question in six children observed longitudinally from the production of single words to the production of two-word combinations.

1.2   Gesture in the one-word period of language development

At a time when children are limited in what they can say, there is another avenue of expression that may be open to them. In addition to speaking, the child can also gesture (cf. Bates 1976; Bates, Benigni, Bretherton, Camaioni & Volterra 1979; Petitto 1988). The use of gesture during the one-word period can extend the range of ideas children can express. For example, Acredolo & Goodwyn (1985) describe a young language-learner in the one-word period who used gestures rather than words to refer to certain objects; for this child, a referent object was symbolized by either a gesture or a word, but not both (see also Acredolo & Goodwyn 1988, who describe this same phenomenon in a larger sample of children). In fact, in a study of twelve Italian children in the one-word period, Iverson, Capirci & Caselli (1994) showed that eight of the children exhibited a clear preference for communication in the gestural modality over the verbal modality.

Combining gesture and speech within a single utterance can also increase the communicative range available to the child. Most of the gesture–speech combinations that young children produce contain gestures that convey information redundant with the information conveyed in speech; for example, pointing at an object while naming it (de Laguna 1927; Greenfield & Smith 1976; Guillaume 1927; Leopold 1949). However, young children have also been found to produce gesture–speech combinations in which gesture conveys information that is different from the information conveyed in speech; for example, gesturing at an object while describing in speech the action to be done on the object (pointing to an apple and saying, "Give"), or gesturing at an object and describing in speech the owner of that object (pointing at a toy and saying, "Mine"; Boswell 1988; Goldin-Meadow & Morford 1985; Greenfield & Smith 1976; Masur 1982, 1983; Morford & Goldin-Meadow 1992; Volterra & Iverson 1995; Zinober & Martlew 1985). This second type of gesture–speech combination allows a child to express two elements of a sentence (one in gesture and one in speech) at a time when the child may not be able to express those elements within a single spoken utterance.

Given that young children do use gesture communicatively during the one-word period of language development, and given that adults' gestures are integrated with speech in both timing and meaning, the question naturally arises as to whether communicative gesture forms an integrated system with speech in the one-word speaker as well. Is there a time early in development when communicative gesture is used primarily without speech? If young children do produce gesture in combination with speech, are the two modalities integrated both temporally and semantically, as they are in adult systems? This study was designed to address these questions.

2   Method

2.1   Subjects and procedure

The subjects for this study were six children, three boys and three girls, videotaped in their homes over a period of months. Videotaping began

Table 12.1. *Subject information*

First name	Sex	Ages observed	No. of sessions observed	Age of first meaningful word	Age of two-word combination
Christopher	M	12 to 23.5 mo.	11	13.0	21.0
Emily	F	13.5 to 19 mo.	9	13.5[a]	18.0
Nicholas	M	15.5 to 21 mo.	11	15.5[a]	18.5
Beth	F	15.5 to 21 mo.	5	15.5[a]	18.0
Ann	F	15.5 to 25 mo.	6	16.5	22.5
Joseph	M	21 to 27.5 mo.	10	21.0[a]	26.5

Note:
[a] These four children produced meaningful words during their first observation sessions.

when each child was in the one-word period of language development, and continued until the child began producing two-word combinations. Four of the six children were seen approximately every 2 weeks (except when weather, illness, vacations, etc. delayed taping sessions); the remaining two subjects were seen approximately every 6 to 8 weeks. Table 12.1 reports the age range during which each child was observed and the number of video-taped sessions conducted during this period.[1]

All of the data were collected in spontaneous play situations during which the children interacted with their primary caregivers and/or the experimenter. In order to facilitate conversation and provide consistent stimuli across subjects, two large bags of toys and books were brought to the child's home by the experimenter (see Goldin-Meadow 1979 and Goldin-Meadow & Morford 1985 for further information on the toys and procedures). The play session was not structured by the experimenter, and parents were encouraged to engage their children in conversation. The play sessions lasted approximately one hour.

2.2   *Identifying and coding communicative utterances*

We focused in this study on gesture and speech that was used communicatively. All of the communicative gestures and vocalizations produced by each child during a half-hour of videotape were transcribed and coded. If that half-hour did not yield one hundred communicative behaviors, additional tape was coded until one hundred behaviors were transcribed. A communicative behavior was defined as either a gesture on its own, speech on its own (either meaningless or meaningful; see below), or a gesture and speech produced together. The mean number of minutes transcribed per session for each child was: Ann, 41 minutes; Beth, 48; Emily, 30; Christopher, 33; Nicholas, 31; and Joseph, 39.

2.2.1   Coding speech. All of the communicative vocalizations that each child produced were coded and classified into one of two categories. (1) Meaningful vocalizations were either actual English words (e.g., "dog," "cat," "duck," "hot," "walking") or speech sounds that were consistently used by a particular child to refer to a specific object or event (e.g., using "bah" to refer to a bottle). (2) Meaningless vocalizations were speech sounds that were not used consistently to refer to a particular referent but appeared to be communicative nonetheless; that is, they were directed toward another individual (e.g., the child looks at a picture, produces the sound "buh," and looks up at the adult; "buh" does not have any apparent relation to the object in the picture, which was neither a ball, a book, nor anything whose name began with 'b', but it does appear to have been produced for the benefit of the listener).

2.2.2   Coding gesture. The criteria for isolating gestures grew out of a concern that the gestures meet the minimal requirements for a communicative symbol (see Goldin-Meadow & Mylander 1984 and Butcher, Mylander & Goldin-Meadow 1991 for discussion) and were as follows:

(1) The gesture must be directed to another individual; that is, it must be communicative. In particular, we required that the child establish eye contact with a communication partner, or be assured of the partner's attention, in order for the child's act to be considered a gesture.

(2) The gesture must not itself be a direct manipulation of some relevant person or object (i.e., it must be empty-handed; cf. Petitto 1988). When a child puts a telephone to the ear and pretends to have a conversation, it is not clear whether that act should be regarded as designating the act of telephoning (and therefore a symbol), or as the child's attempts to practice the act of telephoning (and therefore not symbolic at all; cf. Huttenlocher & Higgins 1978). To be conservative, all acts that were done on objects were excluded, with one exception – if a child held up an object to bring it to another's attention, an act that serves the same function as the pointing gesture, it was counted as a gesture. In addition, functional acts were not considered gestures; for example, neither holding out an object to transfer it to another person nor reaching for an object was considered a gesture. However, if the child extended a hand toward the desired object (but did not try to capture it) and looked at the experimenter, this act was not a direct act on the object and thus was considered a gesture (cf. Masur 1983).

(3) The gesture must not be part of a ritual act (e.g., to blow a kiss as someone leaves the house) or game (e.g., patty-cake). In general, the

symbolic nature of language allows for a particular type of communicative flexibility: a word can be used for multiple discourse functions. Acts that are tied to stereotyped contexts of use clearly do not have this flexibility and thus were not considered gestures.

(4) The gesture must not be an imitation of the communication partner's preceding gesture. This criterion assured that the child was not merely copying – with little or no comprehension – the gestures his or her communication partners produced.

Note that these criteria for identifying gestures are somewhat more stringent than those that have been used in some studies of gesture in young children (e.g., Volterra, Bates, Benigni & Camaioni 1979, who did not require a gesture to be communicative, nor did they require a gesture to be divorced from the actual manipulation of an object). The criteria used in this study closely follow those used by Acredolo & Goodwyn (1988), Petitto (1988), and Morford & Goldin-Meadow (1992).

The form of each gesture was described in terms of the shape of the hand, the type of movement, and the place of articulation. At this age, gestures typically consist of pointing, holding up objects to call attention to them, holding out an open flat palm as if to receive an object, which signifies "Give" or "Gimme," and a very small number of iconic gestures (e.g., a pointing handshape held at the nose and arced upward and off the nose to represent an elephant; see Goldin-Meadow & Morford 1985; Morford & Goldin-Meadow 1992). Meanings were assigned to gestures on the basis of non-linguistic context. The object, person, or place toward which a pointing gesture was directed was considered to be the referent of that point, and the action or attribute depicted by the motion or handshape of an iconic gesture was considered to be the referent of that iconic (see Goldin-Meadow & Mylander 1984 for a detailed description of how meaning was assigned to gesture).

2.3   Coding the relationship between gesture and speech

Gestures produced without speech, and vocalizations produced without gesture, were identified and categorized but coded no further. Gestures combined with speech were divided into two types: those in which gesture was combined with a meaningful word – that is, combinations in which gesture had a *semantic relationship* to the speech it accompanied – and those in which gesture was combined with a meaningless vocalization. In addition, the *temporal relationship* between gesture and the speech it accompanied was coded to the nearest video frame (1/30 second) for all gesture–speech combinations (gestures combined with meaningful words and gestures combined with meaningless vocalizations). Following

McNeill (1992) and Kendon (1972, 1980), gesture–speech combinations were considered synchronous if the vocalization occurred on the stroke of the gesture or at the peak of the gesture (the farthest extension before the hand began to retract).

2.4   Coding reliability

Reliability between two independent coders was assessed on a subset of the videotaped sessions. Reliability was 92% agreement between the two coders ($N = 142$) for isolating and identifying an utterance, 95% ($N = 120$) for classifying these utterances as speech alone, gesture alone, or gesture and speech in combination, 96% ($N = 98$) for dividing speech into meaningless and meaningful vocalizations and for assigning particular meanings to the meaningful vocalizations, 96% ($N = 49$) for assigning meanings to the gestures, 84% ($N = 45$) for coding the semantic relationship between gesture and the meaningful vocalization it accompanied, and 100% (N = 32) for coding the timing between the gesture and vocalization in a gesture–speech combination.

3   Results

3.1   Characteristics of the children's speech

Table 12.1 presents the age at which each child first produced a meaningful vocalization (with or without a gesture) on our videotapes, and the age at which the child first produced a two-word combination on the videotapes. Note that since our videotaped sessions necessarily represent a small sample of each child's communications, the onset ages listed in Table 12.1 may inflate the actual ages at which these children began producing meaningful words and two-word combinations. Four of the children (Beth, Emily, Nicholas, and Joseph) were already producing meaningful words during their first observation sessions; the remaining two (Ann and Christopher) were not and produced their first meaningful words on the videotapes at ages 16.5 and 13 months, respectively. The ages at which the children began producing two-word combinations on our videotapes ranged from 18 to 26.5 months, an age span that falls within the range typically reported for the onset of two-word speech (cf. Bloom & Capatides 1987; Bowerman 1973; Braine 1976).

3.2   Gesture production during the one-word period

Figure 12.1 presents the number of communicative symbolic gestures each of the six children produced, expressed as a proportion of the total number

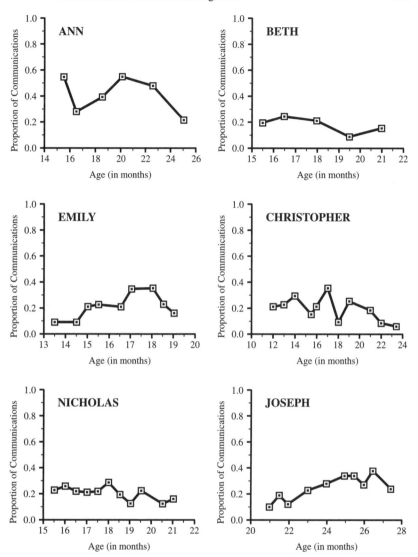

Figure 12.1. Proportion of gesture in each child's communications. The figure displays the number of communications containing gesture as a proportion of the total number of communications that the child produced at each session. Note that, for each child, the proportion of communications containing gesture remains relatively stable over time.

of communications (speech and/or gesture) the child produced at each observation session. There were some individual differences across children in the level of gesture production. Five of the children produced gestures in approximately 20% of their communications, while the sixth child, Ann, produced gestures in approximately 40% of her communications across the observational period. However, for each child, the proportion of gesture produced was relatively stable over the period of observations.

3.3   Is gesture produced without speech during the one-word period?

One of the characteristics of adult gesture that lead McNeill (1992) to suggest that gesture and speech form an integrated system is the fact that gesture is rarely produced on its own without speech. Approximately 10 percent of the gestures adults produce occur without speech. We first ask whether the children in our study looked like adults in this regard, or whether their gestures frequently occurred on their own without speech.

Figure 12.2 presents the number of gestures produced without speech as a proportion of the total number of gestures the child produced at each observation session. Five of the six children produced a large proportion of gestures without speech during their initial observation sessions. Of Ann's gestures ($N = 34$), 0.97 were produced without speech during her first observation session, as were 0.80 of Beth's ($N = 38$); these two children were seen once every two months, and at their second sessions, the majority of their gestures were produced *with* speech. The decline in production of gesture without speech was also evident in the children observed at shorter intervals. Emily produced 0.60 of her gestures ($N = 27$) without speech during her first two observation sessions and then slowly began producing more and more gestures with speech. Joseph produced from 0.60 to 0.90 of his gestures without speech during his first three sessions ($N = 39$) and then began to consistently produce more gestures with speech. Christopher exhibited a more erratic pattern, producing approximately 0.70 of his gestures without speech during his first two sessions ($N = 41$) but not showing a consistent decline in gesture without speech until the sixth observation session. The final child, Nicholas, produced a relatively small proportion of gestures without speech (0.30) at his first observation session ($N = 54$) and continued to do so throughout the study.

Thus, while the proportion of communications containing gesture remained relatively stable over development (cf. Figure 12.1), the way in which the children used gesture during this time period (Figure 12.2) did not. Five children began the period producing gestures without speech. By the end of the one-word period, when the child used gesture it was primarily used in combination with speech. The sixth child, Nicholas, was produc-

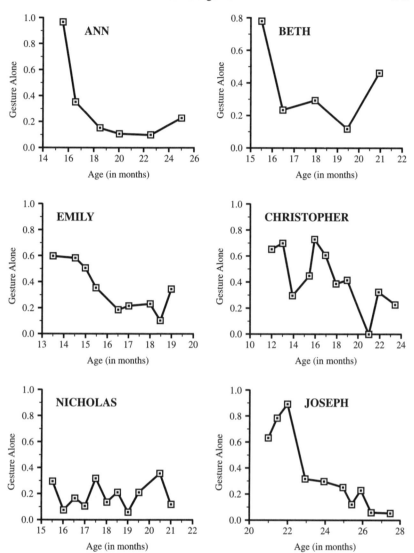

Figure 12.2. Proportion of communications containing gesture alone. The number of communications containing gesture without speech is shown as a proportion of the total number of communications containing gesture (i.e., gesture with or without speech) that each child produced. Note that the proportion of gesture-alone communications decreased over time for five of the six children (the sixth child, Nicholas, produced very few gesture-alone communications from the beginning of the study).

ing a large proportion of gestures with speech at the start of our study. We speculate, though of course we cannot be certain, that he had already shifted to an integrated gesture–speech system before our first videotaping session at 15.5 months. One obvious implication of these data is that there appears to be a time early in the one-word period when communicative gesture is *not* yet fully integrated with speech. We now turn to the characteristics of the integration process.

3.4   When gesture is combined with speech, is it synchronous with that speech?

McNeill (1992) noted that one characteristic of gesture–speech integration in adults is the fact that gesture is synchronously timed with respect to the speech it accompanies. We asked whether the children in our study, when they produced their first gesture–speech combinations, timed those gestures in a synchronous fashion with respect to speech.

Figure 12.3 presents the proportion of gesture–speech combinations that were synchronous (i.e., the stroke of the gesture co-occurred with the speech) at each observation session for the six children. The proportions in Figure 12.3 included all gesture–speech combinations, even those in which gesture was combined with a meaningless (as opposed to a meaningful) vocalization. Five of the six children initially produced gesture–speech combinations in which gesture was *not* synchronous with speech. The sixth child, again Nicholas, produced gesture–speech combinations that were synchronously timed throughout the period when he was observed. The fact that most of the children experienced a period when their gestures were not synchronized with the speech they accompanied further suggests that gesture and speech do not form a completely integrated system from the start but may require some time to become aligned with one another.

3.5   When gesture is combined with speech, is it semantically coherent with that speech?

The final piece of evidence suggesting that gesture and speech form an integrated system in adults (McNeill 1992) is the fact that gesture is semantically coherent with respect to the speech it accompanies. Although gesture does not always convey precisely the same information as does speech, the information conveyed by gesture tends to be related in some way to the information conveyed by speech – the two "cover the same idea unit" (McNeill 1992: 27), thus creating semantic coherence across the modalities. We therefore explore the onset and developmental trajectory of communicative symbolic gesture combined with *meaningful* words.

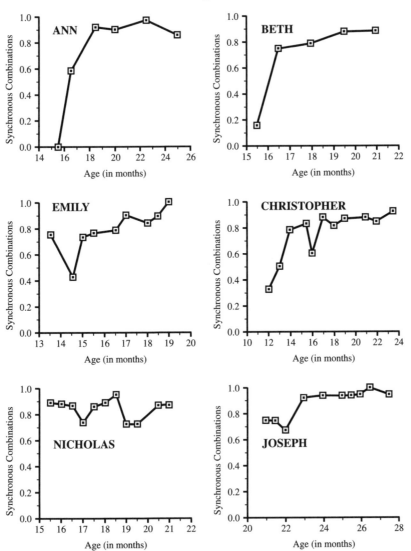

Figure 12.3. Timing in gesture–speech combinations. The figure displays
the number of synchronous gesture–speech combinations as a proportion
of the total number of gesture–speech combinations that the child produced at each session (the total includes gesture combined with meaningless vocalizations as well as meaningful vocalizations). Note that the
proportion of synchronous combinations increased over time for all of
the children except Nicholas, whose combinations tended to be synchronous from the start.

Figure 12.4 presents the number of gestures combined with meaningful speech as a proportion of all gesture–speech combinations produced by the six children at each observation session. Gesture-plus-meaningful-word combinations increased during this period in each of the six children. All of the children produced combinations in which gesture conveyed the same information as speech (e.g., point at box + "Box"), as well as combinations in which gesture conveyed different, but related, information from speech (e.g., point at box + "Open"). Note that in this second type of combination, the child is conveying two elements of a single proposition, albeit across two modalities. Thus, the ability to combine gesture and meaningful speech in a single utterance greatly expands the child's communicative range.

It is important to note that the relatively late onset of communicative symbolic gesture combined with meaningful speech is *not* due to the absence of meaningful words in the child's repertoires. All of the children except Ann and Christopher were producing meaningful words during session 1, and even Christopher produced his first meaningful words during session 2, one session prior to his first gesture-plus-meaningful-word combination.

3.6   *The convergence point: when gesture and speech come together*

More interesting than the fact that gesture-plus-meaningful-word combinations increase over time is the developmental moment at which these combinations first appear. Figure 12.5 presents three pieces of data superimposed on a single graph: (1) the proportion of gesture-alone communications, which declines over time; (2) the proportion of synchronized gesture–speech combinations, which increases over time; and (3) the onset of combinations containing gesture plus meaningful words, shown as a vertical line on each graph. Note that, for each of the five children who began to produce gesture-plus-meaningful-word combinations during our observation sessions, the three events converge: gesture-alone combinations began to decline and synchronous gesture–speech combinations began to increase at just the moment when gesture was first combined in the same utterance with a meaningful word (the sixth child, Nicholas, had presumably gone through this convergence point prior to our observations). Thus, the age at which each of the children began to produce communicative gestures in combination with meaningful words was precisely the age when timing began to improve dramatically in each child's gesture–speech combinations.

Note that in Figure 12.5 the measures of synchronization prior to the onset of gesture combined with meaningful speech (i.e., left of the vertical line) are based only on combinations of gesture with meaningless vocaliza-

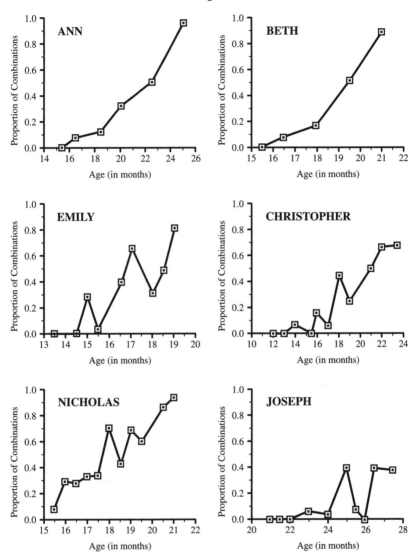

Figure 12.4. Onset of gesture combined with meaningful words. The figure displays the number of combinations containing gesture plus meaningful words as a proportion of all gesture–speech combinations (including those containing meaningless vocalizations) that the child produced at each session.

250   *Cynthia Butcher & Susan Goldin-Meadow*

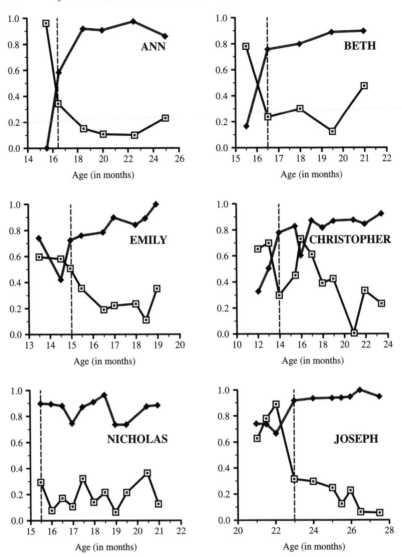

Figure 12.5. The convergence point. The figure displays the proportion of gesture-alone combinations (black diamonds) and the proportion of synchronous gesture–speech combinations (white squares) for each child. The vertical line demarcates the age at which each child first produced gestures in combination with meaningful words. The convergence point of the three marks the integration of gesture and speech in terms of temporal synchrony and semantic coherence.

tions, since, by definition, this is the only type of combination the child produced at that point. In contrast, the synchronization measures at this point and beyond (i.e., to the right of the line) are based on combinations of gesture with either meaningful or meaningless speech. It is therefore important to note that, after gesture began to be combined with meaningful speech, the proportion of synchronous combinations was the same in combinations of gesture with *meaningless* vocalizations as it was in combinations of gesture with *meaningful* words for each of the six children (Ann 0.91 vs. 0.89; Beth 0.80 vs. 0.84; Emily 0.79 vs. 0.89; Christopher 0.83 vs. 0.86; Nicholas 0.86 vs. 0.89; Joseph 0.93 vs. 0.98). In other words, there was an increase in synchrony in combinations of gesture plus meaningless vocalizations over this time period – an increase that coincided with the children's first gesture-plus-meaningful-word combinations.

Thus, the two characteristics that define gesture–speech integration in adult speakers – temporal synchrony and semantic coherence – appear to be absent at the onset of one-word speech and converge later during the one-word period. When children begin to combine gestures with meaningful words, they also begin to synchronize their gestures with respect to speech (both meaningful and meaningless vocalizations).

In sum, we have observed the following developmental sequence. First, there is a period when the child produces communicative symbolic gestures that function relatively independently of speech. During this period, gesture is frequently produced without speech, and, even when it is combined with speech, that speech is meaningless and not synchronized with the accompanying gesture. Next, gesture and speech become more fully integrated – the child begins to produce gesture in combination with meaningful words and to synchronize gesture in relation to speech (both meaningful and meaningless speech). Thus, the combination of gesture and meaningful speech and the synchronization of gesture with speech appear to mark the beginning of gesture–speech integration.

4   Discussion

This study explored the relationship between communicative symbolic gesture and speech in young children at the beginning stages of language development. Our findings suggest that there is a period when children produce communicative symbolic gestures independent of speech. Initially, most of the communicative symbolic gestures produced by the children in our study were unaccompanied by speech sounds of any sort (meaningful or not). Moreover, during this period (when gesture appeared to be operating independently of speech), even for the few times children combined their gestures with speech sounds, the gestures were not synchronous with those sounds and the sounds themselves were not meaningful. It was not until the children began combining gesture with meaningful words that gesture became appropriately timed with respect to speech. Note that the children had been producing meaningful words on their own (i.e., without gesture) for some time. Thus, the novel ability here is the ability to *combine* gesture with meaningful words, rather than the ability to produce meaningful words or meaningful gestures per se.

It is possible that the convergence we see across gesture and speech during the one-word period reflects a newly developed motoric skill in the child, one that allows hand and mouth to work together. If so, what is impressive is that this putative skill, which results in synchrony across the two modalities, is temporally linked to changes in the semantic system. For the first time, the child is able to convey meaningful information in two distinct modalities within a single communicative act. This finding reinforces the premises of McNeill's (1992) view of gesture–speech integration – that gesture and speech come together to form an integrated system both in terms of temporal synchrony and in terms of semantic coherence. Both are central to establishing a unified gesture–speech system.

Further evidence that the relationship between communicative symbolic gesture and speech changes during the early stages of language development comes from an experimental study conducted by Bates, Thal, Whitesell, Fenson & Oakes (1989). Bates et al. modeled gestures for 13- to 15-month-olds and varied the words that accompanied each gesture.[2] They found that the children in an early period of lexical development imitated the modeled gestures at the same rate regardless of the speech that accompanied those gestures. In other words, their performance on a gesture was unaffected by the type of speech with which that gesture occurred, suggesting that these children had not yet unified gesture and speech into a single system. In contrast, the children in later stages of lexical development imitated gestures at different rates, depending upon the words that accompanied the gestures. These children did not treat gesture and speech as independent sources but rather unified the two into a single message – as would be expected if they had already begun to integrate gesture and speech into a single system.

The Bates et al. (1989) study underscores two important points. First, the findings confirm that there is a point early in development when communicative symbolic gesture and speech do *not* yet form a fully integrated system. Second, the findings make it clear that the integration seen across modalities is not limited to production but is evident in comprehension as well (see Morford & Goldin-Meadow 1992, who also found evidence for gesture–speech integration in comprehension in one-word speakers).

In their studies of gesture and language in 9- to 13-month-olds, Bates et al. (1979) found a correlation between gesture production at 9 months (an age several months prior to the age at which we have found that gesture and speech become integrated into a single system) and word comprehension at the later ages. It is important to point out that early gesture use can be correlated with later word use (both reflecting a shared underlying cognitive ability) and still not be integrated with speech in the sense that we use the term. Indeed, Bates et al. (1979: 128) argue that the correlation they have found between gesture and speech reflects just such an ability, in particular an underlying capacity for communication via conventional signals.

Bringing together gesture and speech into a single well-integrated system allows the child to produce utterances in which words and gestures work together to produce a single message. Indeed, in additional analyses conducted on these same six children, Goldin-Meadow & Butcher (n.d.) found that the integration of gesture and speech set the stage for a novel type of combination – combinations in which gesture conveyed different (but related) information from that conveyed in speech. For example, after integration (but not before), each of the children produced combinations of the following type: gesture conveyed the object of a desired action (e.g., point at a box), and speech conveyed the action itself ("Open"); together, the two modalities conveyed a single proposition (open box). As another example, one child produced a FALL DOWN gesture (a palm flipping over in the air) and said, "Mouse," thus describing both the action and the actor of the proposition he intended to communicate. These new types of gesture + speech combinations represent a communicative, and perhaps even a conceptual, breakthrough for the child – a breakthrough that at the least is made evident, and might even be facilitated, by the integration of gesture and speech.

The appearance of these new types of gesture–speech combinations, in turn, heralded the onset of two-word speech. In these six children, the correlation between the onset of combinations in which gesture and speech conveyed different information and the onset of two-word combinations was high ($r_s = .90$) and reliable (p < .05; Goldin-Meadow & Butcher n.d.). Thus, the children who were first to produce combinations in which gesture and speech conveyed different, yet conceptually related, information were also first to produce two-word combinations. It makes intuitive sense to expect a child who can convey two elements of a single proposition across modalities to be closer to developing the ability to produce those two elements within a single spoken utterance – certainly closer than a child who has not yet demonstrated the ability to produce those two elements within a single communicative act in any form at all. The positive correlation confirms this intuition and makes it clear that the cognitive ability to concatenate elements of a proposition within a single communicative act, although necessary, is not sufficient to guarantee two-word speech – all of the children we have observed thus far were able to concatenate elements of a proposition across gesture and speech at a time when they were unable to accomplish this feat in speech alone.

We have shown that when, early in development, children use communicative symbolic gesture, they use it relatively independently of speech. In other words, gesture does not form a fully integrated system with speech from the outset. At some point during the one-word period, children begin to combine their communicative symbolic gestures with meaningful speech and at the same moment produce those gestures in temporal synchrony with that speech. We take the convergence of the semantic union and the temporal union of the two modalities to be the beginning of gesture–speech integration in the young child. This integration sets the stage for the onset of gesture–speech combinations in which gesture conveys different (but related) information from the information that is conveyed in speech. These combinations, in turn, herald the onset of two-word speech. Thus, gesture provides the child with an important vehicle for information that is not yet expressed in speech, and, as such, it provides the listener (as well as the experimenter) with a unique window into the child's mind.

NOTES

This work was supported by grants from the March of Dimes Foundation and the National Institute on Deafness and Other Communication Disorders (RO1 DC00491) to Goldin-Meadow, and by funding from the Home Health Care Foundation of Chicago through the section of Neonatology, Department of Pediatrics, at the University of Chicago. We thank Samar Ali, Vera Joanna Burton, and Beth Stare for their help in coding the videotapes and establishing reliability; Janellen Huttenlocher, Susan Levine, David McNeill, and William Meadow for their intellectual contributions throughout the project; and David McNeill and Jana Iverson for their incisive comments on the manuscript itself. Address correspondence to Susan Goldin-Meadow, Department of Psychology, University of Chicago, 5730 South Woodlawn Avenue, Chicago, IL 60637.

1 Two of the subjects in this study, Ann and Beth, were described by Goldin-Meadow & Morford (1985). The current study differs from the previous account in that additional videotapes were included in the data set and a variety of new analyses were performed on that entire set.

2 The gestures Bates et al. (1989) modeled for the children in their study were different from the gestures we observed in our study in that they were performed with objects. For example, for the phone gesture, a block was held to the ear as if it were a receiver. Although these gestures were not 'empty-handed', which was a requirement for a gesture in our study (cf. Petitto 1988), all of the actions were performed on blocks of different sizes, shapes, and colors and thus could not have been functional acts. In this sense, the gestures used in the Bates et al. study were comparable to the behaviors we took to be gestures in our study.

REFERENCES

Acredolo, L. P. & Goodwyn, S. W. 1985. Symbolic gesture in language development: a case study. *Human Development* 28: 40–49.

Acredolo, L. P. & Goodwyn, S. W. 1988. Symbolic gesturing in normal infants. *Child Development* 59: 450–466.

Alibali, M., Flevares, L. & Goldin-Meadow, S. 1997. Assessing knowledge conveyed in gesture: do teachers have the upper hand? *Journal of Educational Psychology* 89: 183–193.

Bates, E. 1976. *Language and Context.* New York: Academic Press.

Bates, E. with Benigni, L., Bretherton, I., Camaioni, L. & Volterra, V. (eds.) 1979. *The Emergence of Symbols: Cognition and Communication in Infancy.* New York: Academic Press.

Bates, E., Thal, D., Whitesell, K., Fenson, L. & Oakes, L. 1989. Integrating language and gesture in infancy. *Developmental Psychology* 25: 1004–1019.

Bloom, L. & Capatides, J. B. 1987. Expression of affect and the emergence of language. *Child Development* 58: 1513–1522.

Boswell, M. 1988. Gesture and speech in the one-word stage. Unpublished Ph.D. dissertation, University of Chicago.

Bowerman, M. 1973. *Early Syntactic Development: A Cross-Linguistic Study with Special Reference to Finnish.* New York: Cambridge University Press.

Braine, M. D. S. 1976. Children's first word combinations. *Monographs of the Society for Research in Child Development* 41 (164).

Butcher, C., Mylander, C. & Goldin-Meadow, S. 1991. Displaced communication in a self-styled gesture system: pointing at the nonpresent. *Cognitive Development* 6: 315–342.

Collins, A. (ed.) 1978. *Minnesota Symposia on Child Psychology*, vol. 13. Hillsdale, NJ: Erlbaum.

de Laguna, G. 1927. *Speech: Its Function and Development.* Bloomington: Indiana University Press.

Emmorey, K. & Reilly, J. S. (eds.) 1995. *Language, Gesture, and Space.* Hillsdale, NJ: Erlbaum.

Goldin-Meadow, S. 1979. Structure in a manual communication system developed without a conventional language model: language without a helping hand. In Whitaker & Whitaker (eds.), pp. 125–209.

Goldin-Meadow, S. 1997. When gesture and words speak differently. *Current Directions in Psychological Science* 6: 138–143.

Goldin-Meadow, S., Alibali, M. W. & Church, R. B. 1993. Transitions in concept acquisition: using the hand to read the mind. *Psychological Review* 100: 279–297.

Goldin-Meadow, S. & Butcher, C. n.d. Pointing toward two-word speech in young children. In Kita (ed.).

Goldin-Meadow, S. & Morford, M. 1985. Gesture in early child language: studies of deaf and hearing children. *Merrill-Palmer Quarterly* 31: 145–176.

Goldin-Meadow, S. & Mylander, C. 1984. Gestural communication in deaf children: the effects and non-effects of parental input on early language development. *Monographs of the Society for Research in Child Development* 49: 1–121.

Goldin-Meadow, S. & Sandhofer, C. M. 1999. Gesture conveys substantive information about a child's thoughts to ordinary listeners. *Developmental Science* 2: 67–74.

Goldin-Meadow, S., Wein, D. & Chang, C. 1992. Assessing knowledge through gesture: using children's hands to read their minds. *Cognition and Instruction* 9: 201–219.

Greenfield, P. & Smith, J. 1976. *The Structure of Communication in Early Language Development*. New York: Academic Press.

Guillaume, P. 1927. Les débuts de la phrase dans le langage de l'enfant. *Journal de Psychologie* 24: 1–25.

Huttenlocher, J. & Higgins, E. T. 1978. Issues in the study of symbolic development. In Collins (ed.), pp. 98–104.

Iverson, J. M., Capirci, O. & Caselli, M. C. 1994. From communication to language in two modalities. *Cognitive Development* 9: 23–43.

Iverson, J. & Goldin-Meadow, S. (eds.) 1998. *Nature and Functions of Gesture in Children's Communication*. San Francisco: Jossey-Bass.

Kendon, A. 1972. Some relationships between body motion and speech: an analysis of an example. In Seigman & Pope (eds.), pp. 177–210.

Kendon, A. 1980. Gesticulation and speech: two aspects of the process of utterance. In Key (ed.), pp. 207–227.

Kendon, A. 1981. The geography of gesture. *Semiotica* 37: 129–163.

Kessel, F. (ed.) 1988. *The Development of Language and Language Researchers: Essays in Honor of Roger Brown*. Hillsdale, NJ: Erlbaum.

Key, M. R. (ed.) 1980. *The Relationship of Verbal and Nonverbal Communication*. The Hague: Mouton.

Kita, S. 1993. Language and thought interface: a study of spontaneous gestures and Japanese mimetics. Unpublished Ph.D. dissertation, University of Chicago.

Kita, S. (ed.) n.d. Pointing: where language, culture and cognition meet. Unpublished manuscript.

Leopold, W. 1949. *Speech Development of a Bilingual Child: A Linguist's Record*, vol. III. Evanston, IL: Northwestern University Press.

Masur, E. F. 1982. Mothers' responses to infants' object-related gestures: influences on lexical development. *Journal of Child Language* 9: 23–30.

Masur, E. F. 1983. Gestural development, dual-directional signaling and the transition to words. *Journal of Psycholinguistic Research* 12: 93–109.

Mayberry, R. I., Jaques, J. & DeDe, G. 1998. What stuttering reveals about the development of the gesture–speech relationship. In Iverson & Goldin-Meadow (eds.), pp. 89–100.

McNeill, D. 1985. So you think gestures are nonverbal? *Psychological Review* 92: 350–371.

McNeill, D. 1992. *Hand and Mind: What Gestures Reveal about Thought*. Chicago: University of Chicago Press.

McNeill, D., Cassell, J. & McCullough, K.-E. 1994. Communicative effects of speech-mismatched gestures. *Research on Language and Social Interaction* 27: 223–238.

Morford, M. & Goldin-Meadow, S. 1992. Comprehension and production of gesture in combination with speech in one-word speakers. *Journal of Child Language* 9: 559–580.

Morrel-Samuels, P. & Krauss, R. M. 1992. Word familiarity predicts temporal asyn-
    chrony of hand gestures and speech. *Journal of Experimental Psychology:
    Learning, Memory and Cognition* 18: 615–622.
Petitto, L. A. 1988. 'Language' in the pre-linguistic child. In Kessel (ed.), pp.
    187–221.
Seigman, A. & Pope, B. (eds.) 1972. *Studies in Dyadic Communication.* Elmsford,
    NY: Pergamon.
Volterra, V., Bates, E., Benigni, L. & Camaioni, C. 1979. First words in language
    and action. In Bates et al. (eds.), pp. 141–222.
Volterra, V. & Iverson, J. M. 1995. When do modality factors affect the course of
    language acquisition? In Emmorey & Reilly (eds.), pp. 371–390.
Whitaker, H. & Whitaker, H. A. (eds.) 1979. *Studies in Neurolinguistics*, vol. IV. New
    York: Academic Press.
Zinober, B. & Martlew, M. 1985. Developmental changes in four types of gesture in
    relation to acts and vocalizations from 10 to 21 months. *British Journal of
    Developmental Psychology* 3: 293–306.

Part 3

Modeling gesture performance

The chapters in this part agree that modeling sets a standard for theories of gesture performance. If a process is well understood, it should be possible to design a model of it. If the model is computational, there is the further possibility of actually running the model and comparing its output to nature – observed gestures and speech in our case. Two models are described in this part. Neither is yet a running computational model, though both have been conceptualized with this goal in mind. The Krauss et al. and de Ruiter models propose ways to add gesture to the *Speaking* model presented by Levelt in 1989, a computer-like information-processing model of speech that did not make provision for gesture performance (see Gigerenzer & Goldstein 1996 for analysis of the *Speaking* model as part of the tradition of computer-like models in psychology). The Krauss et al. and de Ruiter models, while agreeing on the general framework, differ in a number of details that affect both the scope of the models and their internal organization. The chapters themselves point out these differences. Each chapter can be read in part as a presentation of its model and in part as a critical discussion of the other model. The third chapter, by McNeill, raises a question for both of the other chapters and for information-processing-type models in general. The question concerns how the context of speaking is to be handled. Gestures show that every utterance, even though a seemingly self-contained grammatical unit, incorporates content from outside its own structure (called a 'catchment', an extended example of which is described in the chapter). A model should explain the catchment content of the utterance as well as the linguistically formatted content. But information-processing models seem incapable in principle of incorporating catchments. A dynamic systems approach might offer a more inclusive approach, but models along these lines have not yet been devised for speech–gesture phenomena.

REFERENCE

Gigerenzer, G. & Goldstein, D. G. 1996. Mind as computer: birth of a metaphor. *Creativity Research Journal* 9: 131–144.

13   Lexical gestures and lexical access: a process model

Robert M. Krauss

Department of Psychology, Columbia University

Yihsiu Chen

Department of Psychology, Columbia University

Rebecca F. Gottesman

Department of Psychology, Columbia University

1   Introduction

Observers of human behavior have long been fascinated by the gestures that accompany speech, and by the contributions to communication they purportedly make.[1] Yet, despite this long-standing fascination, remarkably little about such gestures is well understood. The list of things we don't understand is long, but some of the most important open questions concern their form and function: *Why do different gestures take the particular form they do,* and *What is it that these ubiquitous behaviors accomplish?* Traditionally, answers to the function question have focused on the communicative value of gesture, and that view is at least implicit in most contemporary thinking on the topic. Although we do not question the idea that gestures *can* play a role in communication, we believe that their contribution to communication has been overstated, and that the assumption that communication is gesture's only (or even primary) function has impeded progress in understanding the process by which they are generated.

Our goal in this chapter is to provide a partial answer to the question of the origin and function of gesture. It is a partial answer because we suspect that different kinds of gestures have different origins and serve different functions, and the model we propose attempts to account neither for all gestural behavior nor for all of the functions gestures serve. Our account also must be regarded as tentative, because formulating a model requires us to make a number of assumptions for which we lack substantial empirical warrant.

Our concern is with what we will call *lexical gestures*,[2] and we will begin

by discussing the kinds of distinctions among gestures we find useful
and the functions different types of gestures are hypothesized to serve.
Following this, we will describe a model of the process by which lexical gestures are produced and through which they accomplish what we believe to
be their primary function. Then we will examine some of the empirical evidence that bears on our model, and briefly consider alternative approaches.

2   Gesture typologies and functions

The lexical gestures that are the main focus of our model are only one of the
kinds of gestures speakers make, and it probably would be a mistake to
assume that all gestures are produced by the same process or that they serve
the same functions. In the next two sections, we will describe what we
believe to be the major kinds of gestures and the functions the different
types of gestures might serve.

2.1   Gesture types

Gestural typologies abound in the literature, virtually all of them deriving
from the category system initially proposed in Efron's (1972 [1941]) seminal
monograph. We espouse a minimalist approach to gesture categories, based
on our belief that some of the proposed typologies make distinctions of
questionable utility and reliability. However, we do believe that some distinctions are needed.

2.1.1   Symbolic gestures. Virtually all typologies distinguish a category of
gestural signs – hand configurations and movements with widely recognized conventionalized meanings – that we will call *symbolic gestures* (Ricci
Bitti & Poggi 1991). Other terms that have been used are *emblems* (Efron
1972 [1941]; Johnson, Ekman & Friesen 1975), *autonomous gestures*
(Kendon 1983), and *semiotic gestures* (Barakat, 1973). Symbolic gestures
frequently occur in the absence of speech – indeed, they often are used to
communicate when distance or noise renders vocal communication impossible – but they also are commonly found as accompaniments to speech,
expressing concepts that also are expressed verbally.[3]

2.1.2   Deictic gestures. A second class of gestures, called *deictic gestures*,
consists of indicative or pointing movements, typically formed with the
index finger extended and the remaining fingers closed. Deictic gestures
usually are used to indicate persons, objects, directions, or locations, but
they may also be used to 'point to' unseen, abstract, or imaginary things.

Unlike symbolic gestures, which generally have fixed meanings, the 'meaning' of a deictic gesture is the act of indicating the things pointed to. They function in a way that is similar to demonstrative pronouns like *this* and *that*.[4] Deictic gestures often accompany speech, but they may also be used to substitute for it. Such autonomous uses may be especially common when the gesture constitutes the response to a question about a location or direction. Often it's easier to reply to a question like "Where's the Psych Department office?" by pointing to the appropriate door than it is to describe its location. Sometimes the speaker will add, "It's right over there" if the non-verbal response alone seems too brusque or impolite, but in such cases the verbal message really has little meaning in the absence of the accompanying deictic gesture. Questions of politeness aside, the gesture adequately answers the question.

2.1.3   Motor gestures. A third gestural type consists of simple, repetitive, rhythmic movements that bear no obvious relation to the semantic content of the accompanying speech (Feyereisen, Van de Wiele & Dubois 1988). Typically the gesturer's handshape remains fixed, and the movement may be repeated several times. We will refer to such gestures as *motor gestures;*[5] they have also been called "batons" (Efron 1972 [1941]; Ekman & Friesen 1972) and "beats" (Kendon 1983; McNeill 1987). According to Bull & Connelly (1985), motor gestures are coordinated with the speech prosody and tend to fall on stressed syllables (but see McClave 1994), although the synchrony is far from perfect.

2.1.4   Lexical gestures. The three gesture categories we have discussed are relatively uncontroversial, and most gesture researchers acknowledge them as distinct gesture types. The fourth major category is less easy to define, and there is considerable disagreement among researchers as to their origins and functions. What we will call *lexical gestures* are similar to what have been called "representational gestures" (McNeill, Cassell & McCullough 1994), "gesticulations" (Kendon 1980, 1983), "ideational ges- tures" (Hadar, Burstein, Krauss & Soroker 1998; Hadar & Butterworth 1997), and "illustrators" (Ekman & Friesen 1972). Like motor gestures, lexical gestures occur only as accompaniments to speech, but unlike motor gestures, they vary considerably in length and are non-repetitive, complex, and changing in form, and many appear to bear a meaningful relation to the semantic content of the speech they accompany. Providing a formal definition for this class of gestures has proved difficult – Hadar (1989) has defined ideational gestures as hand–arm movements that consist of more than two independent vectorial components – and it is tempting to define them as a residual category: co-speech gestures that are not deictic, symbolic, or motor gestures.

This is not to suggest that lexical gestures are nothing more than what remains in a speaker's gestural output when symbolic, deictic, and motor gestures (along with other, non-gestural hand movements) are eliminated. As the model sketched below makes clear, we believe lexical gestures to be a coherent category of movements, generated by a uniform process, that play a role in speech production. It is relevant that although we do not have a mechanical technique that can distinguish lexical gestures from other types of gestures solely on the basis of their form, naive judges can identify them with impressive reliability (Feyereisen et al. 1988).

2.2   Functions of gestures

2.2.1   Communication. The traditional view that gestures function as communicative devices is so widespread and well accepted that comparatively little research has been directed toward assessing the magnitude of gestures' contribution to communication, or toward ascertaining the kinds of information different types of gestures convey. Reviewing such evidence as exists, Kendon has concluded that:

> The gestures that people produce when they talk do play a part in communication and they do provide information to co-participants about the semantic content of the utterances, although there clearly is variation about when and how they do so. (1994: 192)

After considering the same studies, we have concluded that the evidence is inconclusive at best, and is equally consistent with the view that the gestural contribution is, on average, negligible. (See Krauss, Dushay, Chen & Rauscher 1995 for a discussion of the evidence.) We will return to this issue below in our discussion of the origins of lexical gestures.

2.2.2   Tension reduction. Noting that people often gesture when they are having difficulty retrieving an elusive word from memory, Dittmann & Llewelyn (1969) have suggested that at least some gestures may be more-or-less random movements whose function is to dissipate tension during lexical search. The idea is that failures of word retrieval are frustrating, and that unless dealt with, this frustration-generated tension could interfere with the speaker's ability to produce coherent speech. Hand movements provide a means for doing this. Other investigators (Butterworth 1975; Freedman & Hoffman 1967) have noted the co-occurrence of gestures and retrieval problems, although they have not attributed this to tension management. We are unaware of any evidence supporting the hypothesis that people gesture in order to reduce tension, and find the idea itself somewhat implausible. However, we do think that the association of gesturing and word-retrieval failures is noteworthy.

2.2.3   Lexical retrieval. Gesturing may be common when speakers are trying to access words from their lexicons because it plays a direct role in the process of lexical retrieval. This is not a new idea and has been suggested by a remarkably diverse group of scholars over the last seventy-five years (de Laguna 1927; Freedman 1972; Mead 1934; Moscovici 1967; Werner & Kaplan 1963). Empirical support for the notion that gesturing affects lexical access is mixed. In the earliest published study, Dobrogaev (1929) reported that speakers instructed to curb facial expressions, head movements, and gestural movements of the extremities found it difficult to produce articulate speech, but the experiment apparently lacked the necessary controls.[6] More recently, Graham & Heywood (1975) analyzed the speech of five speakers who were prevented from gesturing as they described abstract line drawings, and concluded that "elimination of gesture has no particularly marked effects on speech performance" (p. 194). On the other hand, Rimé (1982) and Rauscher, Krauss & Chen (1996) have found that restricting gesturing adversely affects speech. See Krauss et al. (1996) for a review of the relevant studies.

Although the idea that gesturing facilitates lexical retrieval is not a new one, none of the writers who have suggested this possibility has described the mechanism by which gestures affect lexical access. The model presented below describes an architecture that accounts for both the production of lexical gestures and their facilitative effects on lexical retrieval.

3   The production of speech and gesture

3.1   Speech production

We assume that lexical gestures and speech involve two production systems that operate in concert. It may be helpful to begin by reviewing briefly our understanding of the process by which speech is generated. Of course, the nature of speech production is not uncontroversial, and several production models have been proposed. These models differ in significant ways, but for our purposes their differences are less important than their similarities. Although we will follow the account of Levelt (1989), all of the models with which we are familiar distinguish three stages of the process. Levelt refers to the three stages as *conceptualizing, formulating,* and *articulating.*

Conceptualizing involves, among other things, drawing upon declarative and procedural knowledge to construct a communicative intention. The output of the conceptualizing stage – what Levelt refers to as a *preverbal message* – is a conceptual structure containing a set of semantic specifications. At the formulating stage, the preverbal message is transformed in two ways. First, a grammatical encoder maps the to-be-lexicalized concept onto a lemma (i.e., an abstract symbol representing the selected word as a semantic-syntactic entity) in the mental lexicon whose meaning matches the content of the preverbal message. Using syntactic information contained in the lemma, the conceptual structure is transformed into a *surface structure* (see also Bierwisch & Schrueder 1992). Then, by accessing word forms stored in lexical memory and constructing an appropriate plan for the utterance's prosody, a phonological encoder transforms this surface structure into a *phonetic plan* (essentially a set of instructions to the articulatory system). The output of the articulatory stage is overt speech, which the speaker monitors and uses as a source of corrective feedback. The process is illustrated schematically in the right-hand (shaded) portion of Figure 13.1, which is based on Levelt (1989).

3.2   Gesture production

Our account of the origins of gesture begins with the representations in working memory that come to be expressed in speech. An example may help explicate our view. Kendon (1980) describes a speaker saying, ". . . with a big cake on it . . ." while making a series of circular motions of the forearm with the index finger extended pointing downward. In terms of the speech-production model, the word "cake" derives from a memorial representation we will call the *source concept*. In this example, the source concept is the representation of a particular cake in the speaker's memory. The conceptual representation that is outputted by the conceptualizer and that the grammatical encoder transforms into a linguistic representation typically incorporates only a subset of the source concept's features.[7] Presumably the particular cake in the example was large and round, but it also had other properties – color, flavor, texture, and so on – that might have been mentioned but weren't, presumably because, unlike the cake's size, they were not relevant to the speaker's goals in the discourse. A central theoretical question is whether or not the information that the cake was round – i.e., the information contained in the gesture – was part of the speaker's communicative intention. We assume that it was not. Below we will consider some of the implications of assuming that such gestures are communicatively intended.

In developing our model we have made the following assumptions about memory and mental representation:
(1) Memory employs a number of different formats to represent knowledge, and much of the content of memory is multiply encoded in more than one representational format.

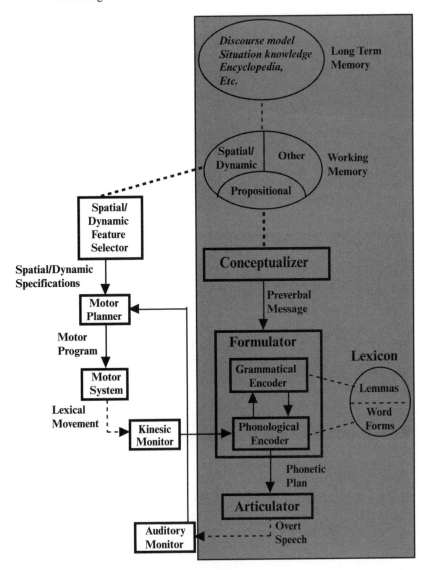

Figure 13.1. A cognitive architecture for the speech–gesture production process (speech processor redrawn from Levelt 1989).

(2) Activation of a concept in one representational format tends to activate related concepts in other formats.
(3) Concepts differ in how adequately (i.e., efficiently, completely, accessibly, etc.) they can be represented in one or another format. The complete mental representation of some concepts may require inputs from more than one representational format.
(4) Some representations in one format can be translated into the representational form of another format (e.g., a verbal description can give rise to a visual image, and vice versa).

None of these assumptions is particularly controversial, at least at this level of generality.

We follow Levelt in assuming that inputs from working memory to the conceptualizing stage of the speech processor must be in propositional form. However, the knowledge that constitutes a source concept may be multiply encoded in both propositional and non-propositional representational formats, or may be encoded exclusively in non-propositional formats. In order to be reflected in speech, non-propositionally encoded information must be 'translated' into propositional form.

We have tried to illustrate this schematically in Figure 13.2. In that figure, the hypothetical source concept *A* is made up of a set of features (features *A1 – A10*) that are encoded in propositional and/or spatial format. Some features (e.g., *A1* and *A4*) are multiply encoded in both formats. Others are represented exclusively in propositional (e.g., *A3* and *A6*) or in spatial form (*A2* and *A5*) form. Our central hypothesis is that *lexical gestures derive from non-propositional representations of the source concept.* Just as a linguistic representation may not incorporate all of the features of the source concept's mental representation, lexical gestures reflect these features even more narrowly. The features they incorporate are primarily spatio-dynamic. As Figure 13.2 illustrates, in the hypothetical example the lexical item the speaker selects to represent concept *A* incorporates six of its propositionally encoded features. The gesture that accompanies it incorporates three features, two of which are also part of the lexical representation.

How do these non-propositionally represented features come to be reflected gesturally? Our model assumes that a spatial/dynamic feature selector transforms information stored in spatial or dynamic formats into a set of *spatial/dynamic specifications* – essentially abstract properties of movements.[8] These abstract specifications are, in turn, translated by a motor planner into a *motor program* that provides the motor system with a set of instructions for executing the lexical gesture. The output of the motor system is a gestural movement, which is monitored kinesthetically. The model is shown as the left-hand (unshaded) portion of Figure 13.1.

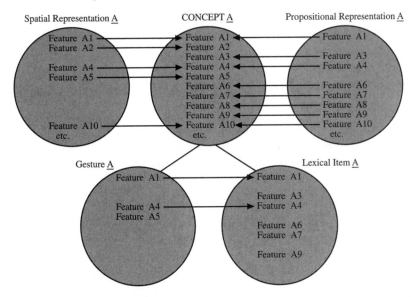

Figure 13.2. Mental representation of a hypothetical source concept and its reflection in speech and gesture.

3.3   Gestural facilitation of speech

We believe that an important function of lexical gestures is to facilitate lexical retrieval. How does the gesture-production system accomplish this? The process is illustrated in Figure 13.1, which shows the output of the gesture-production system, mediated by the kinesic monitor, feeding into the phonological encoder where it facilitates retrieval of the word form.[9]

In our model, the lexical gesture provides input to the phonological encoder via the kinesic monitor. The input consists of features of the source concept represented in motoric or kinesic form. As discussed above, the features contained in the lexical gesture may or may not also be features of the sought-for lexical item, which is to say that they may or may not be elements of the speaker's communicative intention. These features, represented in motoric form, facilitate retrieval of the word form by a process of cross-modal priming. This is represented in Figure 13.1 by the path from the kinesic monitor to the phonological encoder. The figure also shows a path from the auditory monitor to the motor planner. This path (or its equivalent) is necessary in order to account for gesture termination. Since a gesture's duration is closely timed to articulation of its lexical affiliate (Morrel-Samuels & Krauss 1992), a mechanism that informs the motor system when to terminate the gesture is required. Essentially, we are proposing that hearing the lexical affiliate being articulated serves as the signal to terminate the gesture.[10]

4   Some theoretical alternatives

Formulating a theoretical model requires choosing among alternative conceptualizations, often in the absence of compelling evidence on which to base those choices. In this section we will examine a number of the theoretical choices we made and indicate our reasons for choosing them.

4.1   *Autonomous vs. interactive processes*

A question that any model attempting to account for the production of gesture and speech must address is how the two systems function relative to each other. At the most fundamental level, the two systems can be either *autonomous* or *interactive.* Autonomous processes operate independently once they have been initiated; interactive systems can affect each other during the production process. Clearly, we have opted for an interactive model. In our view, an autonomous model is inconsistent with two kinds of data.

(1) *Evidence from studies of the temporal relations of gesture and speech:* It is reasonably well established that lexical gestures precede their 'lexical affiliates' – the word or phrase in the accompanying speech to which they are related (Butterworth & Beattie 1978; Morrel-Samuels & Krauss 1992; Schegloff 1984). Morrel-Samuels & Krauss (1992) examined sixty carefully selected lexical gestures and found their asynchrony (the time interval between the onset of the lexical gesture and the onset of the lexical affiliate) to range from 0 to 3.75 s, with a mean of 0.99 s and a median of 0.75 s; none of the sixty gestures was initiated after articulation of the lexical affiliate had begun. The gestures' durations ranged from 0.54 s to 7.71 s. (mean = 2.49 s), and only three of the sixty terminated before articulation of the lexical affiliate had begun. The product-moment correlation between gestural duration and asynchrony is +0.71. We can think of only two ways in which such a temporal relation could exist without interaction between the gesture and speech production systems: (a) gestures of long duration are associated with unfamiliar words; (b) speakers somehow can predict *a priori* how long it will take them to retrieve a particular word form, and enter this variable into the formula that determines the gesture's duration. We know of no data that support either proposition, and neither strikes us as plausible.

(2) *Evidence of the effects of preventing gesturing on speech:* Rauscher, Krauss & Chen (1996) found that preventing speakers from gesturing reduced the fluency of their speech with spatial content, compared with their speech when they could gesture. Non-spatial speech was unaffected. Rauscher et al. interpret this finding as support for the proposition that gesturing facilitates lexical access, something that is incompatible with an autonomous model of speech and gesture production. The finding by Frick-Horbury & Guttentag (1998) that preventing gesturing increases the rate of retrieval failures in a tip-of-the-tongue (TOT) situation also is relevant.

To explain the association of gesturing with lexical retrieval failures, de Ruiter (this volume) hypothesizes that speakers anticipating problems in accessing a lexical item will try "to compensate for the speech failure by transmitting a larger part of the communicative intention in the gesture modality." However, Frick-Horbury & Guttentag (1998) found that subjects were likely to gesture in a TOT state – i.e., unable to retrieve a sought-for word. It would be odd if these gestures were intended for the benefit of the addressee, since the addressee (the experimenter) already knew what the target word was.

If one takes de Ruiter's proposal seriously, it would follow that the gestures speakers make when they can't be seen by their conversational partners are different from those that are visually accessible, since the former couldn't possibly transmit information. Not much relevant data exists, but the little we are aware of is not supportive. For example, we have coded the grammatical types of 12,425 gestural lexical affiliates from a previously reported experiment (Krauss, Dushay, Chen, & Rauscher 1995). In that experiment, subjects described abstract graphic designs and novel synthesized sounds to a partner who was either seated face-to-face with the speaker or in another room, using an intercom. Not surprisingly, the grammatical categories of gestural lexical affiliates differed reliably depending on whether the stimulus described was an abstract design or a sound. However, they did not differ as a function of whether or not the speaker could be seen by their partners (Krauss, Gottesman, Chen & Zhang n.d.).

It also is relevant that people speaking a language they have not mastered do not attempt to compensate for their deficiency by gesturing. Dushay (1991) found that native English-speakers taking second-year Spanish gestured significantly *less* when speaking Spanish than when they spoke English in a referential communication task, and allowing listeners to see speakers' gestures did not enhance their communicative effectiveness.

Certainly it is possible that speakers rely on gestures to convey information they cannot convey verbally, as de Ruiter contends, but we know of no

attempt to ascertain whether (or how frequently) they do. Our guess is that
it is not a common occurrence, and that another explanation for the frequency of lexical gestures is needed.

4.2   *Conceptualizer vs. origins in working memory*

Our model specifies the speaker's working memory as the source of the representations that come to be reflected in lexical gestures. An alternative
source is the speech processor itself. Logically, there are two stages at which
this could occur: the conceptualizing stage, where the preverbal message is
constructed, and the formulating stage (more specifically during grammatical encoding), where the surface structure of the message is constructed. We
regard both as dubious candidates. To explain why, we need to consider the
nature of the information in the two systems.

The speech processor is assumed to operate on information that is part of
the speaker's communicative intention. If that is so, and if gestures originate in the speech processor, gestural information would consist *exclusively*
of information that was part of the communicative intention. However, we
believe that gestures can contain information that is not part of the communicative intention expressed in speech. Recall Kendon's previously
described example of the speaker saying, ". . . with a big cake on it . . ."
accompanied by a circular motion of the forearm. Although it may well
have been the case that the particular cake the speaker was talking about
was round, ROUND is not a semantic feature of the word *cake* (cakes come
in a variety of shapes), and for that reason ROUND was not part of the
speaker's communicative intention *as it was reflected in the spoken message.*

The reader may wonder (as did a reader of an earlier draft of this
chapter) how a feature that was not part of the word's feature set could aid
in lexical retrieval. For example, if ROUND is not a feature of *cake,* how
could gesture incorporating that feature help the speaker access the lexical
entry? We agree that it could not, and we do not believe that all of the lexical
gestures speakers make facilitate retrieval, or that speakers make them with
that purpose in mind. It is only when the gesture derives from features that
are part of the lexical item's semantic that gesturing will have this facilitative effect. In our view, gestures are a product of the same conceptual processes that ultimately result in speech, but the two production systems
diverge very early on. Because gestures reflect representations in memory, it
would not be surprising if some of the time the most accessible features of
those representations (i.e., the ones that are manifested in gestures) were
products of the speaker's unique experience and not part of the lexical
entry's semantic. Depending on the speaker's goals in the situation, these

features may or may not be relevant. When they are, we would expect the speaker to incorporate them into the spoken message; when they are not, we would expect the spoken message and the gesture to contain different information. Note that in Kendon's example the speaker elected to incorporate the feature LARGE (which could have been represented gesturally) but not ROUND in the verbal message. In some cases, an attentive addressee will be able to interpret the gestural information (e.g., to discern that the cake was both large and round), although the bulk of the gestures speakers make are difficult to interpret straightforwardly (Feyereisen et al. 1988; Krauss, Morrel-Samuels & Colasante 1991). Evidence that viewers are able to do this (e.g., McNeill et al. 1994) really does not address the question of whether such gestures are communicatively intended.

Kendon and others (e.g., Clark 1996; de Ruiter, this volume; Schegloff, 1984) implicitly reject this view of gestures' function and assume that speakers partition the information that constitutes their communicative intentions, conveying some information verbally in the spoken message, some visibly via gesture, facial expression, etc., and some in both modalities. In the *cake* example, Kendon presumably would have the speaker *intending* to convey the idea that the cake was both big *and* round, and choosing to convey ROUND gesturally. No doubt speakers can do this, and occasionally they probably do.[11] However, we see no reason to assume that *most* of the speech-accompanying gestures speakers make are communicatively intended. Apart from the intuitive impressions of observers, we know of no evidence that directly supports this notion, and much of the indirect evidence is unsupportive. For example, speakers gesture when their listeners cannot see them, albeit somewhat less than they do when they are visually accessible (Cohen 1977; Cohen & Harrison 1972; Krauss et al. 1995). Gestures that are unseen (e.g., made while speaking on the telephone) cannot convey information, and yet speakers make them.[12] In addition, experimental findings suggest that on average lexical gestures convey relatively little information (Feyereisen et al. 1988; Krauss et al. 1991: experiments 1 and 2), that their contribution to the semantic interpretation of the utterance is negligible (Krauss et al. 1991: experiment 5), and that having access to them does not enhance the effectiveness of communication as that is indexed by a referential communication task (Krauss et al. 1995). So if such gestures are communicatively intended, the evidence we have suggests that they are not notably effective.

De Ruiter argues that the occurrence of gesturing by speakers who cannot be seen and findings that gestures have relatively little communicative value do not reduce the plausibility of the idea that they are communicatively intended.

Gesture may well be intended by the speaker to communicate and yet fail to do so in some or even most cases. The fact that people gesture on the telephone is also not necessarily in conflict with the view that gestures are generally intended to be communicative. It is conceivable that people gesture on the telephone because they always gesture when they speak spontaneously – they simply cannot suppress it. (de Ruiter, this volume)

The idea that such gestures reflect overlearned habits is not intrinsically implausible. However, the notion that gestures are both communicatively intended *and* largely ineffective is incompatible with a modern understanding of how language (and other behaviors) are used communicatively. The argument is rather an involved one, and space constraints prevent us from reviewing it here.[13] Suffice it to say that de Ruiter is implicitly espousing a view of communication that conceptualizes participants as autonomous information processors. Such a view stands in sharp contrast with what Clark (1996) has termed a collaborative view of language use, in which communicative exchange is a *joint* accomplishment of the participants, who work together to achieve some set of communicative goals. From the collaborative perspective, speakers and hearers endeavor to ensure that they have similar conceptions of the meaning of each message before they proceed to the next one. The idea that some element of a message is communicatively intended but consistently goes uncomprehended makes little sense from such a perspective.

We do not believe that de Ruiter (and others who share the view that gestures are communicatively intended) can have it both ways. If such gestures are part of the communicative intention and convey information that is important for constructing that intention, speaker/gesturers should make an effort to insure that gestural meanings have been correctly apprehended, and it should be possible to demonstrate straightforwardly that the gestures make a contribution to communication. Again, at the risk of being redundant, let us reiterate our belief that there certainly are some gestures (e.g., symbolic gestures, some iconic gestures, some pantomimic-enactive gestures) that are both communicatively intended *and* communicatively effective; that much is not controversial. The question we raise is whether there is adequate justification for assuming that all or most co-speech gestures are so intended. In our view, such a justification is lacking.

The issue of whether we should assume that gestures are part of the speaker's communicative intention is not simply an esoteric theoretical detail. The assumption is important precisely because of the implications it has for an explanation of gestural origins. If gestures are communicatively intended, they must originate within the speech processor – in the conceptualizer or formulator. If they are not, they can originate elsewhere. Note that an origin outside the speech processor would not preclude gestures from containing information that is part of the communicative intention, or from conveying such information to a perceptive observer.[14] However, that would constrain a rather different sort of cognitive architecture.

4.3   Does gestural facilitation affect retrieval of the lemma or lexeme?

Lexical retrieval is a two-step process, and difficulties might be encountered at either stage – during grammatical encoding (when the lemma is retrieved) or during phonological encoding (when the word form or lexeme is retrieved). Do lexical gestures affect retrieval of the lemma, the word form, or both? At this point there is some evidence that gestures affect the phonological encoder, although the evidence does not preclude the possibility that they also can affect retrieval of the lemma. Our choice of the phonological encoder is based on findings from research on lexical retrieval, especially studies using the tip-of-the-tongue (TOT) paradigm, that retrieval failures in normal subjects tend to be phonological rather than semantic (A. S. Brown 1991; R. Brown & McNeill 1966; Jones 1989; Jones & Langford 1987; Kohn, Wingfield, Menn, Goodglass et al. 1987; Meyer & Bock 1992). It is especially significant that preventing gesturing increases retrieval failures in the TOT situation (Frick-Horbury & Guttentag 1998). Since the definitions by means of which the TOT state is induced are roughly equivalent to the information in the lemma, the finding suggests that preventing subjects from gesturing interferes with access at the level of the word form.[15]

4.4   Lexical, iconic, and metaphoric gestures

The movements we are calling lexical gestures are often partitioned into subcategories, although there is relatively little consensus as to what those subcategories should include. Probably the most widely accepted is the subcategory of 'iconic gestures' – gestures that represent their meanings pictographically, in the sense that the gesture's form is conceptually related to the semantic content of the speech it accompanies. For example, in a videotape of a TV program about regional dialects we have studied, the sociolinguist Roger Shuey, explaining how topographic features come to mark boundaries between dialects, is shown saying: ". . . if the settlers were stopped by a natural barrier or boundary, *such as a mountain range* or a river . . ." As he articulates the italicized words, his right hand traces a shape resembling the outline of a mountain peak.

However, not all lexical gestures are iconic. Many speech-accompanying movements clearly are not deictic, symbolic, or motor gestures but still seem to have no obvious formal relationship to the conceptual content of the accompanying speech.[16] What can be said of these gestures? McNeill

(1985, 1992) deals with this problem by drawing a distinction between iconic and *metaphoric* gestures.

Metaphoric gestures exhibit images of abstract concepts. In form and manner of execution, metaphoric gestures depict the vehicles of metaphors . . . The metaphors are independently motivated on the basis of cultural and linguistic knowledge. (McNeill 1985: 356)

Despite their widespread acceptance, we have reservations about the utility of such distinctions. Our own observations have led us to conclude that iconicity (or *apparent* iconicity) is a matter of degree rather than kind. While the forms of some lexical gestures do seem to have a direct and transparent relationship to the content of the accompanying speech, for others the relationship is more tenuous, and for still others the observer is hard pressed to find any relationship at all. So in our view it makes more sense to think of gestures as being more or less iconic rather than either iconic or metaphoric (or non-iconic). Moreover, the iconicity of many gestures seems to exist primarily in the eyes of their beholders. Viewers will disagree about the 'meanings' they impute to gestures, even when viewing them along with the accompanying speech.[17] In the absence of speech, their imputed meanings evidence little iconicity (Feyereisen et al. 1988; Krauss et al. 1991).

We find the iconic/metaphoric distinction even more problematic. The argument that metaphoric gestures are produced in the same way linguistic metaphors are generated does not lead to a tractable explanation of the process by which these gestures are produced. Since our understanding of the processes by which linguistic metaphors are produced and comprehended is incomplete at best (cf. Glucksberg & Keysar 1993), to say that such gestures are visual metaphors may be little more than a way of saying that their iconicity is not obvious.

In what ways might such classifications be useful? The idea that a gesture is iconic provides a principled basis for explaining why it takes the form it does. Presumably the form of Shuey's gesture was determined by the prototypical form of the concept with which it was associated – the mountain range. Calling a gesture metaphoric can be seen as an attempt to accomplish the same thing for gestures that lack a formal relationship to the accompanying speech. We believe that a featural model provides a more satisfactory way of accounting for a gesture's form.

4.5   Featural vs. imagistic models

Our model assumes that the memorial representations that come to be reflected in gesture are made up of sets of elementary features. This 'compositional' view of concepts is an old one in psychology, and it is not without its problems (see Smith & Medin 1981 for a discussion of theories of the structure of concepts). An alternative to featural models of gestural origins is a model that views memorial representations as integrated and non-decomposable units that are retrieved holistically. We will refer to these as *imagistic* models. This approach has been employed by de Ruiter (this volume), Hadar & Butterworth (1997), and McNeill (1992, this volume), among others.

We find a number of problems with imagistic models of gesture production. In the first place, specifying an imagistic origin for a gesture does not eliminate the need for a principled account of how the image comes to be represented by a set of hand movements. That is to say, some mechanism must abstract relevant aspects of the image and 'translate' them into a set of instructions to the motor system. This is the function of the 'sketch generation' module in de Ruiter's Sketch Model. Secondly, images are concrete and specific – one cannot have an image of a generic cake. Finally, although imagistic models of gesture production may offer a plausible account of the production of so-called iconic gestures, many gestures lack apparent *physical isomorphy* with the conceptual content of the speech they accompany, among them the class of gestures McNeill has termed *metaphoric*. It is not obvious how an imagistic production model can account for the production of such gestures.

5   Concluding comment

It is probably unnecessary for us to point out that the cognitive architecture we describe is only one of a number of possible arrangements that would be consistent with what we know about gestures. As things currently stand, there is such a dearth of firm data on gesture production to constrain theory that any processing model must be both tentative and highly speculative. Nevertheless, we believe that model-building in such circumstances is not an empty activity. In the first place, models provide a convenient way of systematizing available data. Secondly, they force theorists to make explicit the assumptions that underlie their formulations, making it easier to assess in what ways, and to what extent, apparently different formulations actually differ. Finally, and arguably most importantly, models lead investigators to collect data that will confirm or disconfirm one or another model.

We have few illusions that our account is correct in every detail, or that all of the assumptions we have made will ultimately prove to have been justified. Indeed, our own view of how lexical gestures are generated has changed considerably over the last several years as data have accumulated. Nor do we believe that our research strategy, which rests heavily on controlled experimentation, is the only one capable of providing useful information. Experimentation is a powerful method for generating certain kinds of data, but it also has serious limitations, and an investigator who does not recognize these limitations may be committing the same error as the savants in the parable of the blind men and the elephant. Observational studies have enhanced our understanding of what gestures accomplish, and the conclusions of careful and seasoned observers deserve to be taken seriously.

At the same time, we are uncomfortable with the idea that experimental evidence is irrelevant to some propositions about gesture, whose validity can only be established by interpretations of observed natural behavior. Ultimately we look for the emergence of an account of the process by which gestures are generated, and the functions they serve, that is capable of accommodating the results of both experimental and systematic-observational studies.

NOTES

Sam Glucksberg, Uri Hadar, Julian Hochberg, Willem Levelt, David NcNeill, Robert Remez, Lois Putnam, and the late Stanley Schachter made helpful comments and suggestions as our theoretical approach was evolving. Needless to say, they are not responsible for the uses we made of their ideas. We are also happy to acknowledge the contributions of our colleagues Purnima Chawla, Robert Dushay, Palmer Morrel-Samuels, Frances Rauscher, and Flora Zhang to this program of research. Jan Peter de Ruiter generously provided us with an advance copy of his chapter, and we found to be helpful notes on relevant matters that Susan Duncan shared with us. The research described here and preparation of this report were supported by Grant SBR 93–10586 from the National Science Foundation. Yihsiu Chen is now at AT&T Laboratories; Rebecca F. Gottesman is at the Columbia College of Physicians and Surgeons.

1 See Kendon (1982) for an informative review of the history of the study of gesture.
2 In previous publications (Chawla & Krauss 1994; Krauss 1995; Krauss, Chen & Chawla 1996) we used the term lexical *movements* for what we are now calling lexical gestures.
3 For example, in a videotape of a birthday party we have studied, a man can be seen extending his arm in a "Stop" sign toward another man, who is offering a box of chocolates. At the same time, the gesturer is saying, "No, thanks, not right now."
4 In the birthday party videotape, a woman points to a child whose face is smeared with cake, exclaiming, "Will you look at her!" to her conversational partner, who then looks in the direction she has indicated.
5 We previously called these motor *movements* (Chawla & Krauss 1994; Krauss 1995; Krauss et al. 1996).
6 As was commonly done in that era, Dobrogaev fails to report procedural details, and describes his results in impressionistic, qualitative terms.
7 The difference between the source concept and the linguistic representation can

most clearly be seen in reference, where the linguistic representation is formulated specifically to direct a listener's attention to something and typically will incorporate only as much information as is necessary to accomplish this. Hence one may refer to a person as "the tall guy with red hair," an expression that incorporates only a few features of the far more complex and differentiated conceptual representation.

8 We can only speculate as to what such abstract specifications might consist of. One might expect articulation of lexical items representing concepts that incorporate the features STRAIGHT and CURVED to be accompanied by rectilinear and curvilinear movements, respectively; that lexical items representing concepts that incorporate the feature FAST would be represented by rapid movements; that lexical items representing concepts that incorporate the feature LARGE would be represented by movements with large linear displacements, etc. However, we are unaware of any successful attempts to establish systematic relations between abstract dimensions of movement and dimensions of meaning. For a less-than-successful attempt, see Morrel-Samuels (1989).

9 This represents a minor change from an earlier version of the model (Krauss et al. 1996), in which the output of the gesture-production system went to the grammatical encoder.

10 Hadar & Butterworth (1997) propose a somewhat different mechanism for gesture initiation and termination: lexical movements are initiated by failures in lexical retrieval and terminated when the sought-for word is accessed. In our architecture, the two systems would appear quite similar structurally, but their operation would be somewhat different. For Hadar & Butterworth, the path from the phonological encoder to the motor planner would carry a signal that lexical access had not occurred and would initiate the gesture; the termination of the signal would terminate the gesture.

11 This is often the case with deictic gestures. For example, a speaker may say, "You want to go through that door over there," and point at the particular door.

12 As we have noted above, the distribution of grammatical types of the lexical affiliates of gestures that cannot be seen does not appear to differ from that of gestures that can be seen.

13 Some of the relevant issues are discussed by Clark (1996) and Krauss & Fussell (1996).

14 Of course it is possible that gestures convey information (e.g., about the speaker's internal state) that is *not* part of the communicative intention but may be of value to the addressee, in much the same way that an elevated pitch level conveys information about a speaker's emotional state. We have explored this idea elsewhere (Chawla & Krauss 1994; Krauss et al. 1996).

15 However, since the grammatical and phonological encoders interact in the formulator module (see Figure 13.1), information inputted to the grammatical encoder could affect retrieval of the lexeme.

16 The proportion of lexical movements that are iconic is difficult to determine and probably depends greatly on the conceptual content of the speech.

17 We have found considerable disagreement among naive viewers about what apparently iconic gestures convey. As part of a pretest for a recent study, we selected 140 gestures that seem to us iconic from narratives on a variety of topics (e.g., directions to campus destinations, descriptions of the layouts of apart-

ments, instructions on how to make a sandwich, etc.). Following the method used by Morrel-Samuels & Krauss (1992), subjects saw the video clips containing the gestures and heard the accompanying speech and underlined the gestures' lexical affiliates on a transcript. Despite the fact that these gestures had been selected because we judged them to be iconic, subjects' agreement on their lexical affiliates averaged 43.86% (SD = 23.34%). On only 12% of the gestures was there agreement among 80% or more of our subjects. These results suggest that even iconic gestures convey somewhat different things to different people, making them an unreliable vehicle for communication.

REFERENCES

Atkinson, J. M. & Heritage, J. (eds.) 1984. *Structures of Social Action.* Cambridge: Cambridge University Press.
Barakat, R. 1973. Arabic gestures. *Journal of Popular Culture* 6: 749–792.
Berkowitz, L. (ed.) 1967. *Advances in Experimental Social Psychology,* vol. III. New York: Academic Press.
Bierwisch, M. & Schrueder, R. 1992. From concepts to lexical items. *Cognition* 42: 23–60.
Brown, A. S. 1991. A review of the tip-of-the-tongue experience. *Psychological Bulletin* 109: 204–223.
Brown, R. & McNeill, D. 1966. The 'tip of the tongue' phenomenon. *Journal of Verbal Learning and Verbal Behavior* 4: 325–337.
Bull, P. & Connelly, G. 1985. Body movement and emphasis in speech. *Journal of Nonverbal Behavior* 9: 169–187.
Butterworth, B. 1975. Hesitation and semantic planning in speech. *Journal of Psycholinguistic Research* 4: 75–87.
Butterworth, B. & Beattie, G. 1978. Gesture and silence as indicators of planning in speech. In Campbell & Smith (eds.), pp. 347–360.
Campbell, R. N. & Smith, P. T. (eds.) 1978. *Recent Advances in the Psychology of Language: Formal and Experimental Approaches.* New York: Plenum.
Chawla, P. & Krauss, R. M. 1994. Gesture and speech in spontaneous and rehearsed narratives. *Journal of Experimental Social Psychology* 30: 580–601.
Clark, H. H. 1996. *Using Language.* Cambridge: Cambridge University Press.
Cohen, A. A. 1977. The communicative functions of hand illustrators. *Journal of Communication* 27: 54–63.
Cohen, A. A. & Harrison, R. P. 1972. Intentionality in the use of hand illustrators in face-to-face communication situations. *Journal of Personality and Social Psychology* 28: 276–279.
de Laguna, G. 1927. *Speech: Its Function and Development.* New Haven, CT: Yale University Press.
Dittmann, A. T. & Llewelyn, L. G. 1969. Body movement and speech rhythm in social conversation. *Journal of Personality and Social Psychology* 23: 283–292.
Dobrogaev, S. M. 1929. Uchenie o reflekse v problemakh iazykovedeniia [Observations on reflexes and issues in language study]. *Iazykovedenie i Materializm*: 105–173.
Dushay, R. D. 1991. The association of gestures with speech: a reassessment. Unpublished Ph.D. dissertation, Columbia University.

Efron, D. 1972 [1941]. *Gesture, Race and Culture*. The Hague: Mouton.

Ekman, P. & Friesen, W. V. 1972. Hand movements. *Journal of Communication* 22: 353–374.

Feldman, R. S. & Rimé, B. (eds.) 1991. *Fundamentals of Nonverbal Behavior*. New York: Cambridge University Press.

Feyereisen, P., Van de Wiele, M. & Dubois, F. 1988. The meaning of gestures: what can be understood without speech? *Cahiers de Psychologie Cognitive* 8: 3–25.

Freedman, N. 1972. The analysis of movement behavior during the clinical interview. In Siegman & Pope (eds.), pp. 153–175.

Freedman, N. & Hoffman, S. 1967. Kinetic behavior in altered clinical states: approach to objective analysis of motor behavior during clinical interviews. *Perceptual and Motor Skills* 24: 527–539.

Frick-Horbury, D. & Guttentag, R. E. 1998. The effects of restricting hand gesture production on lexical retrieval and free recall. *American Journal of Psychology* 3: 43–62.

Glucksberg, S. 1991. Beyond literal meanings: the psychology of allusion. *Psychological Science* 2: 146–152.

Glucksberg, S. & Keysar, B. 1993. How metaphors work. In Ortony (ed.), pp. 401–424.

Graham, J. A. & Heywood, S. 1975. The effects of elimination of hand gestures and of verbal codability on speech performance. *European Journal of Social Psychology* 5: 185–195.

Hadar, U. 1989. Two types of gesture and their role in speech production. *Journal of Language and Social Psychology* 8: 221–228.

Hadar, U., Burstein, A., Krauss, R. M. & Soroker, N. 1998. Ideational gestures and speech: a neurolinguistic investigation. *Language and Cognitive Processes* 13: 56–76.

Hadar, U. & Butterworth, B. 1997. Iconic gestures, imagery and word retrieval in speech. *Semiotica* 115: 147–172.

Higgins, E. T. & Kruglanski, A. (eds.) 1996. *Social Psychology: A Handbook of Basic Principles*. New York: Guilford.

Johnson, H., Ekman, P. & Friesen, W. V. 1975. Communicative body movements: American emblems. *Semiotica* 15: 335–353.

Jones, G. V. 1989. Back to Woodworth: role of interlopers in the tip-of-the-tongue phenomenon. *Memory and Cognition* 17: 69–76.

Jones, G. V. & Langford, S. 1987. Phonological blocking in the tip of the tongue state. *Cognition* 26: 115–122.

Kendon, A. 1980. Gesticulation and speech: two aspects of the process of utterance. In Key (ed.), pp. 207–227.

Kendon, A. 1982. The study of gesture: some observations on its history. *Recherches Sémiotiqués/Semiotic Inquiry* 2: 45–62.

Kendon, A. 1983. Gesture and speech: how they interact. In Weimann & Harrison (eds.), pp. 14–35.

Kendon, A. 1994. Do gestures communicate? A review. *Research on Language and Social Interaction* 27: 175–200.

Key, M. R. (ed.) 1980. *Relationship of Verbal and Nonverbal Communication*. The Hague: Mouton.

Kohn, S. E., Wingfield, A., Menn, L., Goodglass, H. et al. 1987. Lexical retrieval: the tip-of-the-tongue phenomenon. *Applied Psycholinguistics* 8: 245–266.

Krauss, R. M. 1995. Gesture, speech and lexical access. Talk given at the conference 'Gestures Compared Cross-Linguistically', Linguistics Institute, Albuquerque, NM, July.

Krauss, R. M., Chen, Y. & Chawla, P. 1996. Nonverbal behavior and nonverbal communication: what do conversational hand gestures tell us? In Zanna (ed.), pp. 389–450.

Krauss, R. M., Dushay, R. A., Chen, Y. & Rauscher, F. 1995. The communicative value of conversational hand gestures. *Journal of Experimental Social Psychology* 31: 533–552.

Krauss, R. M. & Fussell, S. R. 1996. Social psychological models of interpersonal communication. In Higgins & Kruglanski (eds.), pp. 655–701.

Krauss, R. M., Gottesman, R. F., Chen, Y. & Zhang, E. F. n.d. What are speakers saying when they gesture? Grammatical and conceptual properties of gestural lexical affiliates. Unpublished paper, Columbia University.

Krauss, R. M., Morrel-Samuels, P. & Colasante, C. 1991. Do conversational hand gestures communicate? *Journal of Personality and Social Psychology* 61: 743–754.

Levelt, W. J. M. 1989. *Speaking: From Intention to Articulation.* Cambridge, MA: MIT Press.

McClave, E. 1994. Gestural beats: the rhythm hypothesis. *Journal of Psycholinguistic Research* 23: 45–66.

McNeill, D. 1985. So you think gestures are nonverbal? *Psychological Review* 92: 350–371.

McNeill, D. 1987. *Psycholinguistics: A New Approach.* New York: Harper & Row.

McNeill, D. 1992. *Hand and Mind: What Gestures Reveal about Thought.* Chicago: University of Chicago Press.

McNeill, D., Cassell, J. & McCullough, K.-E. 1994. Communicative effects of speech-mismatched gestures. *Language and Social Interaction* 27: 223–237.

Mead, G. H. 1934. *Mind, Self and Society.* Chicago: University of Chicago Press.

Meyer, A. S. & Bock, K. 1992. The tip-of-the-tongue phenomenon: blocking or partial activation? *Memory and Cognition* 20: 715–726.

Morrel-Samuels, P. 1989. Gesture, word and meaning: the role of gesture in speech production and comprehension. Unpublished doctoral dissertation, Columbia University.

Morrel-Samuels, P. & Krauss, R. M. 1992. Word familiarity predicts temporal asynchrony of hand gestures and speech. *Journal of Experimental Psychology: Learning, Memory and Cognition* 18: 615–623.

Moscovici, S. 1967. Communication processes and the properties of language. In Berkowitz (ed.), pp. 226–270.

Ortony, A. (ed.) 1993. *Metaphor and Thought,* 2nd ed. Cambridge: Cambridge University Press.

Rauscher, F. B., Krauss, R. M. & Chen, Y. 1996. Gesture, speech and lexical access: the role of lexical movements in speech production. *Psychological Science* 7: 226–231.

Ricci Bitti, P. E. & Poggi, I. A. 1991. Symbolic nonverbal behavior: talking through gestures. In Feldman & Rimé (eds.), pp. 433–457.

Rimé, B. 1982. The elimination of visible behaviour from social interactions: effects on verbal, nonverbal and interpersonal behaviour. *European Journal of Social Psychology* 12: 113–129.

Schegloff, E. 1984. On some gestures' relation to speech. In Atkinson & Heritage (eds.), pp. 266–296.

Siegman, A. W. & Pope, B. (eds.) 1972. *Studies in Dyadic Communication*. New York: Pergamon.

Smith, E. E. & Medin, D. L. 1981. *Categories and Concepts*. Cambridge, MA: Harvard University Press.

Weimann, J. M. & Harrison, R. P. (eds.) 1983. *Nonverbal Interaction*. Beverly Hills, CA: Sage.

Werner, H. & Kaplan, B. 1963. *Symbol Formation*. New York: Wiley.

Zanna, M. (ed.) 1996. *Advances in Experimental Social Psychology*, vol. XXVIII. San Diego, CA: Academic Press.

14 The production of gesture and speech

Jan Peter de Ruiter

Max Planck Institute for Psycholinguistics, Nijmegen

1 Introduction

Research topics in the field of speech-related gesture that have received considerable attention are the function of gesture, its synchronization with speech, and its semiotic properties. While the findings of these studies often have interesting implications for theories about the processing of gesture in the human brain, few studies have addressed this issue in the framework of information processing.

In this chapter, I will present a general processing architecture for gesture production. It can be used as a starting point for investigating the processes and representations involved in gesture and speech. For convenience, I will use the term 'model' when referring to 'processing architecture' throughout this chapter.

Since the use of information-processing models is not believed by every gesture researcher to be an appropriate way of investigating gesture (see, e.g., McNeill 1992), I will first argue that information-processing models are essential theoretical tools for understanding the processing involved in gesture and speech. I will then proceed to formulate a new model for the production of gesture and speech, called the Sketch Model. It is an extension of Levelt's (1989) model for speech production. The modifications and additions to Levelt's model are discussed in detail. At the end of the section, the working of the Sketch Model is demonstrated, using a number of illustrative gesture/speech fragments as examples.

Subsequently, I will compare the Sketch Model with both McNeill's (1992) growth-point theory and with the information-processing model by Krauss, Chen & Gottesman (this volume). While the Sketch Model and the model by Krauss et al. are formulated within the same framework, they are based on fundamentally different assumptions. A comparison between the Sketch Model and growth-point theory is hard to make, since growth-point theory is not an information-processing theory. Nevertheless, the Sketch Model and growth-point theory share a number of fundamental assumptions.

284

An important conclusion is that information-processing theories are essential theoretical tools for exploring the processing involved in gesture and speech. The presented Sketch Model is an example of such a tool. It accommodates a broad range of gesture phenomena and can be used to explain or predict these phenomena within a consistent formal framework.

1.1 Terminology

In this chapter, the word 'gesture' is used in the restricted sense of spontaneous body movements that occur during speech and often appear to represent aspects of the topic of the accompanying speech. Although most gestures are hand gestures, other body parts, such as the head, are also often used for gesture. The typology I will use for distinguishing different kinds of hand gestures is similar to McNeill's (1992) typology, but because it is not based on semiotic properties, but rather on the representations underlying the processing of gesture, it is different in important ways. I distinguish the following types of gestures:

> **Iconic gestures**: Depicting aspects of the accompanying speech topic. This category includes what McNeill calls *metaphoric* gestures, because from the perspective of gesture production it is of no relevance whether the imagery underlying the gesture is related to abstract or to real entities.
> **Pantomimes**: Gestures that are imitations of functional motor activities.
> **Deictic gestures**: Pointing gestures.
> **Beat gestures**: Biphasic movements of the hands or fingers that do not represent anything.
> **Emblems**: Gestures whose form–meaning relation is lexicalized.

2 Information processing

A common way to formulate theories in cognitive psychology is to use the *information-processing approach*. In this approach, theories are often specified by using highly suggestive box and arrow drawings. These 'boxologies' may be helpful visual tools, but they do not reveal the underlying assumptions of the information-processing approach. I will therefore clarify and justify these assumptions before presenting a model for gesture and speech.

The term information-processing itself is precise: the core assumption of the approach is that the brain does its job by processing information. This is a weak, but highly plausible, assumption supported by a wealth of neurobiological data. In the formal definition of information by Shannon &

Weaver (1949), information is defined to be anything that reduces the uncertainty about a number of possible alternatives. The general nature of this definition is the main reason why the Information Processing assumption is relatively weak. Neural networks, Artificial Intelligence models, and spreading activation models, to name just a few, are all information-processing models, even though they differ wildly in the way they represent and process information.

In a stronger version of this approach, the word 'information' is taken to mean 'representation'. A representation is some information that is stored as a retrievable entity. The fact that the sun shines is information in Shannon & Weaver's sense of the word, but if I note down in my diary "sun shines today," the entry in my diary will be a representation. The difference between the fact that the sun is shining and my note of that fact is the possibility of retrieving my note at a later time, even when at that time weather conditions have changed. I will use the abbreviation R P (Representations and Processes) for this approach.

The extra assumption implicit in the R P approach is that we can view representations and the processes operating on those representations as *functionally* distinct entities. From this assumption it does not follow necessarily that processes and representations have different spatial locations in the brain, or that the processes involved operate in a certain order. All the assumption states is that once we have a description of the processes and the representations involved in a certain cognitive activity, we know what computations are performed in order to perform this cognitive activity. Often the term 'symbolic' or 'classic' is used to refer to this approach. However, 'classical' theorists usually make stronger assumptions about representations and processes than those of the R P approach (see Fodor & Pylyshyn 1988).

Even when an R P theory is correct, we have no complete knowledge about the cognitive domain of interest. For example, we do not know how the processes are carried out by our neural hardware, or how the representations are stored in the brain. From the R P perspective, to answer those questions it is necessary to know *what* the brain does before trying to figure out *how* it does it.

Needless to say, it is possible to make mistakes in developing an R P theory. If such a mistake is made, researchers investigating lower levels of processing (e.g., neuroscientists) can be wrong-footed in their research, because they have an incorrect view of the computation involved. In that case we have no choice but to hypothesize *another* R P theory, and try again. It is impossible to find out how the brain works only by looking 'under the hood'. If there is no understanding of the computations the brain has to perform, even detailed knowledge about the anatomical structure of the brain will hardly be interpretable.

However, it is possible (and desirable) for neuroscientific knowledge to guide and constrain the development of a functional description. For instance, knowledge of the human retina influences our ideas about the kinds of representations involved in vision, and neuropsychological knowledge about human motor control could constrain and inspire theories about gesture. As Churchland (1986) has argued persuasively, cognitive scientists and neuroscientists can and should cooperate in order to arrive at a full understanding of the workings of the brain.

Assuming that cognitive faculties can be described by specifying representations and processes at some level of abstraction has many advantages. First, the formal properties of processes operating on representations have been studied extensively by mathematicians and information scientists (e.g., in formal languages and automata). It is possible to use this knowledge in proving certain properties of an information-processing model. Second, as with all information-processing models, it is often possible to use computer simulations to explore an RP model or parts of it. Simulations are an effective way of checking the coherence of an RP theory. Something important could be missing from an RP theory, or there could be inconsistencies in it. Simulation will reveal such faults, simply because the simulation will either not run or will produce the wrong kind of output. This forces the researcher to track down and address the problem. Another advantage of using computer simulations is that the processing assumptions are fully specified in the computer program. Verbal theories or processing accounts often have multiple interpretations, which tends to make them immune to potential falsification.

Many RP theorists make the additional assumption that one or more subprocesses of their model are "informationally encapsulated" (Fodor 1983). Models of this kind are often called *modular*. This means, roughly, that computations performed by the subprocess are not affected by computations that take place elsewhere in the system. It should be emphasized that the assumption of informational encapsulation, although it is adopted in the model presented below, does not follow automatically from the assumptions of RP processing.

Modular models are highly vulnerable to falsification, because they prohibit certain interactions between subprocesses. Any data showing an interaction between two encapsulated processes will be sufficient to falsify the model, or parts of it. Without any modularity, every computation can potentially influence every other computation. This makes both the formulation and experimental falsification of predictions considerably more prone to multiple interpretations. Thus, for any specific case, it makes sense to carry on with a modular RP model until it has been proven beyond reasonable doubt that the modularity assumption is false.

Some researchers believe that making the assumption of modularity is dangerous, for if this assumption is wrong, the knowledge accumulated by means of experimentation can be misleading. For instance, in Levelt's (1989) model of speech production, the phonological representations used by the process of word–form encoding are stored in a lexicon. If lexical retrieval were not a relatively independent process, the knowledge obtained from picture-naming experiments could not be generalized to the process of spontaneous speech (S. Duncan, pers. com.). However, there is empirical evidence that the results obtained using experimental tasks are comparable to results found under more naturalistic conditions. For instance, the well-known effects of semantic priming in reaction-time research (see Neely 1991) have been replicated using the Event Related Potential methodology (Hagoort, Brown, & Swaab, in press), even though subjects in ERP experiments typically perform no explicit task – they just passively listen to or read language fragments. Another source of support for modularity is the amazing speed and fluency of speech, which makes it likely that there are specialized subprocesses that operate in highly automated, reflex-like fashion, enabling important subprocesses to operate in parallel (Levelt 1989: 2).

McNeill (1987) argues that information processing has certain built-in limitations that make it impossible to apply it to language behavior:

The most basic [limitation] is that information-processing operations are carried out on signifiers alone, on *contentless* symbols.[1] Given this limitation the only way to take account of 'meaning' and 'context' is to treat them as inputs that are needed as triggers to get the machinery moving, but that are not modeled by the information processor itself. (133; emphasis in original)

However, the fact that the elements of a computation (symbols) do not have inherent content is not a limitation of information-processing theories. As Pylyshyn puts it:

[Turing's notion of *computation*] provided a reference point for the scientific ideal of a mechanistic process which could be understood without raising the specter of vital forces or elusive homunculi, but which at the same time was sufficiently rich to cover every conceivable informal notion of mechanism. (1979: 42)

In other words, it is necessary to define computation as operations on form rather than on meaning (or content), for if symbols have inherent meaning, there also needs to be an entity to whom those symbols mean something. This would introduce a homunculus in the theory.

Context information should obviously be incorporated in theories of language processing. The information-processing framework allows for that, provided there is sufficient knowledge about the role context plays in speech production. For instance, in Levelt's model, the conceptualizer keeps track of anaphoric references and previously produced speech (the 'newness' of information) in the form of a discourse record. The information stored in the discourse record can be used by the conceptualizer to take contextual factors into account while producing speech and gesture (see Levelt 1989 for details).

The only limitation on information processing in general is that it does not allow 'vital forces' or 'homunculi' to be used as explanatory devices. This limitation is in fact one of the main virtues of the approach.

3   A model for gesture and speech

The gestures of interest in this chapter usually occur during speaking and are meaningfully related to the content of the speech. It is therefore plausible that these gestures are initiated by a process that is in some way linked to the speaking process. Sometimes people do gesture without speaking, for instance when speech is not possible (e.g., in a noisy factory), but for the moment I will ignore this phenomenon. The fact that gesturing and speaking are in many ways related to each other led to the choice of extending an existing model for speaking to incorporate gesture processing. Another reason for doing this is to make use of, and be compatible with, existing knowledge about the speaking process. The model of the speaking process that is extended to incorporate gesture processing is Levelt's (1989) model of speech production. This model consists of a number of subprocesses (or 'modules') that each have a specific type of input and output. Given a communicative intention, the *conceptualizer* collects and orders the information needed to realize this intention. It retrieves this information from a general knowledge base. The output of the conceptualizer is a representation called the *preverbal message* (or 'message', for short), which contains a propositional representation of the content of the speech. The message is the input for the *formulator*. The formulator will produce an articulatory plan. In order to do that, the first subprocess of the formulator, *grammatical encoding*, will build a (syntactic) *surface structure* that corresponds to the message. It will access a *lexicon* in which the semantic and syntactic properties of lexical items are stored. The second subprocess of the formulator is *phonological encoding*. During phonological encoding, the surface structure built by the grammatical encoder will be transformed into an *articulatory plan* by accessing phonological and morphological representations in the lexicon. The resulting articulatory plan will be sent to the *articulator*, which is responsible for the generation of overt speech. Overt speech is available to the comprehension system because the speaker can hear it. Internal speech is also fed back to the speech-comprehension system, allowing the conceptualizer to monitor internal speech as well,[2] and possibly correct it before the overt speech has been fully realized.

In order to extend Levelt's model to incorporate gesture, it is important to make an assumption about the *function* of gesture. Some authors (most notably Kendon 1994) argue that gesture is a communicative device, whereas others (Krauss, Morrel-Samuels & Colasante 1991; Rimé & Schiaratura 1991) believe that it is not. There are several arguments for either view. The fact that people gesture when there is no visual contact between speaker and listener (e.g., on the telephone), while this does not present any problems for the listener, is often used as an argument for the non-communicative view. Furthermore, Krauss et al. (1991) argue that iconic gestures (lexical gestures, in their terminology) are hardly interpretable without the accompanying speech. As I have argued in de Ruiter (1995a), there is no real conflict between the two views. Gestures may well be intended by the speaker to communicate and yet fail to do so in some or even most cases. However, one cannot draw the conclusion that gestures do not communicate from the fact that iconic gestures are hard to interpret without the accompanying speech, as Krauss et al. (this volume) do. Gestures are normally perceived *together with* the accompanying speech, and then seem to be an interpretable and non-redundant source of information (see for instance McNeill 1992).

The fact that people gesture on the telephone is also not necessarily in conflict with the view that gestures are generally intended to be communicative. It is conceivable that people gesture on the telephone because they always gesture while they speak spontaneously – they simply cannot suppress it. Speakers could adapt to the lack of visual contact by producing more explicit spatial information in the verbal channel, but they need not suppress their gesturing. Finally, there is evidence for the view that gesturing facilitates the speaking process (Morrel-Samuels & Krauss 1992; Rimé & Schiaratura 1991; de Ruiter 1995b, 1998), implying that communication could indirectly benefit from the gesturing of the speaker. This could be the reason why speakers do not suppress their gesturing in situations without visual contact.

To conclude, I will assume that gesture is a communicative device from the speaker's point of view. The *effectiveness* of gestural communication is another issue that will not be addressed here.

To extend Levelt's model for speaking to incorporate gesture, the first question to be answered is where gestures originate from. In information-processing terminology, what process is responsible for the initiation of a gesture? People do not gesture all the time, nor do they gesture about every-

thing that is being said, so some process must 'decide' whether or not to
gesture and what to gesture about.

Considering the formulation of Levelt's model for speaking, the main
candidates in that model for the initiation of gesture are the conceptualizer
and the grammatical encoder (the first subprocess of the formulator).
Butterworth & Hadar (1989) have suggested that iconic gestures are generated from lexical items. If they are correct, the process of lemma retrieval (a
subprocess of grammatical encoding) would be responsible for the initiation of gesture. However, there is ample evidence that most gestures cannot
be associated with single lexical items. In a corpus of gestures by Dutch
subjects (de Ruiter 1998), many subjects drew a horizontal ellipse in the air
with the index finger, while saying, "liggend ei" [ENG 'lying egg']. The
gesture did not represent the concept of 'lying', nor did it express the
concept 'egg'. Rather it represented simultaneously the concepts of 'lying'
and 'egg' together. Similarly, in data from the McNeill Gesture Laboratory
in Chicago, a subject speaks about a small bird in a cartoon throwing a
bowling ball down into a drainpipe (see McNeill & Duncan, this volume;
McNeill, this volume). During the utterance, the subject performs a 'pantomimic' gesture of this action. The gesture reveals aspects of the bowling
ball itself, of holding it, of throwing it, and of throwing it in a downwards
direction. If gestures were associated with lexical items, one would expect
that a gesture would reveal only information that is semantically equivalent
to the meaning of the 'lexical affiliate'.

Given the fact that many iconic gestures reveal properties that can, at
best, only be represented by phrases, the conclusion is that gestures do not
have lexical affiliates but rather 'conceptual affiliates'. While it is possible to
argue that gestures do have a lexical affiliate, such a proposal would be
neither parsimonious nor empirically supported even when there is more
information in the gesture than in the affiliate. There is much evidence, most
notably from McNeill (1992), that gestures are synchronized with and
meaningfully related to higher-level discourse information. The notion of a
conceptual affiliate can also explain the occurrence of the occasional
gesture that seems to be related to a single word (such as pointing upwards
while saying "up"). All content words have an underlying conceptual representation, but not all conceptual representations have a corresponding
content word.

Another reason why the grammatical encoder is an unlikely candidate
for initiating gestures is the fact that the formulator's input is a *preverbal
message* which is a propositional representation. In other words, it does not
have access to imagistic information in working memory.

Gestures often represent spatial information that cannot be part of the
preverbal message. While it is possible to grant the formulator access to

non-propositional information, that would imply a radical change in Levelt's speaking model. My goal is to leave the core assumptions of the speaking model unchanged as much as possible, for a number of reasons. First, there is an extensive body of literature devoted to testing and investigating Levelt's model and its underlying assumptions. This literature will, for a large part, still be relevant to the speech/gesture model if the speech/gesture model is compatible with it. Second, developing a new speaking model is not only beyond the scope of the present chapter, but also unnecessary, as I hope to demonstrate below.

Aside from these considerations, the conceptualizer is the most natural candidate for the initiation of gesture. Many of the problems the conceptualizer has to solve for speech (e.g., perspective-taking) also apply to the gesture modality. Furthermore, selecting which information should be expressed in which modality is a task that is very similar to Levelt's notion of *Macroplanning*, which ". . . consist[s] in the elaborating of the communicative intention as a sequence of subgoals and the selection of information to be expressed (asserted, questioned, etc.) in order to realize these communicative goals" (1989: 107).

Because the conceptualizer has access to *working memory*, it can access both propositional knowledge for the generation of preverbal messages and imagistic (or spatio-temporal) information for the generation of gestures. The conceptualizer will be extended to send a representation called a *sketch* to subsequent processing modules. Because of the central role the sketch plays in the model, I will call it the Sketch Model.

3.1   The conceptualizer

3.1.1   When to gesture. People do not gesture all the time, nor do they gesture about everything they speak about. McNeill (1997) has proposed that gestures occur when new elements are introduced in the discourse. While I have no reason to disagree with this analysis, there are other factors involved as well. In some cases, it might be necessary to express certain information in gesture, as is most notably the case in pointing gestures that accompany deictic expressions. If someone says, "John is over there," without pointing to a location, or when someone says, "It is shaped like this," without in some way providing shape information by gesture, the utterance as a whole is semantically incomplete.

Even when gesturing is not obligatory, the conceptualizer can generate a gesture which would serve the function of enhancing the quality of the communication. The communicative intention is split in two parts: a propositional part that is transformed into a preverbal message, and an imagistic part that is transformed into a sketch.

People are often found to gesture when their speech is failing in some way. Krauss et al. (1991) and Butterworth & Hadar (1989) claim that gesturing in case of a speech failure helps the speech system resolve the problem, for instance by providing the lexical search process with a cross-modal accessing cue. Another interpretation, which I prefer, is that the temporary speech failure is recognized in the conceptualizer (e.g., by means of internal or external feedback, as in Levelt's model). This recognized speech failure could then be compensated for by the transmission of a larger part of the communicative intention to the gesture modality. Similarly, when circumstances are such that it is difficult to express a communicative intention in speech (e.g. in a noisy environment or when one does not speak the language), gestures can be generated to compensate for the lack of communicative efficiency in the verbal modality.

The assumption that information that is hard to encode as a preverbal message is encoded in a sketch would also explain why narratives involving salient imagery such as motion events will usually evoke many iconic gestures: the conceptualizer applies the principle that a gesture can be worth a thousand words. As mentioned above, the question whether transmitting information by gesture is always *effective*, i.e., whether the listener will detect and process the information represented in gesture, is another issue.

3.1.2   What to gesture. If imagistic information from working memory has to be expressed in an *iconic* gesture, the shape of the gesture will be largely determined by the content of the imagery. It is the conceptualizer's task to extract the relevant information from a spatio-temporal representation and create a representation that can be transformed into a motor program. The result of this extraction process will be one or more spatio-temporal representations that will be stored in the sketch. Because these representations can involve spatial elements combined with motion, I will call these 'trajectories', for lack of a better term.

Emblems have a lexicalized, hence conventional, shape, so they cannot be generated from imagery. I will assume that the conceptualizer has access to a knowledge store that I will call the *gestuary*. In the gestuary, a number of emblematic gesture shapes are stored, indexed by the concept they represent. If a certain propositional concept is to be expressed, or a certain rhetorical effect intended, the conceptualizer can access the gestuary to see if there is an emblematic gesture available that will do the job. If there is, a reference (e.g., a 'pointer') to this emblematic gesture will be put into the sketch.

A third possibility is that the conceptualizer generates a *pantomimic* gesture. A pantomimic gesture is an enactment of a certain movement performed by a person or animate object in the imagistic representation. A good example from the McNeill Gesture Laboratory in Chicago is a Tweety Bird narration in which a subject says, "and Tweety drops the bowling ball into the drainpipe" while moving both hands as if the subject herself is throwing a bowling ball down. This kind of gesture cannot be generated from imagery alone, but has to be generated from (procedural) motoric knowledge. The example makes clear why this is the case; Tweety is about half a bowling ball high, and therefore the movement that Tweety makes when throwing the bowling ball is quite different from the movement the (much larger) subject in the study makes in enacting the throwing. For encoding pantomimic gestures, a reference to a motor program (e.g., an action schema; Schmidt 1975) will be encoded in the sketch.

Finally, it is also possible to encode a *pointing* gesture into the sketch. This is done by encoding a vector in the direction of the location of the referent. Since the handshape of the pointing gesture is conventionalized (Wilkins 1995), and for some languages different types of pointing handshapes indicate the level of proximity of the referent, the conceptualizer will have to encode a reference to the appropriate pointing template in the gestuary.

As with the production of speech, another important issue that has to be resolved by the conceptualizer is that of *perspective*. If spatio-temporal information is stored in four dimensions (three for space and one for time), different perspectives can be used to represent the information using gesture. For instance, if a gesture is accompanying a route description (assuming that speaker and listener are facing each other), the gesture that might accompany the speech "taking a right turn" might be made to the speaker's right (speaker-centered perspective) or to the speaker's left (listener-centered perspective).

In some cultures, iconic gestures preserve *absolute* orientation (Haviland 1993, this volume; Levinson 1996), so in that case the conceptualizer has to specify the orientation of the gesture within an absolute-coordinate system. For details about gestural perspectives, see McNeill (1992). A convenient way of encoding perspective in the sketch is by specifying in the sketch the position of the speaker's body relative to the encoded trajectories.

To summarize, the final output of the conceptualizer, called a *sketch*, contains the information in Table 14.1. The sketch, which will be sent to the *gesture planner*, might contain more than one of the representations above. How multiple sketch entries are processed will be described below.

3.2   The gesture planner

The gesture planner's task is to build a motor program out of the received sketch. The gesture planner has access to the gestuary, motor procedures

Table 14.1. *Gesture output of the conceptualizer*

Gesture type	Sketch content
Iconic	One or more spatio-temporal trajectories
	Location of speaker relative to trajectory
Deictic	Vector
	Reference to gestuary
Emblem	Reference to gestuary
Pantomime	Reference to motor-action schema

(schemata), and information about the environment. One of the reasons a separate module is specified for gesture planning is that the constraints that have to be satisfied in gesturing are radically different from those of manipulating the environment in 'standard' motor behavior.

A problem that the gesture planner has to solve, for all gestures, is that of *body-part allocation*. One hand may be occupied, in which case either the other hand must be used for the gesture, or the occupied hand must first be made available. If both hands are unavailable, a head gesture can sometimes be generated. For example Levelt, Richardson & La Heij (1985) had subjects point to one of a few lights while saying, "This light" or "That light." In one of their conditions, subjects were not allowed to point. The authors note that "When no hand gesture is made, the speaker will still direct his gaze or head toward the target LED; there will always be some form of pointing" (p. 143).

This illustrates one of the problems the gesture planner has to solve. The sketch specifies a location to be expressed in a deictic gesture, but the hands are not allowed to move. Therefore, the gesture planner selects another 'pointing device' to perform the (in this case obligatory) gesture. The fact that the same 'logical' gesture can often be realized overtly by different physical gestures provides support for the assumption that gesture sketch generation and the generation of a motor program are separate processes.

Another task of the gesture planner is to take into account restrictions that objects in the environment impose upon body movements. At a crowded party, too large a gesture could result in hitting another person. Although it probably happens, it seems reasonable to assume that people normally do not hit other people or objects during gesturing. If the environment imposes certain restrictions, the gesture will either be canceled or adapted to fit the circumstances.

For the generation of emblems and pointing gestures, the gestuary plays an important role in the creation of a motor program from the sketch. In the gestuary, information is stored about gestural conventions. For instance, while it is possible to point to a location using the elbow or the little finger, in most Western European cultures people point with the index finger. There is a 'soft rule' that specifies that the preferred way to point is to use the index finger of the hand. However, when pointing to a location behind the back, Europeans will usually use the thumb (Calbris 1990). Speakers of Arrernte (a Central Australian language) will use the index finger for such backward pointing (Wilkins 1995).

It is not possible to have complete motor programs stored in the gestuary for any of these gesture types. Both pointing gestures and emblems have a number of degrees of freedom. In performing the emblematic OK gesture, there is freedom in the location of the hand and the duration of the gesture. The only aspect of this gesture that is fixed is the shape and orientation of the hand. The same holds for pointing: while the shape of the hand is subject to certain conventions, the location that the hand points to is dependent upon where the object of interest happens to be. It is therefore necessary to store gestures in the gestuary in the form of *templates*. A template is an abstract motor program that is specified only insofar as it needs to be. Taking the emblematic OK gesture as an example, the handshape is fully specified in the template, while duration, hand (left or right), and location (where the hand is held) are free parameters. The gesture planner will bind these free parameters to the desired values in order to obtain a fully specified motor program.

If the sketch contains one or more trajectories, the gesture planner has to convert them to motor programs that represent the information in these trajectories. In the simple case of one trajectory, the body part (usually the hand) can often be used to 'trace out' the trajectory, but things can be far more complicated. A more complex problem the gesture planner will have to solve is the generation of so-called *fusions* of different gestures. To take an example from data from Sotaro Kita (pers. com.), a subject is enacting a throwing movement, but adds a directional vector on top of the throwing enactment by 'throwing' the ball sideways, which was not the way the person in the stimulus film threw the ball. However, the movement sideways indicated that (from the speaker's viewpoint) the ball flew off in that particular direction. We must therefore conclude that there has been a fusion of a deictic component (indicating the direction of the ball) and an enactment. This type of fusion of different information in one gesture occurs frequently. If the fusion gesture involves a gestuary entry or an action schema, it is hypothesized that the unbound parameters of the template or action schema (i.e., its degrees of freedom) will be employed, if possible, to encode additional sketch elements. Example C below serves to illustrate this mechanism.

Further research is needed to find out which types of gesture can be fused together, and under which circumstances fusion of information is likely to occur. Of specific interest is also the question in what order information in the sketch will be encoded in case of a fusion gesture. If, for instance, the sketch contains both a pointing vector and an iconic trajectory, the degrees of freedom left over by the pointing template could be used to represent the iconic component; but the reverse is also possible: the degrees of freedom left over by the iconic gesture might be used to encode a deictic component into the gesture.

Once the gesture planner has finished building a motor program, this program can be sent to lower-level motor control units, resulting in overt movement.

To summarize the definition of the gesture planner: upon receiving a sketch, it will

• Generate a gesture from the sketch by retrieving a template from the gestuary (for pointing gestures and emblems), by retrieving an action schema from motoric memory (for pantomimes), or by generating a gesture from the trajectories (for iconic gestures) in the sketch.
• Allocate one or more body parts for execution of the gesture.
• Try to encode other sketch entries into the gesture as well.
• Assess potential physical constraints posed by objects in the environment.
• Send the motor program to the lower-level motor-control module(s).

The complete Sketch Model is graphically represented in Figure 14.1. Boxes represent processes, arrows represent representations that are sent from one process to another, ellipses represent knowledge stores, and dotted lines represent access to a particular knowledge store.

4   Synchronization

So far, nothing has been said about the temporal synchronization of gesture and speech. The Sketch Model provides the opportunity to hypothesize in detail how synchronization is achieved.

It should be pointed out that the issue of temporal synchronization is a nebulous one. It is problematic even to define synchronization. The conceptual representation (the 'state of affairs' [Levelt 1989] or the 'Idea Unit' [McNeill 1992]) from which the gesture is derived might be overtly realized in speech as a (possibly complex) phrase, and is not necessarily realized overtly as a single word. Therefore, it is by no means straightforward to unambiguously identify the affiliate of a given gesture. Even if a speech fragment has been identified as being the affiliate, it has a certain duration, and so does the gesture. The synchrony between gesture and speech is the

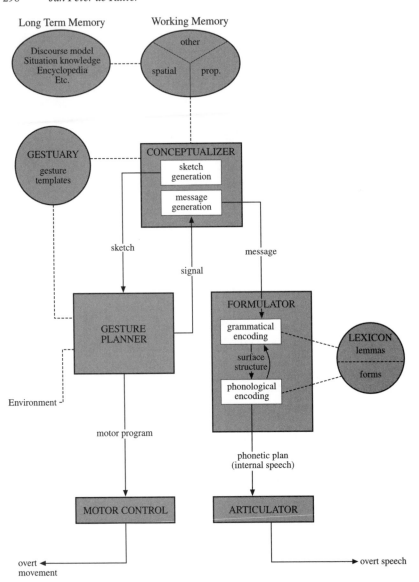

Figure 14.1. The Sketch Model.

synchrony between two time intervals that are often hard to define. However, there is evidence that the *onset* of gesture usually precedes the *onset* of the accompanying speech by a duration of less than a second (e.g., Morrel-Samuels & Krauss 1992; Butterworth & Beattie 1978; Nobe 1996, this volume). Butterworth & Hadar (1989) conclude that

despite the fact that gestures may continue until after speech onset, the beginnings of movements must be considered as events potentially separable from speech onsets, and any processing model must take this fact into account. (P. 170)

The Sketch Model accounts for this phenomenon by assuming that although the preverbal message and the sketch are constructed simultaneously, the preverbal message is sent to the formulator only after the gesture planner has finished constructing a motor program and is about to send it to the motor-execution unit. Once the motor program for the gesture has been constructed, the gesture planner will send a message to the conceptualizer specifying when the generation of speech can be initiated.

This mechanism also accounts for other empirical findings, such as Levelt et al.'s (1985) finding that the onset of speech is adjusted to the duration of the gesture even though the gesture is not yet performed.

However, other synchronization phenomena need to be explained. The first to be addressed is the *gestural hold*, which comes in two varieties. In the *pre-stroke* hold, the gesturing hand moves towards its initial position and then waits for the accompanying speech to be produced before performing the stroke (meaningful part) of the gesture. In the *post-stroke* hold, the hand remains motionless after the stroke has been completed until the related speech has been fully produced. This phenomenon led Kita (1990) to claim that gesture is waiting for the accompanying speech to catch up.

The pre-stroke hold can be accounted for by assuming that the sketch can be sent to the gesture planner before the construction of the preverbal message has been finished. This allows the gesture planner to prepare the motor program for the sketch and put the hand(s) in the initial position for the stroke of the gesture.[3] When the preverbal message is finally sent to the formulator, the conceptualizer will send a 'resume' signal to the gesture planner, which will then send the rest of the motor program (the stroke of the gesture, corresponding to the sketch) to the motor units.

The post-stroke hold can be explained by assuming that the conceptualizer refrains from sending a retract signal to the gesture planner until the production of a preverbal message has been completed. The conceptualizer can detect the completion of a preverbal message fragment, owing to the internal and external feedback loop in the speech-production model. This mechanism does not only offer an account for the occurrence of the post-stroke hold, but also for another interesting finding by Kita (1990). He found that repetitive gestures (e.g., a pantomimic gesture for sawing or hammering) are less likely to have post-stroke holds than are non-repetitive gestures. Instead of the hand stopping at the final position, the repetitive movement is repeated until the related speech fragment has been completed. This difference between repetitive and non-repetitive gestures could be a consequence of the motor programs that are constructed by the gesture planner. For a repetitive gesture, the motor program is specified as a 'loop' – when the stroke has been completed, it starts all over again. Therefore, it will continue to repeat until it receives a retract signal. If non-repetitive gestures are completed before the retract signal, there are no motor instructions left, so the hand stays in its stroke-final position.

Another phenomenon that could be seen as a kind of synchronization is the finding by Kita (1993) that if speakers interrupt their own speech because they detect an error in it, the gesture is often interrupted simultaneously with the speech. In the sketch model, the interruption of both the speech and the gesture is initiated by the conceptualizer. Upon detection of an error in the speech, the conceptualizer sends a stop signal to the formulator and to the gesture planner. These modules pass on this stop signal to lower processing modules.

If future studies reveal a tighter synchronization between iconic gestures and speech than the model accounts for at the moment, the Sketch Model will have to be adapted to incorporate these findings (and will be, in its present formulation, falsified). However, such studies will have to address a number of problems. First of all, synchronization should be defined in such a way that it is possible to locate the affiliate of any iconic gesture unambiguously. Second, synchronization should be defined carefully. Butterworth & Hadar (1989) pointed out that there are thirteen types of temporal relation between two time intervals. Since we can ignore the possibility that two points in time will be *exactly* synchronous, we are still left with six types of temporal relation from which to choose in defining the meaning of 'synchrony'. Finally, there is a measurement problem. Once the affiliate has been defined, the relevant speech interval can be measured to some degree of accuracy, but for gestures this is much harder. Locating the beginnings and ends of gestures (even if restricted to the stroke) is often problematic, especially when gestures follow each other rapidly.

It is tempting to interpret synchronization phenomena as evidence for interactive theories of speech/gesture production, in which lower-level speech and gesture processing continuously exchange information. To paraphrase Kita (1993), because interactive theories assume that speech processes and gesture processes always have access to each other's internal states, gesture can stop when speech stops. Plausible as this may seem, the explanation is incomplete as long as it does not specify what information about what processes is shared in the course of processing. There are a multitude of ways in which speech and gesture processes could share information about their respective internal states. As I hope to have demonstrated in the formulation of the Sketch Model, the computational problems to be solved in the generation of gesture on the one hand and speech on the other are of an entirely different nature. Therefore, sharing all internal state information all the time is not necessary, and probably amounts to interactive 'overkill'. For the same reason, the assumption in growth-point theory that the generation of gesture and the generation of speech are the same process is suspect. It might be the same *general* process, but then this process must perform two rather different computations: one for gesture and one for speech. That again raises the question what information is shared between these two computations.

5   Some examples

A few examples will be helpful in illustrating the mechanics of the proposed model.[4] I will illustrate the Sketch Model by explaining what happens in case of (a) an iconic gesture, (b) a pantomimic gesture, and (c) an Arrernte pointing gesture.

Example A: an iconic gesture. A Dutch subject talks about a Sylvester and Tweety Bird cartoon she just saw. The fragment she is going to describe starts with a big sign saying, "Bird watchers society." She says:

"Op den duur zie je zo'n eh, eh, <u>vogelkijkersvereniging</u> ofzo . . ."
(After a while one sees a eh eh bird watchers' society or something)

Roughly during production of the compound "vogelkijkersvereniging" (ENG 'bird watchers' society') the subject uses both index fingers to draw a large rectangle in front of her body.

Computations in the conceptualizer result in the encoding of the introduction of the bird watchers' society in the speech channel. However, the fact that the bird watchers' society was introduced in the cartoon by showing a sign affixed to a building was encoded in the gesture channel. Therefore, a preverbal message corresponding to "vogelkijkersvereniging ofzo" (ENG 'bird watchers' society or something') is sent to the formulator, while a sketch containing the large rectangle is sent to the gesture planner. The hesitation before and after the described gesture/speech fragment was produced suggests that this part of the communicative intention was a separate fragment (or 'chunk', as Levelt 1989 calls it). Because the sketch and the preverbal message are sent at the same time, the gesture and the speech are synchronized roughly. Interestingly, the speech does contain enough information to understand the cartoon fragment, but only by observing the gesture can the listener tell that there was a sign involved in the cartoon.

This example also illustrates how the conceptualizer can distribute information over different output modalities.

Example B: a pantomimic gesture. Another subject describing the Sylvester and Tweety Bird cartoon says:

> ". . . enne, da's dus Sylvester die zit <u>met een verrekijker naar</u> de overkant te kijken"
> (and eh so that is Sylvester who is watching the other side with binoculars)

During the production of "met een verrekijker naar" (ENG 'with binoculars at') the subject raises his hands in front of his eyes as if lifting binoculars to his eyes.

This example illustrates how difficult it can be to establish what the speech affiliate of the gesture is. In this fragment, it is hard to decide whether the gesture corresponds to "met een verrekijker" (ENG 'with binoculars') or to "zit met een verrekijker naar de overkant te kijken" (ENG 'who is watching the other side with binoculars'). In the latter case, the synchronization of gesture and speech violates the tendency formulated by Butterworth & Hadar (1989) that gesture onset precedes speech onset. We could therefore assume that the affiliate is the stretch of speech that is synchronized with the gesture. However, this leads inevitably to circular reasoning. Either we infer the affiliate from synchronization, or we infer synchronization from the affiliate. It can't be both at the same time, unless the meaning relation of a gesture and the accompanying speech can be established unambiguously, as is for instance the case with most deictic gestures. As example A illustrates, gesture and speech can communicate different aspects of the communicative intention, so the affiliate is not necessarily semantically related to the gesture. In case the meaning relation between gesture and speech is not clearcut, the logic of the Sketch Model requires one to infer the affiliate from the synchronized speech, because in the Sketch model the assumption is made that the sketch and the preverbal message are sent at the same time. In this example the conceptualizer, according to the Sketch Model, encodes a preverbal message corresponding to "met een verrekijker," or possibly "met een verrekijker naar de overkant." At the same time, a sketch is prepared with an entry to the motor schema for holding binoculars. The formulator then processes the preverbal message, and the gesture planner constructs a motor program from the specified motor schema.

Example C: an Arrernte pointing gesture. A (right-handed) speaker of Arrernte and Anmatyerre (Central Australia) is holding a baby in her right arm. (Prior to holding the baby she had made a pointing gesture with her right hand.) Now she says:

> Ilewerre, yanhe-thayte, Anmatyerre
> [place-name] [that/there(mid)-SIDE] [language/group name]
> "(The place called) Ilewerre, on the mid-distant side there, is Anmatyerre (people's country)."

Roughly during the utterance of "yanhe-thayte" she points to the southeast with her left arm. The hand is spread, and the arm is at an angle of approximately 90 degrees from the body.

Wilkins (pers. com.) has observed that the orientation of the palm of the Arrernte spread-hand pointing gesture matches the orientation of the surface that is being referred to. To paraphrase one of Wilkins' field notes, if the palm of the hand is facing out and vertical, it could indicate (for instance) paintings spread out over a cliff face.

Such a gesture can be interpreted as a fusion of an iconic gesture (representing the surface orientation) and a conventionalized deictic gesture. This provides support for the hypothesis that the way the gesture planner realizes fusions is to utilize degrees of freedom in gesture templates to represent additional iconic elements represented in the sketch.

Using the Sketch Model, this fragment can be described in the following way. On the basis of geographical knowledge, the conceptualizer chooses the mid-distant proximity for the deictic reference, and encodes it in the preverbal message. The indication of proximity is not sufficient to realize the communicative intention, so the conceptualizer will generate a sketch containing a vector in the direction of the location of the indicated place. The conceptualizer accesses the gestuary to find the appropriate pointing gesture. In Arrernte, both the shape of the hand and the angle of the arm in pointing are meaningful and conventionalized. The pointing gesture that is selected from the gestuary in this example is one with an arm angle of 90 degrees. Given that the indicated place is not visually available from that vantage point, and is at a significant distance away, the 90-degree angle corresponds with the mid-distant proximity. The spread hand is used to identify a region, something spread out over an area. The entry in the gestuary for this type of pointing gesture specifies hand shape and arm angle, but leaves the parameters specifying the planar angle of the gesture, the handedness of the gesture, and the orientation of the palm of the hand undefined. Finally, the sketch will contain a trajectory that represents a horizontal plane, indicating that the region is spread out over the ground.

The sketch containing the vector, the entry into the gestuary, and the horizontal plane trajectory is sent to the gesture planner. The gesture planner will retrieve the template for the pointing gesture. It will also notice that the right hand is occupied holding a baby, so it will bind the handedness parameter of the gesture template to 'left'. It will bind the parameter specifying the planar angle of the gesture to the angle of the vector that is specified in the sketch, in this case, the southeast. Finally, since the indicated region is an area (flat), the orientation of the hand will be specified as horizontal. Now all free parameters of the template are specified, yielding a complete motor program to be executed.

6   Discussion

To summarize, the most important assumptions of the Sketch Model are:
* The conceptualizer is responsible for the initiation of gesture.
* Iconic gestures are generated from imagistic representations in working memory.
* Gestures are produced in three stages:
    1. The selection of the information that has to be expressed in gesture (the sketch).
    2. The generation of a motor program for an overt gesture.
    3. The execution of the motor program.
* Different gestures can be 'fused' by an incremental utilization of degrees of freedom in the motor program.
* Apart from the conceptualizer, gesture and speech are processed independently and in parallel.

The model covers a large number of gesture types: iconic gestures (including what McNeill 1992 calls *metaphoric* gestures), pantomimes, emblems, and pointing gestures. The Sketch Model also accounts for a number of important empirical findings about gesture. The semantic synchrony of gesture and speech follows from the fact that both gesture and speech ultimately derive from the same communicative intention. Iconic gestures are derived from imagistic representations, while speech output is generated from propositional representations. The global temporal synchrony of iconic gestures and speech is a consequence of preverbal message (speech) and sketch (gesture) being created at approximately the same moment, while the tight temporal synchrony of (obligatory) deictic gestures is accomplished by a signal from the motor unit to the phonological encoder.

As has been mentioned before, it is important to note that in this model, iconic and metaphoric gestures as defined by McNeill (1992) are indistinguishable. Both types of gestures are generated from spatio-temporal representations in working memory. The fact that in the case of a metaphoric gesture the spatio-temporal representation is about abstract entities has no consequence for the transformation of this representation into an overt gesture. On the other hand, pantomimic gestures, while being a subclass of iconic gestures in McNeill's taxonomy, have to be treated in a different way from other iconic gestures, owing to the fact that pantomimic gestures can't be generated from an imagistic representation alone, as explained in section 3.1.2.

There is one category of gestures that is not incorporated by the Sketch Model, namely, beats. The reason for this omission is that there is, at present, insufficient knowledge available about beats. McNeill (1992) has proposed that beat gestures serve metanarrative functions. Lacking detailed processing accounts for the metanarrative level of speech production, incorporating McNeill's proposal in the model is, at present, not possible. While it is sometimes possible to hypothesize the role of beats in a given speech/gesture fragment, it is still impossible to *predict* their occurrence using convenient landmarks: "Beats . . . cannot be predicted on the basis of stress, word class, or even vocalization itself" (McClave 1994: 65).

Since a major advantage of an information-processing model is its vulnerability to potential falsification, it is important to point out a number of predictions that can be derived from the model.

First, the model predicts that people sometimes do *not* gesture. When people read written material aloud, or when they are quoting (repeating) someone, they are predicted not to generate spontaneous gestures.[5] In quoting or reading, the conceptualizer is not constructing a new preverbal message and/or sketch. As the Sketch Model assumes that the generation of gestures is tightly coupled with the generation of preverbal messages, there will be no spontaneous gestures either.

With respect to the synchronization of iconic gestures with the related speech, the model makes the prediction that the onset of the iconic gesture is (roughly) synchronized with the onset of the overt realization of the conceptual affiliate in speech (usually a noun phrase or a verb phrase), independent of the syntax of the language. For example, if an English-speaker says, "He runs across the street," the onset of the iconic gesture that represents 'running across something' is predicted to be roughly co-occurring with the onset of the first word of the verb phrase, in this case "runs." If a Japanese-speaker says "miti o wata te" (street go-across), the onset of the iconic gesture is predicted to be synchronized with the onset of "miti" (street); although it has a different meaning from the first word in the English sentence, it is again the first word of the verb phrase.[6]

Another prediction concerning the synchronization of gesture and speech is that the model does not permit representations active in the formulator to influence the timing of the gesture. Lexical stress or pitch accent, for instance, are therefore predicted to have no effect on gesture/speech synchronization.

A final, rather straightforward prediction of the Sketch Model is that gestures can only be interrupted (e.g., when there is a problem in the generation of speech) during the preparation phase of the gesture. Once the gesture stroke has started to execute, it can no longer be interrupted.

6.1   A comparison with growth-point theory

In comparing the Sketch Model with McNeill's (1992) growth-point (GP) theory, it is possible to point out both similarities and differences. The main similarity is that according to both the Sketch Model and GP theory, gesture and speech originate from the same representation. In the Sketch Model this is the communicative intention, while in GP theory it is the growth point. "The growth point is the speaker's minimal idea unit that can develop into a full utterance together with a gesture" (McNeill 1992: 220).

McNeill (1992) discusses and dismisses theoretical alternatives (pp. 30–35) for GP theory. His analysis applies equally well to the Sketch Model, because of two important assumptions that underlie both GP theory and the gesture model: gestures and speech are part of the same communicative intention, and are planned by the same process.

However, GP theory does not give any account of how (in terms of processing) growth points develop into overt gestures and speech. The growth point is an entity whose existence and properties are inferred from careful analyses of gestures, speech fragments, and their relation (McNeill 1992: 220). However, without a theory of how a GP develops into gesture and speech, gesture and speech data can neither support nor contradict GP theory. This also introduces the risk of circularity. If a fragment of speech that is accompanied by a gesture is interpreted as a growth point, and the growth point is also the entity responsible for the observed (semantic and temporal) synchronization, the observation and the explanation are identical. Therefore, GP theory in its present form does not explain how the speech/gesture system actually accomplishes the observed synchrony (cf. McNeill, this volume).

6.2   A comparison with the model of Krauss et al. (1996, this volume)

Krauss, Chen & Chawla (1996) and also Krauss, Chen & Gottesman (this volume) have also formulated a model that is based on Levelt's (1989) model. (For convenience, I will call their model the KCG model.) The most important difference from the Sketch Model is that in the KCG model the conceptualizer from Levelt's model is left unchanged, whereas in the Sketch

Model it is modified extensively. In the KCG model, gestures are not generated by the conceptualizer, but by a separate process called the spatial/dynamic feature selector. These features are transformed into a motor program which helps the grammatical encoder retrieve the correct lemma for the speech. Synchronization is accounted for in the KCG model by the assumption that the auditory monitor can terminate gestures upon perceiving the (spoken) lexical affiliate.[7] In the Sketch Model the assumption by Levelt (1989) is adopted that the monitor can use both overt speech and the output of the phonological encoder ('inner speech') to terminate gestures.

The main assumption of the KCG model is that iconic gestures (lexical gestures, in their terminology) are not part of the communicative intention, but serve to facilitate lemma selection. However, if the spatio-dynamic features in the generated gesture are to facilitate lemma selection, it is essential that the features that, taken together, single out a particular lemma are identifiably present in the motoric realization of the gesture. If the gesture contains features that are not associated with the lemma that is to be retrieved, these features will very likely *confuse* (hence slow down) lemma selection, because more than one lemma will be activated by the features in the gesture. The example given by Krauss et al. is a gesture about a vortex. A gesture representing a vortex might indeed contain features that, taken together, would help in retrieving the lemma for 'vortex'. Interestingly, a gesture containing these features will be very easy to identify as representing a vortex, even by a listener who does not have access to the accompanying speech. Especially when, as Krauss et al. assume, the features present in the gesture are to be apprehended proprioceptively, these features must be clearly present in the overt realization of the gesture.

This is in contradiction to the experimental findings reported in Krauss et al. that indicate that most iconic or lexical gestures are not easily recognizable at all without access to the accompanying speech. The paradox here is that those gestures that could facilitate lemma selection must be gestures whose meaning is largely unambiguous (such as the gesture for 'vortex'). Gestures that are hard to interpret without the accompanying speech will usually not contain enough information to facilitate lexical selection.

Another problem with the KCG model is that if gestures are indeed derived from spatio-dynamic working memory (an assumption their model shares with the Sketch Model), there is no reason to expect that there exists a single lemma that has the same meaning as the gesture. As mentioned above, in many cases *phrases* are needed to describe or approximate the meaning of a gesture. Therefore, if gesturing facilitates the speaking process, this is more likely to involve more complex (higher-level) representations than lemmas. For instance, de Ruiter (1995b, 1998) found evidence suggesting that performing iconic gestures facilitates the retrieval of imagery from working memory.

Synchronization in the KCG model also differs from that of the Sketch Model. While the mechanism Krauss et al. propose is more parsimonious than that of the Sketch Model, it is doubtful whether it will explain all synchronization phenomena. The KCG model does not provide an account for the post- and pre-stroke hold phenomenon. In the KCG model, gestures are terminated once the corresponding lexical affiliate has been articulated, but especially the pre-stroke hold phenomenon indicates that gestures can also be *initiated* in synchronization with speech.

7   Conclusions

In investigating the processing involved in gesture and speech production, it is a great advantage to develop theories in the framework of information processing. IP theories are less prone to multiple interpretations, easier to falsify, and facilitate the generation of new research questions. These advantages become even more salient when the theory is in a stage of development that allows for computer simulations. The IP approach is a theoretically neutral formalism that enhances the resolution of our theories without restricting their content, apart from the fact that the IP approach does not allow the use of homunculi as explanatory devices.

The Sketch Model is an attempt to incorporate and explain many well-established findings in the area of gesture and speech with a largely modular IP model. It incorporates a large amount of knowledge about gesture and speech in a consistent framework. As has been shown, predictions can be generated from the Sketch Model that can be tested in future experiments. The Sketch Model allows for detailed specification of hypotheses about the synchronization between gesture and speech. It can also accommodate cross-cultural variation in gesture behavior, and proposes a new and detailed account for the fusion of information in gestures. Because the Sketch Model is an extension of Levelt's (1989) model, the model implicitly incorporates a large amount of accumulated knowledge about speech production.

While the formalism used to specify the Sketch Model is similar to the formalism used by Krauss et al. (1996), the underlying assumptions of the Sketch Model are more similar to growth-point theory. Most notably, the assumption that gestures and speech are planned together by the same process and ultimately derive from the same representation is made in both the Sketch Model and in growth-point theory. However, in contrast to the Sketch Model, growth-point theory does not specify how a growth point develops into overt speech and gesture.

NOTES

This research was supported by a grant from the Max-Planck-Gesellschaft zur Förderung der Wissenschaften, Munich. I wish to thank Asli Özyürek for initially suggesting to me that I write about this topic. The chapter owes a great deal to many interesting discussions with Susan Duncan about information processing and growth-point theory. Finally, I wish to thank (in alphabetical order) Martha Alibali, Susan Duncan, Sotaro Kita, Pim Levelt, Stephen Levinson, David McNeill, Asli Özyürek, Theo Vosse, and David Wilkins for their invaluable comments on earlier versions of the chapter.

1 Here McNeill cites J. A. Fodor (1980), 'Methodological solipsism considered as a research strategy in cognitive psychology', *Behavioral and Brain Sciences* 3: 63–73.

2 Wheeldon & Levelt (1995) found evidence suggesting that internal speech consists of a syllabified phonological representation.

3 The gesture planner knows which part of the motor program is the meaningful part (stroke) because only the stroke is constructed from the information in the sketch.

4 Examples A and B are taken from videotaped narrations collected at the Max Planck Institute for Psycholinguistics by Sotaro Kita. David Wilkins kindly provided a transcript from his Arrernte field data for example C. Any errors in representing or interpreting these examples are my responsibility.

5 Of course, it is conceivable that people will 'quote' the gestures made by the quotee, but these gestures are not spontaneous.

6 I took these example sentences from McNeill (1992).

7 This is a change from the assumption made in Krauss, Chen & Chawla (1996), where the phonological encoder terminates gestures by sending a signal to the motor planner unit once the affiliated lexical item has been encoded phonologically.

REFERENCES

Besner, D. & Humphreys, G. (eds.) 1991. *Basic Processes in Reading*. Hillsdale, NJ: Erlbaum.

Biemans, M. & Woutersen, M. (eds.) 1995. *Proceedings of the CLS Opening Academic Year 95–96*. University of Nijmegen.

Butterworth, B. & Beattie, G. W. 1978. Gesture and silence as indicators of planning in speech. In Campbell &. Smith (eds.), pp. 347–360.

Butterworth, B. & Hadar, U. 1989. Gesture, speech, and computational stages: a reply to McNeill. *Psychological Review* 96: 168–174.

Calbris, G. 1990. *The Semiotics of French Gesture*. Bloomington: Indiana University Press.

Campbell, R. N. & Smith, P. T. (eds.) 1978. *Recent Advances in the Psychology of Language*, vol. IV: *Formal and Experimental Approaches*. London: Plenum.

Churchland, P. 1986. *Neurophilosophy*. Cambridge, MA: MIT Press.

de Ruiter, J. P. A. 1995a. Classifying gestures by function and content. Paper presented at the Conference on 'Gestures Compared Cross-Linguistically', Linguistic Institute, Albuquerque, July.

310   *Jan Peter de Ruiter*

de Ruiter, J. P. A. 1995b. Why do people gesture at the telephone? In Biemans & Woutersen (eds.), pp. 49–56.

de Ruiter, J. P. A. 1998. Gesture and speech production. Unpublished doctoral dissertation, University of Nijmegen.

Feldman, R. & Rimé, B. (eds.) 1991. *Fundamentals of Nonverbal Behavior*. New York: Cambridge University Press.

Fodor, J. A. 1983. *The Modularity of Mind*. Cambridge, MA: MIT Press.

Fodor, J. A. & Pylyshyn, Z. W. 1988. Connectionism and cognitive architecture: a critical analysis. *Cognition* 28: 3–71.

Hagoort, P., Brown, C. M. & Swaab, T. M., in press. Lexical-semantic event-related potential effects in left hemisphere patients with aphasia and right hemisphere patients without aphasia. *Brain*.

Haviland, J. B. 1993. Anchoring, iconicity, and orientation in Guugu Yimithirr pointing gestures. *Journal of Linguistic Anthropology* 3: 3–45.

Kendon, A. 1994. Do gestures communicate? A review. *Research on Language and Social Interaction* 27: 175–200.

Kita, S. 1990. The temporal relationship between gesture and speech: a study of Japanese–English bilinguals. Unpublished master's thesis, Department of Psychology, University of Chicago.

Kita, S. 1993. Language and thought interface: a study of spontaneous gestures and Japanese mimetics. Unpublished Ph.D. dissertation, University of Chicago.

Krauss, R. M., Chen, Y. & Chawla, P. 1996. Nonverbal behavior and nonverbal communication: what do conversational hand gestures tell us? In Zanna (ed.), pp. 389–450.

Krauss, R. M., Morrel-Samuels, P. & Colasante, C. 1991. Do conversational hand gestures communicate? *Journal of Personality and Social Psychology* 61: 743–754.

Levelt, W. J. M. 1989. *Speaking*. Cambridge, MA: MIT Press.

Levelt, W. J. M., Richardson, G. & La Heij, W. 1985. Pointing and voicing in deictic expressions. *Journal of Memory and Language* 24: 133–164.

Levinson, S. C. 1996. The body in space: cultural differences in the use of body-schema for spatial thinking and gesture. Paper prepared for the Fyssen Colloquium: Culture and the Uses of the Body, Paris, December.

McClave, E. 1994. Gestural beats: the rhythm hypothesis. *Journal of Psycholinguistic Research* 23: 45–66.

McNeill, D. 1987. *Psycholinguistics: A New Approach*. New York: Harper & Row.

McNeill, D. 1992. *Hand and Mind: What Gestures Reveal about Thought*. Chicago: University of Chicago Press.

McNeill, D. 1997. Growth points cross-linguistically. In Nuyts & Pederson (eds.), pp. 190–212.

Morrel-Samuels, P. & Krauss, R.M. 1992. Word familiarity predicts temporal asynchrony of hand gestures and speech. *Journal of Experimental Psychology: Learning, Memory and Cognition* 18: 615–622.

Neely, J. H. 1991. Semantic priming effects in visual word recognition: a selective review of current findings and theories. In Besner & Humphreys (eds.), pp. 264–336.

Nobe, S. 1996. Cognitive rhythms, gestures, and acoustic aspects of speech. Unpublished Ph.D. dissertation, University of Chicago.

Nuyts, J. & Pederson, E. (eds.) 1997. *Language and Conceptualization.* Cambridge: Cambridge University Press.

Pylyshyn, Z. W. 1979. Complexity and the study of human and artificial intelligence. In Ringle (ed.), pp. 23–56.

Rimé, B. & Schiaratura, L. 1991. Gesture and speech. In Feldman & Rimé (eds.), pp. 239–281.

Ringle, M. (ed.) 1979. *Philosophical Perspectives in Artificial Intelligence.* Brighton, Sussex: Harvester.

Schmidt, R. 1975. A schema theory of discrete motor skill learning. *Psychological Review* 82: 225–260.

Shannon, C. E. & Weaver, W. 1949. *The Mathematical Theory of Communication.* Urbana: University of Illinois Press.

Wheeldon, L. & Levelt, W. 1995. Monitoring the time course of phonological encoding. *Journal of Memory and Language* 34: 311–334.

Wilkins, D. 1995. What's 'the point'? The significance of gestures of orientation in Arrernte. Paper presented at the Institute for Aboriginal Developments, Alice Springs, July.

Zanna, M. (ed.) 1996. *Advances in Experimental Social Psychology*, vol. XXVII. Tampa, FL: Academic Press.

15 Catchments and contexts: non-modular factors in speech and gesture production

David McNeill

Departments of Psychology and Linguistics, University of Chicago

1 Introduction

The present chapter joins that by McNeill & Duncan in this volume to present the concept of a growth point. The aim of the chapter is to articulate some of the implications of this concept for models of speaking. When concrete utterances are examined for their growth-point sources, they are found to include information and groupings of information that are inconsistent with modularity-based information-processing models. What growth points can model naturally, information-processing models are systematically prevented from modeling – the contextualization of speech, gesture, and the thinking-for-speaking which they embody. Thus, I present the current chapter as a challenge to modular information-processing-type explanations of speech–gesture productions. Incorporating context conflicts with the encapsulation axiom shared by modular models. This axiom can be stated in something like the following terms: a complex mental process is modeled by breaking it down into a series of less complex processes (modules) each of which is encapsulated in the sense that it reacts only to specific inputs and has no information about or influence upon the internal operations of the other modules. Incorporating context conflicts with encapsulation because it means allowing the internal structure of a module to be altered by the context of speaking. The problem can't be solved by programming context into the module, because modularity requires the recurrence of internal steps (cf. Gigerenzer & Goldstein 1996), while context is precisely that which is unpredictable and non-recurrent. In contrast, growth points incorporate context at a foundational level; they are undefined without it. The current chapter states the concept of a growth point, or GP, explains how it explicates communicative dynamism, considers at length how it incorporates context as a fundamental component of thinking-for-speaking, and compares this incorporation to three information-processing, or IP, models, where context is inevitably excluded. The specific examples to be analyzed pose seemingly insuperable difficulties for modularity accounts where a module would have to alter its internal

312

grammar. How a growth point can be unpacked into a surface utterance is also considered. Finally, by taking context into account, we see an extraordinary level of speech–gesture synchrony that, disregarding context, has been overlooked or misinterpreted by previous gesture researchers.

2   Summary of growth points

This section recapitulates the fuller exposition of growth points in McNeill & Duncan. A GP combines imagery and linguistic categorial content into a single unit. GPs are inferred from all communicative events that can be observed, with special emphasis on speech–gesture synchrony and co-expressivity.

We regard a GP as a *minimal* psychological unit in Vygotsky's (1987) sense; that is, a smallest unit that retains the essential properties of a whole. The whole preserved in this case is an image and a linguistically codified meaning category; it is such a unit that we find in the speech–gesture window.

The psycholinguistic reality of the GP is shown in that it remains intact through delayed auditory feedback and clinical stuttering (Mayberry & Jaques, this volume), and in that information that was conveyed in gesture is interchangeable with that through speech in memory, as would be expected of a multi-modal unit (McNeill et al. 1994; Cassell et al. 1999).

To understand the incorporation of context into the GP, it is first necessary to understand how the GP is a product of differentiation. Growth points emerge as the newsworthy elements in the immediate context of speaking. They are, to adopt another Vygotsky concept, *psychological predicates* (not always grammatical predicates). The concept of a psychological predicate expresses the link between a GP and its immediate context of speaking; they are mutually defining: (1) A psychological predicate (and GP) marks a significant departure in the immediate context and at the same time (2) implies this context as a background.

These relationships suggest a mechanism of GP formation in which differentiation of a focus from a background is the key operation. Thus, for the purposes of the GP, 'context' is the background from which a psychological predicate is differentiated. This background is partially under the control of the speaker. It is a *mental construction* that is part of the speaker's effort to construct a meaningful context and idea units within it. The background is updated by the speaker's own activities, and thus is a continuously shifting part of the meaning structure. The speaker shapes the background in a certain way in order to give the intended contrast significance. The joint product of background and differentiation is a new meaning which exists only in relation to a background. I will use the terms *field of oppositions* and

Table 15.1. *Catchment structure*

Line	Catchment	Utterance	Gesture Feature
1	C1	he tries going [up the inside of the drainpipe and]	1 hand (right)
2	C2	Tweety Bird runs and gets a bowling ba[ll and drops **it** do_wn_ the drai]npipe	2 similar hands
3	C3	[and as he's coming up]	2 different hands
4	C3	[and the bowling ball's coming d]	2 different hands
5	C3	[own he swallows it]	2 different hands
6	C1, C3	[and he comes out the bottom of the drai]	1 hand (left)
7	C2	[npipe and he's got this big bowling ball inside h]im	2 similar hands
8	C2	[and he rolls on down into a bowling all]	2 similar hands
9	C2	[ey and then you hear a stri]ke	2 similar hands

significant (newsworthy) contrast to refer to this constructed background and the differentiation of a psychological predicate. All of this is meant to be a dynamic, continuously updated process in which new fields of oppositions are formed and new G P s or psychological predicates are differentiated in ongoing cycles of thinking-for-speaking.

2.1   Note on terminology

A GP is called a growth point since it is meant to be the initial form of thinking out of which speech–gesture organization emerges.

It is also called a GP since it is a theoretical unit in which principles that explain the mental growth of children – differentiation, internalization, dialectic, and reorganization – also apply to realtime utterance generation by adults (and children). That is, the process of utterance formulation is viewed as a process akin to mental growth.

A final reason for calling it a GP is that it addresses the concept that there is a definite starting point for an idea unit. An idea unit is not always present; it comes into being at a certain moment. It has roots in the previous context, but the idea unit itself does not exist before this moment.[1] The growth point is a *point* in this sense.

3   Case study of a growth point

The narrative text in Table 15.1 will be used to illustrate a number of features important for explaining the G P. Most details of the gesture transcription, with the exception of line 2, have been omitted from the table. Each line contains one gesture phrase (Kendon 1980), which is indicated by square brackets.[2]

To focus on one item for analysis, consider the utterance and gesture in (2). My purpose will be to show how this utterance can be explained utilizing GP as the model and how it conflicts with IP.

First, to explain the inferred GP itself. The gesture in (2) was made with two symmetrical hands – the palms loosely cupped and facing downward as if placed on top of a large spherical object, and the hands moved down during the linguistic segments "it do(wn)." The inferred GP is this image of downward movement *plus* the linguistic content of the "it" (i.e., the bowling ball) and the PATH particle "down." The GP is both image and linguistic categorial content: an image, as it were, with a foot inside the door of language. Such imagery is important, since it grounds the linguistic categories in a specific visuo-spatial context. It may also provide the GP with the property of 'chunking', a hallmark of expert performance (cf. Chase & Ericsson 1981), whereby a chunk of linguistic output is organized around the presentation of an image. The downward content of the gesture is a specific case of "down," the linguistic category – a specific visualization of it – in which imagery is the context of the category and possibly the unit of performance. The linguistic categorization is also crucial, since it brings the image into the system of categories of the language, which is both a system of classification and a way of patterning action. The speech and its synchronized gesture are the key to this theoretical unit.

3.1   Incorporating context

A GP is a psycholinguistic unit based on contrast, and this concept brings in context as a fundamental component. As mentioned above, I use the terms field of oppositions and significant contrast to analyze the role of context in thinking while speaking. A significant contrast and the field of oppositions within which it is drawn are linked meaning structures that are under the creative control of the speaker at the moment of speaking. Control by the individual ensures that GPs establish meanings true to the speaker's intentions and memory. The formation of a GP is the highlighting or differentiation of what is novel in such a field. The field defines the significance of the contrast; it establishes what is meaningful about it. The contrast itself is the source of the GP.

3.1.1   Catchments.   To explain the utterance in (2) and why it has the growth point we infer, we must consider the complete context above and study how the different parts of it came together in the utterance. A useful approach to this analysis is by means of *catchments* – a phenomenon first

noted by Kendon in 1972 (although he did not use the term catchment). A catchment is recognized from a recurrence of gesture features over a stretch of discourse. It is a kind of thread of consistent visuo-spatial imagery running through a discourse segment that provides a gesture-based window into discourse cohesion. The logic of a catchment is that discourse themes produce gestures with recurring features; these recurrences give rise to the catchment. Thus, working backwards, the catchment offers clues to the cohesive linkages in the text with which it co-occurs. Catchments are recognized from two or more gestures (not necessarily consecutive) with partially or fully recurring features of shape, movement, space, orientation, dynamics, etc. The example text from a cartoon story narration above illustrates three catchments. The catchments in this case are recognized from handedness and shape, and each of the features is based on the thematic content that motivates it: **C1** is a about a single moving entity, and its recurring gesture feature is a single moving hand; **C2** is about a bowling ball and what it does, and its recurring feature is a rounded shape (in gesture transcription terms, '2 similar hands' with shape details added); **C3** is about the relative positions of two entities in a drainpipe, and its recurring feature involves two hands in the appropriate spatial configuration ('2 different hands').

C1. The first is the catchment of one-handed gestures in items (1) and (6). These gestures accompany descriptions of Sylvester's motion, first up the pipe and then out of it with the bowling ball inside him. Thus **C1** ties together references to Sylvester as a solo force. This one-handed catchment differs from the two-handed gestures, which in turn divide into two other catchments:

C2. Two-handed symmetrical gestures in (2), (7), (8), and (9). These gestures group descriptions where the bowling ball is the antagonist, the dominant force. Sylvester becomes what he eats, a kind of living bowling ball, and the symmetric gestures accompany the descriptions where the bowling ball asserts this power. In (2) the bowling ball is beginning its career as antagonist. The rest of the catchment is where it has achieved its result. A two-handed symmetric gesture form highlights the shape of the bowling ball or its motion, an iconicity appropriate for its antagonist role.

C3. Two-handed asymmetrical gestures in items (3), (4), and (5). This catchment groups items in which the bowling ball and Sylvester mutually approach each other in the pipe. Here, in contrast to the symmetric set, Sylvester and the bowling ball are equals differing only in their direction of motion.

With these catchments, we can analyze the realtime origins of the utterance and gesture in (2) in a way that incorporates context as a fundamental component.

The occurrence of (2) in the symmetrical catchment shows one of the factors that comprised its field of oppositions at this point – the various guises in which the bowling ball appeared in the role of an antagonist. This catchment set the bowling ball apart from its role in **C3** where the bowling ball was on a par with Sylvester. The significant contrast in **C2** was the downward motion of the bowling ball toward Sylvester. Because of the field of oppositions at this point, this downward motion had significance as an antagonistic force. We can write this meaning as Antagonistic Force: Downward toward Sylvester; this was the context and contrast. Thus, "it down," unlikely though it may seem as a unit from a grammatical point of view, was the cognitive core of the utterance in (2) – the "it" indexing the bowling ball and the "down" indexing the significant contrast itself in the field of oppositions.

The verb "drops," therefore, was *excluded* from this G P. We can explain this as follows. The verb describes what Tweety did, not what the bowling ball did (it went down), and thus was not a significant contrast in the field of oppositions involving the bowling ball. The core idea at (2) was the bowling ball and its action, not Tweety and his. The detailed synchrony of speech and gesture thus depended on the context at the moment of speaking.

3.2   Unpacking

Unpacking in the G P model is conceptualized as a process of growth – differentiation, internalization, dialectic, and reorganization describe its dimensions – carried out over very short time intervals. The term unpacking refers to reorganization and the attainment of new levels of structure. In this section, I will consider the unpacking of the utterance at (2) and how it emerged out of contexts of speaking. It is growth-like in that it emerges with a new structure that makes manifest in a lexically and syntactically articulated construction the contextual oppositions at work at (2).

The gesture at (2) also contrasted with **C1** – a one-handed gesture depicting Sylvester as a solo force. This significant contrast led to the other parts of the utterance in (2) via a partial repetition of the utterance structure of (1). Contrasting verbal elements appeared in close to equivalent slots (the match is as close as possible given that the verb in (2) is transitive, while that in (1) is intransitive):

(1′) | (Sylvester) | up | in "he tries going up the inside of the drainpipe"
(2′) | (Tweety) | down | in "and (Tweety) drops it down the drainpipe"

The thematic opposition in this paradigm is counterforces – Tweety-down versus Sylvester-up. Our feeling that the paradigm is slightly ajar is due to the shift from spontaneous to caused motion with "drops." This verb does not alter the counterforces paradigm but transfers the counterforce from Tweety to the bowling ball, as appropriate for the gesture with its imagery of downward bowling ball.

The parallel antagonistic forces in (1′) and (2′) made Tweety the subject of (2′), matching Sylvester as subject of (1′). The contrast of (2′) with (1′) thus had two effects on our target utterance. It was the source of the verb "drops," and also why the subject was "Tweety" rather than "bowling ball." The verb expressed Tweety's role in the contrast and shifted the downward-force theme to the field of oppositions about the bowling ball. The subject identity expressed the antagonistic-forces paradigm. The pre-stroke hold over "drops" is thus also explained: the verb, deriving from an antagonistic-forces context, was propaedeutic to the GP, and the stroke was withheld until the way had been prepared for it (the post-stroke hold on the second half of "down" derives differently, as Kita (1990) observed: the mechanical downward stroke was over before the word and was held until the co-expressive content could be discharged).

The choice of verb was "drops", rather than 'throws', 'thrusts', or some other caused-motion option for a downward trajectory from a manual launch, possibly because it, among these options, corresponds most closely to the force dynamics of how Tweety made use of gravity to launch the bowling ball.[3] Thus, a further aspect of the context of (2) is this force dynamics. If this is the case, we have a further argument for the analysis above in which "drops" and "it down" are contrasts in different contexts. This comes from the handshape of the gesture in (2). The speaker made the gesture with her hands facing *down*, in a thrusting position. They were not positioned for a simulation of Tweety's hands when he exploited gravity to launch the bowling ball. Tweety in the cartoon stimulus held the bowling ball from the bottom and chucked it into the pipe, allowing gravity to do the rest. The GP image altered this force dynamics by making the launch into a thrust. The gesture, that is, reflected the speaker's reconceptualizing of the cartoon. The new force dynamics is not appropriate to Tweety, but it does fit the field of oppositions that concentrated on the force dynamics of the bowling ball in its persona as antagonist.

The question of how unpacking leads to grammatically allowable surface forms can be answered in part with filters or templates. The idea unit in a GP, being a point of differentiation from a background, must be realized in a surface position consistent with its communicative dynamism, but this fact does not, in itself, specify a position in a sentence framework. The concepts of "construction grammar" (Goldberg 1995) and of "emergent grammar" (Hopper 1987) may apply here. The contextual weight generated for the initially non-grammatical pair "it down"-plus-gesture was completed by accessing a caused-motion construction:

Subj   V   Obj   Obl
| | | |
Tweety drops it (b-ball) down

This construction type, learned and functioning as a unit, then could ease the GP, despite its dual contextual base, into a single grammatical format and guide the unpacking to a well-formed output type. This is 'emergent' in the sense that the grammatical form was not part of the input (this was the GP, the non-grammatical "it down" plus gesture), yet the output was this grammatical pattern. Thus, constructions, retrievable as wholes, can provide part of the template that unpacking needs.[4]

3.3   One utterance, several contexts

The utterance at (2), though a single grammatical construction, grew out of two distinct contexts. The two contexts were 'clamped together' by the gesture in (2) – the utterance was part of two separate contexts; it gained oppositional meaning from each. The downward-thrusting gesture is the mediating link, or 'clamp', that ties the contexts to the utterance. This gesture put the bowling ball in a field of oppositions in which the significant contrast was what it did (rather than how it was launched) and made the non-grammatical pair "it down" into a unit, yet it also made a place for the other context, that at **C1**, and the thematic shift of downness from Tweety to the bowling ball via "drops," thus providing the basis for the verb choice.

Let's summarize the contexts that brought (2) into being:

1. The field of oppositions in which the significance of the downward motion of the bowling ball was that of an antagonistic force – the contrast of (2) with (3), (4), (5): this gave the growth-point core meaning centered on "it down." It's noteworthy that the preparation for the gesture in (2) began in the preceding clause, concurrent with mentioning the bowling ball for the first time ("Tweety Bird runs and gets a bowling ba[ll and drops it down the drai]npipe"). That is, the new growth point embodying the idea of the bowling ball in its role as the antagonist to Sylvester began to take form as soon as the bowling ball itself entered the discourse.

2. The field of oppositions in which the significance was the counter-forces of Sylvester-up versus Tweety-down. This gave a sentence schema that included the words "drops," "down," "drainpipe," and the repetition of the sentence structure with Tweety in the subject slot.

The unpacking sequence would have begun with the first contrast. This was the core meaning embodied in the gesture. Unpacking then went to the counterforces context in (1) for information on how to unpack the sentence in (2), possibly guided by the gesture clamping the contexts together. The word order ("drops it down") obviously does not correspond to the derivational sequence. This was something more like "it down" → "drops."

A module producing "drops it down" would have to alter its internal structure to make the "it down" into a unit, be open to the contextual forces that require it to be such a unit, and generate it in advance of "drops" in the derivational sequence. These appear to be insuperable obstacles to a modular account.

4   Comparison with information-processing models

4.1   Predicting contexts

A unique accomplishment of the GP model is that it can 'predict' the context of the utterance. The GP includes context as a fundamental component. Incorporating context into the GP means that we can 'predict' what this context *must have been* for this image and category content to have congealed into a unit of thinking-for-speaking. An IP model does not address context at all. I will illustrate the GP/IP difference with three information-processing models all based on Levelt's *Speaking* – de Ruiter's (this volume), Krauss et al.'s (this volume), and Cassell & Prevost's (1996).

4.2   Three IP models

The three models have been proposed with the purpose of extending IP to gesture performance. Gesture is not a phenomenon originally considered in the Levelt model.

4.2.1   *The common element.* All three adopt basically the same strategy for including gesture, which is to attach a new module at some point – a *gesture module* – to the speaking module. Thus all three regard gesture as an outgrowth of more basic sentence-generating operations. All also share the IP design feature of treating contextualized information as peripheral, not as a central component of speech performance. Context or 'situation knowledge' in the Levelt model is in an external information store to which the modular components have access. Context is treated as background information along with such long-term data as encyclopedic information and standards of appropriate discourse. This store is segregated from the conceptualizer–formulator mechanism responsible for the construction of the utterance.

4.2.2   Variations. Though the strategies are the same, the models differ in other ways. In particular, they differ in where on the speaking module the new gesture module is affixed. In fact, all possible ways of hooking gesture onto a hypothetical central module have been adopted:

> Krauss et al. (this volume) – *preconceptualizer* link: the gesture component is linked to the IP structure preconceptually in working memory.
>
> De Ruiter (this volume) – *conceptualizer* link: the gesture component is linked at the conceptualizer to the IP structure at the level of message generation.
>
> Cassell & Prevost (1996) – *postconceptualizer* link: the gesture component is linked to the IP structure at the equivalent of the formulator (called the sentence planner).

4.2.3   Context outside the model. Although there is this variation, none of the models provides a way to include context as a fundamental component of speaking. The consequences of this absence can be demonstrated by examining examples cited by the authors themselves.

Krauss et al.: The key step in this model is the use of gesture to assist lexical retrieval: "In our model, the lexical gesture provides input to the phonological encoder via the kinesic monitor. The input consists of features of the source concept represented in motoric or kinesic form . . . These features, represented in motoric form, facilitate retrieval of the word form by a process of cross-modal priming." If there is some delay in retrieving a word, *drainpipe*, say, a gesture with some of the spatial features of a drain-pipe (e.g., 'verticality', 'hollowness') can be fed into the lexical system and prime the word, and thereby aid retrieval. This mechanism will work to activate missing words but does not explain item (2). The word "drops" had features that matched the downward-thrusting gesture (DOWNWARD, CURVED, etc.), yet this word was *excluded* from the gesture stroke via a pre-stroke hold. Furthermore, the same DOWNWARD and CURVED gesture features matched a different set of lexical features, those of the bowling ball (indexed by "it") and the path ("down"). Why did the gesture target these lexical items and yet exclude "drops"? We know the answer – it was owing to the contextual contrast of **C1** versus **C2**. That is, to achieve its own lexical retrieval goals, the Krauss et al. model must have had access to contextual information. But precisely this content is excluded by a modular design.

De Ruiter: A gesture occurred in which a speaker appeared to hold binoculars before her eyes, synchronized with 'with binoculars at' (part of a longer utterance in Dutch, ". . . enne, da's dus Sylvester die zit met een verrekijker naar (ENG 'with binoculars at') de overkant te kijken" 'and eh so that is Sylvester who is watching the other side with binoculars'). De Ruiter claims that to say that 'with binoculars at' is the linguistic affiliate of the gesture would be circular. But this is because, in his IP model, context is excluded. With context included, we have another source of information that breaks into the logical circle. Moreover, this incorporation of context into the model amounts to a prediction of what the context would have to have been: a context in which the instrument and direction were jointly the newsworthy content (we don't know what the context in fact was, since de Ruiter, thinking in IP terms, doesn't report it). His and the other IP models can't make this type of prediction at all. If the context was not one in which this gesture–speech combination would be newsworthy, we would have the much-sought-after falsifying observation that, according to de Ruiter, is possible only in the IP framework. This potential disproves the claim that IP models alone are falsifiable.

Cassell & Prevost: The sentence-planner plans a sentence like "Road Runner zipped over Coyote"; finds the rheme; chooses a gesture to depict this rheme (driving, say); and puts principal stress on the verb going with this gesture. The process, in other words, starts from the sentence and, in keeping with the peripheral status of the rheme, adds the rheme, the gesture, and finally the stress. A gesture-imbued-with-context approach is more or less the reverse of this. The process starts from the narrative context as it has been built up at the moment of speaking, and differentiates some meaningful step from this context (this is like the rheme). Unpacking the content of the gesture is the process of working out a surface sentence in such a way that it can carry this meaning into a full linguistic realization.

4.2.4   Summary of IP. In all the models described, context has been excluded, and this has created a disparity between what the models are able to do and the facts of human language use. For, if gesture shows anything, speaking and thinking, at their cores, are manipulations of context, both created and interpreted, with meanings and forms in integral contact – the very antithesis of IP modularity.

5   Gesture timing

The GP predicts speech–gesture timing points based on the concept that individual utterances contain content from outside their own structure. This power of prediction, in turn, suggests the validity of the GP, in that it can account for the occurrence of gesture–speech events to a high level of temporal accuracy.[5]

• *Stroke*. The image embodied in the gesture automatically synchronizes with the linguistic categories that are also part of the GP. In the case of (2), the G P comprised downward-motion imagery categorized as 'bowling ball' and 'down'. This timing was a product of the contrast between **C2** and **C3**.

• *Pre-stroke hold.* When two contexts intersect in a single utterance, the context embodied in the growth point can be delayed while the other context is materialized in lexical form. In the case of (2), the verb "drops" emerged from the **C1–C2** contrast, and while it was being articulated, the G P materialization of the **C2–C3** opposition was placed on hold.

• *Preparation onset.* This is explained as the moment when the next G P unit starts to take form. When Vivian mentioned the bowling ball in the preceding clause, "Tweety Bird runs and gets a bowling ba[ll and drops it do<u>wn </u>the drai]npipe," she simultaneously began to move her hands in preparation for the gesture stroke. That is, she began to organize the G P unit in which the bowling ball was conceptualized as a force opposing Sylvester which acted by coming down. The bowling ball took over the opposing-forces paradigm initiated by Tweety. This shift of embodiment occurred precisely when Vivian mentioned the bowling ball in the preceding clause. The point at which the ball was mentioned is the earliest moment for forming the next G P around the bowling ball and its downward path. Again, the timing is derived from the developing context, in this case the contrast between **C1** and **C2**.

Susan Duncan (pers. com.) has pointed out contrasting utterances that demonstrate the systematic shifting of gesture timing as the context varies; the G P predicts this timing shift by generating different G Ps according to their contexts. In the first example, Sylvester is climbing up the outside of the drainpipe – this action is the new content – and the gesture stroke synchronizes with the verb "climbs." In the second example, the speaker describes another scene in which Sylvester is making a second ascent – this time on the inside of the pipe. Again the stroke synchronizes with the new content, and the verb "climbs" is passed over, while the gesture synchronizes with "inside." The gestures themselves are quite similar; thus the timing difference is not due to shifting gesture content but to different fields of opposition and the contrasts within them – Ways of Reaching Tweety ('climbing the drainpipe') and Ways of Climbing Up the Pipe ('inside'), respectively:

(10)   second part [is he **climbs up** the drai]n to get* <uh> try and get Tweety
        Gesture shows Sylvester moving up the pipe

(11)   tries to climb up in through the [drain* / <nn> / **inside the dra<u>in</u>-pipe**]
        Gesture shows Sylvester moving up the pipe

Inasmuch as predicting the exact timing of two gesture phases from basic principles embodied in the G P counts as support for the model, the timing of the preparation and stroke gesture phases (accurately transcribed within three-hundredths of a second) supports the GP model.[6]

6   The moral

All of this implies that every utterance, even though seemingly self-contained, contains content from outside its own structure. This other content ties the utterance to the context at the level of thinking. It is this fact that conflicts with the axioms of modularity yet fits the schema outlined in the GP concept. The GP *predicts* a context rather than adds context as a parameter (the treatment of context in Levelt 1989, for example). A successful prediction, in turn, validates the GP analysis of the utterance and its origins. That two contexts could collaborate to form one grammatical structure also implies that a sense of grammatical form enters into utterances in piecemeal and oblique ways that do not necessarily follow the rule-governed patterns of the utterance's formal linguistic description. The gesture had the role of 'clamping' the contexts together, and this may be one of the functions of gestures.[7]

A further moral is that modularity should be replaced by some more flexible concept of utterance-modeling. Gestures are a crucial test of speech-production models, and models based on modularity fail this test spectacularly. Modular models have the opposite effect – pulling context and gesture/speech as far apart as possible. The odd group of words "it down" must be dismissed as an 'error' or an imprecision of timing (de Ruiter), that is, be set aside as inexplicable in the system. In the GP, on the other hand, this grouping is the key to understanding the relationship of the utterance and its cognition in the context of speaking.[8]

Is some other kind of module possible – one that puts context and propositional content into one package? I think not, for this would fly against the concept of a recurrent process that is essential to an encapsulated modular system. Context is precisely that which is not recurrent but which is constructed in the process of thinking and speaking.

I am not advocating an anti-modeling position. On the contrary, I endorse de Ruiter's call for modeling as a tool in cognitive science. But if a model is to realize its potential it must be appropriate for the domain being modeled. It cannot be based on other-worldly assumptions. In the case of contextualized functions, modularity is an example of the other-worldly.

NOTES

Preparation of this chapter was supported by a grant from the Spencer Foundation.
1 Dennett & Kinsbourne (1992) have argued against such a concept. The temporal anatomy of a gesture however appears to answer part of their argument; namely,

the onset of gesture preparation provides a definite locus for the beginning of a
new thought element seemingly not confounded with the conscious experience of
that element itself.

2 In addition, boldface marks the gesture 'stroke', which is the phase with semantic
content. Underlining marks holds (the hands held in place in midair). In line 2
there is both a 'pre-stroke' hold on "drops" and a 'post-stroke' hold at the end of
"down" as the word is completed (Kita 1990). The full transcript of the narration
in the table is the following (# shows a breath pause):

Battle Plan for Vivian

(1) he tries going [[**up** <u>the insid</u>][e of the **drainpipe** and]]
     1 hand: RH rises up

(2) Tweety Bird runs and gets a bowling ba[ll and <u>drops</u> **it** <u>do**wn**</u> the drai]npipe #
     Symmetrical: 2 similar hands move down

(3) [[<u>and</u> / **as he's** <u>coming up</u>]
     Asymmetrical: 2 different hands, LH holds, RH up

(4) [[<u>and the</u> **bowling** <u>ball's coming d</u>]][own
     Asymmetrical: 2 different hands, RH holds, LH down

(5) he **sss**<u>wallows it</u>]
     Asymmetrical: 2 different hands, RH up, LH down

(6) [# and he comes **out the bot**<u>tom of the drai</u>]npipe
     1 hand: LH comes down

(7) and he's **got this** <u>big bowling ball inside h</u>][im
     Symmetrical: 2 similar hands move down over stomach

(8) [[and **he rolls on down**] [into **a bow**<u>ling all</u>]][ey
     Symmetrical: 2 similar hands circling around each other

(9) and then yo**u hear a** sstri]ke #
     Symmetrical: 2 similar hands move apart

3 Pointed out by Karl-Erik McCullough.

4 Also, 'poetic' aspects, in the Jakobsonian sense, of the discourse provide their
own templates for unpacking and have the important property that they are
created by speakers on-line. The poetic aspects can work in collaboration with
constructions. Speakers deploy a system of contrasts in the code itself to guide
the construction of a surface form as it fulfills a poetic plan. Dayton (1998) has
carried out an analysis from a poetics point of view of the transformation undergone by Sylvester in lines 1–9 of the example analyzed in this chapter.

5 The limit on how accurately hand and other movement segments can be aligned
temporally with speech in videotaped recordings is given by the frame-replace-
ment rate of the video that one is employing. In de Ruiter's European tapes this
is 25 times a second, or 40 ms per video frame; in North American and Japanese
tapes it is slightly better – 30 times a second, or 33 ms per frame. If we think in
terms of electronic devices such as computers, a margin of 33 ms may seem wide
indeed. However, on the scale of speech events, 33 to 40 ms is a small margin.
Syllables take 200 or 300 ms; 33 ms is shorter than the release of a stop conso-
nant (Lehiste & Peterson 1961). Observations of speech–gesture timing are
therefore well within the confines of a syllable, and approach the resolving power
of the phonetic system itself. The evidence on which the inference of the G P in
"Tweety Bird runs and gets a bowling ba[ll and <u>drops</u> **it** <u>do**wn**</u> the drai]npipe" is

based thus has an accuracy well within the durations of the speech segments being considered.

6 That the preparation phase of a gesture signals the initiation point of the GP explains why the onset of a gesture movement (i.e., preparation) often precedes and *never* follows the semantically related speech (Kendon 1972; Morrel-Samuels & Krauss 1992; Nobe, this volume). It also explains why the extent of onset anticipation would be negatively correlated with the frequency of use of the lexical affiliate (Morrel-Samuels & Krauss 1992). A GP can have come into being and the speaker not have found the signifier with which to present it. The tip-of-the-tongue phenomenon demonstrates the reality of having categorized meanings while lacking the word forms with which to express them (Brown & McNeill 1966).

7 After right-hemisphere damage, speakers show tendencies both to decontextualize speech and to reduce gesture output (McNeill 1998). These phenomena may be linked, in that lowered contextualization removes opportunities for gestures to clamp different contexts together.

8 Kita (this volume) has proposed a new hypothesis, similar in some respects to the GP, that he terms the Information Packaging Hypothesis (IPH). An important difference between the GP and the IPH is the concept of a unit. Despite the Information Packaging Hypothesis name, units exist only in the GP. This is because speech and gesture are held to be independent systems in the IPH. Imagery and language intertwine as continuous threads. In the GP, as I have explained, these meaning systems are packaged into bundles with onsets and offsets (the GP unit, while bundled, is far from isolated from context, as explained above).

Kita argues that the IPH takes an 'actional' view of the origin of gestures, in contrast to the 'representational' view assumed by the GP. I consider this difference to be non-fundamental, since (a) the IPH itself has a representational component, the intertwining threads, and (b) the GP for its part can be extended to include actional origins, and indeed such a proposal is made in McNeill & Duncan (this volume).

The unbounded IPH offers advantages in accounting for certain phenomena, especially mismatches of spoken and gestured depictions of Piagetian conservation and arithmetic, as described by Goldin-Meadow and colleagues (Goldin-Meadow et al. 1993). It is easy to see with the IPH how one thread is able to take over and represent meanings not accessible to the other thread. The concept of a GP is, on the other hand, more appropriate for expressing communicative dynamism and differentiation in context, since it provides something that can be differentiated, as a unit, from the background. A possible relationship between the IPH and the GP could be that the GP is temporarily suspended during mismatch phases of development, whereupon the IPH takes over. While the GP is modeled on the mental growth of children, it may, paradoxically, not apply during children's transition points in mental growth. The conceptual instability that characterizes these phases could be a force breaking the GP apart. After negotiating the mismatch (e.g., attaining a new level of cognitive organization), GP units reappear at the new level, that is, the new mental growth dimensions become available on the micro level. This relates the IPH and GP as successive stages. An empirical prediction from this form of relationship is that measures of GP binding power – synchrony during DAF, synchrony during stuttering (if any), and the interchangeability of speech- and gesture-based information – should be weakened in areas of the mismatch. Another implication is that during mismatches communicative dynamism should be conveyed by gesture or speech but not by both (with gesture the more likely vehicle, according to Goldin-Meadow et al.). A third implication is that cognitive instability (e.g., from fatigue or distraction) could erode the GP and bring the IPH to the fore. Finally, in children GPs should be structured differently before and after mismatches.

The striking phenomenon described by Kita to illustrate speech–gesture collaboration (a gesture is repeated with possible modifications to get a match with speech) can be analyzed in similar terms. These examples show transitory states of disorganization where imagery and categorial content have trouble converging. It is important to observe that in both examples of this phenomenon, the speaker hesitated or interrupted her speech not for lexical retrieval purposes but because of conceptual configuration problems; thus it is plausible that achieving a GP was problematic in these cases. Consider one of Kita's examples: an arcing hand showing the path of a catapulted weight which first appeared during a speech-hesitation pause and then was repeated in modified form while speech articulated the situation, "um and he **gets** clobbered by the weight." In GP terms, the speaker is attempting to converge on a GP, which she does manage to do in the final utterance – the image of the flying weight, until then only imagery, is brought into the system of language (categorized) as "gets clobbered." The modification of the gesture in the final GP could show that convergence involved an image–categorial content dialectic (see Dray & McNeill 1990 for other cases of gesture modification during dialectics). Kita's other example of speech–gesture collaboration, which again involved a conceptual configuration problem, can be explained in a similar way.

REFERENCES

Anderson, J. R. (ed.) 1981. *Cognitive Skills and Their Acquisition*. Hillsdale, NJ: Erlbaum.
Atkinson, J. M. & Heritage, J. (eds.) 1984. *Structures of Social Action: Studies in Conversational Analysis*. Cambridge: Cambridge University Press.
Brown, R. & McNeill, D. 1966. The 'tip of the tongue' phenomenon. *Journal of Verbal Learning and Verbal Behavior* 5: 322–337.
Cassell, J., McNeill, D. & McCullough, K.-E. 1999. Speech–gesture mismatches: evidence for one underlying representation of linguistic and nonlinguistic information. *Pragmatics & Cognition* 7: 1–33.
Cassell, J. & Prevost, S. 1996. Distribution of semantic features across speech and gesture by humans and machines. In Messing (ed.), pp. 253–269.
Chase, W. G. & Ericsson, K. A. 1981. Skilled memory. In Anderson (ed.), pp. 227–249.
Dayton, S. 1998. A poetic structure of speech and gesture. Unpublished manuscript, Department of Anthropology, University of Chicago.
Dennett, D. C. & Kinsbourne, M. 1992. Time and the observer: the where and when of consciousness in the brain. *Behavioral and Brain Sciences* 15: 183–247.
Dray, N. L. & McNeill, D. 1990. Gestures during discourse: the contextual structuring of thought. In Tsohatzidis (ed.), pp. 465–487.

Duncan, S. D. 1996. Unpublished comments on de Ruiter's 'Sketch'. Max Planck Institute for Psycholinguistics, Nijmegen.

Gigerenzer, G. & Goldstein, D. G. 1996. Mind as computer: birth of a metaphor. *Creativity Research Journal* 9: 131–144.

Goldberg, A. E. 1995. *Constructions: A Construction Grammar Approach to Argument Structure*. Chicago: University of Chicago Press.

Goldin-Meadow, S., Alibali, M. W. & Church, R. B. 1993. Transitions in concept acquistion: using the hand to read the mind. *Psychological Review* 100: 279–297.

Hopper, P. 1987. Emergent grammar. In J. Aske, N. Beery, L. Michaels & H. Filip (eds.), *Proceedings of the 13th Annual Meeting of the Berkeley Linguistics Society*, pp. 139–157. Berkeley, CA: Berkeley Linguistics Society.

Kendon, A. 1972. Some relationships between body motion and speech: an analysis of an example. In Siegman & Pope (eds.), pp. 177–210.

Kendon, A. 1980. Gesticulation and speech: two aspects of the process of utterance. In M. R. Key (ed.), *The Relation between Verbal and Nonverbal Communication*, pp. 207–227. The Hague: Mouton.

Kita, S. 1990. The temporal relationship between gesture and speech: a study of Japanese–English bilinguals. Unpublished master's thesis, Department of Psychology, University of Chicago.

Lehiste, I. & Peterson, G. E. 1961. Transitions, glides and diphthongs. *Journal of the Acoustic Society of America* 33: 268–277.

Levelt, W. 1989. *Speaking*. Cambridge, MA: MIT Press.

McNeill, D. 1998. Gesture after right hemisphere injury. Paper presented at the European Workshop on Neuropsychology, Bressanone, January.

McNeill, D., Cassell, J. & McCullough, K.-E. 1994. Communicative effects of speech-mismatched gestures. *Research on Language and Social Action* 27: 223–237.

Messing, L. (ed.) 1996. *Proceedings of WIGLS* (Workshop on the Integration of Gesture in Language and Speech). Wilmington, DE: Applied Science and Engineering Laboratories.

Morrel-Samuels, P. & Krauss, R. M. 1992. Word familiarity predicts temporal synchrony of hand gestures and speech. *Journal of Experimental Psychology: Learning, Memory, and Cognition* 18: 615–622.

Rieber, R. W. & Carton, A. S. (eds.) 1987. *The Collected Works of L. S. Vygotsky*, vol. I: *Problems of General Psychology*, trans. N. Minick. New York: Plenum.

Siegman, A. & Pope, B. (eds.) 1972. *Studies in Dyadic Communication*. Elmsford, NY: Pergamon.

Tsohatzidis, S. L. (ed.) 1990. *Meanings and Prototypes: Studies in Linguistic Categorization*. London: Routledge.

Vygotsky, L. S. 1987. Thinking and speech. In Rieber & Carton (eds.), pp. 39–285.

Part 4

From gesture to sign

The topic of gesture gains added importance because of its connections to the topic of sign linguistics. These connections are of interest in part because they are, in fact, problematic. A major question is, Do the deaf make gestures? And beyond this puzzle, what in general is the relationship of sign language to natural gesture? These questions and others are the themes of part 4.

The gesticulations at one end of Kendon's continuum (see the introduction) can be related to sign languages at the other end on three timescales – *real time* (the possibility of a gesture occurring during signed utterances and what constrains it), *historical time* (the emergence of a sign language), and *evolutionary time* (the possible place of signs in the origin of human language abilities). The chapters in this part conveniently focus on these timescales.

Liddell presents an analysis of the 'gestural' in realtime American Sign Language usage. He argues that gesture is incorporated in the form of deixis (thus Liddell makes contact with Haviland's discussion of deixis), a use for which the structure of ASL itself makes provisions.

Morford & Kegl in their chapter take up the historical dimension by describing the remarkable situation that has arisen in Nicaragua since the Sandinista Revolution. Deaf people who previously had been isolated were brought together for the first time, and out of this natural contact a new language has emerged, nearly all of it recorded on video.

Stokoe, finally, brings us to the phylogenetic dimension, proposing a scenario in which (conceivably) *Homo erectus* crossed the symbolic threshold – the conjectured step away from instrumental actions to symbolic representations (similar to the transition described by LeBaron & Streeck's sketch of the same passage in our own species) – and beyond, into the elaboration of representations that become increasingly language-like even while still in the visual-kinesic modality.

16   Blended spaces and deixis in sign language discourse

Scott K. Liddell

American Sign Language, Linguistics, and Interpretation, Gallaudet University

1   Introduction

It is abundantly clear that gestures constitute a highly significant, often indispensable, aspect of spoken language discourse. Can the same be said of sign language discourse, where signs themselves are produced by gestures of the hands, arms, and body? Does sign language discourse make use of spontaneous gestures, distinguishable from lexical signs, that convey meanings such as those conveyed by gesture in spoken language discourse? I will argue that it does. Although I focus on deictic gestures, it will become apparent that sign language discourse also includes gestures in which the actions of the signer illustrate the actions of one of the characters in a narrative. Mental-space theory (Fauconnier 1994, 1997) provides the conceptual structures needed for constructing meaning from the linguistic signal and has been employed to successfully solve numerous previously intractable linguistic problems. Phenomena such as metonymy, reference, co-reference, and presupposition have all been shown to depend on mental-space configurations. I will argue that mental spaces are also essential in understanding the significance of the gestural signal. I will begin by describing the production of signs in some detail. Understanding the nature of the articulation of the signed signal is essential in making the distinction between articulatory gestures of the hands equivalent to gestures of the tongue in the production of speech and other types of spontaneous, non-lexical gestures. Next I will provide a brief history of the treatment of space in the analysis of ASL. The gestures I will treat as pointing gestures have been previously analyzed as ordinary linguistic, articulatory movements. I will argue that such grammatical (phonological) treatments of pointing gestures do not adequately account for the sign language data. I will then introduce mental spaces, the concept of a grounded mental space (Liddell 1995), and finally the concept of a blended mental space (Fauconnier & Turner 1994, 1996). Finally, I will show how these cognitive structures lead to a coherent analysis of the gestures that are part of the sign language discourse.

The signs in signed languages are produced by gestures of the hands, arms, face, and body. Stokoe (1960) was the first to argue that these gestural activities were part of a linguistic system. He demonstrated that the gestures involved in sign production were the surface manifestation of a phonological system, equivalent in its abstract structure to phonological systems in spoken languages.[1] As a result of the process begun by Stokoe, sign languages all over the world are now recognized as real human languages with their own grammars. Sign language grammars include all the types of abstract structure one would expect to see in the grammar of any language, including phonological, morphological, and syntactic systems.

This chapter examines the use of space in American Sign Language. This is an aspect of ASL which has not generally been regarded as being related to gesture. That is, once sign languages were understood to be real languages, virtually all the pointing activities in sign languages were analyzed as driven by linguistic features rather than by the more general ability to point at things. This chapter will argue, based on an examination of some of the cognitive activity which underlies the use of space, that the use of space in sign languages is carried out through a combination of linguistic features and gestural pointing.

I will begin with an articulatory parallel between sign languages and vocally produced languages. In both types of languages a mobile articulator must be correctly placed in articulatory space to produce the words of the language. In the ASL sign THINK, for example, the fingertip makes contact with the forehead. The sign FUNNY makes contact with the nose. In the production of any given sign, the hand can either be in contact with the location, as it is in the sign COLOR (inside of the fingers contact the chin), or the hand can be near a location, as it is in the sign MIRROR (the hand is near the nose, but ahead of it). Such articulatory uses of space in ASL are contrastive. Replacing one location with another results in the production of a different sign or no sign at all. For example, the sign ONION is produced by a twisting motion of the X handshape (forefinger extended with curled tip, other fingers closed over palm and covered by thumb) in contact with the side of the forehead near the eye. Changing the location to the lower cheek while keeping all other aspects of the sign the same produces the sign APPLE. Changing the location to the chin produces a possible but non-existent sign.

Signs are also produced at specific locations in space. The sign CELE-BRATE is made in space ahead of the shoulders at about the level of the neck. The sign THING is produced in space about at the level of the lower chest. Although signs can be made in different locations in space, it is very difficult to find a difference in spatial location which will distinguish one sign from another. The signs POINT and GOAL constitute the only such pair of signs I know of in ASL. Both are two-handed signs. The non-moving hand in both signs has a 1 handshape with the index finger pointing upward. The moving hand has the same handshape, and the index finger of the moving hand is directed toward the tip of the finger of the stationary hand. What distinguishes one sign from the other is the placement of the stationary hand. When performed at the level of the abdomen the sign POINT is produced. When performed at approximately the level of the forehead, the sign produced is GOAL.

The movement or placement of the tongue with respect to location in its articulatory space is also vital in the production of spoken words. Just as the hand must be correctly positioned to articulate signs, the tongue must be correctly positioned to produce spoken words. For example, in producing the word *tick*, the tongue must begin by making contact with the alveolar ridge, behind the upper teeth. It will make contact with the velum at the end of the word. If these two locations were reversed, the word *kit* would be produced instead. This need to correctly place an articulator demonstrates a clear parallel between spoken and signed languages, with the only difference being one of degree. That is, for a spoken language the tongue is the only truly mobile articulator, since it can move to distinctive locations in the mouth. In the case of sign languages, there are two such articulators. Each is highly mobile and, compared with the tongue, can contact a much greater number of locations.

In contrast to the signs described above, a few classes of signs can be made in what appear to be an unlimited number of locations. For these signs the basic meaning of the sign remains the same regardless of the way the sign is directed. In contrast to earlier examples like APPLE and ONION, where a change in location produces a completely different sign, the difference in direction or location in signs which 'use space' leaves the meaning of the basic sign intact. For these signs, directing them spatially *adds* meaning to the basic meaning of the sign. For example, the ASL pronoun PRO has the meaning and syntactic function one expects of a pronoun. In addition, it can be directed toward entities which are present in the signer's environment.[2] A signer could direct PRO toward any one of a large number of people sitting in a room. The direction of the movement of the sign would be different, depending on the location of the person toward whom the sign was directed. Indicating verbs, locative verbs, and classifier predicates present a picture very similar to pronouns, since the signs in these categories also 'use space'. They differ in the details of their interpretation and production but nevertheless are highly variable in how they are directed in space, depending on the location of real or imagined entities they are directed toward. This is no longer parallel with the production of spoken words. This is not a difference of degree, but a difference in kind, since the tongue does not move about the oral cavity pointing at things out in the environment, thereby adding meaning to the word being produced.

2   Grammatical treatments of the signing space

Klima & Bellugi (1979) and Poizner, Klima & Bellugi (1987) describe a 'syntactic' use of space in which the signer makes an association between a locus and a non-present referent. In this analysis, a signer could first mention a referent and then point toward a locus in space on a horizontal plane in front of the signer. It is claimed that signs are subsequently directed toward the locus to refer to that referent. For convenience, I will refer to this as the HP (horizontal plane) theory.

Klima & Bellugi (1979) propose that such loci are used even when referents are present. Lillo-Martin & Klima (1990) refer to such loci as *referential loci* (R-loci), and in that analysis, the location of a present referent determines its R-locus. For example, suppose a signer wishes to produce a pronoun referring to the addressee. If the addressee is standing ahead of the signer but slightly to the left, then the R-locus will be present on the horizontal plane ahead of the signer, slightly to the left of center, between the signer and the addressee. To produce a pronoun referring to the addressee, the signer directs the pronoun toward the R-locus between the signer and the addressee. In the HP theory, whether the thing being described is present or not, signs which 'use space' are directed toward loci on a horizontal plane in the space ahead of the signer in order to refer to the things associated with those loci.

Spatial loci are treated as parts of the grammar of ASL. Fischer (1975), for example, proposes that such spatial loci may cliticize to verbs. Kegl (1985) treats specific locations in space as morphemes. Spatial loci, it is argued, are also used for the expression of morphological-agreement affixes (Neidle et al. 1998, Bahan 1996).

Since the HP theory depends on signs being directed toward spatial loci, this will be the first issue to be examined. We will first look at how signs are directed when the referent is present. When the present referent is a human being, each sign which uses space has a specific part of the body toward which it is directed. PRO is directed toward the sternum. Although this level is higher than the horizontal plane, it is close enough to give the appearance that the sign is being directed toward a locus on that plane. Other signs, however, are produced far enough above the horizontal plane so that it is obvious that the sign is not being directed toward a locus on the horizontal plane. For example, the sign GET-SAME-IDEA-SAME-TIME (Figure 16.1a) is directed toward the forehead of a person who is present.[3] The sign SAY-NO-TO (Figure 16.1b) is made at approximately the level of the nose, and

a. GET-SAME-IDEA-SAME-TIME

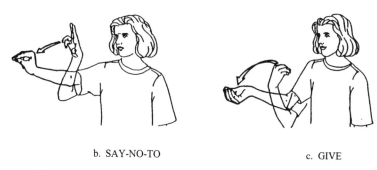

b. SAY-NO-TO   c. GIVE

Figure 16.1. Differing heights of agreement verbs.

the sign GIVE (Figure 16.1c) is made at the level of the sternum (the same level at which pronouns are produced). Even lower still is the sign INVITE, produced at the level of the abdomen. Thus, there is a range of heights at which signs are produced, from the abdomen to the forehead. These facts stand in direct conflict with the claim that signs are directed toward a single locus on the horizontal plane – or a single locus anywhere.

Making the case for loci on a horizontal plane even more difficult is the fact that the person the sign is directed toward can be located not just ahead of the signer, but on the ground, in a tree, behind a window in the third floor of a building, etc. For a referent significantly higher than the signer, none of the signs behave the way the HP theory says they should. For example, suppose that a signer is going to direct a sign toward a referent standing on a ladder. In this circumstance even the lowest signs (e.g., INVITE) will be directed upward, away from the horizontal plane. The general statement we can make about how pronouns and indicating verbs are directed when referents are present is that the signs are directed toward the thing itself. There is no need for a locus on the horizontal plane in this analysis. All one needs is some entity to direct the signs toward. In the case of present referents, the HP theory is not consistent with the facts concerning how signers sign. As a result, the idea that signs are directed toward loci on a horizontal plane when referents are present should be abandoned.

3   Surrogates

In addition to real things, signs can be directed toward entities which are imagined to be present. For example, a signer could imagine that a man much taller than himself is standing nearby. The signer could say that the two of them got the same idea at the same time by directing the sign GET-SAME-IDEA-SAME-TIME toward the forehead of the imagined tall man. Since the imagined referent is much taller than the signer, the sign will be directed upward toward the forehead of the imagined referent. It is easy to see that a locus on the horizontal plane also has no connection with this type of signing. In fact, when referents are imagined to be present, signers behave just as if the imagined referent were real. In the case of an imagined person, signs are directed toward the appropriate part of that imagined person's body.

It is even possible to imagine that a person is present and not direct any signs at all toward that imagined person. Suppose, for example, that a signer is telling a story about how a small child came up to him and that he responded that he was busy. All the signer needs to do is to turn and look at the imagined child and make the statement "PRO.1 BUSY" as if the child were there.[4] The signer could produce a sentence intended for the imaginary child to see and understand, but neither PRO.1 nor BUSY would be directed toward the imagined child. In this case, the imagined child serves as an addressee, with no signs at all being directed toward the area of space associated with the imagined child. Naturally, the signer also has the option of directing signs toward the imagined child. Suppose, as part of that story, the signer wished to represent a conversation in which he told the child, "I will tell you later." The sign TELL would be directed roughly toward the neck or sternum of the imagined child.

Liddell (1994) refers to entities like the imagined child as *surrogates*. The person or thing may be imagined as near, far, on the left or right, high or low, etc. The location of the surrogate, not loci on the horizontal plane, determines how signs are directed. In this respect, directing signs toward either real things or surrogates works in the same way. The sign ASK, for example, would be directed toward the chin of a real person or toward the chin of a surrogate.

Kegl (1976: 30) describes a signing sequence in which a signer pretends to put earrings on an imagined person. To do this, Kegl describes the imaginary equivalent of the signer's own body projected into the space facing the signer. She calls it a 'projected body pronoun'. In her analysis the projected body pronoun is placed in the signing space at the same place where an NP has been 'indexed'. A projected body pronoun might seem to be similar to a surrogate, but their properties are quite different. First, a surrogate is not a pronoun. Signs can be directed toward either a real person or a surrogate. This does not mean that a real person or surrogate is a pronoun.[5] The second major difference is that a surrogate is not 'in' the signing space where something was indexed. A surrogate can be imagined to be anywhere. A surrogate is treated like a real thing. Signers can talk to surrogates or talk about them.

In sum, Real Space and surrogate uses of space have nothing at all to do with pointing toward a meaningful locus on the horizontal plane. There is no need for such a locus when signs are directed toward either real things or surrogate things. Real things in the immediate environment are both physically present and conceived of as present. Surrogates are only conceived of as present. Because both are conceived of as present, both conceptual entities have a location somewhere in the immediate environment, a certain size, shape, etc.

4   Establishing an 'index'

We are ready now to talk about 'establishing an index' in the signing space. To indicate that a boy was standing in a certain place the signer could sign

BOY LOC-AT$_X$.

The sign LOC-AT$_X$ in this example is produced by directing the index finger downward toward some location X in the space ahead of the signer. For purposes of discussion, we will say that X is ahead of and to the right of the signer. The HP theory states that this places a meaningful locus X on a horizontal plane ahead of the signer and on the right at about the level of the abdomen. It further entails that the signer has made an association between the sign BOY and the X locus. If the signer wishes to make reference to the boy, the HP theory holds that the signer will then direct signs toward the X locus, which represents the boy.

Again, however, the theory is not consistent with the facts of signing. Recall that, when directed at a physically present person, every verb has a particular level, or part of the body, toward which it is directed. Such height differences can also appear when talking about referents 'established' in space. The range of height appears to be from about the level of the abdomen to the level of the lower face, though it can be smaller. A sign like KICK is directed at the lower level of this range. The pronoun PRO is directed slightly higher. The sign SAY-NO is higher still, moving outward and downward, ending its movement at about the level of the signer's own

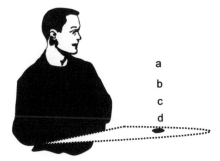

Figure 16.2. The symbols a–d show where an indicating verb could be directed when an entity representing a human is established in the signing space.

chin or neck. The sign GET-SAME-IDEA-SAME-TIME is the highest. Figure 16.2 illustrates the ways that signs point when an index is established ahead of the signer.[6] Some signs are directed as if they were pointing at the spatial locus, the black dot on the horizontal plane, while others are directed well above the level of the locus.

Earlier I provided evidence that if real things are present, signs are directed toward those real things, not to loci in the signing space. Similarly, signs are directed toward surrogates rather than loci in the signing space. In both cases, signs are directed toward things, not loci on a horizontal plane. Suppose we assume that when signers direct a pronoun or verb in space (after establishing an index), these signs are also directed at something. If we make this assumption, then all we need to do is look at how signs are directed and we will have an idea of the size and location of the entity toward which they are directed. This has been done in Figure 16.3a.

The area of space shown in Figure 16.3a has been associated with a standing human. Such entities are referred to as *tokens* in Liddell (1994). The shape and size of any given token seems to depend on the particular type of entity being described. A person assumed to be lying down, for example, will be associated with a much shorter token than one conceived of as standing up.[7]

Both tokens and surrogates are invisible, conceptual entities. Because tokens are limited to the space ahead of the signer, they have a size which fits in that space. The token in Figure 16.3a, which represents a human, does not have the shape of a miniature human. It is merely an area of space. Figure 16.3b illustrates a surrogate – which does have the shape of a person. The signer could direct the sign SAY-NO-TO toward the surrogate's nose or the sign INVITE toward the surrogate's abdomen. One could look down at

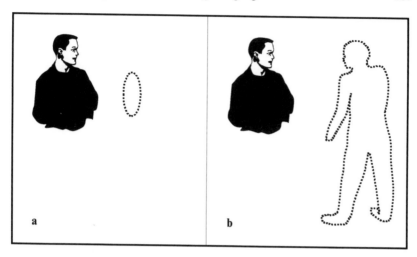

Figure 16.3. Comparing a token and a surrogate representation.

the shoes of a surrogate, tap the surrogate on the shoulder, look at the surrogate's hair, etc. None of these activities are possible with a token. Surrogates can be any size. While a token house would only be inches tall, a surrogate house would be full-sized. Finally, while one can talk about a token, it is not possible to talk to a token. A surrogate, however, can play a first-person, second-person, or third-person role in the discourse. One can easily talk about a surrogate (third-person) or talk to a surrogate (second-person). A surrogate can even play a first-person role in the discourse (Liddell 1995).

Recall that a locus was thought to represent a referent because it was believed that signers directed signs toward a locus to make reference to an entity. Above, however, I have shown that signs are directed toward tokens rather than the spatial locus at which the token was placed. It no longer follows, then, that the locus represents the entity. Instead, when a signer makes an association between an entity and a locus in space, that places a token at that locus. Signs are then directed toward that token to make reference to the entity. It follows, in this new analysis, that the token represents the entity.

Kegl (1985) proposes a treatment of loci in the signing space which is similar in some respects to that proposed by Klima & Bellugi (1979). In Kegl's proposal there are an unlimited number of possible spatial loci, and these loci are not restricted to the horizontal plane. In this analysis, spatial loci are explicitly described as morphemes. This immediately raises two difficult analytical issues – one related to meaning and the other to form.

Would each spatial morpheme have a meaning distinct from each other spatial morpheme? If so, what would the meanings be? If not, then will there be an unlimited number of morphemes which all mean the same thing? Even if the meaning question could be solved, we are still left with no proposal for the phonological description of these morphemes.

Suppose, for the sake of argument, that it were correct that spatial loci on or off the horizontal plane were the targets of pronouns and indicating verbs. A set of phonological features which would capture the various ways that the hand could be directed would seem to be a minimal requirement for an adequate analysis of this phenomenon. Liddell & Johnson (1989) attempted an analysis involving seven vectors radiating away from the signer, several horizontal planes, and four distances away from the signer. Using vector, plane, and distance features, we were able to phonologically define more than a hundred points in space ahead of the signer. In the end, even this elaborate spatial grid proved inadequate. There are simply too many possible ways to direct or place the hand. Currently, there is no adequate system for producing a phonological description of *any* sign which points at things. To put this in more concrete terms, there is no phonological analysis which can even describe the pronoun PRO directed toward addressee, meaning 'you'. As a result, an act of faith is required to hold onto the idea that spatial loci are grammatical entities with morphological and phonological substance. Maintaining that view requires holding onto the idea that some highly variable physical activity which occurs during sign language discourse is the reflection of an unlimited number of morphemes whose meanings and forms cannot be described.

Even assuming that a solution to the semantic and phonological problems could be solved, any proposal which claims that signs are directed toward a single point or locus will be unable to deal with the data described above. First, in the case of present referents, there is no single point toward which signs are directed. That is, signs may be directed toward someone's forehead, nose, chin, sternum, etc. The same applies to surrogates. The same also applies to entities 'established' in space. Some signs are directed at the upper level of a token, while others are directed at other levels. Proposing a single locus toward which all signs are directed is not consistent with the facts concerning how signs are used with present referents, surrogates, or tokens.

5   Mental spaces

In mental space theory, constructing the meanings of sentences depends on the existence of mental spaces – a type of cognitive structure distinct from linguistic representations (Fauconnier 1994 [1985]). For example, when a signer describes the house he lived in as a child, the description is based on a mental representation of that house. Suppose, for example, that an English-speaker says, "In 1970 I lived in a small house on the outskirts of town." The person is not describing the actual house as it exists today, but the house as it existed in 1970. In fact, the house being described may no longer exist, may no longer be small, or may no longer be on the edge of town. This demonstrates that the phrase *a small house* is describing a mental represen-tation of a house at a certain time and place. The situation in 1970 being described is an example of a mental space, and the house as it existed in 1970 is an element of that mental space. In mental space theory, all sen-tences are about mental spaces, and elements of sentences correspond to elements in mental spaces. For example, the phrase *a small house* describes an element of the 1970 mental space. If the physical house no longer exists, then the house being described only exists in the mind of the speaker. If the house does still exist, then it exists not only in the mind of the speaker, but also in the real world. In either case, the sentence is about the house in a mental space. The house in the mental space may or may not correspond to some entity in the real world. Fauconnier demonstrates how the existence of mental spaces allows for elegant solutions to previously insoluble prob-lems of reference, coreference, and ambiguity.[8]

Issues of reference in ASL are intimately tied to the way that signs are directed in space. For example, I argued above that when the referent of a pronoun is present, signs are directed toward the actual referent, thereby identifying that referent. Since no one would want to argue that an actual referent was part of the grammar of a language, it seems incontrovertible that signs can be directed toward entities which are not part of the grammar of the sign language. It might be possible, however, that directing the sign TELL toward an obviously physical thing such as a real person is either con-ceptually or grammatically distinct from directing a sign toward an obvi-ously conceptual thing such as a surrogate or token. I will be arguing below that these are neither conceptually nor grammatically distinct. In all of these cases, signs are directed toward elements of mental spaces by the general cognitive ability to point at things.

When the sign TELL is directed toward the addressee, the sign expresses the meaning "tell you." The person toward whom the sign is directed is made of flesh and blood. This fact seems to be in conflict with the proposal that signs are directed toward elements of mental spaces. How is it possible to consider the person toward whom the sign is directed to be an element of a mental space? The answer comes with an understanding of what is meant by Real Space.

5.1   *The non-linguistic character of Real Space*

A person's mental representation of his or her immediate physical environment is a type of mental space (Lakoff 1987, Liddell 1995). This mental representation includes a person's understanding of what is real, where real entities are located around them, what they look like, and what their properties are. I will use the label 'Real Space' to talk about this mental space.

It is important to distinguish the conceptual elements of Real Space from the physical entities which we assume make up our world. That is, we take it for granted in our everyday lives that our world is composed of physical entities which take up space, have mass, can move, can harm us, etc. Real Space is our conceptual representation of these physical things. The types of conceptual entities which are found in Real Space are just those things which a person understands to be currently present and real. If I see a book ahead of me, my perception of the book adds a conceptual book of the appropriate size, shape, and color to my mental representation of what exists in my immediate environment. When I reach out and grasp the book, the physical sensation of touch confirms the correctness of my mental representation.

Thus far I have tried to make a distinction between physically real things in one's immediate environment and the mental representations of those things. Real Space is the mental representation of the physical elements in one's immediate physical environment. Real Space has a unique characteristic which distinguishes it from other mental spaces. Its elements have conceptual locations in the immediate environment. That is, the conceptual location of a book in Real Space guides my hand in reaching out toward that conceptual element. In general, the location of the conceptual element and the physical element coincide. That is, I reach for a book in its Real Space location and I feel a sensation of touching the book. A fish swimming in a river as perceived by people standing on the shore is an exception to this generalization. The refraction of the light makes the fish appear to be in a different place from where it actually is. In this case the location of the fish in Real Space differs from the location of the physical fish. Throwing a spear toward the location of the fish in Real Space will not produce a satisfactory result. Although real things and elements of Real Space do not always coincide physically, they generally do, and that allows us to function in the world.

The term *grounded* is used to label a mental space whose entities are conceived of as present in the immediate environment (Liddell 1995). Since Real Space has this characteristic, Real Space is a grounded mental space. The difference between a grounded and a non-grounded mental space is an important part of everyday life. That is, humans behave differently toward a grounded mental space than toward a non-grounded mental space. Consider the difference between seeing a book ahead of you and recalling that there was a book ahead of you when you were in another room. Both are examples of mental spaces. They differ in that the former is grounded and the latter is not. Only in the case of a grounded mental space will someone reach out and try to grasp the book. This is because of the unique characteristic of a grounded mental space described earlier. That is, with a grounded mental space, the conceptual entity is conceived of as present. If it is near enough, a reaching gesture will be successful in making contact with both the conceptual and the physical book.[9]

In discourse, there are also consequences to the grounded versus non-grounded distinction. In (1) the phrase *this book* describes a book which does not yet exist. Therefore, *this book* describes an element in a non-grounded mental space. There is no physical book in the immediate environment corresponding to the phrase *this book*.

(1) Tell me more about this book you plan to write.
(2) This book explains everything.

Spoken-language discourse typically relies on a combination of language and gesture when elements in Real Space become part of the discourse. For example, although (2) mentions a book, and the word *this* is used in English to refer to a proximal entity, the mere presence of a book near the speaker is generally insufficient to let the addressee know that the phrase *this book* describes the physically present book. To make this connection clear, the speaker would be expected to produce a gesture identifying the book. Since the book being described is in the immediate environment of the speaker, the phrase *this book* describes an element of Real Space – a grounded mental space. On the other hand, if (2) describes a book which is not physically present (i.e., it is in a non-grounded mental space), then no gesture would be expected.

Assuming that the speaker of (3) was talking about two books on a table, an addressee would have no idea which book was being claimed to be better without a mental representation of the table and the books on it. In addition, the speaker would have to make some type of gesture in the form of a glance, a pointing gesture, grasping or touching each book, etc., in order to make clear which book was being talked about with the phrases *this book* and *that one*.

(3) This book is better than that one.

Understanding utterances about elements of Real Space depends on the addressee also having a Real Space representation which contains the entities being described. The addressee's Real Space would also have to include the two books being talked about in (3) in order to make sense of the utterance. The same applies to constructing a meaning for (4).

(4)   I'll take one of those.

Suppose a shopper enters a store and utters (4). It would be necessary to simultaneously produce a gesture toward the item being requested. The gesture could take the form of a finger pointing, a tilt of the head, an eye gaze at the item, etc. Such a gesture would let the addressee determine which item was being referred to based on the direction of the deictic gesture. The gesture makes clear that the item being requested is in Real Space. If the speaker entered a store and uttered (4) without any kind of gesture, the clerk would not know how to respond.

Notice that (4) is also an acceptable response to the question from a waiter, "Could I bring you a bowl of ice cream?" In response to this question, however, one would not expect a pointing gesture, since the bowl of ice cream is not present and therefore not an element of Real Space. But if in response to the suggestion to order ice cream, the speaker gestured toward a dessert on an adjacent table while uttering (4), the interpretation would be different. The deictic gesture would signify that the element being described by the phrase "one of those" was in Real Space. This would be taken as a rejection of the suggestion to bring ice cream. By following the direction of the deictic gesture, the waiter would be able to identify the element being described by the phrase "one of those."

It seems apparent that Real Space is not part of any language. But ASL and other sign languages take advantage of Real Space by directing signs toward real things. The fact that signs can be directed in an unlimited number of ways toward things which are not part of that language presents a difficult analytical problem. Specifically, the manner in which signs which use space are placed or directed is not listable in the grammar (Lillo-Martin & Klima 1990, Liddell 1995).[10] The problem which arises here relates to having a sufficient number of morphemes to correctly describe the ways that signs are directed in space. There cannot be a discrete morphemic solution, since there are too many possible locations and there could not be a morpheme for each possible location or direction.

Liddell (1995) proposes that directing signs toward things in Real Space is not dependent on any linguistic features. Instead, signs which use space are directed by non-discrete gestural means toward elements of a grounded mental space. This proposal makes such signs combinations of linguistic and gestural elements. The handshapes, certain aspects of the orientation of the hand, and types of movement are all describable by discrete linguistic features. The direction and goal of the movement constitutes a gestural component of the sign.

Spatial representations established ahead of the signer in ASL discourse are also examples of mental spaces (van Hoek 1988, 1989; Liddell 1995, 1996). In the framework of this chapter, tokens have locations in the immediate environment of the signer, and signs can be directed toward these entities. This makes them grounded mental spaces (Liddell 1995, 1996). The same description also applies to representations involving surrogates. They are also elements of grounded mental spaces. We will now turn to an examination of the mental spaces in which tokens and surrogates appear.

6   Mental spaces which include tokens and surrogates

In Figure 16.4 a signer is describing an interaction between a seated Garfield and his standing owner in which Garfield is turning his head and looking up at his owner (Figure 16.4a).[11] The signer partially describes this with the signing shown in Figure 16.4b.

In describing the cartoon, the signer does several things. He produces a narrative description of the event by signing, CAT LOOK. He also looks up and to the right. He also directs the sign LOOK upward and to the right.[12] In reality, there is no one standing to the right of the signer, but based on the direction in which the signer is looking and the direction that the sign LOOK is pointing, the signer has conceptualized a space in which the owner is standing there.

6.1   Physical overlap analysis

Initially, I treated the space containing the surrogate as conceptually independent of, but physically overlapping, Real Space (Liddell 1996). That is, mental space 'a' was analyzed as a grounded mental space which contained a seated surrogate Garfield and a surrogate owner standing to the right of Garfield. This conceptual space would then be superimposed on Real Space such that the surrogate Garfield occupied the same space as the signer and the surrogate owner was located to the right. Since the surrogate Garfield overlapped physically with the signer, the movement of the signer's head and the direction of the signer's eye gaze in Figure 16.4b (Real Space) were to be interpreted as movements of Garfield. In this analysis, the signer is still conceptually the signer. The surrogate space is a grounded space that now overlaps physically with Real Space. The physical overlap between the two spaces is illustrated in Figure 16.4c.[13] This analysis relies on the physical overlapping of two grounded mental spaces to associate the signer with Garfield.

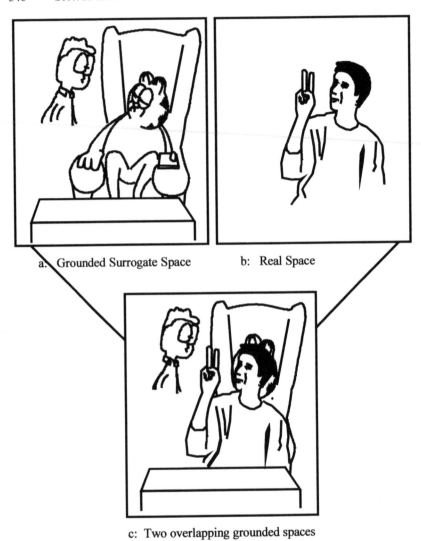

a: Grounded Surrogate Space   b: Real Space

c: Two overlapping grounded spaces

Figure 16.4. Overlapping grounded mental spaces.

6.2   *Analysis of blended mental spaces*

An alternative mental-space analysis is also available. Two mental spaces may blend to create a new space in which selected properties of each of the two input spaces are projected into a third, novel space called a *blend* (Fauconnier & Turner 1994, 1996). Thus, a blend is a partial mapping from two input spaces onto a third space in which the blend takes on novel properties not present in either of the two input spaces.

6.2.1   Blend analysis of surrogates. A blend analysis of the Garfield cartoon episode can be seen in Figure 16.5. The two input spaces are the cartoon space (a) and Real Space (b). Of the two input spaces, only Real Space is a grounded mental space.

In the blended space, elements of the cartoon space are projected onto Real Space. For example, the owner has been projected onto a physical location to the right of the signer, and a TV has been projected onto a physical location ahead of the signer. In this example, aspects of Garfield have also been projected onto the signer himself. The result of this blending is that, within the context of the blend, the signer is partially Garfield. This is shown in Figure 16.5 by the lines joining Garfield in (a) to the signer in (c). In this example, only Garfield's head rotation and the eye gaze have been mapped onto the signer. As a result of the blend, the signer's head rotation and eye gaze are interpreted as actions of Garfield.

For ease of reference, I will bracket the blended elements with the symbol |. Thus, the blend represented in Figure 16.5c contains |Garfield|, |the owner|, |the chair|, and |the TV|. Evidence for the projection of all the elements of the blend shown in Figure 16.5c was found in the narrative from which this example was taken (Liddell & Metzger 1998). The evidence consists of directing signs toward blended elements (e.g., |the owner|, |the TV|, and |the chair|), directing eye gaze or head position toward one of those elements (e.g., |the owner|), or carrying out actions of the entity mapped onto the signer (e.g., head turning, eye gaze, etc.). Note that the processing of the single sign LOOK has to be based on two different mental spaces. The narration takes places in Real Space (16.5b) as an action of the signer, but directing the sign toward |the owner| depends on knowledge of the blended space (c).

The production of the single sign illustrated in Figure 16.5b requires a considerable amount of background cognitive activity.[14] That is, in order to express information about the cartoon, the signer has created a grounded blended space. Creating this blend involves mapping elements of the cartoon space onto Real Space, including the signer himself. By doing so, the signer is aware that some of his actions will be interpreted as his own (e.g., producing the sign LOOK). Other actions will be interpreted within the context of the blend (e.g., turning the head to the side, gazing to the right and up).

Since the blended space involves a mapping onto Real Space, the blend is also grounded. That is, |the owner| is conceptually present for the signer to direct the sign LOOK toward, and for |Garfield| to direct his face and eye

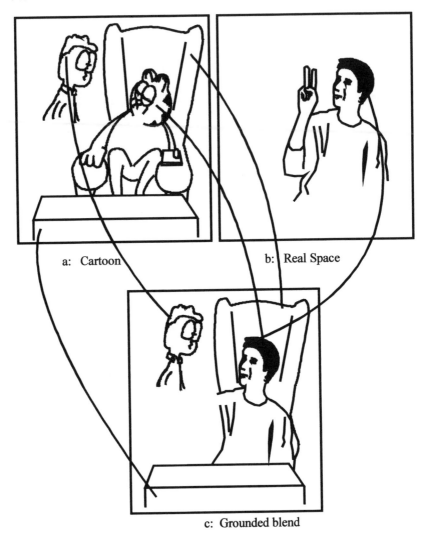

a: Cartoon   b: Real Space

c: Grounded blend

Figure 16.5. Two input spaces and the blend.

gaze toward. Since this is a *grounded* blend, signs are still being directed toward things present. The owner is not physically present with the signer, but |the owner| is conceptually present in a physical location next to the signer in the blended space. Thus, directing signs toward |the owner| is accomplished by a combination of linguistic and gestural elements within the same sign. This is not different from directing signs toward someone or something physically present.[15]

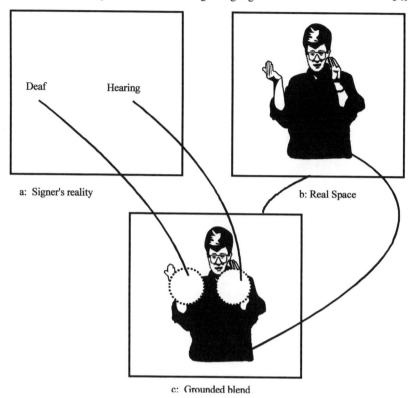

a: Signer's reality

b: Real Space

c: Grounded blend

Figure 16.6. Two input spaces and the grounded blend.

6.2.2   Blend analysis of tokens. The blend analysis also applies in a straightforward way to the elements I have previously described as tokens. The primary difference between a surrogate representation and a token representation is whether or not the signer has been assigned a role in the blend. In the surrogate example we examined earlier, Garfield was mapped onto the signer in the blend. Conceptually, this makes the signer, at least partially, something other than simply the signer.

In Figure 16.6 the signer has created a blend by mapping 'deaf people' and 'hearing people' onto two areas in the space ahead of her. Deaf people and hearing people are two elements of a non-grounded mental space (a). Real Space is represented in (b), and the blend of these two input spaces is shown in (c), where |deaf people| and |hearing people| are represented as spheres. As a result of creating the blend, the signer is able to talk about deaf people and hearing people by directing signs toward the two blended elements. In this example, she directs the sign COMPARE toward |deaf

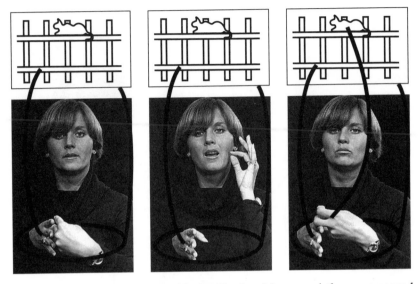

Figure 16.7. A blend with classifier handshapes and the space around them.

people| and |hearing people|. This indicates that she is talking about comparing deaf people and hearing people. This blend adds new elements to Real Space without changing any other aspects of Real Space.

In the next example the signer is stating that a cat is on a fence. This is also accomplished by means of a blended space. The signer maps the fence and the cat onto specific areas in space ahead of her. First the signer explains that she is talking about a fence by signing FENCE.[16] In Figure 16.7a, the hand with the fingers pointed inward will trace out the location and extent of the fence while the other hand remains stationary. Producing the sign FENCE in a location and a direction different from its citation form creates the blended space ahead of the signer. After the completion of the sign, the non-moving hand remains in place as a visible landmark of only part of the fence, since |the fence| extends beyond the fingertips of the signer. The area ahead of the signer to the side of |the fence| is |the surface| surrounding |the fence|. The space near the fence is mapped onto the space near |the fence|. Space further from the fence is mapped onto the space further from |the fence|. This space is represented by the oval drawn around the two handshapes. The line connecting the non-grounded mental space to the space around the two classifier handshapes represents the mapping of the physical setting of the fence from the input space onto Real Space. The size of the oval is not meant to represent the exact size of the mapping, which could be much larger than what is shown in Figure 16.7.

The second sign produced is CAT (b). This identifies the next element to be added to the blended space. The third sign (c) places the hooked V classifier (CL:V") on top of the 4 classifier (CL:4). The hooked V classifier has the meaning 'animal' or 'seated human', and is produced by extending the index and middle fingers from a fist (V) with both extended fingers bent over at the tips ("). Since the signer just signed CAT, the intention to map the cat in the mental space onto the hooked V classifier is clear. As a result of the blending, the hooked V classifier takes on the additional significance 'cat'. The physical relationship between the cat and the fence is shown by the physical relationship of the two classifier handshapes. It is important to note here that this blend includes not just |the cat| and |the fence| but the setting containing those two elements. This could include not only the physical setting but the temporal setting as well. Just as in Real Space and in the previous blended spaces, the blended elements in Figure 16.7 are conceptually present and can have signs directed toward them. Those elements can be located in an unlimited number of places, so once again a morphemic solution to directing signs is not possible. Signs directed toward blended elements will also consist of combinations of linguistic features and gestural pointing.

In the next example, the signer is giving advice about driving a car in New York City. First he explains that one should not simply drive through an intersection (on the assumption that the cross-traffic will be stopped). One should rather first stop and look both ways. Only then should one proceed. In Figure 16.8, the signer describes the vehicle stopped at an intersection using a classifier predicate with a vehicle classifier (the top hand with the thumb, index finger, and middle fingers extended) and a surface classifier (the B handshape with the four fingers extended and straight). The physical arrangement of the two handshapes shows the physical relationship between the vehicle and the street. This creates a blend very much like the cat-on-the-fence blend in Figure 16.7. In this blend, the car from the hypothetical New York streets mental space has been blended with the vehicle classifier. Thus, because of the blend, the vehicle classifier picks up the additional significance 'specific car on streets on New York'. The street from that mental space has been blended with the surface classifier. Although not visible in the blend, the continuation of the street as well as the cross-street is also an important part of the blend. The area around these two classifier handshapes is also part of the setting projected from the New York streets mental space. This blend is shown as blend #1 in Figure 16.8.

This example also contains another grounded blend. The signer looks left and right as if he were in the vehicle. In Figure 16.8 he is looking to the right. The hypothetical driver is blended with the signer, so that the signer's

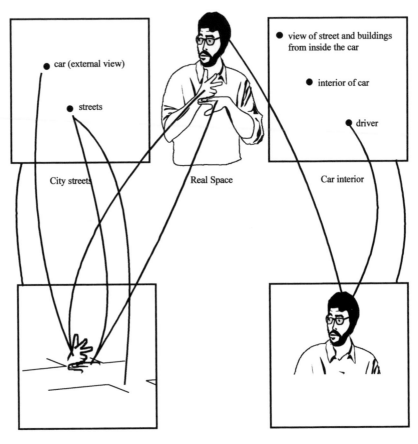

Figure 16.8. Multiple simultaneous grounded blends.

actions illustrate the actions of the hypothetical driver. Note that the signer is not gazing at the scene of blend #1. He is looking to his right as if he were the driver. Thus, he is behaving as if he were in the vehicle and the traffic to be checked were to his right and left. In other words, the hypothetical driver has been partially mapped onto the signer. This creates the blended element |the driver| in blend #2. Because of the blending, the facial expression, head movements, and eye gaze of |the driver| can be seen by looking at the signer. This is equivalent to the previous Garfield example, where |Garfield| looks up and to the right toward |the owner|. Examples such as these have no obvious solution without blended spaces.[17] In the grounded-blend analysis, however, a solution involving two simultaneous blends is available.

In order to understand the intent of the signer, the addressee will have to integrate the significance of grounded blend #1 and grounded blend #2. Grounded blend #1 provides a 'wide angle' point of view of the scene being described, while grounded blend #2 provides a 'close up' view of the signing. In public lectures, Bernard Bragg has frequently discussed the use of 'close up' and 'long range' cinematic techniques in signing. In this example, we have both at once – in two separate but simultaneous physically overlapping grounded blended spaces. The two individual blends are similar to blends examined earlier. The complexity in this example comes from the simultaneity of the two blends.[18] Here we see the equivalent of the mappings in the Garfield example and the cat-on-the-fence example present simultaneously.

6.3   Mental-space theory

Mental-space theory provides a theoretical framework for talking about the meanings being expressed by the signer. Fauconnier (1997: 34) describes language as a "superficial manifestation of hidden, highly abstract, cognitive constructions." He proposes that constructing the meaning of linguistic constructions depends on the interaction of the grammar and mental spaces, frequently in highly abstract and complex ways. His statement about meaning construction applies without modification to the sign language examples we have been discussing. In those examples, it is clear that the grammar provides only pieces of the meanings being expressed by the signers.

7   Sign languages and the need for deictic gestures

A word in a spoken language can be described in terms of a discrete set of features which combine to describe the sound structure of that word.[19] The same can be said for a non-pointing sign in a sign language, which can also be described by a set of linguistically definable features. The same cannot be said for signs which use space. I have proposed that ASL and, by implication, other sign languages have classes of signs which can be directed toward elements of grounded mental spaces. Since the elements in these spaces can be located in what appear to be an unlimited number of places, sign languages must rely on a pointing gesture as a component of these signs. This makes such signs unlike words in spoken languages. This might be thought of as an interesting aberration if it occurred in only one sign language. But it is not just one sign language which operates this way. Every natural sign language we know of functions in the same way.

The nature of the difference between signed and spoken languages may not be as great as it appears. For example, speakers and signers both have the need to make clear to their addressees that elements of a grounded mental space are being discussed. In both circumstances deictic gestures toward those entities have exactly the same significance.[20] They let the addressee know that the entity being described in the grammatical construction is present. Not only does the gesture show that it is present, it identifies the actual entity being described. This statement applies equally well to spoken and signed languages.

In an orally produced language, the linguistic signal and pointing gestures are easily distinguished, since they are carried out by completely different means. The need to gesture during spoken-language discourse is met by making deictic gestures while speaking. How will a sign language be able to distinguish between signs which point to elements in a grounded and a non-grounded mental space? The answer is the same for sign languages as for spoken languages – through gesturing toward the elements of the grounded mental space while signing. The need to gesture toward elements of grounded mental spaces is met in the case of sign languages by creating classes of signs which combine sign and gesture.

Regardless of the modality, there is a need for deictic gestures toward elements of grounded mental spaces. In spoken languages the gesture does not influence the form of the individual spoken words. The one difference I am proposing between signed languages and spoken languages is that signed languages have all developed in ways which allow the gestural component to combine with the linguistically specified features of some classes of signs without interfering with the ability to recognize the signs themselves.

NOTES

This chapter is a revised and expanded version of a 1996 paper, 'El uso del espacio en las lenguas de señas: un marco teorico', in L. Pietrosemoli, (ed.), *Lengua y habla*, vol. II.

1 Stokoe used the term *cherology* as the signed equivalent of spoken-language phonology. This term, however, was not widely adopted. Currently, linguists studying sign language phonology use phonological terminology (and concepts) used in the study of spoken language.

2 Meier (1990) argues that there is no formal distinction between second- and third-person pronouns in ASL. There is a single pronoun which can be directed toward the addressee or some other referent. Meier uses the gloss INDEX for this sign, but since the term 'index' is used in so many different ways in linguistics and descriptions of sign language, I will use the gloss PRO to represent that sign.

3 This figure was drawn by Paul Setzer.

4 The gloss PRO.1 refers to the first-person pronoun directed toward the signer's own chest. The gloss PRO.1 is used rather than I or ME, since each of these alter-

nate glosses reflects an English case distinction. The ASL sign is unmarked for case.

5   I prefer to hold on to the idea that pronouns are parts of sentences, not part of the environment which sentences describe.

6   This represents the levels one would expect to see for a person assumed to be standing.

7   When creating spatial maps (e.g., "Chicago is here, Indianapolis is here," etc.), the locations on the maps appear to be just points on the map 'surface', not three-dimensional entities with skylines, etc.

8   Mental-space theory actually goes well beyond these specific linguistic issues and encompasses not only other linguistic issues, but more general issues of cognition and mental representation. The reader is referred to Fauconnier (1994, 1997) for a detailed discussion of the theory.

9   In our everyday lives we make no distinction between the conceptual and the physical book. We operate as if there are simply real things around us.

10 Lillo-Martin & Klima (1990) make this argument for pronouns in ASL, but the argument is easily extended to include all signs that use space.

11 This example and the narrative it was taken from are more fully discussed in Liddell & Metzger (1998).

12 Winston (1991, 1992) and Metzger (1995) refer to such gestures intended to illustrate the actions of others as "constructed action."

13 In a classroom discussion several years ago, Byron Bridges suggested that in the case of a first-person surrogate, the signer himself was the surrogate. This observation seemed essentially correct, but it was not compatible with the idea of a surrogate as an invisible entity in space. How it is possible for the signer to 'be' the surrogate can be seen in the blend analysis which follows.

14 Fauconnier (1994) describes such activity as "backstage cognition."

15 Kegl (1985) proposes the existence of a grammatical element she calls a *role prominence marker*. The function of the proposed role prominence marker is to identify the grammatical subject of the sentence as the person (or personified animate or inanimate object) with whom empathy is established. It is an abstract grammatical treatment of the type of body tilt and gaze direction I have analyzed here in the Garfield blend. See Liddell & Metzger (1998) for a fuller discussion of the narrative from which this example was taken and of alternative proposals such as that in Kegl (1985).

16 An alternative analysis of this sign would describe it as a stative-descriptive classifier predicate (Liddell & Johnson 1987) which happens to look like the sign FENCE. Making this distinction goes well beyond the scope of this chapter and will not be attempted here. For ease of exposition, I will describe this as an instance of the sign FENCE.

17 Andre Thibeault first identified examples such as this as problematic for my previous mental-space analysis, which had no blending. Paul Dudis has also brought similar examples to my attention in his analysis of role-shifting phenomena. Paul Dudis produced the New York City driving example analyzed in the text.

18 This example may actually be more complex than the discussion in the text indicates. This is because of the nature of the 'hypothetical city streets' and the

'hypothetical car interior' mental spaces. Fauconnier (1997) has shown that analogical counterfactuals depend on blended mental spaces. This suggests the possibility that the 'hypothetical city streets' and the 'hypothetical car interior' spaces are themselves formed from the blending of two mental spaces. These spaces, in turn, would serve as input to the grounded blends illustrated in Figure 16.8. Exploring these blends would go well beyond the focus of this chapter.

19 Linguistic features do not fully describe how a word is pronounced by a given individual on a given occasion. For example, a phonetic description does not normally include things like tone of voice, intonation, speed of production, vocal characteristics unique to the speaker, and the overall pitch level. In this sense, the linguistic features selectively describe certain aspects of the speech signal but not others.

20 I am using the term *deictic* here in a very broad sense, to include even such activities as holding up a pen to bring attention to it.

REFERENCES

Ahlgren, I., Bergman, B. & Brennan, M. (eds.) 1994. *Perspectives on Sign Language Structure: Papers from the Fifth International Symposium on Sign Language Research*, vol. I. University of Durham: International Sign Linguistics Association.

Bahan, B. 1996. Non-manual realization of agreement in American Sign Language. Unpublished Ph.D. dissertation, Boston University.

Emmorey, K. & Reilly, J. (eds.) 1995. *Sign, Gesture, and Space*. Hillsdale, NJ: Erlbaum.

Fauconnier, G. 1994 [1985]. *Mental Spaces*. New York: Cambridge University Press. (Originally published Cambridge, MA: MIT Press.)

Fauconnier, G. 1997. *Mappings in Thought and Language*. Cambridge: Cambridge University Press.

Fauconnier, G. & Turner, M. 1994. Conceptual projection and middle spaces. University of California at San Diego Cognitive Science Technical Report 9401. [Compressed (Unix) Postscript version available from http://cogsci.ucsd.edu or http://www.informumd.edu/EdRes/Colleges/ARHU/Depts/English/engfac/Mturner/.]

Fauconnier, G. & Turner, M. 1996. Blending as a central process of grammar. In Goldberg (ed.), pp. 113–130.

Fischer, S. 1975. Influences on word order change in American Sign Language. In Li (ed.), pp. 1–25.

Fischer, S. & Siple, P. (eds.) 1990. *Theoretical Issues in Sign Language Research*, vol. I: *Linguistics*. Chicago: University of Chicago Press.

Goldberg, A. (ed.) 1996. *Conceptual Structure, Discourse and Language*. Stanford, CA: CSLI Publications.

Kegl, J. 1976. Pronominalization in ASL. Unpublished manuscript, Department of Lingusitics, Massachusetts Institute of Technology.

Kegl, J. 1985. Locative relations in American Sign Language word formation, syntax, and discourse. Unpublished Ph.D. dissertation, Massachusetts Institute of Technology.

Klima, E. S. & Bellugi, U. 1979. *The Signs of Language*. Cambridge, MA: Harvard University Press.

Lakoff, G. 1987. *Women, Fire, and Dangerous Things: What Categories Reveal about the Mind*. Chicago: University of Chicago Press.

Li, C. N. (ed.) 1975. *Word Order and Word Order Change*. Austin: University of Texas Press.

Liddell, S. K. 1994. Tokens and surrogates. In Ahlgren et al. (eds.), pp. 105–119.

Liddell, S. K. 1995. Real, surrogate, and token space: grammatical consequences in ASL. In Emmorey & Reilly (eds.), pp. 19–41.

Liddell, S. K. 1996. Spatial representations in discourse: comparing spoken and signed language. *Lingua* 98: 145–167.

Liddell, S. K. & Johnson, R. 1987. An analysis of spatial-locative predicates in American Sign Language. Paper presented at Fourth International Conference on Sign Language Research, Lapeenranta, Finland, July.

Liddell, S. K. & Johnson, R. E. 1989. American Sign Language: the phonological base. *Sign Language Studies* 64: 195–277.

Liddell, S. K. & Metzger, M. 1998. Gesture in sign language discourse. *Journal of Pragmatics* 30: 657–697.

Lillo-Martin, D. & Klima, E. S. 1990. Pointing out the differences: ASL pronouns in syntactic theory. In Fischer & Siple (eds.), pp. 191–210.

Lucas, C. (ed.) 1995. *Sociolinguistics in Deaf Communities*. Washington, DC: Gallaudet University Press.

Meier, R. 1990. Person deixis in American Sign Language. In Fischer & Siple (eds.), pp. 175–190.

Metzger, M. 1995. Constructed dialogue and constructed action in American Sign Language. In Lucas (ed.), pp. 255–271.

Neidle, C., Bahan, B., MacLaughlin, D., Lee, R. G. & Kegl, J. 1998. Realizations of syntactic agreement in American Sign Language: similarities between the clause and the noun phrase. *Studia Linguistica* 52: 191–226.

Plant-Moeller, J. (ed.) 1992. *Expanding Horizons: Proceedings of the Twelfth National Convention of the Registry of Interpreters for the Deaf*. Silver Spring, MD: RID Publications.

Poizner, H., Klima, E. S. & Bellugi, U. 1987. *What the Hands Reveal about the Brain*. Cambridge, MA: MIT Press.

Stokoe, W. C., Jr. 1960. *Sign Language Structure: An Outline of the Visual Communication Systems of the American Deaf*. Studies in Linguistics: Occasional Papers 8. Buffalo, NY: University of Buffalo. [Rev. ed., Silver Spring, MD: Linstok Press, 1978.]

van Hoek, K. 1988. Mental spaces and sign space. Unpublished manuscript, Salk Institute for Biological Studies, La Jolla, CA.

van Hoek, K. 1989. Locus splitting in American Sign Language. Unpublished manuscript, Salk Institute for Biological Studies, La Jolla, CA.

Winston, E. 1991. Spatial referencing and cohesion in an American Sign Language text. *Sign Language Studies* 73: 397–410.

Winston, E. 1992. Space and involvement in an American Sign Language lecture. In Plant-Moeller (ed.), pp. 93–105.

17 Gestural precursors to linguistic constructs: how input shapes the form of language

Jill P. Morford

Department of Linguistics, University of New Mexico

Judy A. Kegl

Center for Molecular and Behavioral Neuroscience, Rutgers University

1 Introduction

Studies of atypical first-language acquisition have demonstrated the importance of maturation on the outcome of the acquisition process. The age at which individuals are first exposed to a language impacts both language mastery and language-processing abilities in adulthood (Emmorey et al. 1995; Mayberry 1993; Mayberry & Eichen 1991; Newport 1988, 1990). This factor is widely understood to be related to the maturation of the neural substrate for language. Plasticity in neural organization decreases with age, inhibiting late development of sensitivity to linguistic structure. A second factor that has received less attention in the recent literature on language acquisition is the type of input to which the child is exposed. Even when exposure is sufficiently early to influence neural development, the nature of the input can influence the course of acquisition. In the case of spoken language acquisition, it has been suggested that the influence of the input is merely to make the child attend to marked structures in the primary language (e.g., Roeper & Williams 1987). Several cases of very limited input suggest that children will develop more structured systems than they are exposed to (Goldin-Meadow & Mylander 1984, 1990a; Singleton & Newport 1987). These studies might be construed to support the view that input plays little role in the course of acquisition relative to the factor of age of exposure; that is, input only guides a process that is primarily an expression of structure that is already in place, or innate.

Evidence from a newly emerged signed language that has arisen in the last two decades in Nicaragua has been used to argue that language can arise under conditions where no prior language (spoken or signed) was available as input to the acquisition process (Kegl & Iwata 1989; Kegl & McWhorter 1997; Kegl, Senghas & Coppola 1999). In pre-revolutionary

Nicaragua, no target signed language existed, and spoken languages were inaccessible to people who could not hear them. Within a decade of the Sandinista government's establishment of special education schools with dedicated classrooms for deaf children in 1980, Idioma de Señas de Nicaragua (Nicaraguan Sign Language) was rapidly becoming standardized in Managua.

Given the speed with which this language emerged, and the lack of a preexisting signed language as input, some researchers, in the spirit of Bickerton (1984), might be tempted to conclude that Idioma de Señas de Nicaragua constitutes a direct spellout of a bioprogram for language. However, we will demonstrate that, at least at the level of the lexicon, the Nicaraguan evidence argues instead that even in the absence of a target language, preexisting non-linguistic input plays a role in determining certain structural characteristics of the product of first-language acquisition. We view the 'bioprogram' for language as a set of expectations, choices, and tendencies, rather than as a rigid blueprint for language. As a result, characteristics of the non-language input available in the language acquirer's environment can potentially influence the ultimate form of the grammar settled upon. It is this possibility that we will explore in this chapter. Looking back from the fully articulated grammar of Idioma de Señas de Nicaragua we will try to identify in Nicaraguan homesigners those gestural precursors of the eventual grammatical constructs that emerged and trace the process of their grammaticization from their gestural roots.

Researchers come to a task with a particular theoretical perspective that may bias them in one way or another as they collect and analyze data. We are no exception. One of us is biased toward a strongly nativist point of view that sees language as the proprietary domain of the human brain. The other favors an approach that would set language in a continuum with gestural communication.[1] We both see maturation as playing a crucial role in language acquisition. What we have tried to do in this chapter is to exploit our common interest in the question of how language comes to be and where it comes from, balanced by our differing biases, to take a look at some extremely interesting and rarely encountered data collected in 1994 from eleven homesigners on the Atlantic coast of Nicaragua who had been in limited contact for a maximum of two years without the benefit of any exposure to a signed language or any preexisting knowledge of a spoken language.[2]

2   Maturational constraints on language acquisition: the role of age

Lenneberg's (1967) 'critical period hypothesis' proposed, without direct evidence, an optimal period in childhood for language acquisition extending roughly from infancy to puberty. Evidence for this hypothesis has been accumulating ever since, suggesting that age of exposure to language stimulation is a deciding factor in an individual's eventual linguistic knowledge and performance. Since deaf children of hearing parents can vary in terms of the age at which they come into contact with signed language input, they provide a natural experiment with respect to the effects on language acquisition of age of exposure to a first language.

Newport (1988, 1990), looking at the production and comprehension of complex morphology in ASL, confirmed Lenneberg's critical-period hypothesis by showing long-lasting effects of age of exposure on the acquisition of ASL as a first language. However, rather than showing an abrupt cutoff of language acquisition capacities at puberty, she showed a small but gradual decline in language-learning abilities starting at ages 4–6, but a more substantial decline when language exposure began at 12 or older. Mayberry (1993) presents an analysis of first-language acquisition from 0–3 (native), 5–8 (childhood), and 9–13 (late) that showed a similar gradual decline in sentence-processing abilities with increasingly later exposure to ASL as a first language. In addition, she showed the benefits of early first-language acquisition by showing that late-deafened "subjects who acquired ASL as a second language after childhood outperformed those who acquired it as a first language at exactly the same age" (p. 1258). These results combined suggest that there is a gradual loss of sensitivity to the structural patterns of language across childhood, but that the neural structure resulting from exposure to any language can be recruited, at least in part, in the acquisition and processing of another language, even across modalities.

3   Structural constraints on language acquisition: the role of input

A factor that is not explicitly mentioned in Lenneberg's hypothesis is whether the quality of the input to which one is exposed will also affect the outcome of acquisition. This question is difficult to conceive of if one thinks only of spoken language acquisition. There is limited variability in the quality of input to which hearing children are exposed, unless their parents choose not to speak to them in their native languages. By contrast, the type of input deaf children are exposed to varies enormously. They can potentially be exposed to four types of input in the visual modality: (1) gesture, (2) homesign, (3) non-native signing, or (4) native signing. In most cases, deaf children are born to hearing parents and are exposed only to their parents' gestures in the earliest stages of development. When several deaf children are born to hearing parents, or when there is a community of hearing individuals with a high incidence of deafness, we have the potential situation for a child to be exposed to a homesign system from birth. Homesign refers to the gesture communication systems of deaf children who have been exposed only to gesture (see section 3.1). Although it has not yet been documented, the homesign of one child could serve as the language model for another deaf child, and this situation should be distinguished from that of deaf children exposed only to gesture. A very small percentage (under 10 percent in the USA) of deaf children are born to parents who are deaf (Rawlings & Jensema 1977). If their deaf parents have only a limited knowledge of a signed language, these children will have slightly more regular input than those exposed only to gesture or homesign, but they will not be exposed to the range of structures that native signers perceive. Finally, the few children born to native-signing deaf parents receive what in the case of hearing individuals is called 'typical' input – a full model of a language – and unsurprisingly, they attain language milestones at approximately the same ages as hearing children acquiring spoken languages (Chamberlain, Morford & Mayberry 2000; Newport & Meier 1985).

Gee & Goodhart (1988)[3] have argued that the more variable the input, the more clearly we should see the expression of innate structure. They have, more specifically, predicted that owing to the high variability in the input that deaf children are exposed to, we should predict a high degree of similarity in the outcome of the acquisition process in this population. This perspective is similar to the view in spoken language acquisition that the role of the input is to make children attend to marked or non-canonical structures in the primary language. In this section, we will argue, from cases in which the input varies, that this is not the case. Like age of acquisition, the quality of input that children are exposed to directly affects the acquisition process. We find that children exposed only to gesture develop a system with some of the characteristics of language, but only children who are exposed to a community of homesigners or to non-native signing of a conventional signed language develop the full range of linguistic structures identified in signed languages.[4]

3.1   Gesture as input

Goldin-Meadow & Feldman (1975) have shown that deaf children raised in hearing families, with no exposure to an established signed language such as ASL, spontaneously develop gesture systems called homesign that exhibit some of the features of natural language, such as consistency in the lexicon, repeated use of a limited number of morphemes across the system, and ordering and deletion preferences related to the constituent structure.[5] Singleton, Morford & Goldin-Meadow (1993) compare ASL signers, homesigners, and hearing individuals asked to gesture without speaking and show that in homesign systems and ASL, standards of well-formedness can be identified, as they cannot for gestures created on the spur of the moment. However, without exposure to a larger Deaf community, home-signers do not seem to develop the full range of linguistic structures that are found in creoles and well-established languages, such as obligatory morphological marking or syntactic movement.

The structural properties that Goldin-Meadow and her colleagues have identified in homesign are not present in the gestures they have observed to be used by those homesigners' parents (Goldin-Meadow & Mylander 1984, 1990b). However, the homesigners participating in the Goldin-Meadow et al. studies were being raised with an oralist philosophy of education, which generally entails parents being told not to sign to their children. Adherence to this mandate generally results in a withholding not just of signs, but of gestures to some extent as well. This would offer one explanation for the fact that the parents of the homesigners were observed to exhibit a less structured gesture system.

Another explanation for why there is little structure found in the gesture of the parents of homesigners is that these individuals speak while gestur-ing (gesticulate). As McNeill (1992) and others have shown, when gesture and speech are produced simultaneously, they cohere into one coordinated speech act. By analyzing the parents' gesture out of the context of its co-occurring speech, we see only a part of the total communicative act of the parents. Interestingly, when asked to gesture without speaking, hearing individuals' gestures do begin to exhibit some of the structures found in homesign systems (Goldin-Meadow, McNeill & Singleton 1996; Singleton, Goldin-Meadow & McNeill 1995).

On the Atlantic coast of Nicaragua, parents were not told to withhold sign or gesture from their deaf children. In our initial testing of the family, we don't just record free conversation, but actually elicit a gestural narrative from the family members via presentation of a non-verbal cartoon. The family members communicate gesturally in the absence of speech. Preliminary analyses of these narratives indicate that they exhibit the kind of systematic, more structurally complex gesture that Singleton et al. (1995; Goldin-Meadow, McNeill & Singleton 1996) observed when hearing English-speakers were given the task of gesturally describing video vig-nettes without speaking. If these analyses are correct, it even appears that the gesture (as opposed to gesticulation) is richer in the parent and other hearing family members than in the homesigner. This makes sense when we consider that preexisting language competence could be driving the gesture of the hearing family members.[6] Figure 17.1 presents the number and types

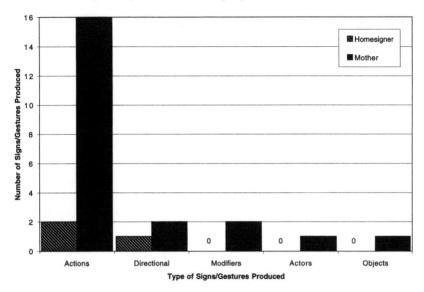

Figure 17.1. Gesture types produced by a homesigner and her mother.

of signs produced at first contact by an eight-year-old homesigner from Corn Island (located fifty miles off the Atlantic coast of Nicaragua) and her mother. In contrast to her daughter, the mother begins her narrative by establishing and describing the main character and goes on to use a great many more signs and uses of space to recount the story. Her daughter only signs FLY (whole body acts out sign) GO-UP (flat hand indicates movement upward) UP (points upward).

Yet when we observe the everyday interaction between parent and child, the parents' communication fails to recruit the language-driven structurally rich gestures we can elicit via the narrative task. Instead we see that, as observed in the Goldin-Meadow et al. homesign studies, the more common form of communication from parent to child is gesticulation with speech, and single gestures. Thus we might more accurately note that the homesigners' gesture is more structured than the gestural input shared with them by their parents – even though the parents are capable of more.

However, the fact that the children's systems end up more structured than the input they get from their parents does not mean that the gestures they are exposed to are irrelevant. To the contrary, cross-cultural differences have been noted in homesign systems, since children integrate conventional gestures into their homesign systems.[7] For example, three homesigners in the USA have been observed to use the gesture meaning "Wait a minute" (extended index finger pointing up, palm out) in references to the future. Note that these children adopt a conventional gesture but change its function. Instead of using the gesture to request that another person wait for them, they combine this gesture with other gestures to express what they are going to do (e.g., one child gestured WAIT (future) TOYBAG, and then walked over to the toybag to retrieve a new toy to play with; Morford & Goldin-Meadow 1997).

Whether or not the elaborateness of the homesign system a child develops can be predictive of successful subsequent language acquisition has yet to be determined, but there is at least evidence that ASL signs for concepts represented in homesign are more easily acquired than ASL signs for concepts that are not represented in homesign (Morford, Singleton & Goldin-Meadow 1995). In other words, it appears that homesign facilitates, rather than interferes with, the subsequent acquisition of a signed language. Nevertheless, these individuals are presumably from the same population as those who participated in Newport's and Mayberry's studies of delayed acquisition of ASL (see section 2). As Mayberry (1993) has demonstrated, these individuals' processing of ASL sentences is significantly poorer than that of second-language learners. Thus, we contend that homesign does not constitute a full primary language.

3.2   Homesign as input

There are very limited data available on how language develops in individuals who are exposed to homesign as input, because the contexts in which it would occur are so rare. Danziger & Keating (1996) described the social context of a Mayan family with multiple deaf children living in a community that is otherwise completely hearing and in which there is no signed language. They concluded that communicative norms in the degree of expressivity acceptable among hearing members of the community influence the use of facial expression and space in homesign. However, there are no developmental linguistic data from this case study, or data relevant to the influence of the older homesigners upon the younger homesigners in this context. The only other reported situation in which deaf children were exposed to homesign as their primary input concerns the case described in the introduction on the Pacific coast of Nicaragua (Kegl & Iwata 1989; Kegl, Senghas & Coppola 1999; Senghas 1995b). When schools for the deaf were first opened in Managua in 1980, homesigners of all ages were brought together, inadvertently forming a deaf community. Although the schools did not promote signing, the youngest members of this community were exposed during their critical period for language acquisition to the homesign of the older members of this community. We discuss the specific relationship between gesture, homesign, and structures in Idioma de Señas de Nicaragua in more detail below. For now, we note merely that, unlike children exposed only to gesture, when children are exposed to a community of homesigners, we find language emergence.

3.3   Non-native ASL as input

Recall from our discussion of the role of age of acquisition (section 2) that deaf children who are not exposed to ASL prior to the age of five do not fully master the grammatical structure. Newport (1982) refers to this population as "first generation deaf," and has concluded that older members of this group acquire predominantly the frozen lexicon of ASL. Despite the fact that these signs are frozen for "first generation deaf," the lexical items themselves encode the complex morphology of ASL.

3.3.1   Second-generation signers. Occasionally, "first generation deaf" have offspring who are deaf, and with whom they communicate, from birth, using their non-native form of ASL. Interestingly, these children, "second generation deaf," surpass their models. In contrast to their parents, who have command over only the frozen lexicon of ASL, the offspring produce forms using productive word-internal morphology, indicating that they have performed a morphological analysis on the frozen input from their parents. Noting that pidgins tend to have isolating morphology while creoles universally include morphology internal to the word, Newport (1982: 480–84) argues that the elaboration in morphology seen in second-generation signers can be viewed as a "recreolization" of the pidgin input of their first-generation deaf parents. She uses the term "recreolization"[8] because the recurrent influx of deaf children born to hearing parents recreates the conditions leading to creolization of pidgin input by their offspring.[9]

Unfortunately, this perspective (as stated) loses sight of the fact that children actually seem to learn language from slightly older peers rather than from parents (Baron 1977), and most of these second-generation deaf children have additional sources of input from the Deaf community at large, including native-signing peers in schools for the deaf. Still, since 90 percent of the deaf population are deaf children of hearing parents, the source of input as a whole is heterogeneous, even though it also may include native signers.

3.3.2   Simon: a more controlled case of non-native input. Singleton & Newport (1987) and Singleton (1989) avoided criticisms such as those

above by focusing upon a case study of Simon, a deaf child whose parents had learned ASL in late adolescence and were, for a time, his sole language input. Until school age, Simon did not have significant contact with other members of the Deaf community. They argued that even after his entry into school Simon was the best signer in his class, in which the primary mode of communication was a form of manually coded English and not ASL. Simon's parents had a vocabulary of frozen signs and used many of the grammatical constructions in ASL unsystematically. By the age of seven, Simon's ASL had already surpassed the input he was receiving from his parents, particularly with respect to verbs of motion and location. Simon did not invent new forms, as frequently occurs in homesign systems. He took morphemes that were used sporadically in his parents' signing, and used them more consistently and systematically in his own signing.

Simon's situation offers a somewhat more controlled case of non-native signing input to a first-language learner, but conditions being as they are in the United States, this case study stands alone, and long-term outcomes for this individual are not yet known.

3.3.3   Non-native input is still language input. Simon's case focuses upon the recreolization of non-native ASL input by a single signer. The recreolization studies focus upon individual cases of recreolization within a broader population of deaf signers, 10 percent of whom are native signers. These cases are similar to the emergence of spoken-language creoles, in that input to the emergence process contains fragments of full-fledged natural languages. Like Simon's case, and the other cases of recreolization, spoken-language creolization constitutes a case of 'language from language', albeit fragmentary. In fact, spoken-language creolization involves language from multiple languages, and could even be considered as hyper-rich input (see Kegl & McWhorter 1997). The fact that Simon and other recreolizers of ASL continually reconverge on the structure of an established language is an additional indication that the input contains structural elements that bias the recreolization process toward the original system from which the frozen forms were extracted. Thus, while innate language expectations could well have been instrumental in guiding the language-acquisition process, we cannot eliminate the contribution of language fragments in the input to the eventual form of the language acquired in these cases. The Nicaraguan case we discuss here is unique in that preexisting language input to the language emergence process *is* eliminated. In contrast to Simon, whose language input was ASL, albeit frozen and fragmented, the input to the first generation of first-language acquirers in Nicaragua was nothing more than homesign systems in contact.

4   How input shaped Idioma de Señas de Nicaragua

4.1   Background on language emergence in Nicaragua

In Nicaragua prior to the 1980s, deaf people did not form a community. For the most part, they lived as linguistic isolates in an otherwise nurturing family environment. Subsequently, as a consequence of a popular revolution, major educational reforms were instituted that included access to public education with a goal of literacy and the minimum of a fourth-grade education for everyone, including deaf people. Schools for special education in the major cities along the Pacific coast of Nicaragua suddenly became centers where large numbers of deaf students came together daily. Prior to this contact, the only means of communication these individuals possessed were idiosyncratic gestures (or homesigns) shared only among themselves and their immediate family members.

In the context of these schools, whose educational program was speech training in Spanish supported by fingerspelling, the homesigners who first came together gradually developed a gestural communication system among themselves – a contact language between their individual idiosyncratic gesture systems. In concert, the highly variable and patchy gesture systems of each individual contributed toward providing a larger communicative milieu that was richer in content and structure than the communication system of any one of its members or any one of the homesign systems these individuals experienced at home. We will refer to this as a *homesign contact form.*

We believe that this intermediate form between homesign and Idioma de Señas de Nicaragua may have fulfilled an important role in the emergence of language. Evidence that the homesign contact form was richer (or at least a better input to language acquisition) than homesign itself is drawn from the differential outcome in the language development of very young children exposed to each. Idiosyncratic gestures used for communication between a deaf person and hearing family members are insufficient to support language acquisition. Homesigners left in the home remain homesigners. Yet young children placed in the context of homesigners in contact with one another do develop language spontaneously. Homesigners under the age of seven (Senghas 1995b) who participated in the first cohort of homesigners in contact in Nicaragua ended up acquiring a signed language – a signed language that did not exist prior to their acquisition of it (Kegl & Iwata 1989; Kegl & McWhorter 1997). In other words, they gave birth to a signed language.

Much of the initial research conducted in Nicaragua has focused upon distinguishing the newly emerged signed language, Idioma de Señas de Nicaragua, from the homesign contact (or more pidgin-like) form typical of students who entered the schools at later ages – ages that placed them beyond the critical period for native acquisition of their first language (Kegl & Iwata 1989; Senghas 1995b). These contact forms ranged between little expansion from their initial homesign systems to contact forms that borrow greatly from the communication systems of their interlocutors.[10] In the remainder of this chapter we will try to fill in an earlier stage in the description of the emergence of Idioma de Señas de Nicaragua by characterizing homesign systems in Nicaragua and the 'source forms' from which many constructions in the homesign contact form and in Idioma de Señas de Nicaragua may have arisen. The gestures that fed the homesigns in contact that served as the input to the first cohort of young deaf acquirers in schools serving deaf children in Nicaragua did not contain within them vestiges of a preexisting signed language. This situation allows us to address the issue of whether non-language input can shape the final outcome of the first-language acquisition process. In this section, we explore how gestural input can function as precursor to natural language grammar.

4.2   Nicaraguan homesign data

While schools for deaf children were being established on the Pacific coast of Nicaragua, much of the Atlantic coast, separated from the Pacific coast by a mountain range, impenetrable rainforest, and a cultural and language barrier, as well as political differences that culminated in a counterrevolution, received less of the benefits of educational reform. What developments were begun in Bluefields – the major city in the southern region of Nicaragua's Atlantic coast – were eradicated on October 7, 1988, when Hurricane Joan flattened the city. Since that point, efforts have been placed on rebuilding the infrastructure. Thus, fifteen years after Idioma de Señas de Nicaragua had begun to spread on the Pacific coast, deaf people on the Atlantic coast continued to rely upon homesigns to communicate. In December 1994, two colleagues traveled to Bluefields and videotaped the signing of eleven deaf students ranging in age from seven to eighteen who had been in extremely limited contact for a maximum of two years. These students all attended a school for war victims that had no curriculum specifically designed for the deaf students and did not attempt to use or teach signing. Classes were held for two hours a day. In an interview with the school director, who was himself a war victim who was physically disabled, he explained that there was little sustained interaction between himself and the deaf students or among the deaf students, since they attended for such a

Table 17.1. *Gender, age, and onset and cause of deafness*

Subject	Gender	Age (yr)	Onset	Cause
1	F	7	Birth	Anoxia at birth
2	F	12	Birth	Rubella
3	M	12	Birth	Rubella
4	F	12	Birth	Meningitis
5	M	13	Birth	Rubella
6	F	13	Birth	Unknown
7	F	13	Birth	Unknown
8	F	13	Birth	Unknown
9	F	13	9 months	High Fever
10	M	15	Birth	Unknown
11	M	18	Birth	Unknown

short time each day and did not socialize outside of class. By their own reports, the deaf students remained homesigners at that point despite their contact with each other.[11] This view is supported by the variability of the elicited gestures they produced, with the exception of the conventional Nicaraguan gestures (see section 4.2.1). Although we cannot rule out the possibility that some individuals in this sample modified some of their gestures after coming into contact with other deaf students, the social circumstances of the contact as well as the variability of the data suggest that the gestures being used in 1994 by these individuals are more representative of homesign than of the type of homesign contact form that developed between 1980 and 1994 in Managua among deaf students who socialized regularly with each other but who were too old to learn Idioma de Señas de Nicaragua. Table 17.1 reports statistics on age, gender, and onset and cause of deafness for the population.

Thirty-three homesigns were elicited from the subjects by showing them black-and-white line drawings of common objects (e.g., animals, fruit, household objects) and action scenes (e.g., swimming, hugging, washing; see Appendix 17.1 for a complete list of pictures). The method consisted of showing a picture to a subject and shrugging, to which subjects replied by describing the picture. Owing to the conditions in which the data were collected (intermittent electricity, use of a handheld camcorder, unfamiliarity of subjects with the equipment, etc.), several homesigns are unclear for each subject. Results are reported only for homesigns which could be clearly viewed on the videotape. The homesigns were transcribed by one of the authors (JM), who had no prior knowledge of Nicaraguan gesture but who was familiar with a variety of homesigners from different countries and cultures. They were then retranscribed (three years later) by one of the subjects in this study, who is now a research assistant to the other author (JK). For the purposes of this analysis, we describe characteristics of individual signs. In future work we will report analyses of larger constituent structures.

Homesign responses were classified into five categories of representation. (1) Handling gestures include homesigns that show how an object is manipulated with the hands, such as how a mop is used or how a fruit is cut. (2) Shape gestures include homesigns that use the hands to represent the shape of the object, such as pressing the palms together to represent a book. (3) Outline gestures include homesigns that trace the shape of an object, such as using the thumb and index finger to outline the form of a hammock. (4) Whole-body gestures include representations that involve acting out an action with the entire body, such as moving the arms and head the way a swimmer does, or moving the hands and feet to represent an animal crawling. (5) Two-sign responses were coded when the homesigner responded with signs from two of the categories above. These combinations are described below.

Although the homesign responses we examined were not identical, their similarities suggest that the form of the homesigns is constrained by features of the gestures of hearing Nicaraguans, as well as by what appear to be conceptual constraints governing how cognitive representations of action and form are best mapped onto the structure of the human hand. Contributing to these constraints is the fact that homesigns must be transparent in order to be understood by hearing family members. We summarize these organizing tendencies here (see Table 17.2 for proportions of responses to picture types).

4.2.1   Conventional gestures. In our data set, several gestures were noteworthy because they did not fit the pattern of responses to related objects. We suggest that these homesigns, EAT/FOOD, DRINK/WATER, BED/SLEEP, are derived from conventional gestures used by hearing Nicaraguans. The homesign for EAT/FOOD, for example, involves holding the hand, palm in, at the mouth, and alternately bending and extending the four fingers from the base knuckle so that the tips of the fingers wave up and down in front of the mouth. This was the only gesture in our data set that did not fit into one of the four gesture categories listed above. Further, it is not an obvious gesture for eating, given an observed tendency among homesigners to represent the handling of objects (see below). However, this gesture is used pervasively throughout Nicaragua.

Table 17.2. *Type of gesture response to each picture category (percentages)*

Picture category	Handling gestures	Shape gestures	Outline gestures	Whole-body gestures	Two-sign responses
Fruit	33	0	2	32	33
Utensils	78	19	3	0	0
Household items	30	43	0	25	2
Animals	0	50	5	41	5
Human action	40	17	0	43	0
Non-human action	0	100	0	0	0

Similarly, the homesign for DRINK/WATER is a fist with thumb extended moving with thumb tip oriented toward the mouth. Again, the typical handling gesture is not used by these homesigners, and again this gesture is universally used and understood by hearing Nicaraguans. The gesture for BED/SLEEP (two flat hands in a praying configuration, supporting the side of the signer's tilted head) is different from gestures for other household items, which typically used the hand to represent the shape of the object. Instead, the homesigners consistently produced a body gesture in response to this picture.

As evidence that the signs discussed above were indeed conventional gestures, consider data collected by Morford in Montreal from homesigners from other countries. A homesigner from Southeast Asia, for example, used an F-handshape (thumb and index finger touching with other fingers extended) as if holding a thin-handled teacup for DRINK. A homesigner from the West Indies held a slightly cupped palm at the mouth (as if drinking from a flattened bowl or from the hand) to refer to drinking water, and a curved handshape as if holding a glass to refer to drinking juice. Such examples illustrate the variability possible for these gestures and support our contention that the consistency we found with gestures like DRINK and EAT in Bluefields cannot be attributed to mere accident.

One striking example that had perplexed investigators of Idioma de Señas de Nicaragua for years was an L-handshape, made to the side of the body, with fingertips pointing to the floor, that was also used by several Bluefields homesigners to represent small animals. The same sign appeared nine years earlier in a fifteen-year-old homesigner in Managua her first day in contact with the Deaf community and is frequent in both the homesign contact form and the full signed language. This is one sign that seemed rather marked and also fairly clearly associated with objects, as opposed to actions, but its origin was unclear, since it was not very iconic. When we saw this 'small animal' sign again in the repertoires of homesigners on the Atlantic coast, our curiosity was again piqued. We tested hearing non-signers in Bluefields and Puerto Cabezas/Bilwi (on the northern Atlantic coast) who had no familiarity with Deaf people, and discovered that they too both used and recognized this gesture to mean 'small animal'. It was a common conventional gesture in Nicaraguan culture that we simply had not been aware of. Interestingly, this gesture was not prevalent on Corn Island, which lies fifty miles off the Atlantic coast, and homesigners living there instead used a flat hand, palm downward, to indicate small animals.

These conventional gestures were also prevalent in the contact form used between homesigners, and have been carried over into the signed language. However, there is a movement to reject or replace signs that are derived from and remain homophenous (look-alikes) with conventional gestures by alternative signs – newly created signs or even ones borrowed from other languages. For example, there is pressure to replace the conventional gesture-based signs for EAT and CLEAN with their ASL counterparts. We feel this shows increased sensitivity to the distinction between conventional gesture versus signed language on the part of the Pacific coast signers and constitutes an attempt to more clearly delineate the distinction between the two.

4.2.2   Human action versus non-human action. Human action exhibits a hand-to-hand mapping priority. In other words, the hands are used to represent the hands rather than the hands being used to represent the whole body in motion or an object that a human is interacting with. Actions involving the upper body such as HUG and SWIM are produced using the hands in an analog fashion. Actions involving the lower body like CLIMB-STEPS or RIDE-A-BIKE are produced either by full-body gestures or with the hands representing the feet. Instruments and use of instruments (such as IRON, SPOON, and MOP) are typically represented by showing how the object is manipulated.[12] All of these gestures depict an action, although they were produced in response to depictions of either actions or objects. This helps to elucidate the finding reported in Senghas, Kegl, Senghas & Coppola (1994), Kegl, Senghas & Coppola (1999), and Senghas (1995a) that in the communication variety used by homesigners in contact, the hands are used for both objects and the handling of objects. In the full form of the language, by contrast, these two uses diverge in production and are represented by distinct morphological forms (handling classifiers and object classifiers), but handling classifiers still maintain a flexible interpretation (as referring to either the handling of an instrument or the instrument itself) in comprehension tests even for signers of Idioma de Señas de

Nicaragua, probably because of the large percentage of late learners in the population (Senghas 1995b).

In contrast to human action, inanimate or non-human themes (the element that moves or is located in an event, as in ANIMAL-RUN or BOAT-SINK) are typically represented by the hand equaling the whole object, taking on the function of semantic or object classifiers. In considering gestural precursors to language, it is worth noting that the divergence between these two classes of actions (human and non-human) almost invariably becomes grammaticized cross-linguistically by a distinction between an unergative versus unaccusative construction. Unergative constructions involve intransitive verbs (typically activity verbs with human subjects) that select for a subject at an abstract underlying level of syntactic representation, while unaccusative constructions involve intransitive verbs (typically inchoative verbs, verbs of appearance, intransitive change-of-state verbs, etc.) that lack a subject, but do select for a direct object at an abstract underlying level of syntactic representation. For example, in English, *John ate* is an unergative construction, while *The bottle broke* ([someone] broke the bottle) is an unaccusative construction. In Idioma de Señas de Nicaragua, this distinction can also be identified by the use of object classifiers for unaccusative forms and handling classifiers or full-body signs for unergatives.

4.2.3   Precursors of compounds. In homesign, most fruits were either consistently signed as some variant of eating, or by a gesture indicating how the fruit is prepared for eating (FRUIT-PREP; e.g., how it is cut, squeezed, or held for eating), or by a sequence of the two (e.g., FRUIT-PREP EAT, as in RUB-ON-SHIRT EAT = 'apple'; SLICE-OFF-TOP-WITH-MACHETE EAT = 'pineapple'; or SLICE-VERTICALLY EAT = 'pear/avocado').[13] While FRUIT-PREP appears to involve a complex series of components, these strings of glosses joined by dashes actually describe a single unitary gesture. Notice that in all two-sign sequences the manner consistently precedes the action. Similarly, animals are represented by their path of movement (e.g., GO-STRAIGHT-PATH) or by some physical characteristic (e.g., HORNS, TEETH, CLAWS, LONG-EARS) or, as with the fruits above, as a sequence of the two, again with the action second (e.g., PHYSICAL-CHARACTERISTIC GO). In the homesign contact form we see the variability give way to a consistent use of sequences that lexicalize members of basic-level categories as well as a broader range of referents. These verb sequences begin to show the formational properties of compounds. In the fully fledged signed language we see compounds as well as signs depicting basic-level, superordinate, and subordinate categories.

Figure 17.2 presents the standard Idioma de Señas de Nicaragua sign for

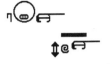

Standard ISN Sign for APPLE

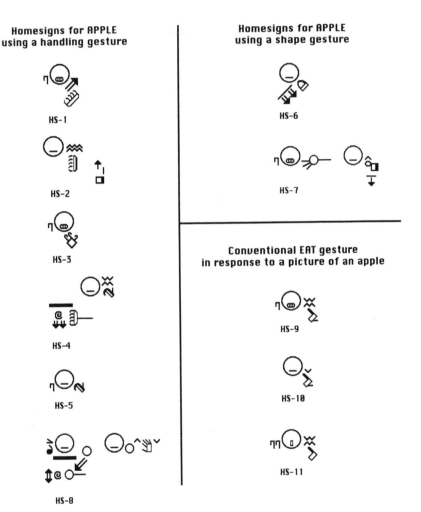

Figure 17.2. Homesign responses to a picture of an apple. See Appendix 17.2 for an explanation of the notation system.

APPLE as well as the variant homesigns produced by each of the eleven homesigners studied in this chapter. The examples in the figure are notated using SignWriter®, a computer program for writing signed languages developed by the Center for Sutton Movement Writing, Inc. (Gleaves 1995). See Appendix 17.2 for an explanation of the symbols. Notice that homesigners 1–5 and 8 use various handling gestures, the most typical response type for object manipulation. Homesigners 6 and 7 use gestures that incorporate the shape of the apple into an eating gesture. The three oldest homesigners, 9–11, use the conventional Nicaraguan gesture for EAT. Although the manual handshape and movement for the three older signers is invariant, we do note variation in the number of hand-internal movements (bent-B hand, palm toward mouth, with fingers bending once or repeatedly), in whether the palm is contacted (in the case where the fingers bend once, they completely contact the signer's palm), and in the facial gestures that accompany the signs (facial expressions vary from person to person between a neutral face and two variants of biting: bared teeth and pursed lips; symbols to the left of the face (circle) indicate the number of biting movements articulated by the mouth). Three homesigners (4, 7, and 8) have two-part signs that first indicate shape (no. 7) or preparation (nos. 4, 8) followed by putting in mouth or holding at mouth (eating). While manner consistently precedes action in the homesigns, notice that the standardized sign for APPLE in Idioma de Señas de Nicaragua reverses this order, sacrificing chronological order of events for phonological constraints applying to lexical compounds that favor fluidity of movement moving from head level to chest level.

4.2.4   *Unitary action gestures.* When shown a picture of a person engaging in an activity (e.g., washing a table, diving, etc.), the homesigners typically produced a single gesture to describe the event, depicting the action from a first-person perspective. In contrast, previous research on non-isolated signers suggests that homesign contact signers most often produce one argument with a verb, whereas signers of Idioma de Señas de Nicaragua typically produce multiple arguments with a single verb (Kegl, Senghas & Coppola 1999; Senghas 1995b). Thus, one process that seems to be at work in the emergence of language is the way a proposition is analyzed into constituent parts. Although the homesigners surely understood the roles of the participants in these scenes, their symbol systems are more context-dependent; it is assumed that who did what to whom is apparent to the interlocutor. Interestingly, the portion of the proposition that they chose to encode in their gestures was the action, suggesting that non-linguistic input is more likely to influence the form of open-class items (or lexical categories – specifically verbs) in an emerging language as opposed to the closed-class items.

4.2.5   Perspective. One direct result of the hand-to-hand mapping priority for human actions is that homesigners have a tendency to express human action from a first-person perspective. This is one feature of homesign systems that, combined with the relatively rare expression of agents, can lead to considerable confusion about who is performing the action. In the homesign contact form, this confusion is abated somewhat by the unambiguous expression of a single argument with the verb. However, the argument expressed in a transitive is usually the object rather than the subject, which is still related to the fact that in general the signer takes on the agent's role, thereby marking the agent with the signer's body. An additional aid to this distinction is added by use of body movement to suggest a change in perspective. Signers of the contact form will recruit their interlocutors to stand in for participants in a narrated event, or shift their body positions by several steps to mark a change in perspective. In the signed language, this shift of perspective becomes considerably reduced to a slight change in shoulder or head orientation. Roleshift splits into roleplay (actually taking on the role) and role prominence (expressing the action in third person but viewing it from that person's perspective). Role prominence in the signed language comes to mark subjects. The fact that several signed languages mark perspective change in precisely this way suggests that the path we have seen from homesign to pidgin to signed language is not uncommon to visuo-spatial languages.

4.3   Linking precursors to their grammatical counterparts

Table 17.3 summarizes our findings. It is important to realize that while certain aspects of homesign may well prefigure grammatical constructs that will emerge later, we cannot determine from a lexical analysis alone at what point precisely in the transition they should be considered grammatical forms. For example, the representation of events in homesign may involve movements and handshapes similar to verb forms we eventually find in the signed language, but they may not function fully as verbs in the homesign system.[14] Similarly, the pointing used by homesigners to identify referents may not be grammatically equivalent to pointing in the signed language, even though pronominals take this same form. While a gesture may move from one position to another, it is not necessarily marking any form of grammatical agreement. However, physical characteristics of these gestures may be perceived by a first-language acquirer as evidence for one versus

Table 17.3. *Gestural precursors to linguistic constructs*

Homesign	Homesign in contact	Signed language
Conventional gestures with some functional shift; pointing used to indicate most nouns	Lexicalization	Addition of bound morphology; pointing used as determiners and adverbials
Hand-to-hand mapping priority	Handling gestures (broad interpretation)	Handling classifiers Object classifiers
Action, descriptor, or both descriptor + action; action = superordinate; descriptor = subordinate	Two-sign sequences, less restricted in terms of category type; terms lexicalized	Compounds
Single gesture depicting actions	Action + one argument	Verb + multiple arguments
Act out event from 1st-person perspective	Torso/role shift	Perspective; grammatical relations

another kind of grammatical option available in the language he or she is learning and as such this input could shape the eventual grammar acquired.

4.3.1   Homesign. We begin with isolated homesign, which draws from the conventional gestures used by hearing Nicaraguans and thereby maintains intelligibility with this group. Lexical items are also influenced by a tendency to map human action onto the body directly, such that the hands represent the hands performing actions or manipulating objects. Non-human action, by contrast, is represented in such a way that the whole hand represents the agent or theme. To identify within-category differences, homesigners will string two gestures together, such that an attribute of the specific referent precedes a gesture that is common to its category. Homesigners tend to use the full body to depict events from a first-person point of view. Despite the overlap with Nicaraguan gestures, homesigners do extend certain of their signs to a wider range of functions. Yet, short of multiple homesigners in a single family, homesign left in the home fails to expand into anything more.

4.3.2   Homesign in contact. As soon as homesigners have regular contact in a context that provides (1) ample opportunities for shared communication, (2) the presence of partners willing to communicate in the visuospatial modality alone, (3) new communication demands associated with preferred accommodation to visually oriented deaf interlocutors, and (4) a multiplicity of means of expression among these deaf interlocutors, these factors all lead to a certain level of shared conventions and an expanded and more regular vocabulary (Kegl, Senghas & Coppola 1999).

Conventional gestures lexicalize into form–meaning pairs that are used consistently across signers. The handling of objects, which before was typically associated with taking on the agent role, gets extended semantically to indicate both the handling of objects and the objects themselves (independent of whether an agent is involved). In other words, a semantic distinction arises before a grammatical device is available to encode the distinction. This constitutes a function shift/expansion for handling gestures. Sequences of signs characterizing a single referent or event become more frequent and begin to be used for a wider range of semantic uses. Full-body acting out of events becomes more restrained, and typically actions that would involve the legs are realized via the arms and hands. Single gestures depicting actions begin to co-occur with other signs. Furthermore, taking on the first-person role becomes more formalized and is extended to the patient in addition to the agent role.

4.3.3   Signed language. In the full-fledged form of Idioma de Señas de Nicaragua, sporadic precursors to linguistic constructions become fully grammaticized (Kegl, Senghas & Coppola 1999). For example, gestures become fully lexicalized and accept agreement and aspect. Handling classifiers become distinct from object classifiers with respect to the type of constructions they appear in. Some sequences of homesigns become formal, formationally consistent compounds, while others surface as a lexical sign plus bound morpheme. Formational constraints on signs themselves and signs in sequence appear. For example, a language-specific phoneme inventory of handshapes, movements, and locations constrains the range of articulations possible. Morpheme-structure constraints on sign articulation can affect what before were chronologically or causally based orderings of the two conjuncts in a compound, resulting not only in assimilations, deletions, and insertions for the sake of making the two conjuncts conform to the fluidity requirements of a single sign, but may even result in reordering of the conjuncts in a semantically implausible order, such as EAT^RUB-ON-SHIRT for the standardized form of APPLE. Most striking in the emergence of language from gesture is the appearance of multiple-argument-taking verbs, grammatical devices for marking grammatical relations, constraints on word order, and movement rules. While we are focusing solely on lexical items here, we have seen relevant precursors to these syntactic phenomena. For example, the acting out of events from the first-person point of view that is strongly characteristic of homesigners ends up as roleplay among multiple characters (spatially distinguished by bodyshifts) in the homesign contact form, and eventually splits into using the body as a marker of taking on a character's role as well as marking a given verb (despite third-person agreement) as being viewed from a particular character's perspective. This perspective marker in Idioma de Señas de Nicaragua also coincides with the grammatical marker for subject. This use of the signer's body as agent may also determine the typological choice made by most signed languages to allow null subjects – not to require an overt noun phrase to occupy subject position.

5   Conclusions

We have argued in this chapter that the role of maturation is given priority over the role of input in current models of language acquisition. While maturation is shown to have robust effects on the outcome of first-language acquisition, we demonstrate here that non-linguistic input influences the form that language takes in important ways as well. Individuals who are exposed only to gesture are unlikely to develop a full language. Yet the output of their learning process, homesign, especially when in contact with other homesign systems, may be sufficiently rich to support the development of language in another set of individuals if they are exposed to it during the critical period for language acquisition.

In this study of eleven homesigners, we identified possible gestural precursors of the signs that are currently used in the signed language that has emerged over the last two decades in Nicaragua via the intermediate step of a contact form of homesigning. We find that conventional gestures are adopted by homesigners and lexicalized in the contact form. Many of these same forms are in use in the full form of the signed language today, but, interestingly, they now accept bound morphology, an indication that their forms have undergone morphological analysis. We also find a strong tendency in the data to represent human actions by using the hands in an analog fashion. Homesigners tend to depict non-human action, by contrast, by mapping the whole object onto the structure of the human hand. This difference in mapping results in a dichotomy which is grammaticized into two different classifier types (handling versus object) in Idioma de Señas de Nicaragua. In homesign, which has a much more restricted lexicon, members of a class of objects are sometimes represented by two coordinated gestures representing an attribute or manner followed by a representative action common to all the members of the category. These gesture strings are sometimes maintained in the contact form, and are subsequently lexicalized into compounds in the full form of the language. We also find that many homesigners used single gestures to encode whole events. Interestingly, the gestures produced in these contexts resemble most closely verb forms in Idioma de Señas de Nicaragua. Two consequences of this tendency to represent human actions in an analog fashion are that we find a systematic progression of event-encoding from no arguments in homesign to a semantically transparent (but not necessarily syntactic) single argument plus action in the homesign contact form to the syntactic encoding of verb plus multiple arguments in the full language form. Similarly, we find a progression from a solely first-person representation by the homesigner, with little regard for distinguishing roles, to shifts of the body that conventionalize roleplay in the homesign contact form. In the full form of the language, we see this precursor split into the pre-existing role-play, which shifts person agreement from third to first person and a more fine-grained marker of perspective without a shift in person marking from third to first person that appears to take on the function of marking grammatical subject. These findings together suggest that the emergence of a language is shaped by many factors, including the structure of the input, be it linguistic or not, and characteristics of the learner, particularly with respect to his or her maturational state.

The question we hope to focus upon in further work is whether the leap to 'language' occurs when the lexical conceptual structure possessed by each homesigner demands some form of linguistic encoding – however variable – or whether that leap is reserved for the point where characteristics of the input are recognized by the expectations of the human brain as sufficiently linguistic to initiate the first-language acquisition process. The former would set language in a continuum with gestural communication; the latter would demonstrate that language is a unique capacity of the modern human brain.

APPENDIX 17.1. STIMULUS LIST (N = 33)

Objects	Actions
<u>Fruit</u>	<u>Human action</u>
Apple	Brush teeth
Banana	Ride a bike
Pear	Erase
Pineapple	Hug
	Swim
<u>Utensils</u>	Dive
Dishes	Wash table
Glass	Sweep
Fork	Eat
Knife	Walk up steps
Iron	Pour from a bottle
Mop	
Scrub brush	
Spoon	<u>Non-human action</u>
	Boat sinking
<u>Household items</u>	Cat chasing mouse
TV	
Book	
Hammock	
Bed	
<u>Animals</u>	
Horned animal	
Burro	
Cat	
Mouse	

APPENDIX 17.2. EXPLANATION OF SIGNWRITER® NOTATION SYMBOLS
USED IN FIGURE 17.2.

neutral mouth

neutral mouth
open and shut once

neutral mouth,
rapid inhale

O-shaped mouth

O-shaped mouth
closing twice

gritting teeth

gritting teeth closing once

right hand claw,
palm toward signer,
hand angled to right

right hand claw,
profile orientation,
parallel to floor,
with fingers wiggling

3-finger claw
(thumb, index & middle fingers)

O-shaped hand,
palm toward signer,
forearm vertical

O-shaped hand,
palm toward signer,
forearm horizontal

O-shaped hand,
palm toward signer,
open and close once

C-shaped hand,
palm toward signer,
forearm vertical

C-shaped hand,
palm toward signer,
thumb extended,
multiple partial closings

right hand moves
upward diagonally

right hand moves
downward diagonally

right hand
inward wrist flex (2 times)

right hand rubs
up and down on left side of chest

2-fingered O
(index and thumb touching)
palm toward signer forearm vertical

fisted 2-fingered O,
profile orientation

fisted 2-fingered O,
fingers open as wrist flexes inward

flat-O,
palm toward signer

flat C-shaped hand,
palm toward signer,
thumb extended, closes once

flat C-shaped hand,
palm toward signer,
multiple partial closings

flat C-shaped hand,
palm toward signer,
thumb extended,
multiple partial closings

NOTES

We are deeply grateful to all the individuals and their families who participated in this study. The investigation was supported in part by National Science Foundation Grant #SBR-9513762 to Rutgers University. We would like to thank Gene Mirus and James Shepard-Kegl for their efforts in collecting these data, Zoila Garcia Cantero for collection and verification of background information, Nicaraguan Sign Language Projects, Inc., for access to the Nicaraguan Sign Language archive, and Anselmo Agustin Alvarado Alemán and Enrique Javier Marley Ellis for helpful discussion and clarification regarding the home-signs collected. Parts of this chapter were presented at the conference 'Gestures Compared Cross-Linguistically' organized by David McNeill and Adam Kendon which was held at the University of New Mexico in July 1995. We would like to thank the participants in the conference for their lively discussion and continued interest in this project. Address correspondence to Jill P. Morford, Department of Linguistics, University of New Mexico, Humanities 526, Albuquerque, NM 87131.

1 The argumentation that bears on deciding between these two approaches or finding a common ground between them requires more debate than we are prepared to address in the confines of this chapter. See Elman et al. (1996) for just the tip of the iceberg.

2 Many of these eleven homesigners spent at least a little time over the prior two years in a school for victims of the war populated primarily by hearing children with a variety of disabilities. This school had limited capacities to serve these deaf children. Neither a program in signed language nor speech training was offered. Students report knowledge of each other but no significant gestural communication or cohesion as a self-identified group. Socialization did not occur outside the school context.

3 Related studies include Goodhart (1984), Mounty (1986, 1990), and Gee & Mounty (1991).

4 We view homesign or non-native signed input as necessary but not sufficient for developing native ability across the full range of linguistic structures. Other factors such as the size and social structure of the community in which the child lives may constitute additional requirements upon language emergence (cf. Washabaugh 1978, 1980, 1986a, b).

5 The Goldin-Meadow & Feldman article has been followed by numerous studies that further examine the characteristics of homesign systems: among others, Butcher, Mylander & Goldin-Meadow (1991), Feldman, Goldin-Meadow & Gleitman (1978); Goldin-Meadow (1982, 1993); Goldin-Meadow & Feldman (1977); Goldin-Meadow & Mylander (1983, 1984, 1990a, 1998).

6 We are not claiming that the gestures these hearing family members produce are organized according to the rules of their spoken language, but rather that certain language-based constructions such as action/relational element plus argument (usually no more than one) may appear.

7 But see also Goldin-Meadow & Mylander (1998) for a discussion of interesting similarities in homesign systems across cultures.

8 The term *recreolization* actually goes back to a paper on sign languages as creoles by Fischer (1978: 329), where she noted the large proportion of non-native speakers in the communication environment of deaf children (including,

but not limited to, their parents) and pointed out that "most deaf children are forced to *re*-creolize ASL in every generation."

9 Newport's analysis also fails to account for the fact that these second-generation deaf not only recreolize, but recreolize to a language-specific target. Kegl (1986) and Kegl & McWhorter (1997) argue that language fragments of ASL, however frozen, allow the native acquirer to reconstruct the grammar of ASL.

10 Now that the language environment includes more than just homesigning in contact, some late learners who are exposed to input that includes both contact forms and the language output of early learners may even incorporate many features of Idioma de Señas de Nicaragua while failing to use these linguistic features and constructions in the consistent and effortless fashion characteristic of early learners. It is important to note that some homesigners who enter the Deaf community at points beyond the optimal critical period for language acquisition may nonetheless exhibit partial mastery of the target signed language.

11 Subsequent to first contact in 1994, when these data were collected, a school was set up in Bluefields (in the summer of 1995) by Nicaraguan Sign Language Projects, Inc., ANSNIC (The Nicaraguan National Deaf Association), and Los Pipitos, Bluefields Chapter (an advocacy group of parents of disabled children). Deaf students living in Bluefields and surrounding areas were invited to attend classes taught by deaf teachers from Managua using Idioma de Señas de Nicaragua. Participants in the study reported here currently use a form of Idioma de Señas de Nicaragua as a result of their participation in the school.

12 There were two exceptions to the representation of instruments by showing how they are manipulated. There was a stronger tendency to use the hand (an extended index finger) to represent the object for KNIFE and for BRUSH-TEETH. These cases illustrate that both the structure of the hand and the conception of the event may influence the choice of gesture. Both a knife and a toothbrush are easily represented by an extended index finger, but it is less obvious how to form one's hand into the shape of an iron or a scrub brush.

13 'Pear' is the creole word for an avocado.

14 See Goldin-Meadow, Butcher, Mylander & Dodge (1994) for an analysis of one child's homesign system which revealed a systematic treatment of nouns and verbs.

REFERENCES

Baron, N. 1977. Trade jargons and pidgins: a functionalist approach. *Journal of Creole Studies* 1(1): 5–28.

Bickerton, D. 1984. The language bioprogram hypothesis. *Behavioral and Brain Sciences* 7: 173–221.

Butcher, C., Mylander, C. & Goldin-Meadow, S. 1991. Displaced communication in a self-styled gesture system: pointing at the non-present. *Cognitive Development* 6: 315–342.

Carlson, R., DeLancey, S. Gildea, S., Payne, D. & Saxena, A. (eds.) 1989. *Proceedings of the Fourth Meetings of the Pacific Linguistics Conference.* Eugene: Department of Linguistics, University of Oregon.

Chamberlain, C., Morford, J. P. & Mayberry, R. I. (eds.) 2000. *Language Acquisition by Eye.* Mahwah, NJ: Erlbaum.

Danziger, E. & Keating, E. 1996. Between anthropology and cognitive science: a re-emerging dialogue. Symposium presented at the meetings of the American Anthropological Association, San Francisco, November.

DeGraff, M. (ed.) 1999. *Language Creation and Language Change: Creolization, Diachrony, and Development*. Cambridge, MA: MIT Press.

Edmondson, W. H. & Karlsson, F. (eds.) 1990. *SLR '87: Papers from the Fourth International Symposium on Sign Language Research*. Hamburg: Signum-Press.

Elman, J. L., Bates, E. L., Johnson, M. H., Karmiloff-Smith, A., Parisi, D. & Plunkett, K. 1996. *Rethinking Innateness: A Connectionist Perspective on Development*. Cambridge, MA: MIT Press.

Emmorey, K., Bellugi, U., Frederici, A. & Horn, P. 1995. Effects of age of acquisition on grammatical sensitivity: evidence from on-line and off-line tasks. *Applied Psycholinguistics* 16: 1–23.

Feldman, H., Goldin-Meadow, S. & Gleitman, L. 1978. Beyond Herodotus: the creation of language by linguistically deprived deaf children. In Lock (ed.), pp. 351–414.

Fischer, S. 1978. Sign language and creoles. In Siple (ed.), pp. 309–331.

Gee, J. & Goodhart, W. 1988. American Sign Language and the human biological capacity for language. In Strong (ed.), pp. 49–74.

Gee, J. & Mounty, J. 1991. Nativization, variability, and style shifting in the sign language development of deaf children. In Siple & Fischer (eds.), pp. 65–84.

Gibson, K. R. & Ingold, T. (eds.) 1993. *Tools, Language, and Cognition in Human Evolution*. New York: Cambridge University Press.

Gleaves, R. 1995. *SignWriter® Computer Program*. La Jolla, CA: Deaf Action Committee for SignWriting®.

Goldin-Meadow, S. 1982. The resilience of recursion: a study of a communication system developed without a conventional language model. In Wanner & Gleitman (eds.), pp. 51–77.

Goldin-Meadow, S. 1993. When does gesture become language? A study of gesture used as a primary communication system by deaf children of hearing parents. In Gibson & Ingold (eds.), pp. 63–85.

Goldin-Meadow, S., Butcher, C., Mylander, C. & Dodge, M. 1994. Nouns and verbs in a self-styled gesture system: what's in a name? *Cognitive Psychology* 27: 259–319.

Goldin-Meadow, S. J. & Feldman, H. 1975. The creation of a communication system: a study of deaf children of hearing parents. Presented at the Society for Research in Child Development meeting, Denver, April.

Goldin-Meadow, S. & Feldman, H. 1977. The development of language-like communication without a language model. *Science* (Washington, DC) 197: 401–403.

Goldin-Meadow, S., McNeill, D. & Singleton, J. 1996. Silence is liberating: removing the handcuffs on grammatical expression in the manual modality. *Psychological Review* 103: 34–55.

Goldin-Meadow, S. & Mylander, C. 1983. Gestural communication in deaf children: the non-effects of parental input on language development. *Science* (Washington, DC) 221: 372–374.

Goldin-Meadow, S. & Mylander, C. 1984. Gestural communication in deaf children: the effects and non-effects of parental input on early language development. *Monographs of the Society for Research in Child Development* 49: 1–121.

Goldin-Meadow, S. & Mylander, C. 1990a. Beyond the input given: the child's role in the acquisition of language. *Language* 66: 323–355.

Goldin-Meadow, S. & Mylander, C. 1990b. The role of parental input in the development of a morphological system. *Journal of Child Language* 17: 527–563.

Goldin-Meadow, S. & Mylander, C. 1998. Spontaneous sign systems created by deaf children in two cultures. *Nature* 391: 279–281.

Goodhart, W. 1984. Morphological complexity, ASL, and the acquisition of sign language in deaf children. Unpublished Ph.D. dissertation, Boston University.

Kegl, J. 1986. The role of sub-lexical structure in recreolization. Presented at the 18th Annual Stanford Child Language Research Forum, Stanford University, April.

Kegl, J. & Iwata, G. 1989. Lenguaje de Signos Nicaragüense: a pidgin sheds light on the 'creole?' ASL. In Carlson et al. (eds.), pp. 266–294.

Kegl, J. & McWhorter, J. 1997. Perspectives on an emerging language. In *Proceedings of the Stanford Child Language Research Forum*, pp. 15–36. Palo Alto, CA: Center for the Study of Language and Information.

Kegl, J., Senghas, A. & Coppola, M., 1999. Creation through contact: sign language emergence and sign language change in Nicaragua. In DeGraff (ed.), pp. 179–237.

Lenneberg, E. 1967. *Biological Foundations of Language*. New York: Wiley.

Lock, A. (ed.) 1978. *Action, Gesture, and Symbol*. New York: Academic Press.

MacLaughlin, D. & McEwen, S. (eds.) 1995. *Proceedings of the 19th Boston University Conference on Language Development*. Somerville, MA: Cascadilla Press.

Mayberry, R. 1993. First-language acquisition after childhood differs from second-language acquisition: the case of American Sign Language. *Journal of Speech and Hearing Research* 36: 1258–1270.

Mayberry, R. & Eichen, E. 1991. The long-lasting advantage of learning sign language in childhood: another look at the critical period for language acquisition. *Journal of Memory & Language* 30: 486–512.

McNeill, D. 1992. *Hand and Mind: What Gestures Reveal about Thought*. Chicago: University of Chicago Press.

Morford, J. P. & Goldin-Meadow, S. 1997. From here and now to there and then: the development of displaced reference in homesign and English. *Child Development* 68: 420–435.

Morford, J. P., Singleton, J. L. & Goldin-Meadow, S. 1995. From homesign to ASL: identifying the influences of a self-generated childhood gesture system upon language proficiency in adulthood. In MacLaughlin & McEwen (eds.), pp. 104–113.

Mounty, J. 1986. Nativization and input in the language development of two deaf children of hearing parents. Unpublished Ph.D. dissertation, Boston University.

Mounty, J. L. 1990. Grammar and style in the sign language development of two deaf children of hearing parents. In Edmondson & Karlsson (eds.), pp. 212–223.

Newport, E. L. 1982. Task specificity in language learning? Evidence from speech perception and American Sign Language. In Wanner & Gleitman (eds.), pp. 450–486.

Newport, E. L. 1988. Constraints on learning and their role in language acquisition: studies on the acquisition of American Sign Language. *Language Science* 10: 147–172.

Newport, E. L. 1990. Maturational constraints on language learning. *Cognitive Science* 14: 11–28.

Newport, E. L. & Meier, R. P. 1985. The acquisition of American Sign Language. In D. Slobin (ed.), *The Cross-Linguistic Study of Language Acquisition*, vol. I: *The Data*, pp. 881–938. Hillsdale, NJ: Erlbaum.

Rawlings, B. & Jensema, C. 1977. *Two Studies of the Families of Hearing Impaired Children*. Office of Demographic Studies, ser. R, no. 5. Washington, DC: Gallaudet College.

Roeper, T. & Williams, E. (eds.) 1987. *Parameter Setting*. Dordrecht: Reidel.

Senghas, A. 1995a. The development of Nicaraguan Sign Language via the language acquisition process. In MacLaughlin & McEwen (eds.), pp. 543–552.

Senghas, A. 1995b. *Children's Contribution to the Birth of Nicaraguan Sign Language*. Doctoral dissertation. Cambridge, MA: MIT Working Papers in Linguistics.

Senghas, A., Kegl, J., Senghas, R. J. & Coppola, M. 1994. Sign language emergence and sign language change: children's contribution to the birth of a language. Poster presented at the Winter Meeting of the Linguistics Society of America, Boston, January.

Singleton, J. 1989. Restructuring of language from impoverished input. Unpublished doctoral dissertation, University of Illinois at Urbana–Champaign.

Singleton, J., Goldin-Meadow, S. & McNeill, D. 1995. The 'cataclysmic break' between gesticulation and sign. In K. Emmorey & J. Reilly (eds.), *Sign, Gesture, and Space*, pp. 287–311. Hillsdale NJ: Erlbaum.

Singleton, J., Morford, J. & Goldin-Meadow, S. 1993. Once is not enough: standards of well-formedness over three different time spans. *Language* 69: 683–715.

Singleton, J. & Newport, E. 1987. When learners surpass their models: the acquisition of American Sign Language from impoverished input. Poster presented at the Biennial Meeting of the Society for Research in Child Development, Baltimore, April.

Siple, P. (ed.) 1978. *Understanding Language through Sign Language Research*. New York: Academic Press.

Siple, P. & Fischer, S. (eds.) 1991. *Theoretical Issues in Sign Language Research*, vol. II: *Psychology*. Chicago: University of Chicago Press.

Strong, M. (ed.) 1988. *Language Learning and Deafness*. Cambridge: Cambridge University Press.

Wanner, E. & Gleitman, L. (eds.) 1982. *Language Acquisition: The State of the Art*. New York: Cambridge University Press.

Washabaugh, W. 1978. Providence Island Sign: a context-dependent language. *Anthropological Linguistics* 20: 95–109.

Washabaugh, W. 1980. The manu-facturing of a language. *Semiotica* 29: 1–37.

Washabaugh, W. 1986a. The acquisition of communicative skills by the deaf of Providence Island, *Semiotica* 62: 179–190.

Washabaugh, W. 1986b. *Five Fingers for Survival*. Ann Arbor: Karoma.

18   Gesture to sign (language)

William C. Stokoe

Editor, 'Sign Language Studies'; Emeritus, Gallaudet University

1   Introduction

When gesture is defined as body movement that communicates more or less consciously, and Sign is taken as a generic term for natural sign languages, the progression from gesture to Sign is entirely natural. What makes it so is the nature of the hominid phenotype and its attributes – its vision and the physical structure and use of hands, arms, faces, and bodies. The nature of the physical universe is also involved, because an early cognitive advance was/is to see the world composed of *things* that persist and *actions* that disappear even as they appear. Animals gain information from what they see. Social animals learn to survive as they do by watching and aping movements of parents and elders. Higher animals make movements for specific purposes. Chimpanzees make a few gestures; e.g., movements reliably interpreted as asking for food or for grooming. Humans turn gesture into Sign when they perceive that a gesture made of a hand and its movement may depict things (animate and inanimate) and at the same time duplicate features of actions done by or to such things. Foveal vision discriminates among the many forms a hand can assume, and peripheral vision faithfully interprets the multiplicity of differences in limb movements. Thus a gesture may express both noun-like and verb-like meanings and at the same time show them related. Words and sentences appeared simultaneously when gesture became Sign. It is doubtful, however, that hand–arm gestures would have become Sign were it not that the gesture-maker was in full view, allowing face and body changes to add essential features to the expression of feeling–thought. Once it was common practice to recombine hand-shapes with different movements – i.e., NPs with different VPs and VPs with different NPs – Sign had fully become language.

2   Seeing a gesture

The term gesture has been used in a variety of ways. I am treating it here as a hand–arm movement seen to stand as a symbol for something else. Thomas A. Sebeok, in *Signs: An Introduction to Semiotics*, defines a symbol as "a sign without either similarity or contiguity, but only with a conventional link between its signifier and its denotata" (1994: 33). That clearly distinguishes symbol from five other major kinds of signs, some of which, as Sebeok points out, have natural links to what they signify (their denotata); but he adds:

It should be clearly understood . . . that it is not signs that are actually being classified, but more precisely, aspects of signs: in other words, a given sign may – and more often than not does – exhibit more than one aspect . . . (P. 21)

A major fact about manual gestures is that they do exhibit more than one aspect: they are symbols but more often than not are also icons or indexes or both. They are symbols because of conventional linkage: they mean (denote) what they mean because a small group, a larger community, a whole nation, or even most people everywhere tacitly agree that they do. But they are also icons when something about the appearance of the hands and the way they are held resembles in some way what they denote. They are indexes if they are close to or retrace the movement of the action that they denote. Gestures can be all these kinds of signs at once.

From this point, I will use the term *represent* instead of the semiotic term *denote*, because the latter connotes the formal study of signs, sign relations, sign denotata, and sign interpretation. *Represent* suggests current cognitive studies, which seek to integrate psychology and physiology and sociology and even sign behavior with linguistics. When an animal sees an object, one may suppose that the object is *present* in whatever mind, or modeling of the world, that organism is capable of. Chimpanzees, as Gerald Edelman has pointed out, probably have reached an evolutionary stage which enables them to form concepts:

These animals definitely show the ability to classify and generalize on relations – whether of things or of actions. They can also decide on sameness or difference, make analogies, and assess intentions, guiding their actions by such processes. (1989: 142)

Much of the evidence for this ability comes from an animal's identical reaction whether something (e.g., dog, bird, doll, soft-drink can) is *present* to its sense of sight or is *represented* by a photograph or a token or a manual gesture, i.e., a sign in American Sign Language (Premack 1976; Gardner, Gardner & Van Cantfort 1989; Fouts 1997).

My argument is not that language as such evolves, but that cognitive abilities of the kind Edelman enumerates do evolve. These he identifies with "primary consciousness." Primary consciousness in his view evolved into "higher-order consciousness," which includes language and also needed language to evolve. Thus the claim is not that gestures evolved directly into a (sign) language, but that gestures, as easily manipulated representations of things and actions seen, could have provided the material needed for the cognitive abilities to evolve. Like dentition, which evolves because of what is bitten and chewed, cognition has evolved because of what it cognizes. Dental anthropology may be a 'harder' science than cognitive science, but both show us that a species' abilities to operate evolve as they do because of what they operate on.

Gestural representations as they relate to language, therefore, deserve more careful consideration than they have heretofore received, for they may have provided the additional something needed by the cognitive abilities of our and chimpanzees' common ancestor to evolve into higher-order consciousness and language.

Things and actions directly presented to the senses suffice for the generalizing and classifying that chimpanzees accomplish, but when things and actions are supplemented by gestural representation, then deciding on sameness or difference, making analogies, assessing intentions – all such cognitive acts become more efficient. The physical foundations for such representation are innate in human bodies, in the visual system, the upper-body anatomy, and the exquisite coordination of vision with facial, eye, head, hand, and arm movements.

Vision was possibly the first system of this complex to evolve: from primitive eyespots that detect difference between light and darkness to the human eye with its retinal circuits to the brain (which outnumber the circuits from all the other sensory end organs) is a long evolutionary story indeed (see Gibson 1966). The most pertinent part of the story of gesture's metamorphosis into sign language is the relatively recent-to-evolve operation of the two kinds of cells lining the retinas of our eyes. Cone cells clustered at the retinal center, or fovea, permit detail-by-detail comparison (classifying) and contrast (distinguishing) of things. Rod cells all around them are adapted for seeing and analyzing movement, its speed, direction, and other features. These two subsystems of vision combine (with the addition of color detection; Zeki 1993) to give us the full-color moving picture we have of the world we live in.

Because of the way we see, we become aware to a degree of how the world around us works. We discover early (in infancy as in phylogeny) that some things 'out there' are relatively passive and others are alive and can act; also that most of these things and creatures are permanent or long-lived. We also (with the other kind of vision) see actions and movements that vanish almost as soon as they appear. In the philosophers' terms, we learn that the world is substance and accident.

3   Gestures, the world, and social animals

This knowledge of the world does not come to us because we have a soul separate from our body or a mind ready equipped with all the ideas Plato and

Descartes thought of as composing the real world. It is more likely instead that our pragmatic, bodily integrated knowledge is formed from the information our sensory systems seize on and our brain interprets. Leaving aside one philosophical speculation – that the world exists only in our consciousness of it, we know, or safely assume, that indeed there are creatures and objects in the world and that creatures and unseen natural forces can and do act on objects and other creatures, making, changing, even destroying them.

This brief excursion into epistemology has shown at least that there is a remarkable congruence, which we might symbolize $a + b = c$, between the way things happen in the visible world and the way our two-part visual system informs us about them. We are not alone, however, in seeing and interpreting the world in this fashion. Chimpanzees and other animals who live socially in families or troops also know the difference between things and actions and between animate and inanimate things, as their behavior shows. They also know that some among their own kind make good allies and others are better avoided. In the argument for the evolution of language from gesture, it is important to see how such social life is arranged and maintained, especially among primates most like ourselves.

Zoologists and primatologists discover that real similarity, including conceptualization, and not just homology of physical form, gives rise to similar social arrangements – 'cultures'. The human visual system is no less remarkable for guiding motor activity than for importing information about the world around us. In primate species that live above ground as well as in chimpanzees, who are equally at home on the ground and in trees, this eye–brain–hand coordination is a spectacular part of existence. In the human species, however, long adaptation to upright walking and different uses of the hands and arms have led to different hand structure and, as archaeology suggests, different uses of the hands – more toolmaking and other manipulations than tree climbing and swinging.

Despite this difference, however, there is a remarkable similarity in the process by which an infant of the human and an infant of other primate and mammalian social species becomes a viable participant in its society. This is the process of social information transfer, which Barbara King has explored (1994). Each infant is helped by a parent, parents, and others, to the best of their ability. (The extent of elders' participation in this socialization or enculturation correlates well with the intelligence and evolutionary 'height' of the species.) Nevertheless, and apart from 'instinct', or genetically transmitted reflexes, the infant on its own spends a great deal of its waking life learning to become a member of its troop, family, or other social group.

In primates the infant's activity is mainly that of watching what others do and imitating their actions. Chimpanzees, as King has found, supplement this see-and-do activity with what she calls donation. Donation is not teaching as we normally understand it. It is a special activity of the elder animal, usually the mother. Reliable repeated observations show that the mother becomes aware that the infant is copying her actions, and may also slow down her own movements as she watches the infant's imitative movements. As I understand King's careful distinction, 'donation' occurs while the mother is engaged in some instrumental activity, such as digging a tuber or cracking open a nut. It would become actual teaching if the mother set out specifically to show the infant how to do some task and not primarily to accomplish that task; but apparently teaching thus defined occurs only in our species.

What the infant observes and copies is mainly activity of hands and arms and faces; but among non-human primates, all or most of it appears to be instrumental activity: the hands being used to groom, get food, prepare it by peeling, digging, cracking, and so on. Not all of the actions are copied, however. King reports that chimpanzee mothers may actually snatch away something harmful an infant is about to eat. It is my guess that this manual action of the vigilant mother is accompanied by facial and other body activity that signals danger or disgust or the like. Thus, we might translate the message her action transmits as 'Don't ever eat that stuff; it will make you sick!' This is a broad interpretation, to be sure, but it seems to be true that the infant does not repeat the mother's intervening action until she herself is a mother watching her own infant try to eat something poisonous. I for one am willing to join Edelman in supposing that chimpanzees' conceptual abilities are up to seeing this prophylactic action as symbolic. The mother's startling appearance and snatching action are not copied, but they may be repeated far in the future when the infant is a mother or elder sister.

King's major thesis in *The Information Continuum* is that donation of social information, which is rare to non-occurring in monkeys but is reliably observed in the higher apes, is likely to have been even more frequently used by hominid species. This extrapolation is well supported by her own fieldwork and by the work of other primatologists, but I would like to take it a step further and speculate on what it implies.

Like other speculations about the possible origins of language, this one may be dismissed by critics as another 'just-so story'. However, before it is consigned to the fiction shelf, anyone at all disposed to believe that we and our language have evolved naturally and are not the product of supernatural or miraculous mutational intervention will find rich food for thought in *Next of Kin*, by Roger Fouts (with Stephen T. Mills). It describes the social behavior of chimpanzees, both cross-fostered in human homes and living in a minimally disturbed group in naturalistic surroundings. The fund of personal knowledge Fouts has gained in three decades of work complements and adds to the estimate that neuroscientist Gerald Edelman makes of chimpanzees' primary consciousness. But to the conjecture:

Let us suppose a hominid mother of the species *Homo erectus* is confronting a similar scene: her infant is about to ingest something she knows is indigestible or poisonous. From the same ancestor as the chimpanzee, this mother reacts in the same way. She snatches away the offending morsel as her face expresses alarm, distaste, anger – something like that. Later, when the two are some distance apart, the mother sees the infant looking at or picking up something else not good for it. Too far away now to snatch it, she looks directly at the child and makes a snatching and throwing movement of her hand while displaying the same frightening face. This mother's action, though similar, is now significantly different from the chimpanzee's; no longer instrumental, it is wholly symbolic. It is symbolic even though the convention linking sign to what it represents is tenuous: mother and child remember very well what this action and appearance meant moments earlier.

Once a gesture has been used to represent symbolically, the watching and aping that prepare a youngster to be a social animal turn into something new. Young creatures 'know' instinctively but not consciously that the actions of elders they are playfully copying and performing are important. By acting thus they learn to live as social animals. But when some of these actions become symbolic, they keep for a time at least their natural relationship to what they represent: digging roots, stripping leaves from twigs, eating, interrupted eating, bending branches down to pick fruit, and so on. But as symbols now, the manual actions do not have to be actually doing things as they had been. Digging movements can be made by a hand even if it contains no digging implement; the fingers and thumb will be configured *as if* the hand were holding a stick; the movements will be identical. The handshape and actions of cracking a nut can likewise be performed with empty hands. Thus, both handshape and movement have become indexes. Similarly, many kinds of activities can be represented in gesture by appropriately configuring and moving the hand or hands. To be icons and indexes, hand and movement need only be what they naturally would be in performing the instrumental action, and the continuum perceived by King and Fouts and Edelman sufficiently accounts for the rise of the convention linking gestures to what they symbolize.

4   Next step: language

We have been considering instrumental manual actions becoming transformed into symbolic gestures. This transformation would have had a physical aspect: the empty hand not used to perform an actual task but retaining the characteristic configuration and movement. There would also be a cognitive aspect, a new way of looking at what the hands were doing – not performing a practical action as they had been doing, but representing that action.

For such representative gestures to become language symbols, no magic, no language organ, no special module or set of modules would have been necessary. Instead, the cognitive ability of early humans would have grasped that the handshape definitely represented something and that its movement represented what that something did or what happened to it. This slightly enhanced interpretation of manual actions, which had been clearly visible and familiar in eons of repetitions of similar actions, required only a new use of the vision, upper-body structure, control, and concept formation the species had inherited. Innate rules and Universal Grammar have nothing to do with this step from a gestural representation to a language utterance.

One exception might be that the first rule in Chomsky's *Syntactic Structures* (1957) elegantly represents this stage of gesture language in abstract, formal symbols:

$$S \rightarrow NP + VP.$$

The rubric Chomsky gives, "A sentence may be rewritten as a noun phrase followed by a verb phrase," is expressed as it must be so that the rule can begin to generate a (perhaps infinitely downward-growing) tree. In the present context it would be more accurate to say, 'A sentence is a noun phrase (naturally) united with a verb phrase', or

$$S = NP \cup VP.$$

This formalization is possible and appropriate because, as we have seen, the handshape of a gesture represents what the gesture is about, and its movement represents (both naturally and symbolically) what or how the subject acted or what happened to it or how it changed. We can see that this two-part structure, the basis of syntax, is shared with foveal–peripheral vision, with manual gestures, and with the way visible actions take place in the world. This structure, repeated and maintained in human physiology, vision, motor action, and cognitive ability, is all that language needs. From $S = NP \cup VP$ the rest of the structure of a language can develop naturally. There is no need to postulate an innate language faculty that puts the Cartesian cart before the very physical and un-Platonic horse. Language comes from the body, not from an airy-fairy world separate from the world of flesh and blood, and of matter and energy.

5   How language grew

All that was needed for the elaboration of the basic hand–movement structure into full-blown syntax existed in the nature of vision. As an information-gathering device, vision is superbly capable of parallel processing. We have already seen how one part interprets detail and another analyzes movement. But in addition, at any given moment a field of view contains a great deal of information. Vision is not limited, as hearing is, to receiving disparate signs in temporal succession. At the moment one sees a hand moving (in an instrumental or symbolic way), one also sees the face and body of the mover and the information they may transmit.

Much of the information thus expressed, as Darwin long ago pointed out (1873), displays the emotion felt by the one seen. Such a display is the kind of sign that Peirce and Sebeok, and Herodotus before them, call the symptom. It is the visible outward appearance of the inner state of one being observed, and it participates in the development of gesture-symbolized language in the simple additive way available only to vision.

Suppose a group of early humans use hand–movement gestures and understand their full potential (NP united with VP) to make a statement or pose a question. And suppose that two of the group in turn relate similar experiences. (The translation below into English of this highly imaginative episode is to be read in the manner of a scenario or play script. What is gesturally represented is shown in single quotes. Stage directions and the description of the manual actions and non-manual displays are enclosed in brackets).

> First signer
> 'Me' [The signer glances down front of self] 'digging, digging, digging – tired' [Whole body expresses fatigue].
>
> 'Find nothing' [Hand drops digging-tool grip and lifts as if holding something in fingertips; hand turns palm up, spreads open; other hand parallels it; whole upper body shrugs, face and posture express utter frustration].
>
> Second signer
> 'Me digging too' [Glances at other, may move forearm horizontally toward that one and back toward self].
>
> 'Digging, digging; suddenly stop; excited!' [The digging motion stops abruptly; signer displays the excitement with face and posture and manner].
>
> 'Pick up something big; wow!' [Both hands scoop up an imagined large object and hold it up in front of face expressing amazement, awe].

When language came to be largely vocal activity, it was necessary to turn all this bodily expressed 'adverbial' material into vocalizations, spoken words, adverbs, adverbial phrases, etc. But with vision the channel for language reception, adverbial modifications are naturally and effectively expressed simultaneously with the manual expression of the primary components of the sentence. In the same way that the verb phrase is expanded by what can be seen, the noun phrase represented by the symbolism, iconicity, or pointing of the handshape can be given adjectival modification. A good mango or yam or banana is represented with an iconic and symbolic (because conventionally understood) handshape and the face expressing pleasure. Rotten or bad-tasting fruit uses the same manual action, but the simultaneous facial expression is one of disgust.

Of course there is no direct evidence that language began with gesture and changed over largely (but not completely) to the vocal–auditory channel. However, the paragraph above describes accurately the way languages are still expressed by deaf people and by those hearing peoples who preserve a traditional sign language. The sign languages of deaf populations, primary sign languages, have had to keep up with cultural change and have done so in societies where deaf people actually are permitted full participation. (Alternative sign languages may be reserved for ceremonial or other special purposes and need not keep up with the times.) Thus, primary sign languages have added a great many conventional representations to the natural representations that are the basis of gestural-language signs. Nevertheless, primary sign languages make good use of non-manual activity, and if *Homo erectus* did use a gesture language, it is hardly conceivable that it would have been exclusively manual.

There is not space here to chronicle the whole story of gesture's contribution to developing cognitive ability and language (Stokoe, in press). Even before gestures could have been interpreted as two-part structures, they must have played a major role in getting an unprecedented bipedal, upright-walking species oriented to terrestrial living. Just as human infants now learn up from down (their initial position) and later learn to stand and walk, a fully human species would have had to adapt to the world its physical and locomotive attributes made brand new. The task of becoming human – that is, acting human – would have been greatly aided by hand and arm use. Pointing is certainly a first representation of the cognitive recognition of directions and spatial relations. Up and down, forward and back, near and far, and a host of other binary contrasts on which a human modeling of the world is based are likely to have been gesturally represented long before two-part language-expressing gestures were used – just as all children (hearing and deaf) communicate gesturally for months before they use parental language (Volterra & Iverson 1995).

Once space could be handled as well as seen and moved through, extension of the original metaphor would produce an even more significant cognitive jump. Gestures themselves are metaphoric, in the sense that any sign perceived as a sign is metaphoric, because a gesture is not in fact the action

it represents by looking like it. Once gestures as natural indexes representing different places relative to the gesturer were used habitually, conventionally, they could then have become metaphoric instead of indexic. An
imaginative person or group might, for example, use the gestures that represented 'here' and 'not here' to mean, respectively, 'now' and 'not now'.

In describing children's acquisition of language, specifically language
about space and spatial relations, Herbert Clark (1973) demonstrates that
perceptual space (P-space) is first understood via vision, movement, and
gestural representation, and that P-space is mapped into L-space (words in
the language of the child's society). Philosophers and psychologists agree
generally that understanding time is more difficult than understanding
space, but arguably having a way to represent dimensions of space helps in
achieving an understanding of time. The ability to move across different
distances by walking or running would certainly contribute to understanding time differences, but having a set of easily performed visible representations for units of this understanding would contribute even more.

To come back from epistemology to language, familiar languages not
only have words for time and time relations but also use grammatical representations of time in tenses and the tricky business called in school grammars the 'sequence of tenses'. Language scholars familiar with the kind of
gesturing or gesticulation speakers engage in but unacquainted with sign
languages have the mistaken impression that grammatical management of
time with any precision is impossible in a language that does not have the
contrastive power of speech production and reception. Familiar only with
the linear processing to which the nature of sound and hearing is limited,
and unaware of the parallel processing of vision (which sees manual action
and much else besides at the same time), they suppose that spoken languages alone have the grammatical processes needed to express complex
time sequences and embedding.

Consider the following sentence:

> The people I talked with yesterday are leaving town tomorrow, but
> they said that they will be glad to discuss last year's report with you
> if you meet them at their hotel tomorrow morning.

This can be represented precisely in American Sign Language, which proves
nothing about the nature of primal gestural languages. Visual representation, however, by its very nature resists change. The line of sight from the
signer to the person addressed as 'you' is obvious to both, and always would
have been. Representing 'the people I talked with', however, calls for sign
movement toward one side (if the signer's left, then 'they' are on the
addressee's right). The idea 'meet' naturally brings the hands together; if
'you meet me', my hands move in the sagittal plane. If 'you meet them,' one

hand will move from the side where 'they' were indicated and the other hand from where 'you' are (out in front of 'me'). Time is represented with movements that, as noted above, also represent places, but it requires only two explicit time designations: past and future, or 'yesterday', 'tomorrow', and 'tomorrow morning'. (The time of the signer's report does not need specification; many spoken languages, in contrast, require proper choice of verb form.)

This brief explanation, much longer than the original sentence, is no substitute for a live or videotaped performance by a signer; but even simply speaking the words of the example would take about twice as much time as signing the ASL version. The time needed is shorter because manual signs, with or without facial and other accompaniment, are seldom co-extensive with words in English or any other spoken language. A moment of signing (which includes the whole appearance of the signer at a given instant) can and often does represent what requires several words to represent in speech. The different principals (I, they, you) and the different times involved (yesterday, now, tomorrow) are being indicated while other meanings are being represented. Information can be transferred at a higher rate via vision than via hearing, and information encoded in language is no exception.

6   Summary

Returning to an ancient idea, that language may have begun with gestural expression, and combining that idea with knowledge about evolution and human physiology and cognitive functioning, has led to some radical notions:

- Vision and gesture must first have given a new fully bipedal species a new way to model its world, especially three-dimensional space and time;
- Syntax may have been born when a hand was seen to represent substance (NP) and its movement to represent accident (its conjoined VP);
- The initial classification, 'noun' and 'verb', must have occurred at the same time as their manifestation in 'sentence'; neither word nor sentence would exist without its counterpart;
- Language and discursive thought are to related emotion as active (manual) movements are to passive (facial and postural) movements;
- Motoric expression and visual reception of connected thought and emotion could have begun language and naturally expanded its initial structure – hand + movement, NP + VP, noun + (conjoined) verb – as non-manual displays added modification;
- And finally, language is a natural consequence, requiring no extraordinary intervention, of the evolving body, senses, and cognitive powers of the new genus *Homo*.

REFERENCES

Chomsky, N. 1957. *Syntactic Structures.* Cambridge, MA: MIT Press.

Clark, Herbert. 1973. Space, time, semantics, and the child. In Timothy Moore (ed.), *Cognitive Development and the Acquisition of Language,* pp. 27–63. New York: Academic Press.

Darwin, C. 1873. *The Expression of Emotion in Man and Animals.* New York: Appleton.

Edelman, G. 1989. *The Remembered Present.* New York: Basic.

Emmorey, K. & Reilly, J. (eds.) 1995. *Language, Gesture and Space.* New York: Academic Press.

Fouts, R. (with S. Mills) 1997. *Next of Kin.* New York: Morrow.

Gardner, R. A., Gardner, B. T. & Van Cantfort, T. E. (eds.) 1989. *Teaching Sign Language to Chimpanzees.* Albany: State University of New York Press.

Gibson, J. J. 1966. *The Senses Considered as Perceptual Systems.* Boston: Houghton Mifflin.

King, B. 1994. *The Information Continuum.* Santa Fe, NM: SAR Press.

Premack, D. 1976. *Intelligence in Ape and Man.* Hillsdale, NJ: Erlbaum.

Sebeok, T. A. 1994. *Signs: An Introduction to Semiotics.* Toronto: University of Toronto Press.

Stokoe, W., in press. *Language in Hand: or Chasing the Language Butterfly.* Washington, DC: Gallaudet University Press.

Volterra, V. & Iverson, J. 1995. When do modality factors affect the course of language acquisition? In Emmorey & Riley (eds.), pp. 371–390.

Zeki, S. 1993. *A Vision of the Brain.* New York: Oxford University Press.

Index

400